Accounting, Finance, Sustainability, Governance & Fraud: Theory and Application

Series Editor

Kıymet Tunca Çalıyurt, Iktisadi ve Idari Bilimler Fakultes, Trakya University
Balkan Yerleskesi, Edirne, Turkey

This series acts as a forum for book publications on current research arising from debates about key topics that have emerged from global economic crises during the past several years. The importance of governance and the will to deal with corruption, fraud, and bad practice, are themes featured in volumes published in the series. These topics are not only of concern to businesses and their investors, but also to governments and supranational organizations, such as the United Nations and the European Union. Accounting, Finance, Sustainability, Governance & Fraud: Theory and Application takes on a distinctive perspective to explore crucial issues that currently have little or no coverage. Thus the series integrates both theoretical developments and practical experiences to feature themes that are topical, or are deemed to become topical within a short time. The series welcomes interdisciplinary research covering the topics of accounting, auditing, governance, and fraud.

More information about this series at http://www.springer.com/series/13615

Halis Kıral · Tekin Akdemir
Editors

Public Financial Management Reforms in Turkey: Progress and Challenges, Volume 1

Springer

Editors
Halis Kıral
Faculty of Political Sciences
Social Sciences University of Ankara
Ankara, Turkey

Tekin Akdemir
Ankara Yıldırım Beyazıt University
Ankara, Turkey

ISSN 2509-7873 ISSN 2509-7881 (electronic)
Accounting, Finance, Sustainability, Governance & Fraud: Theory and Application
ISBN 978-981-15-1913-0 ISBN 978-981-15-1914-7 (eBook)
https://doi.org/10.1007/978-981-15-1914-7

This Springer imprint is published by the registered company Springer Nature Singapore Pte Ltd.
The registered company address is: 152 Beach Road, #21-01/04 Gateway East, Singapore 189721, Singapore

Foreword

A well-functioning Public Financial Management (PFM) system is essential for promoting macroeconomic stability and the efficiency of public expenditure. It can also foster good governance, including transparency and accountability in managing public funds.

The 2008/09 global financial crisis dramatically affected many developed and developing countries, creating vulnerable fiscal positions and weakening financial structures. The high costs of the crisis and weakened financial structures prompted renewed recognition of the need for robust PFM systems that encourage countries everywhere to establish the need for, and then design and implement, critical PFM reform measures. To these ends, many countries are looking outwards to learn from international best practice, while recognizing the need to adapt and tailor international good practices to their own unique socio-political institutional environments. Countries are also looking inwards to better understand the constraints and opportunities in their own countries that determine success in improving the quality of their PFM systems.

In recent years, there has been a growing body of literature on PFM reforms. This has focused on specific PFM reforms both in broad cross-country and more narrow country-specific contexts. While these studies have been extremely insightful, there is also value in understanding integrated reform packages appropriate for high- and middle-income developing countries. Such an in-depth, context-specific study would help identify the challenges in designing and implementing sustainable PFM reforms in these countries.

Public Financial Management Reforms in Turkey: Progress and Challenges, Volume 1 is just such a study. The two volumes of the study focus on the PFM reform strategy, together with recent shifts on PFM policies and administration, in Turkey. Discussion of the challenges faced and progress achieved in Turkey should be of relevance and interest to other developing countries facing similar challenges and seeking similar progress.

Turkey has pursued comprehensive PFM reforms since the early 2000s to promote fiscal discipline and macroeconomic stability. These reforms, implemented as part of fiscal consolidation, not only made a remarkable contribution to the reduction of the budget deficit and debt stock but they also enhanced economic growth. In the second decade of the 2000s, the Turkish economy experienced an economic contraction due to various external changes in the global environment, as well as internal structural problems. This prompted a renewed focus on the need to ensuring a robust and responsive PFM system to address the emerging challenges, including a need for expenditure rationalization. However, as with many other countries, the lack of a comprehensive analysis of the existing PFM policies, systems, and procedures in Turkey made it difficult to ensure consistency and integrity among the different components of these reforms, and to mitigate some of the complex problems that arose in the process of reform.

Public Financial Management Reforms in Turkey: Progress and Challenges, Volume 1 provides a comprehensive analysis of different PFM reform components, and reveals the challenges faced in designing and implementing PFM reforms in Turkey and other developing countries. Bringing together academics and practitioners, the two-volume study includes papers by PFM experts with differing perspectives on the ongoing PFM reforms affecting revenue management, expenditure management, public budgeting, financial management information systems, asset and liability management, intergovernmental fiscal relations, and accounting, financial reporting, and auditing.

Durham, NC, USA

Richard Hemming
Visiting Professor of the Practice in the Sanford School of Public Policy

Roy Kelly
Professor of the Practice of Public Policy in the Sanford School of Public Policy

Acknowledgements

First and foremost, we would like to express our sincere gratitude to all the chapter authors for submitting their high-quality work in an effective and timely manner.

We would like to express our special thanks to all the anonymous reviewers including academics, experts as well as bureaucrats for their constructive comments and valuable suggestions on earlier versions of this book.

We are also grateful to Barış Alpaslan and Hüseyin Şen for their helpful comments and to Richard Hemming and Roy Kelly for the foreword of this book, and to Kıymet Çalıyurt for her endless support and encouragement at every single stage of the book project. Last but not least, we would like to express our sincere gratitude to our family members, without whom this book would have never come to an end.

Introduction

Since the late 1980s, the interest in and need for performance management and budgetary reforms has increased. These reforms aimed at the establishment of a sustainable financial structure, efficient allocation of resources, and efficient provision of public services. They have been also implemented to meet the social expectations for greater accountability in the public sector (Diamond 2005; Wescott 2008; Allen 2009; Shah and Shen 2007; Cangiano et al. 2013). Following the budget reform efforts in New Zealand, many countries including the US, Australia, Denmark, France, the Netherlands, England, Sweden, and Canada have embarked on similar reforms and restructured their public financial systems (Allen 2009). These reforms, which aim to transform input-oriented public budget systems into output and result-oriented systems, have encouraged result-oriented accountability to increase operational efficiency (Shah and Shen 2007).

Many countries that have reformed their public financial management (PFM) system have implemented reforms with different methods and tools, depending on their circumstances (Diamond 2013). Differences in the scope of the reforms and their reflection in practice have also been reflected in the general framework of public financial management, which has produced different definitions in literature; as a result, the term PFM and public expenditure management are used interchangeably (Prakash et al. 2008; Allen et al. 2004). The concept is also defined as the efficient management of the acquisition and expenditure of public resources by the government (Commonwealth Secretariat 2005), or the way governments manage public revenue and expenditure and its impact on the economy and society (Andrews et al. 2014). Allen et al. (2004) define the concept as limited to the phases of the budget process other than policy-making, budget preparation, and approval activities such as budget implementation, control, accounting, reporting, monitoring, and evaluation. However, Lawson (2015) makes a more comprehensive definition saying that the PFM refers to the transactions performed by governments in the budget cycle and the laws, rules, systems, and processes that regulate them. Focusing on the contribution of the PFM in achieving strategic and operational objectives, the Chartered Institute of Public Finance and Accountancy (CIPFA) defines the concept as a system in which financial resources are planned, directed, and controlled to ensure the effective and efficient fulfillment of public service objectives (Garcia-Sanchez and Cuadrado-Ballesteros 2016).

The narrowest definition of the PFM has limited the concept to processes and procedures covering all aspects of public expenditure management, ignoring the revenue part of the budget and other components of financial management (such as risk analysis, debt management, accounting of public assets, and liabilities). Over time, this definition has enlarged to cover all phases of the budget cycle and all aspects of the management of public resources. Moreover, efficient management of public resources is no longer just a task attributed to the ministry of finance. Every manager responsible for the provision of public service has been held responsible for the efficient and effective use of resources under his/her responsibility. Thus, financial management is not only limited to characterizing the central government's budget management, but is also used to characterize the activities of the public sector in a broad sense, including local governments and state economic enterprises, and public–private partnerships (Pretorius 2011; Cangiano et al. 2013; Allen et al. 2013).

These differences in definitions have led to different approaches to the overall framework of the PFM. For example, Potter and Diamond (1999) argue that the PFM is related to how the expenditure side of the budget is planned, prepared, and implemented, while the World Bank (2005) states that it includes the stages of the budget process covering budget preparation, implementation, accounting, reporting, and auditing. Premchand (1990) restricts the scope of the PFM to budgeting, expenditure control, accounting, and financial reporting. Schiavo-Campo and Tommasi (1999) in contrast to Premchand (1990) take a broader perspective to the general framework of the concept to include setting fiscal policy, budget preparation, budget implementation, management of financial transactions, accounting, and auditing and evaluation. Andrews (2007) includes resource management in the scope of the PFM. Witt and Müller (2006) also consider intergovernmental relations as a subcomponent of the PFM. The Manila Consensus on the PFM states that public financial management encompasses all stages of the public resources management cycle (OECD 2011).

As can be seen from the definitions and explanations on general framework of the PFM above, there is no clear-cut consensus over the PFM concept. Accordingly, the PFM tends to be more complex and wider in scope. In this respect, the concept not only covers all stages of the budget process but also includes the management of extra-budgetary financial transactions, intergovernmental relations, and the management of financial management information systems.

In the last 30 years, it has become impossible to develop a standard approach to guide implementation in the reform process, with the effect of different approaches to the definition of the PFM and the overall framework of financial management reform. Nevertheless, the questions that the modern financial management seeks to answer have partially directed the implementation of reforms. As argued by Allen et al. (2013), traditional public finance seeks to answer the question of what reforms to implement, while modern public finance seeks to answer the question of how to implement reforms.

Reforms on budget and financial system became widespread in the 1990s with the reflection of the new public administration approach on the financial field. The successful results of output-oriented budget systems and medium-term spending programs in developed countries have led developing countries to reform their PFM systems. These reforms have generally come to the fore with comprehensive public service reforms (Pretorius and Pretorius 2008).

Like many other countries, Turkey was also affected by the change in the world. Furthermore, the macroeconomic stability threatened by the deterioration in the financial structure forced Turkey to make the PFM reforms. In the second half of the 1990s, many studies on the PFM reforms were conducted with the contribution of international financial organizations such as the IMF and the World Bank.

The PFM reforms in Turkey was launched by the Public Financial Management Project signed with the World Bank in 1995. This project aimed at increasing fiscal consolidation and reform efforts initiated by the Turkish Government in 1994 by increasing the efficiency of tax administration, expenditure, and personnel management (World Bank 1995). However, serious steps could not be taken to overcome the problems faced in the financial management system in the Project period.

Before and after the stand-by agreement concluded with the IMF at the end of 1999, the restructuring of public administration was brought to the agenda once again; the stand-by agreement and the preparatory work for the 8th Five-Year Development Plan highlighted the need for the PFM reform (DPT 2000).

The Restructuring of Public Financial Management and Financial Transparency Specialized Commission Report published in 1999 within the framework of the preparation of the 8th Development Plan and the Public Expenditures and Institutional Review Report issued by the World Bank in 2001 emphasized the need for restructuring of the PFM. These documents established the basis for the legal, institutional, and systematic reform of the financial management system (Ağar 2009).

After 2001, great effort has been made to modernize Turkey's PFM system, and the reform initiatives have been supported by international organizations such as the World Bank and the IMF. To make the PFM system more robust, various reforms were put into practice. In this scope, a series of legal and institutional arrangements were introduced between 2001 and 2010 to establish a fiscal discipline and make macroeconomic stability sustainable. For instance, extra-budgetary funds were abolished in 2001, the e-accounting system was adopted and some arrangements were made to ensure the independence of the Central Bank. In 2002, with the Public Finance and Debt Management Law, the disintegration of borrowing legislation was eliminated and an important step was taken towards the establishment of modern debt management. In 2003, the Public Procurement Law and public procurement processes were harmonized with the EU legislation, and procurement processes, principles, and methods were made competitive. In the same year, the Public Financial Management and Control Law No. 5018 was enacted. With this law, a performance-based budgeting system was introduced, the scope of the budget was expanded further and a number of innovations including internal control, internal audit, and multi-year budgeting came into force.

In addition to these reforms, comprehensive changes were made to the local government laws to ensure compliance with the changes in the PFM system in 2003, the budget code structure was altered in 2004 and the revenue administration was reformed in 2005. While these reforms—made between 2001 and 2005—brought about fundamental changes in the field of the PFM, the regulations in the administrative pillar of financial reform could not be fully implemented since the Law on Basic Principles and Restructuring of Public Administration adopted by the legislature in 2004 was rejected by the Constitutional Court. In addition, all the provisions of Law No. 5018 became effective from the beginning of 2006 and some amendments had been made before the law came into force. With the Law, the internal audit entered into the financial management system, but the full implementation of the regulations regarding the auditing aspect of financial management was made possible by the amendment made to the Court of Accounts Law in 2010.

The series of reforms have made significant contributions to the establishment of fiscal discipline and macroeconomic stability in the short and medium term since the day on which they were first implemented. However, since the budgetary resources could not be allocated in compliance with the targets envisaged in the medium-term program due to a failure to transform the administrative structure as required by Law No. 5018 as well as economic crises and resource constraints, the review and re-evaluation in the field of the PFM has become a necessity after 15 years. As a consequence, the third generation reforms in the performance-based budgeting system come to the agenda and are discussed, since the arrangements made in the PFM system have not been fully reflected in practice due to the deficiencies in institutional and financial structure in Turkey. Moreover, with the arrangements made in the financial legislation, the executive power on the budget has expanded. Particularly considering the significant changes to the administrative structure made by the constitutional reform of 2017, it is required to restore the balance of power and authority in the financial structure accordingly. The provisions added to Law No. 5018, the budget laws, and Law No. 4734 has loosened the restrictive regulations of the financial legislation. Furthermore, it could have been not possible to ensure effective accountability due to the lack of fiscal transparency in practice. This required the revision of the PFM system, assessments of the impact of the reforms, and an overall review of the system.

In this regard, our study aims to identify problematic areas in current reforms and implementation, and to form the basis for the next reform studies by providing possible solutions. The study also aims to contribute to the best practices through revealing the achievements and challenges of the PFM reforms in developing countries, for example in Turkey.

Although studies evaluating the PFM reforms on an international scale were published in the last decade, they included almost no country-specific evaluation. In fact, reviewing the country-specific good practices, risks, and challenges in the PFM reforms can guide other countries, which are considering the implementation of similar reforms. Starting from this idea, our study is prepared in two volumes in order to reveal the process leading to the financial management reform in Turkey, reform practices, the challenges faced in this process, and steps to overcome these challenges. In this context, the first volume of the book provides an assessment of revenue and expenditure management in Turkey, reform of budget financial management information systems, and compliance of the PFM reform with EU standards. The Second Volume evaluates the reforms on asset and liability management, intergovernmental relations, accounting, financial reporting, and auditing.

Part I of Volume 1 focuses on Revenue Management. Three papers are presented in this part. The very first chapter of this part is titled "Tax System and Tax Reforms in Turkey". In this chapter, Gerçek and Bakar Türegün analyze the structure of the Turkish tax system, which has an important role in the PFM, and the stages it has gone through from past to present day. The tax system is shaped according to the economic, social, legal, and administrative structure of a country, and it directly affects the PFM. The Turkish tax system is also based on income, consumption, and wealth taxes. Especially from 1950 onwards, many taxes have been levied and after the 1980s, many changes have been made in compliance with the international policies. The chapter reveals that there are several fundamental tax reforms and many revision processes in the Turkish tax system.

In Chap. 2, Budak and Benk investigate the restructuring of the Turkish revenue administration in terms of its organization and management within a historical perspective and through stages in which the proposed changes occurred. When the historical development of the Turkish revenue administration is examined, 2005 represents an important turning point in terms of radical changes to its organizational structure and working method. In 2005, the entire system of the Turkish revenue administration was re-organized. Accordingly, the authors focus on the reorganization of the administration within the framework of the year before and after 2005.

In Chap. 3, Karataş Durmuş and Arıtı Erdem present the tax audit system and recent tax audit reform in Turkey. They provide general information on the aims, functions, features, and types of tax audits in Turkey, and they review the four basic types of tax audits—physical inquiry, tax inspection, inquiry, and gathering information. In this chapter, they also evaluate the process of tax audit reform in Turkey dated 2011, and this evaluation involves the change in the units of tax audit and a tendency to build a risk analysis-based tax audit system. Within this context, the authors compare the structures of the tax audit units before and after this reform. They also explain how Turkey gives priority to information technologies in the process of tax audit as in developed countries.

Part II covers Public Expenditure Management in Turkey within four chapters. Demirbaş provides a comprehensive analysis of Medium-Term Expenditure Framework (MTEF) in Turkey in Chap. 4, "The Experience of a Medium-Term Expenditure Framework in Turkey". In this chapter, he examines the experience of MTEF, which is one of the main components of public expenditure management reform in Turkey. After providing brief theoretical information, Demirbaş summarizes the history of Turkey's adoption of MTEF. He then discusses the specific objectives, characteristics, and basic stages of MTEF in Turkey. The chapter contains both qualitative and quantitative evaluations on MTEF implementation over a period of almost 15 years.

In Chap. 5, "An Assessment of How the Public Procurement System Works in Turkey", Çetinkaya and Eroğlu assess the Public Procurement Law, which is one of the most specifically focused areas in the restructuring process of the PFM through the good governance model. Considering that a major part of the state budget is allocated for construction work and the purchase of goods and services, the significance of the procurement law is well-understood for efficient and effective use of resources. Having a good procurement system in place increases the efficiency and performance of the PFM and reduces prodigality. Accordingly, Çetinkaya and Eroğlu evaluate the efficiency of the public procurement system in Turkey in terms of the results of implementation within the perspective of the process in question and make suggestions for the improvement of defective aspects.

Public–Private Partnership (P3) has become increasingly popular as a means of procuring and maintaining public sector infrastructure including transportation projects such as roads, tunnels, bridges, railways, airports, schools, hospitals, social housing, and government offices projects since the 1980s. In Chap. 6, Açıkgöz evaluates the P3's practices around the world to overcome the traditional drawbacks of public procurement. Afterwards, the author explores the P3 practices in Turkey intensively used in transportation (highways and airports), the healthcare, and energy sectors and offers some policy suggestions for Turkey.

In Chap. 7, Akdemir, Alpaslan, and Kıral first provide a general overview of conditional cash transfers and then review in detail the available information on conditional cash transfers for education and conditional health benefits in Turkey in order to reduce poverty and improve the public expenditure system. The program was primarily initiated to alleviate the effects of the Turkish 2000–2001 banking crisis on the poor. In addition, it was aimed at increasing the enrolment rate and duration of schooling of children living in low-income families as well as ensuring that women, during and after pregnancy, benefit from basic healthcare and nutrition services.

Part III of the volume evaluates the budget reforms in Turkey. Four chapters are presented in this part. In Chap. 8, "Program Budgeting in Turkey", Yenice provides a comprehensive analysis of the cornerstones of the program budget classification reforms in Turkey in terms of program classification, program performance identification, and program evaluation. The chapter starts with the Public Financial Management and Control Law No. 5018 which was adopted in 2003 and introduced fundamental changes in the Turkish financial management system. One of them is the shifting of the budget system from being input-oriented to output and result-oriented. Public institutions have prepared 5-year strategic plans, annual performance plans, and accountability reports in the context of a performance-based budgeting system in Turkey. The author evaluates the reform studies, which have been so far carried out in the Turkish budgeting system, and discusses the future steps for comprehensive program budgeting reforms.

In Chap. 9, "Judicial Review of Budget in Turkish Law", Yüksel discusses the power of the purse and the intellectual sources of budgetary practices and how it has historically developed in terms of legal framework and practice. In addition, he evaluates over a century of judicial review of the budget by the Court of Accounts and over half a century of the constitutional judicial audit of Constitutional Court. The author examines the regulations in the Constitutional Laws, Court of Accounts Law, General Accounting Law, and Public Financial Management and Control Law No. 5018 and how the Court of Account's audit of the budget has changed over time.

In democracies, one of the main functions of the parliament is to oversee the executive body of the government. As a political document, a budget is an important tool ensuring the parliament's oversight function. Parliaments can also reflect the public demands in the budget documents and increase accountability through budget scrutiny, approval, and auditing of the public accounts. Therefore, playing an active role in the budget process is crucial for the parliaments to perform their oversight function. In this regard, in Chap. 10, "The Role of Parliament in Budget Process", Tezcan outlines the Turkish budget process and the legislative oversight function of the Grand National Assembly of Turkey, in light of the transition of the governmental system from parliamentary to presidential.

In Chap. 11, "Fiscal Transparency in Turkey: Lessons Learned from International Evaluations", Eker suggests some steps that can be taken to improve fiscal transparency in Turkey by highlighting its importance. The author firstly emphasizes the importance of the concept and makes a current situation analysis which includes the steps taken to ensure fiscal transparency. Lastly, Eker determines the matters that need to be improved, in the light of fiscal transparency evaluations made by international organizations for Turkey.

Part IV of the volume looks at the Government Financial Management Information Systems in Turkey. In this context, in Chap. 12, Demirhan discusses the rapid change in information and communication technologies, which gives governments an opportunity to develop their financial systems. This chapter focuses on the Integrated Public Financial Management System (IFMIS), its benefits, and challenges as well as the integrated financial management experiences of Turkey. The author also evaluates the IFMIS Policy Paper and Action Plan, New Accounting Information System, New Expenditure Management System, and e-documents Standards & Standard Documents and Reporting in terms of implementation of IFMIS in Turkey.

Turkey was accepted as a candidate country of the European Union (EU) at the Helsinki Summit held on 10–11 December 1999. Obviously, the pre-conditions for EU accession emphasized the requirement to establish a strong public administration to transpose and implement the EU *Acquis* effectively. The PFM is one of the most important reforms made by Turkey in the EU accession process. In this regard, in Chap. 13 of Part V, "Alignment of Turkey with the European Union in Public Financial Management and Control", Karabacak reviews the general EU accession requirements and Turkey's level of alignment in the field of the PFM and its sub-systems that are covered under different chapters, namely taxation, economic and monetary policy, and financial control, all of which have been opened to negotiations. Finally, the author discusses the progress achieved so far and further work to be done in these areas.

Halis Kıral
Tekin Akdemir

References

Ağar, M. (2009), Turkey, in: Performance-Based Budgeting and Medium-Term Expenditure Frameworks in Emerging Europe, Leszek Kąsek and David Webber (ed), The World Bank, 2009) pp-207–219, p.208.

Allen, R., Schiavo-Campo, S., and Garrity T.C., (2004), Assessing and reforming public financial management: a new approach, The World Bank, 2004, p.2.

Allen, R. (2009), The Challenge of Reforming Budgetary Institutions in Developing Countries, (No. 9–96). International Monetary Fund, p.7.

Allen, R., Hemming, R., & Potter, B. H. (2013). Introduction: The meaning, content and objectives of public financial management. In: *The international handbook of public financial management* (pp. 1–12). Palgrave Macmillan, London., p.1.

Andrews, M. (2007) What Would an Ideal Public Financial Management System Look Like? In Shah, A. ed. Budgeting and Budgetary Institutions. Washington: World Bank.

Andrews, M., Cangiano, M., Cole, N., de Renzio, P., Krause, P., & Seligmann, R. (2014). *This is PFM* (No. 285). Center for International Development at Harvard University.

Cangiano, M., Curristine, T., & Lazardo, M. (2013). Introduction: The Emerging Architecture of Public Financial Management, in: *Public Financial Management and Its Emerging Architecture (Ed:* Cangiano, M. M., Curristine, M. T. R., & Lazare, M. M., International Monetary Fund.

Commonwealth Secretariat (2005), Guidelines for Public Financial Management Reform. *Marlborough House Pall Mall London SW1Y 5HX. UK.*

Diamond, J. (2005). *Reforming the Russian Budget System: A Move to More Devolved Budget Management?* (Vol. 5). International Monetary Fund., p.16.

Diamond, J. (2013), Background Paper 1: Sequencing PFM Reforms, January 2013, p.7.

DPT (2000), *Sekizinci Beş Yıllık Kalkınma Planı Kamu Mali Yönetiminin Yeniden Yapılandırılması ve Mali Saydamlık Özel ihtisas Komisyonu raporu.* Devlet Planlama Teşkilatı.

Garcia-Sanchez IM., Cuadrado-Ballesteros B. (2016) New Public Financial Management. In: Farazmand A. (eds) Global Encyclopedia of Public Administration, Public Policy, and Governance. Springer, Cham.

Lawson, A. (2015), Public Financial Management, GSDRC C Professional Development Reading Pack no. 6. Birmingham, UK: GSDRC, University of Birmingham.

OECD (2011), Manila Consensus on Public Financial Management: Partnering to Strengthen Public Financial Management for Effective States, https://www.oecd.org/dac/effectiveness/48780763.pdf.

Potter, B., and Diamond, J. (1999). *Guidelines for Public Expenditure Management.* Washington: International Monetary Fund., pp. 3–50.

Prakash, T., & Cabezon, E. R. (2008). Public financial management and fiscal outcomes in sub-Saharan African heavily-indebted poor countries. *IMF Working Papers*, 1–46.

Premchand, A. (Ed.). (1990). *Government Financial Management: Issues and Country Studies.* International Monetary Fund.

Pretorius, C. and Pretorius, N. (2008) A Review of PFM Reform Literature. London: DFID.

Pretorius, C., Quist, R., Dendura, J.M., & Dehove, M. (2011). Supporting Capacity Development in PFM - A Practitioner's Guide.

Schiavo-Campo, S. and Tommasi, D. (1999), Managing Government Expenditure, Asian Development Bank, Manila.

Shah, A. and C. Shen (2007) A Primer on Performance Budgeting. Budgeting and Budgetary Institutions. A. Shah. Washington, D.C., World Bank 137–176., p.137.

Wescott, C. G. (2008). World Bank Support for Public Financial Management: Conceptual Roots and Evidence of Impact. *Available at SSRN 1169783*., p.2.

Witt, M. and Müller, I. (2006) Implementing the Paris Declaration in Public Finance- Challenges by Capacity Development, Fiscal Studies No 4, GTZ: Eschborn.

World Bank (1995), Legal Dept of World Bank. 1995. *Conformed Copy - L3942 - Public Financial Management Project - Loan Agreement (English)*. Washington, DC: World Bank. http://documents.worldbank.org/curated/en/471561468312861765/Conformed-Copy-L3942-Public-Financial-Management-Project-Loan-Agreement.

World Bank (2005), Strengthened Approach to Public Financial Management Reform, http://www1.worldbank.org/publicsector/pe/StrengthenedApproach/#Note2.

Contents

Editors and Contributors

About the Editors

Halis Kıral is an assistant professor at the Social Sciences University of Ankara (ASBU) in Turkey. He is also Head of Audit and Risk Management Department and Director of Center for Audit and Risk Management (ASBUDRM) at the ASBU. He was a visiting scholar in Duke Center for International Development (DCID) for the 2017–2018 academic year. He worked in the Ministry of Finance of Turkey as a state budget expert, public finance expert, head of the department of Central Harmonization for Internal Audit, and head of the Budget Policy Department. As the Head of Central Harmonization Unit for Internal Audit, his main responsibilities were to prepare and develop public internal audit and reporting standards, internal audit manuals, to arrange the certification and training programs of internal auditors and internal auditor candidates, to prepare quality assurance and development program and to evaluate the internal audit units within external quality assurance scope, to carry out designing, training, and monitoring processes of Public Internal Audit Software (İçDen©), and to identify and disseminate best practices of public internal audit units for 250 public institutions and almost a thousand public internal auditors and two thousand public internal auditor candidates.

He has led several projects including developing Public Internal Audit Software (İçDen©) for public internal auditors and publishing Public Internal Audit Manual, Information Technology Audit Manual, Quality Assurance and Improvement Manual and Performance Audit Manual for Public Internal Auditors (the first manual in the world adopting the perspective of internal audit on performance audit).

He has written a number of articles, books and book chapters on topics such as public finance, public financial management and control, specifically internal audit and risk management, and applied economics. Currently, he is also working on impact analysis, monitoring and evaluation. He received his Ph.D. in economics from Hacettepe University.

Tekin Akdemir is Professor of Public Finance at the Ankara Yıldırım Beyazıt University, Faculty of Political Sciences, He is also co-head of Public Finance Department. Before this post he was an Associate Professor at the Erciyes University. Prof. Akdemir is also a member of the Turkish Tax Council. He received his Ph.D. in public finance department at the Institute of Social Sciences, Dokuz Eylul University in 2006. His research focuses on Budgeting and financial management, Government cash and debt management, and local govenment finance. Prof. Akdemir has authored and contributed to numerous books, book chapters, articles, and reports on intergovernmental finance, public financial management, and public debt and cash management. In addition to his academic research and expertise in the management and provision of technical assistance, Prof. Akdemir has considerable experience in the development and delivery of academic courses and professional training programs in the areas of public sector finance, (fiscal) decentralization and government budgeting and financial management issues.

Contributors

Bernur Açıkgöz İzmir Katip Çelebi University, İzmir, Turkey

Tekin Akdemir Ankara Yıldırım Beyazıt University, Ankara, Turkey

Barış Alpaslan Social Sciences University of Ankara, Ankara, Turkey

Feride Bakar Türegün Department of Public Finance, Faculty of Economics and Administrative Sciences, Bursa Uludağ University, Bursa, Turkey

Serkan Benk Department of Public Finance, İnönü University, Malatya, Turkey

Tamer Budak Department of Fiscal Law, İnönü University, Malatya, Turkey

Özhan Çetinkaya Department of Public Finance, Faculty of Economics and Administrative Sciences, Bursa Uludağ University, Bursa, Turkey

Tolga Demirbaş Department of Public Finance, Bursa Uludag University, Bursa, Turkey

Habip Demirhan Hakkari University, Hakkari, Turkey

Neslihan Karataş Durmuş Educational Consultant, Republic of Turkey Ministry of National Education, Brussels, Belgium

Ali Yıldırım Eker Ministry of Treasury and Finance, Ankara, Turkey

İmran Arıtı Erdem Faculty of Political Sciences, Yıldırım Beyazıt University, Ankara, Turkey

Erdal Eroğlu Department of Public Finance, Faculty of Economics and Administrative Sciences, Çanakkale Onsekiz Mart University, Çanakkale, Turkey

Adnan Gerçek Department of Public Finance, Faculty of Economics and Administrative Sciences, Bursa Uludağ University, Bursa, Turkey

Halis Kıral Social Sciences University of Ankara, Ankara, Turkey

Nihal Samsun Karabacak Directorate for European Union Affairs, Ankara, Turkey

Hilal Tezcan Head of Department, Presidency of Strategy and Budget, Ankara, Turkey

Ebru Yenice Ministry of Treasury and Finance, Ankara, Turkey

Nahit Yüksel Ministry of Treasury and Finance, Ankara, Turkey

List of Figures

List of Tables

Part I
Revenue Management

Chapter 1
Tax System and Tax Reforms in Turkey

Adnan Gerçek and Feride Bakar Türegün

1.1 Introduction

Tax reforms are defined as fundamental changes in the tax system for simplification, effectiveness, fairness, and other reasons. Fundamental changes are needed to ensure that the tax system adapts to developments in the economy. For this reason, tax reforms are always on the agenda. The Turkish tax system has passed through many stages, including tax reforms until today. While these reforms aimed to create a simple, modern, and effective tax system, to adopt the tax system to the EU and global developments, in some cases it led to clogging the system. Therefore, the process and problems of the Turkish tax system must be considered as a whole.

This study aims to evaluate the general view of today's Turkish tax system and to identify the current problems by considering the reform processes. For this purpose, firstly, fundamental reforms were discussed, and then the current structure of the Turkish tax system was presented in the framework of the tax procedure law, income taxes, taxes on expenditure, taxes on wealth, and taxes on foreign trade. This structure caused some problems to be detected. For this reason, the last part of the study was divided for the main problems of the Turkish tax system and recommendations. Finally, the general evaluation and discussion of the study were made.

A. Gerçek (✉) · F. Bakar Türegün
Department of Public Finance, Faculty of Economics and Administrative Sciences, Bursa Uludağ University, Bursa, Turkey
e-mail: agercek@uludag.edu.tr

F. Bakar Türegün
e-mail: feridebakar@uludag.edu.tr

H. Kıral and T. Akdemir (eds.), *Public Financial Management Reforms in Turkey: Progress and Challenges, Volume 1*, Accounting, Finance, Sustainability, Governance & Fraud: Theory and Application, https://doi.org/10.1007/978-981-15-1914-7_1

1.2 The Main Reforms in the Turkish Tax System

Tax reform generally includes observing multiple targets and evaluating interactions between different tax tools and their bases. It is generally handled with optimal taxation theory (The World Bank 1991: 6; Thirsk 1991: 8). Tax reforms should be carefully designed considering with existing tax system and economies. The presence of a shadow economy can negatively affect the results of any reform intended at decreasing tax deterioration (Annicchiarico and Cesaroni 2017: 459). Reasons for application of tax reform are generally complex, inelastic, inefficient, inequitable, quite merely, and unfair tax systems; one or more of them are possible (Khalilzadeh-Shirazi and Shah 1995: xv).

Tax reform aims at developing the system by making marginal changes to the tax system and structure. All changes of a tax system are not considered tax reform; it involves "significant" changes. Others can be accepted to be revision (Jha 2010: 384). So, there are several fundamental tax reform and many revision processes in the Turkish tax system.

The tax system, which was inherited by the Turkish Republic from Ottoman Empire, was rather based on the theocratic state structure. Tax system included two groups: religious taxes that consist of the offering, tithe, jizya as well as tithe paid by Non-Muslims and customary taxes that are the civil taxes (Başpınar 2009: 97).

After the abolition of tithe in 1925 and the dividend tax replacing with profit tax in 1926, the first fundamental tax reform process in Turkey started (Özker and Esener 2010: 23). Religious taxes are removed, in this way more modern taxation approach has begun. Protective tariffs for customs duties were applied during this period. It is seen that some temporary taxes were implemented due to the developments in the world from 1931 to 1945 (Taş 1995: 357–363). Besides, seven tax amnesty laws entered into force during the first fundamental tax reform period. Therefore, 1925–1950 period can be regarded as a preparatory period for transition to modern the tax system in Turkey.

At the early stages of the Republic, land and agricultural tax system remained from Ottoman Empire continued to be implemented; some parts of this system changed in time, but the fundamental changes in Turkish tax system occurred in 1950. Those were the years when the second reforms to set the basis for the modern Turkish tax system of today were made (Başpınar 2009: 97). The advice of Fritz Neumark and hallmarks of Germany's tax system were effective to make second fundamental tax reform. Personal and corporate income tax together instead of profit tax with inheritance and gift tax were included in the Turkish tax system in this period. After 1950, the protection measures in foreign trade were reduced (Taş 1995: 368). Tax procedure law was also enacted. By the planned period, income tax extended to agriculture and tax incentives entered into the system for the first time. In the 1970s, some new taxes were introduced like retail sales tax on services and luxury goods, capital gains tax on real property, sports lottery tax, building and construction acquisition tax, etc. In this period, the real estate tax and motor vehicles tax were included in the tax system. Also, the constitutional amendment were enabled to empower the government to amend the percentages of exemption, exceptions, and reductions in taxes within the minimum and maximum limits prescribed by law (Bulutoğlu and Thirsk 1999: 362). Furthermore, nine tax amnesty law entered into force during the second fundamental tax reform period.

By the liberalization policies of our country in the 1980s, the other fundamental reform was implemented with the inclusion of VAT in our tax system in 1985. After 1980, adopted liberal policies also affected tax reforms. In this reform period, many changes in the tax rate and new sales taxes occurred; taxes on real property replaced real estate duty on both buyer and seller. The living standard assessment system that applied until 2001, for a minimum tax on income tax filers were announced (Bulutoğlu and Thirsk 1999: 363). Liberalization policies and the customs union process with the EU has affected import duties to be declined. In order to comply with the EU acquis, the Customs Law No. 4458 was enacted in 2000 to reform the foreign trade taxes.

This process has continued with the Special Consumption Tax (SCT) which entered into force in 2002. The tax reform strategy in 2002 had the main objective to make better the sustainability, transparency, and fairness of the system through precautions including correcting the tax system-related problems, increasing the tax base, and ensuring the efficiency of the tax administration (OECD 2006: 7–8). Indirect taxation was simplified with replacing several taxes with the special consumption tax. With the Special Consumption Tax Law, 16 items including taxes, fees, funds, and shares were abolished (Ateş 2008: 9). In the period that beginning with the implementation of VAT and continuing with acceptance of SCT is an important step to adapt to the EU harmonization process (Demirli 2011: 285).

Besides, the corporate tax law was rewritten to adapt to the global world and became applicable in 2006. The reform set new corporate taxation schemes and clarified the implementation of some of the previously regulated fields. The significant changes occurred in transfer pricing, thin capitalization, anti-avoidance measures, foreign participation exemptions, and provisions specific to controlled foreign companies (Otonglo and Trumbic 2006: 68–69). In the last tax reform period from 1980 to 2018, 21 tax amnesty laws that generally aim to resolve tax controversies by restructuring and to achieve fiscal goals entered into force.

The main reforms in the Turkish tax system are shown in Fig. 1.1.

1.3 General Information About Turkish Tax System

In Turkey, the tax system includes various taxes and its regime can be categorized under five main headings; Tax Procedure Law, Income Taxes, Taxes on Expenditure, Taxes on Wealth, and Taxes on Foreign Trade. Detailed information about these headings will be given below:

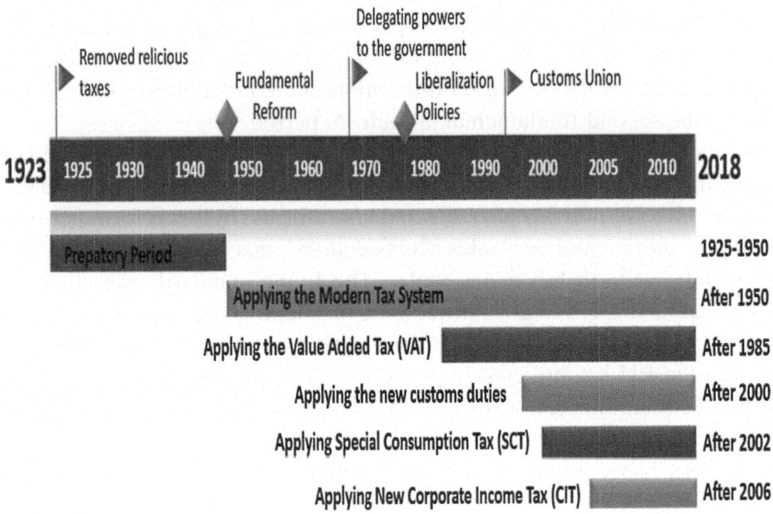

Fig. 1.1 Timeline of tax reform in Turkey. *Source* Own elaboration based on the information above

1.3.1 Tax Procedure Law

Tax Procedure (TP) Law regulates taxation stages, liabilities of taxpayers, the process of the administration to implement its obligations, mutual responsibilities and rights as well as results arising from the operation of the system. Law No 213 which regulated Turkey's TP legislation, entered into force on January 1 1961. Scope of this Law is procedural and formal regulations of all laws related to taxation. This Law includes taxes, duties and charges, and the others that belong to provincial private administrations and municipalities except for taxes, duties, and fees collected by customs administrations (Karakoç 2017: 23).

The TP Law is divided into five main sections including the following headings. The first section named "Taxation" (Articles 4–152) contains regulations relevant to main issues such as taxpayer, the person responsible for the tax, legal representative, time limits, types of assessment, notifications, payment, errors and the ways of correction, tax inspections (Revenue Administration 2016: 1). The second section named "Taxpayer Duties" (Articles 153–257) edits regulations about taxpayer duties, declarations, books, and records, also the documents to be issued. The third section named "Valuation" (Articles 258–330) includes regulations related to ways of validating economic assets and wealth of taxpayer and its depreciation. The next section named "Penalty Provisions" (Articles 331–376) comprises penalties for breaking the rules by taxpayers, their payment and abolishment also the conciliation process regulations. The last section named "Tax Cases" (Articles 377–417) edits regulations related to the lawsuit process filed by taxpayers and persons who are punished with tax penalties (See Şenyüz et al. 2018a).

1.3.2 Income Taxes

Taxation of income is made by collecting two separate taxes in Turkey: personal income tax and corporate income tax. Personal Income Tax (PIT) Law came into force in 1960 which regulates the taxation of personal income and earnings. On the other hand, Corporate Income Tax (CIT) aiming at the taxation of corporations was introduced in 1949 and a new CIT Law making essential changes came into force in 2006.

Personal Income Tax

Personal income tax (PIT) is applied for taxation of individuals' income. Law No 193 regulating PIT came into force on January 1, 1961. Partnerships are not considered as separate legal entities when applying the income tax law, and each share is individually taxed over the profit share. The elements of an individual's income are classified into seven categories. These are (Revenue Administration 2006: 17): "business profits, agricultural profits, salaries and wages, incomes from independent personal services, incomes from immovable property and rights (rental income), incomes from capital investment, and other incomes and earnings without considering the source of income."

Individuals who earn income from one or more of these seven categories are taxed according to PIT. Those individuals who earn such incomes are considered as "personal income taxpayers". Both people who have income as an employee and people who have earnings as a self-employed are obliged to pay tax in Turkey. People under the rules of "permanent resident" are taxed earned income on both in Turkey and other countries. A worker who is a resident of another country is only responsible for income tax of earned in Turkey (Şenyüz et al. 2018b: 10–12).

The authority to change the PIT rates belongs to the central government. Rates of PIT which starting from 15 to 35% are progressive. The dividend income that does not exceed a certain limit is not subject to tax, for example, the limit for 2018 is 34.000 TRL (PWC 2018: 17). The declaration is used for income tax and there are three different tax returns.

Annual Tax Return: People use the declaration to collect and declare profits and earnings from each income elements in one calendar year. Some incomes are not included in the declaration such as wage received from one employer. After each calendar year, the annual tax return for the previous year must be submitted by March 31. The payment of the tax is made in two installments, March and July (Başpınar 2009: 206).

Special Tax Return: The annual tax return is not required for nonresident taxpayers if they have certain profits and earnings regulated by Law. These taxpayers who obtain certain incomes and earnings must declare them via the special tax return (PWC 2018: 14).

Withholding Tax Return: In cases where the rules in law-related withholding taxes such as taxes withheld by employers and other people, they must declare their withholding tax through the tax return. These taxes should be added to the tax return and declared within the 26th of the following month, and they are paid within the same day of the month on which the declaration was made (Oktar 2018: 103–104).

Corporate Income Tax

The corporate tax is applied for taxation of income and earnings obtained by corporations and corporate bodies. Corporate Income Tax (CIT) Law No 5520 making significant changes to the previous law came into force on January 1, 2006. The main objective of the new law is to establish a corporate tax structure that facilitates the international integration of the economy (Otonglo and Trumbic 2006: 69–70).

In the law, companies and corporate bodies which are considered as taxpayers are regulated and these are as follows: "Capital companies, Cooperative companies, State Economic Enterprises (public corporations), Economic entities owned by foundations and associations, and Joint Ventures."

In the taxation of corporations, all obtained income and profits are included in the taxable income except the exemption of domestic profit share. Expenses incurred during operation are considered as deductible, excluding those that are not allowed to be deducted by law. By international rules, the new corporate tax law included regulations such as transfer pricing, thin capitalization rules, and controlled foreign companies. Turkey does not allow the filing of consolidated tax return. Each company in a group is considered separate (Deloitte 2011: 11).

As of January 1, 2006, the tax rate was decreased from 30 to 20% by Law No 5520 on CIT. As a result of this law, the final tax burden on corporate profits decreased to 44% to 34 (Ateş 2008: 7). However, the corporate tax rate was raised from 20 to 22% for 2018, 2019, and 2020 fiscal years after tax periods beginning on January 1, 2018. Therefore, the tax rate is no longer competitive.

In general, the person having the regal responsibility declare the CIT by the tax return. Three different tax returns are used to declare CIT, as follows:

The Annual Corporate Income Tax Return: Net corporate profits in an accounting period are included in this tax return. After each calendar year, the tax return for the previous year must be submitted by the end of April. The payment of the tax is made until the same time (Şenyüz et al. 2018b: 218).

Special Tax Return: The annual corporate income tax return is not required for nonresident foreign corporations if they have certain profits and earnings regulated by Law. The tax return is given in 15 days after the deriving of these earnings and profits.

Withholding Tax Return: Taxpayers who are responsible for making tax withholding must declare themselves to the tax office related to the place of payment which they have made during the month by this tax return until the 23rd day of the following month. They are paid until the 26th day of the month on which the declaration was made (Bicer 2009: 549).

1.3.3 Taxes on Expenditure

There are several indirect taxes in the Turkish taxation system, but the most important of these are "value-added tax, special consumption tax, banking, and insurance transaction taxes and special communication tax."

Value Added Tax

The Value Added Tax (VAT) Law came into force on January 1, 1985. The VAT is imposed on the supply of most goods and the provision of services in the context of commercial, industrial, agricultural, and professional activities. The VAT is a tax that extends to every stage of the production and distribution process. Taxpayers who provide or import the goods or service are responsible for payment but VAT mechanism enables to transfer real tax burden to the final consumer (Revenue Administration, 2016: 19).

Taxpayers of VAT are generally deliverers and importers of the goods or service providers. The VAT Law regulated standard VAT rate for taxable areas to be 10%; however, the rate was raised to 18% after May 15, 2001. At the same time, two reduced rates of VAT are accepted. One of these is 8% for "basic foodstuffs, pharmaceutical products, and other items," and the other is 1% for "journals, newspapers, certain farm products and certain machine/equipment acquired under finance leases." Some products are also covered by the exemption (Hodzic and Celebi 2017: 81).

Tax returns for VAT are used for declaration. The tax returns must be submitted by the 26th day after each taxation period. The payment of the tax is made until the 26th day of the same month (Oktar 2018: 222).

Special Consumption Tax

Goods in one stage of consumption process located in four lists regulated by law are subject to tax. Special consumption tax (SCT) is located in Law No 4760 which came into force after August 1, 2002.

The Law has four attached lists which determine the goods forming the subject of tax. SCT is taken only once from goods in the lists. Different tax rates and amounts are determined for each product groups. These groups are as follows (Revenue Administration 2006. 22).

- The List I consists of "petroleum products, natural gas, lubricating oil, solvents, and derivatives of solvents."
- The List II consists of "automobiles and other vehicles, motorcycles, planes, helicopters, yachts."
- The List III consists of "tobacco and tobacco products, alcoholic beverages and cola."
- The List IV consists of "luxury products."

Products in the lists have tax rates and amounts or both regulated by the lists. The tax is generally calculated at the stage of import or end of production to be from 0.5 to 160% of the value (Şenyüz et al. 2018b: 325–327).

Banking and Insurance Transaction Taxes

Banking and insurance transactions tax (BITT) aims at taxation of all transactions and services submitted by banks and insurance companies. Because of this, taxpayers of BITT are "banks, bankers and insurance companies, financing companies, lenders and factoring companies" (Revenue Administration 2006: 23).

The transactions of banks and insurance companies have exemption related to VAT. However, these transactions are subject to BITT. Banks and insurance companies pay VAT for the purchase of goods and services, but they are accepted to be expenses or costs.

The general BITT rate is 5%, and some specific transactions are taxed at 1%. Also, BITT is calculated on 0 (zero)% for foreign exchange transactions after the Council of Ministers Decision since 2008 (Revenue Administration 2006: 29).

Taxation period of BITT is monthly. Banks and insurance companies submit their tax returns and pay their taxes until the 15th day of the following month.

Special Communication Tax

The subject of special communication tax is generally "services of a mobile phone, cable radio and television broadcasts, internet providing services, and telecommunication." Providing this service occurs a taxable event. Special communication tax rate on all these services is 7.5% (Şenyüz et al. 2018b: 328).

The taxpayer of the tax is companies which provide these services. VAT base is used to detect tax base of special communication tax. Taxation period of special communication tax is monthly. Taxpayers submit their tax returns and pay their taxes until the 15th day of the following month. Deducting of a payment for a special communication is not acceptable as an expense for income and corporate tax (Oktar 2018: 258).

Stamp Tax

Stamp tax aims at taxation transaction of many documents such as contracts, agreements, notes payable, letters of credit and letters of guarantee, financial statements, and payrolls. Different tax rates ranging from 0.189 to 0.948% or lump-sum amount depending on the type of document listed in Annex I of the Stamp Tax Law are used to calculate (Revenue Administration 2016: 31).

Documents which are accepted to be exemption takes place in Annex II. All parties involved in the document have liability for payment of the stamp tax. All different document is subject to the tax apart from each other.

If a person who signs a document regulated in law, he/she will be a taxpayer for stamp tax. The tax can be paid in three ways as follows: by putting the printed stamp, in respond of receipt, and by withholding (Şenyüz et al. 2018b: 357–358).

1.3.4 Taxes on Wealth

Turkish taxation system comprises three wealth taxes; motor vehicle tax, property tax, and inheritance and gift taxes.

Motor Vehicle Tax

The subject of the tax is "land motor vehicles registered to traffic bureaus or offices, helicopters and airplanes registered to the Directorate General of Civil Aviation." Registration of the motor vehicles in the traffic, municipality, and docks occur in the taxable event (Revenue Administration 2006: 26).

Taxpayers are individuals and the legal person who have motor vehicles that are registered to their own names in the traffic register and the civilian air-vehicle register maintained by the Ministry of Transport and Infrastructure (Revenue Administration 2016: 31). The tax is calculated and accrued every year, and it can be paid in two equal installments: in January and July.

There are three main classifications for motor vehicles for accepting in the subject of tax (Şenyüz et al. 2018b: 387–391): List 1: "cars, motorcycles, and terrain vehicles, etc.," List 2: "minibuses, panel vans, motorized caravans, buses, trucks, etc.," and List 3: "planes and helicopters."

The age, value, type, the number of seats, cylinder capacity, maximum gross weight are used to calculate motor vehicle tax for land vehicles and maximum takeoff weight is used to calculate for planes and helicopters (Oktar 2018: 372).

Property Tax

Property tax aims at taxation of the buildings and lands in Turkey. The tax value of the building/land calculated under Property Tax Law No 1319 is used to be the tax base. The owner of the building/land, the owner of any usufruct over the building/land or if no one is the owner, any person that uses them are a taxpayer for the tax (Revenue Administration 2016: 30).

Property taxes are assessed every year depending on municipality according to rates from 0.1 to 0.3% of the tax values of land and buildings. Increased rates being 100% are used for calculation in the metropolitan municipality (Şenyüz et al. 2018b: 377).

Local municipalities take payments every year in two equal installments. The first is paid during the period from March through May, and the second in November. Payment can be made at banks, online, or in cash (Oktar 2018: 365).

Inheritance and Gift Taxes

Inheritance and gift given to Turkish citizens not only in Turkey but also in other countries are taxed. The inheritance tax is applicable for resident foreigners. The subject of tax based on a gift on Turkey or another country is assets received from Turkish citizens and or assets located in Turkey. The inheritance and gift tax based on assets located in Turkey is used for nonresident foreigners (Revenue Administration 2016: 30). Assets being gift or inheritance are taxed according to a progressive tax rate which is from 10 to 30% and 1 to 10% of the value. If a taxpayer pays any tax for inherited in a foreign country, the tax may be deducted from the taxable value of the asset (Şenyüz et al. 2018b: 405).

A tax return is used for the declaration by the taxpayers to submit inheritance and gift tax. The tax return for inheritance tax must be given four months after the date of death. If the death occurs in Turkey and the taxpayer is outside of Turkey, the declaration period is extended to six months (Revenue Administration 2016: 24–25).

The payment of the tax is made in 3 years in six equal installments. The installments are paid in a biannual period; the first in May, and the second in November each year.

1.3.5 Taxes on Foreign Trade

Turkish taxation system composes of many taxes on foreign trade, but the most important of these are Customs Duty, and Single and Cut off Tax.

Customs Duty
Customs Duty aims to be taxed on import goods. Turkey's Customs Duty legislation is regulated by Law No 4458 which came into force on January 1, 2000. Customs duties are not included in the scope of the Tax Procedures Law. The procedural provisions of the customs duty are regulated by the Customs Duty Law No 4458, which is its own law (Şenyüz et al. 2018b: 337).

The law regulates "free circulation of goods, registration of customs declaration, and temporary importation in case of partial exemption" to be taxable events. As a taxpayer, those who make these transactions are responsible for making a declaration to the customs office. Customs duties are calculated through tariffs, declared and paid by the taxpayer until ten days dating from notification (Revenue Administration 2016: 32).

Single and Cut off Tax
Goods, especially those that come with passengers or via mail or fast shipping transportation are the subject of Single and Cut off Tax (SCT). SCT is levied on goods that are sent by mail or fast shipping by purchasing over the internet from a foreign country between € 30–1500 or goods included in the exemption of personal belongings and brought to the passenger and the value between € 430–1500 per shipment and each passenger.

SCT tax rate about the goods coming from the EU countries is 18%, and the goods coming from other countries are 20%. Imports of these goods are allowed from customs after payment of SCT (Terzi 2017: 96–97).

1.4 The Main Problems of Turkish Tax System and Need for Reform

The Main Problems Of Turkish Tax System
There have been many changes and reforms in the Turkish tax system, but they could not be sufficient to solve the problems. Even some of the regulations have led to the root of new problems. In Turkey, especially the legal regulations called "tax reform" have made the tax system more complicated than improving the system and increased bureaucratic procedures. Tax reforms have led to deformations in the

system (Aktan 2009: 55). Therefore, The Turkish tax system has some problems. One of the problems is complexity.

The complexity of the tax system leads to problems related to predictability, manageability, difficulty, and applicability (Slemrod 1989). Many factors lead to the complexity of the tax system such as tax expenditures, complex economic relations, measures to prevent tax avoidance, and regulations to ensure tax justice (Budak and James 2018: 28–29). Tax expenditures not only complicate tax laws but also lead to loss of income. For example, in Turkey, due to the exemption, exclusions, and discounts the state renounces of the tax income approximately 24% of total tax revenues (Hazine ve Maliye Bakanlığı 2018: 285).

There are several methods to calculate complexity and to make comparative analyses. According to Budak and James (2018), level of legal complexity of Turkish tax system is lower, but the level of operational complexity that is related with the implementation of the laws is higher than in developed countries, this analysis is based on Office of Tax Simplification (OTS) index. TMF Group Financial Complexity Index (2017) report observed that Turkey is the jurisdiction with the world's most complex tax and accounting requirements. The other indicator for tax complexity is "time to comply," and Turkey has 216 h total tax time in a year. This score is close to the world average (based on 190 economies) but above in the developed countries (PWC and World Bank 2018: 97).

Another problem of the Turkish tax system is that the tax base is limited and the number of taxpayers is low. The income tax is based on the principle of the declaration, and as a requirement of the global system, all elements of income must be declared. However, the last situation reached by the system has observed that Turkish tax system is a divergence from the global system. Therefore, the ratio of active income taxpayers to the total citizen population in Turkey is only 2, 3% (OECD 2017: 77). Average 95% of the personal income tax is collected through withholding. The other reason for this deficiency is determining taxable income. There are two theories to determine: source theory and net accretion theory. The tax base is limited because the source theory is accepted in Turkey.

Despite the implementation of similar tax structure, direct taxes are 32%, and indirect taxes are 68% of tax revenues collected in Turkey, contrary to other OECD countries. The main reason for the high share of indirect taxes in Turkey is not high rates; its reason is that direct tax revenues are not sufficient. Indeed, the share of direct taxes in GDP is 13.9% including social security payments (OECD 2018: 150). This rate is so below the OECD average. Inadequate collection of direct taxes leads to a shift in the tax revenue composition toward indirect taxes; damages principle of justice in taxation and causes to increase in the informal economy.

When considered together with other reasons, it is observed that the informality is high and tax reforms are not effective in reducing this. The rate of the informal economy in Turkey is 31.4% which is the highest rate in the 34 OECD countries in 2017 (Medina and Schneider 2018: 46).

Tax amnesties issued to adapt to the new tax regulations have convicted the tax system to periodic amnesties in Turkey. The process of implementation of tax amnesties which started with the first tax reform in 1924, 37 laws containing tax amnesties have entered into force until today. The tax amnesty was issued approximately once every three years, but especially after the 2000s, it has been made every two years. The negative effects of tax amnesties on the taxpayers' attitudes and behaviors have also caused a decline in their volunteer tax compliance behavior (Çetin Gerger 2012: 107).

In addition, there are some specific problems with the tax system. For example, the personal income tax tariff has a strong progressive structure, the principle of differentiation is not implemented effectively, and the corporate tax rate is not competitive in today's conditions in Turkey. Another problem is that the structure of wealth taxes is not appropriate to the modern tax system and their application is inefficiency.

Recommendations For The Reform In Turkish Tax System

As a result of frequent changes in tax laws for many years, the Turkish tax system has become complex, unjust, and unenforceable. Therefore a fundamental tax reform should be made in the tax system instead of minor changes.

First of all "New Generation Tax System" should be created in our country and should be given the assurance that a retrospective review of the activities, revenues or assets of taxpayers will not be made. In this process, the shadow economy should be prevented by expanding the tax base and providing more taxpayer to give a declaration.

The most important step that should be taken for the expansion of the tax base is to pass from the source theory to the net accretion theory in the definition of income. With the transition to the net accretion theory, the definition and scope of the income will expand, and the tax system will increase its ability to capture tax economic activities.

In addition, to ensure justice in taxation and to implement taxation on financial power, according to the person's civil and family status, the minimum subsistence allowance should be considered in income tax. The minimum subsistence allowance is a social exemption method applied in modern tax systems.

After the minimum subsistence allowance is put into effect, the number of exemptions and exceptions in tax laws should be reduced. Thus, the complexity of the tax system will be eliminated, and the tax system will become simpler, more comprehensible, and effective. Also, it would be useful to rewrite the basic tax laws to make the tax system understandable and feasible and to provide a simple and clear text. In order to make the tax system more competitive, arrangements should be made to enable consolidation in corporate tax and VAT in accordance with global developments.

When comprehensive tax reform is made in our country, tax amnesty must be made for the last time to eliminate the injustice of the old tax system. The content of this amnesty law should be determined very well and should be supported by a good inspection mechanism.

1.5 Conclusion

Turkey has a modern tax system based on taxation of income, expenditure, and wealth. The Turkish tax system achieved this modern structure with the fundamental tax reform in 1950. In order to adapt to the EU and global developments, significant reforms were made in the field of VAT, SCT, foreign trade taxes, and corporate tax after the 1980s. Also, many changes have been made to various economic, social, and political aims.

As a result, the Turkish tax system includes all taxes in modern tax systems but is extremely complex and incomprehensible regarding implementation. As a matter of fact, according to TMF Group Financial Complexity Index, it is determined that the Turkish tax system is the most complicated tax system in the world.

In the Turkish tax system, source theory is essential in the definition of income. Therefore the tax base is limited, the number of taxpayers is low, and the informal economy is widespread in Turkey. Also, because income taxes cannot be effectively applied and sufficient tax revenues cannot be collected, the rate of indirect tax in Turkey is very high. As a result of all this, frequent tax amnesties come to the agenda in Turkey. Thus, the Turkish tax system has entered into a "vortex of failure."

To make the Turkish tax system simpler, more comprehensible, and effective, the "New Generation Tax System" should be created. The following reforms should be made in this process:

- In the definition of income, the net accretion theory should be accepted instead of the source theory.
- According to the person's civil and family status, the minimum subsistence allowance should be considered in income tax.
- The number of exemptions and exceptions in tax laws should be reduced.
- The basic tax laws should be rewritten to make the tax system understandable and feasible.
- Arrangements should be made to enable consolidation in corporate tax and VAT in accordance with global developments.
- A final tax amnesty must be made with comprehensive tax reform.
- All these reforms should be supported by a good inspection mechanism.

If these policy proposals are implemented, many problems in the tax system will be solved. This situation will increase tax compliance and tax awareness of taxpayers.

References

Aktan, C. C. (2009). "Bitmeyen Senfoni ve Vokal Katkılar", *Ekonomi Bilimleri Dergisi*, 1 (1): 39–58.

Annicchiarico, B. & Cesaroni, C. (2018). "Tax Reforms and The Underground Economy: A Simulation-Based Analysis", *International Tax and Public Finance*, 25: 458–518.

Ateş, L. (2008). "Recent Tax Reform in Turkey", ECPR Joint Sessions Rennes Workshop 5, Retrieved from https://ecpr.eu/Filestore/PaperProposal/3e99b74f-a40f-495c-9fb4-2e63f74a4cfc.pdf.

Başpınar, A. (2009). *Tax Law & Turkish Tax System*, Ankara, Turkey: Republic of Turkey Ministry of Finance Strategy Development Unit.

Bicer, R. (2009). "Withholding Taxes under Turkish Corporate Income Tax Law", *IBFD European Taxation*, 542–552.

Budak, T. & James, S. (2018). "The Level of Tax Complexity: A Comparative Analysis Between the UK and Turkey Based on the OTS Index", *International Tax Journal*, January–February.

Bulutoğlu, K. & Thirsk, W. (1999). "Turkey's Struggle for a Better Tax System", in Thirsk, W. (Ed.), *Tax Reform in Developing Countries*, pp. 1–32, Washington D.C., USA: World Bank.

Çetin Gerger, G. (2012). "Tax Amnesties and Tax Compliance in Turkey", *International Journal of Multidisciplinary Thought*, 2 (3): 107–113.

Deloitte. (2011). *Turkey International Tax and Business Guide*, Retrieved from https://www.verginet.net/dokumanlar/2011/dtt_tax_guide_2011_turkey.pdf.

Demirli, Y. (2011). *Gelişmekte Olan Ülkelerde Vergi Reformları ve Türkiye'de Gelir Üzerinden Alınan Vergiler Açısından Değerlendirme*, Ankara, Turkey: Maliye Bakanlığı Strateji Geliştirme Başkanlığı Yayını.

Hazine ve Maliye Bakanlığı. (2018). *Vergi Harcamaları Raporu*, Ankara, Turkey: Hazine ve Maliye Bakanlığı Gelir Düzenlemeleri Genel Müdürlüğü.

Hodzic, S. & Celebi, H. (2017). "Value-Added Tax and Its Efficiency: EU–28 and Turkey", *UTMS Journal of Economics*, 8 (2): 79–90.

Jha, R. (2010). *Modern Public Economics*, Second Edition, New York, USA: Routledge.

Karakoç, Y. (2017). *Genel Vergi Hukuku*, Ankara, Turkey: Yetkin Yayınları.

Khalilzadeh-Shirazi, J. & Shah, A. (1995). *Tax Policy in Developing Countries*, Third Edition, Washington D.C., USA: World Bank.

Medina, L. & Schneider, F. (2018). *Shadow Economies Around the World: What Did We Learn Over the Last 20 Years?* IMF Working Paper No. WP/18/17, Retrieved from https://www.imf.org/en/Publications/WP/Issues/2018/01/25/Shadow-Economies-Around-the-World-What-Did-We-Learn-Over-the-Last-20-Years-45583.

OECD. (2006). "Tax Policy Reforms in Turkey", Retrieved from https://www.oecd.org/tax/tax-policy/37154710.pdf.

OECD. (2017). *Tax Administration 2017: Comparative Information on OECD and Other Advanced and Emerging Economies*, Paris, France: OECD Publishing.

OECD. (2018). *Revenue Statistics 1965–2017*, Paris, France: OECD Publishing.

Oktar, A. (2018). *Türk Vergi Sistemi*, 2. Edition, İstanbul, Turkey: Türkmen Kitabevi.

Otonglo, C. & Trumbic, T. (2006). "Giving a Facelift to the Turkish Tax System", *Paying Taxes Case Study: Turkey*, Washington DC, USA: World Bank, 68–71. Retrieved from http://www.doingbusiness.org/content/dam/doingBusiness/media/Reforms/Case-Studies/2008/DB08-CS-Turkey.pdf.

Özker, A. N. & Esener, S. Ç. (2010). "Kurumsal Bir Vergi Reformu Sürecinde Hedefler ve Vergilemeye Yönelik Beklentiler", *Hukuk ve İktisat Araştırmaları Dergisi*, 2 (1): 21–32.

PWC & World Bank. (2018). *Paying Taxes 2018*, Retrieved from https://www.pwc.com/gx/en/paying-taxes/pdf/pwc_paying_taxes_2018_full_report.pdf.

PWC. (2018). *Global Mobility Services: Taxation of International Assignees – Turkey*, Retrieved from https://www.pwc.com/gx/en/services/people-organisation/global-employee-mobility/global-mobility-country-guides/assets/pwc-gm-folio-turkey.pdf.

Revenue Administration. (2006). *Taxation in Turkey*, Ankara, Turkey: The Presidency of Revenue Administration Department of Taxpayer Services Publication No: 21.

Revenue Administration. (2016). *Turkish Taxation System*, Retrieved from http://www.gib.gov.tr/sites/default/files/fileadmin/taxation_system2016.pdf.

Şenyüz, D., Yüce, M. & Gerçek, A. (2018a). *Vergi Hukuku*, 9. Edition, Bursa, Turkey: Ekin Basım Yayın Dağıtım.

Şenyüz, D., Yüce, M. & Gerçek, A. (2018b). *Türk Vergi Sistemi*, 15. Edition, Bursa, Turkey: Ekin Basım Yayın Dağıtım.
Slemrod, J. (1989). "The Return to Tax Simplification: An Econometric Analysis", *Public Finance Quarterly*, 17(1): 3–27.
Taş, R. (1995). "Türk Mali Sisteminin Uzun Dönem (1923–1980) Gelişiminin Yapısal ve Oransal Analiz Yöntemleriyle Değerlendirilmesi", *Ankara Üniversitesi SBF Dergisi*, 50 (1): 355–382.
Terzi, G. (2017). "Dış Ticarette Tek ve Maktu Vergi Uygulaması", *Mali Çözüm Dergisi*, Eylül-Ekim 2017, 143: 93–102.
The World Bank. (1991). *Lessons of Tax Reform*, Washington D.C., USA: The World Bank Publication.
Thirsk, W. (1991), "Overview: The Substance and Process of Tax Reform in Eight Developing Countries", in Thirsk, W. (Ed.), *Tax Reform in Developing Countries*, pp. 1–32, Washington D.C., USA: World Bank.
TMF Group. (2017). "The Financial Complexity Index 2017", Retrieved from https://www.tmf-group.com/en/news-insights/publications/2017/financial-complexity-index-2017/.

Adnan Gerçek is a Professor of Fiscal Law at Bursa Uludağ University, Faculty of Economics and Administrative Sciences, Department of Public Finance, Bursa, Turkey. Prof. Gerçek is a member of the Turkish Tax Council, and an editor of the International Journal of Public Finance. He is also a member of the Scientific Board of International Public Finance Conference/Turkey. He received his Ph.D. in public finance department at the Institute of Social Sciences, Bursa Uludağ University in 2001. His research focuses on tax law, tax system, tax administration, tax collection procedure, taxpayers' rights, tax responsibility, discretionary power of tax administration, and the e-taxation system. Prof. Gerçek has considerable experience in reform of tax system and tax administration in Turkey, development of e-taxation system, and taxation of companies.

Feride Bakar Türegün is an Assistant Professor of Fiscal Law at Bursa Uludağ University, Faculty of Economics and Administrative Sciences, Department of Public Finance. Dr. Bakar Türegün is a member of Publication Committee of International Journal of Public Finance. Through the scholarship of The Scientific and Technological Research Council of Turkey, she has been at Vienna University of Economics and Business Institute for Austrian and International Tax Law as a guest researcher in 2015. She received her Ph.D. in the public finance department at the Institute of Social Sciences, Bursa Uludağ University in 2017. She took part in tax-related projects and she has authored many articles. In her research, she focuses on taxpayers' rights, tax audits, comparative tax law, taxation of companies and tax risk management.

Chapter 2
Restructuring of Revenue Administration in Turkey

Tamer Budak and Serkan Benk

2.1 Introduction: A Brief Historical Setting

The foundations of the Turkish Revenue Administration go back to the era of the Ottoman Empire. The first financial organization in the Ottoman Empire era was established during the reign of Murat I (1359–1389), which was subsequently developed by Suleiman the Magnificent in a way to bring about a more efficient revenue and spending structure of the state. However, it is not possible to speak of a Ministry of Finance in the Ottoman State in its fullest sense until 1838. Prior to it, the functions of the Ministry of Finance had been carried out by an administration known as "*Hazine-i Amire*" headed by a person in charge called "*birinci sınıf muhasip* (first-class accountant)" or "*defterdar* (head of the financial department)". There was also "*Darphane Nezareti* (Bank Note Printing House Supervision)", acting as an independent body from Hazine-i Amire and "*Mansure Hazinesi* (Mansura Treasury)" to manage military income and expenses (Tezcan 2003, pp. 126–128).

The Ministry of Finance was officially founded in 1838. It was made up of departments, each headed by a high-ranking official called "*reis* (chairman)." *Harac Dairesi* (Tribute Department) charged with the duties of revenue administration in modern sense was also part of the Ministry of Finance. The main task of the Tribute Department was to collect charges received from municipalities from each neighborhood called "*Avarız* (extraordinary tax in the Ottoman Empire)" and "*Bedeli Nuzul* (Nuzul Levy)." It is observed that in 1881, the Ministry of Finance was divided into two units, being called "*Heyet-i Merkeziye*" and "*Heyet-i Mülhaka,*" respectively. Within this structure, initially the General Directorate of Revenues was included in *Heyet-i*

T. Budak (✉)
Department of Fiscal Law, İnönü University, Malatya, Turkey
e-mail: tamer.budak@inonu.edu.tr

S. Benk
Department of Public Finance, İnönü University, Malatya, Turkey

H. Kıral and T. Akdemir (eds.), *Public Financial Management Reforms in Turkey: Progress and Challenges, Volume 1*, Accounting, Finance, Sustainability, Governance & Fraud: Theory and Application, https://doi.org/10.1007/978-981-15-1914-7_2

Merkeziye. However, subsequent changes in the functional and organizational structure of the Ministry of Finance were made in 1908 to the effect that such structural modifications somewhat formed the basis of the current system. Interestingly, the very first decree by the first Turkish Grand National Assembly passed simultaneously with the proclamation of the Republic in 1923 was itself a tax law (www.gib.gov.tr).

Although the Ministry of Finance was founded by the modern Turkish Republic in 1923; it is noted that Law no. 2996 concerning Finance Power Organization and Duties (Official Gazette: July 7, 1936; 1349), a legal regulation of the Ministry's organizational structure and duties, was enacted in 1936 (GİB 2010, p. 1). With this statute, a triple system of organization was formed comprising the Directorate of Public Revenue (General Directorate of Revenues), the Directorate of Collection and the Commissions of Tax Objection and Appeal. While the duty of the Directorate of Public Revenue was to prepare the revenue budget and laws of the state to manage the tax organization, the Directorate of Collection was entrusted with the application of laws relating to revenue collection, receiving tax assessment forms, and gathering accounts coming from provinces. The Commissions of Objection and Appeal were assigned to deal with tax disputes and carry out procedures for judgements on tax payment.

With an amendment in 1942, the Directorate of Public Revenue was abolished and two separate general directorates under the names of "Public Directorate of Indirect Taxes" and "Public Directorate of Direct Taxes" were instead created. However, in 1946, by virtue of Law no. 4910 Related to the Change of Articles of Law no. 2996 Related to the Foundation and Duties of the Ministry of Finance and to the Addition of Some Articles to this Law (Official Gazette: June 7, 1946: 6327), the Turkish Revenue Administration was brought under an umbrella regime and rebranded as General Directorate of Revenues. In 1950, Law no. 5655 amending the Articles of Law no. 2996 Related to the Foundation and Duties of the Ministry of Finance and the Addition of Some Articles to this Law (Official Gazette: April 3, 1950; 7473) also overhauled the provincial organizational structure of the revenue administration, resulting in abolishment of the "General Directorate of Collection" and replacement of the Directorate of Public Revenue with the General Directorate of Revenues. Another significant outcome was the introduction of new independent tax offices (DPT 1996, p. 60).

Notably, the most radical change in the organizational structure of the Turkish Revenue Administration was made by Statutory Decree no. 178 of 1983 (Official Gazette: December 14, 1983; 18251, which combined the Ministry of Finance, the Ministry of Customs, and the Ministry of Monopolies under a single unified structure to streamline the operations. While the remit of the General Directorate of Revenues was extended to include direct and indirect taxes; the General Directorate of Customs and the General Directorate of Control were assigned to respectively carry out all procedures relating to customs duties (www.gib.gov.tr).

A comparable attempt to fundamentally restructure the Turkish Revenue Administration was another legislation through the Law on the Organization and Tasks of Presidency of Revenue Administration, No. 5345 (Official Gazette: May 16, 2005;

25817) which came into force in 2005 marking a new period into which the Turkish Revenue Administration entered under a framework of restructuring, only to be reorganized as a semi-autonomous administration affiliated with the Ministry of Finance.

2.2 Efforts to Transform the Turkish Revenue Administration

A brief historical summary above shows a strong desire to constantly modernize the revenue system. To that end, early meaningful efforts to restructure the Revenue Administration can be seen as early as in the 1950s. They were initially reactive in the sense that the groundwork for such efforts mainly targeted the problems that the revenue administration faced and consisted of corrective proposals aimed at solving them. Not only did remedial solutions come from experiences with domestic practice, but international institutions, researchers, and practitioners played an influential role shaping relevant policies (Karayılan and Alantar 2003, p. 64). In fact, the first of such studies by the latter was a report presented by James Martin and Frank Cush to the Ministry in 1951 (Ünal 2014, p. 60). In this report, the staff regime and budget structure of the revenue administration as well as the problems related to the central and provincial administration were raised and pertinent solutions were proposed to solve them. In the 1960s, the restructuring of the revenue administration came to the fore again and in 1963, a report entitled "Report on the White Mission on Tax Administration in Turkey" was prepared by Frank White to advise the Ministry. In the report, it was emphasized that the revenue administration had to be transformed into an independent organization (Kırım, 2001, pp. 105–107). Moreover, White's proposal included a new Undersecretariat of Revenue and severance of the relations between the governor, provincial treasurer and district revenue officers, and tax administration in provincial organizations (Sevik 2006, p. 8).

The draft law of "Revenue Administration" prepared in 1964 is another important study carried out by the Ministry of Finance, allowing the Tax Reform Commission to be formed in 1960s. Pursuant to this study, a draft law aiming to organize the Revenue Administration as "General Secretariat of Revenue" was sent to the parliament, but failed to become law. The 1980s marked another attempt in the form of a report by Adnan Baser Kafaoglu who pointed to a need for the Revenue Administration to be restructured; however, his proposals were not followed and no regulation came to frutation (Öner 2005a). From the mid-1980s, a number of studies, draft laws, and reports on restructuring the Revenue Administration were prepared, but none was put into effect (Oz and Karakurt 2007, p. 82).

By the 1990s, disagreements over the restructuring of the Revenue Administration resurfaced again due to Turkey's budget deficits and financing problems experienced. In 1991, a panel themed "The Restructuring of Turkish Revenue Administration" was arranged by Marmara University Financial Research and Implementation

Center. In this panel, the participants expressed their views on how an effective revenue administration would be created (Milliyet 26.01.1991: 5). A Taxation Specialization Commission Report prepared by the Turkish Union of Chambers and Exchange Commodities in 1992, stressed that the Revenue Administration did not have a healthy organization to carry out its functions adequately. Again, in 1996, the report of Taxation Specialization Commission of TOBB (Turkish Union of Chambers and Exchange Commodities) drew attention to persistence of "The Problems of the Revenue Administration" which called for urgent action. In the Taxation Specialization Commission Report of 2001, the State Planning Organization (DPT) in 2001 highlighted the problems of the Revenue Administration and presented its own assessments on how to enhance the effectiveness of the administration (http://www.sbb.gov.tr/wp-content/uploads/2018/11/08_Vergi.pdf).

The common trait of all these studies aimed at restructuring the Revenue Administration at different levels is the desirability of restructuring the general framework for the superstructure of institutions. It can be stated that the primary elements emphasized in these studies were for the strengthening of the administration, the development of its technological infrastructure, making the organizational structure more functional, the restoration of the relation between the center and the provinces, and the realization of an administrative mentality with the taxpayer in its focus. Also in these studies, the harmony between the units making up economical policies was mentioned to the extent that tax policies could not be created independently from economical policies.

However, the Turkish Revenue Administration that was largely formed by way of regulations in the 1950s profoundly retained its structure until 2005 (Öner 2005a, p. 38). Efforts directed at reshaping and developing its shortcomings always remained on the agenda mainly stimulated by the studies carried out before 2005, but the reason why no satisfactory resolution was materialized is because the problem could never be treated from a holistic perspective. Moreover, the fact that public sector deficits increased continuously and the taxes could not be collected on time and sufficiently, causing increase in indebtedness gradually but surely revealed the need for a powerful revenue administration.

It is observed that concrete steps to ensure the restructuring of the revenue administration in the real sense began to be taken in the 2000s. In that vein, the passage of Law no. 5345 in 2005 provided a much needed legal framework for structural, organizational, and functional transformation of the Revenue Administration (Güzelsarı 2007, pp. 204–205). It is only with this law that a more holistic approach to the process of restructuring the Turkish Revenue Administration was adopted for the first time (Arıoğlu 2005, pp. 69–70). Thus, this study examines the restructuring process of Turkish Revenue Administration in two distinct stages, before and after the law of 2005.

2.2.1 *Pre-2005*

Before 2005, the central organization of Turkish Revenue Administration took the form of a general directorate of revenues as a main service unit, headed by the deputy secretary of the Ministry of Finance, together with "Regional Directorates of Revenues" as its peripherals. This administrative structure was, as can be seen in Fig. 2.1, made up of a sufficient number of assistant general managers, heads of department, managers of branches, officials and other staff working under the supervision of a general director (Tezcan 2003, p. 136).

The General Directorate of Revenues was seemingly organized in a relatively simple way. Its main duties were initially set out by a legal framework as "preparing and carrying out the policy of state revenue" in accordance with article 12 of Decree no. 178 and later expanded by two subsequent statutory Decrees no. 516 and 543 in 1993 and 1994, respectively, to entail the following duties:

(a) It prepares and carries out the policy of state revenue,
(b) It prepares laws related to state revenue and all kinds of changes related to these,
(c) It arranges the revenue budget of the state with its intended legislative goals,
(d) It takes precautions that will provide the harmony of the taxation system of local administrations with that of the state,
(e) It examines all kinds of laws, offers. and drafts that would have an effect on the revenue and expresses its opinions on these and ensures the appropriateness of the drafts to the policy of state revenue and taxation technique,
(f) It sustains international taxation relations, carries out dual or multilateral tax agreements,
(g) It ensures the implementation of laws pertinent to the state revenue,

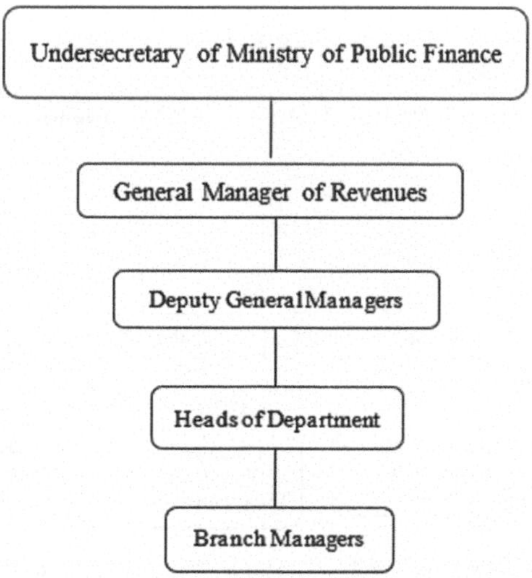

Fig. 2.1 Turkish revenue administration before 2005

(h) It takes necessary precautions for the state receivables to be collected on time and in a way that is compatible with laws,
(i) It carries out tax supervision,
(j) It improves the services of tax technique implementation and carries out procedures related to other taxes,
(k) It replies to questions about the disagreements and hesitations in practical implementation of rules and procedures,
(l) It carries out procedures relating to taxes to be written off and the writing off the receivables of the treasury that cannot be collected and become overdue in accordance with the laws,
(m) It collects, assesses, publishes assessment and collection accounts and statistics,
(n) It cooperates with international institutions on issues concerning taxation, attends meetings, and expresses views,
(o) It provides taxation intelligence services,
(p) It designs and carries out data processing services for the procedures within the scope of its functions and determines what duties to be carried out, ensuring that the organization has the necessary capacity for this purpose,
(q) It devises enabling procedures within the organizational field to allow duties to be examined and checked by its controllers.

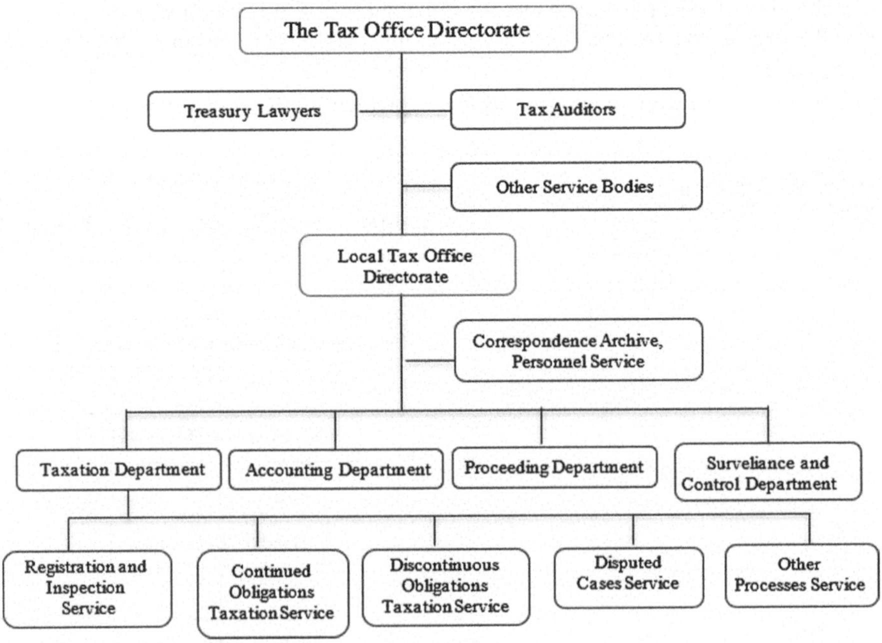

Fig. 2.2 Pre-2005 provincial organization of directorates of tax administration

As seen in Fig. 2.2, the total of 111 Directorates of Revenue were set up within the scope of Statutory Decree no. 178 together with a tax office provincial organization. To make sure the above-specified duties discharged at a level of regions by Regional Directorates of Revenue, it was projected to establish Regional Directorates of Revenue in 12 regions in accordance with Statutory Decree no. 543. From June 1, 1998 onwards, six regional directorates were put into operation in Adana, Ankara, Antalya, Erzurum, Izmir, and Samsun. Further tax office directorates, taxation directorates and directorates of revenue were set up in accordance with Statutory Decrees no. 516 and 543, comprising the provincial organization of revenue administration.

The way in which the Turkish Revenue Administration is organized in the form of a General Directorate caused some important problems within the organizational scope hindering its effectiveness. Of all the problems perhaps the foremost is that it became no longer possible for revenue administration to carry out its duties with the existing central and provincial structures of organization. The General Directorate of Revenue was responsible for carrying out a wide range of significant duties including keeping up with developments in economical and social life, creating policies of taxation, preparing and carrying out appropriate regulations and the taxation policies for minimizing risks in the process of implementation, preparing international taxation agreements for realizing tax supervision, creating and improving the necessary infrastructure for tax practices, and using modern technology in tax practices. Ever-expanding scope of operations made it impossible to carry out such a broad spectrum of duties requiring expertise at different levels between fragmented departments within the single structure of general directorate. Hence the lack of productivity became an issue (DPT 2001, p. 28).

Another significant problem with the pre-2005 structure was that the central and provincial organizations of the revenue administration were not organized in a complete hierarchical integrity. For instance, although there was not a hierarchical relationship between the General Director of Revenue and provincial treasurers, the most authorized people in provincial regions, tax offices, and the provincial organization of the revenue administration were administratively accountable to provincial treasurers (Gerçek et al. 2006, p. 3). This situation also adversely affected the connection between the General Directorate of Revenue and the provincial organization of the general directorate. In other words, it was not possible for the central organization of the revenue administration—pursuant to Law for Provincial Administration no. 5442 (Official Gazette; May 18, 1949: 7236)—to exert a direct authority on "provincial treasurers" who were placed within the provincial organization of the revenue administration. Despite having a broad authority in local tax matters, provincial treasurers could not deal with the procedural aspects of taxation properly because they were overburdened with other duties. As for the Regional Directorates of Revenue, they failed to discharge their duties properly because they were not sufficiently authorized to act in matters falling under their operational remit which were described mainly as functions aimed at their regional tax offices (Bureau of Tax Auditors 2002, p. 27).

Another problem seemed to relate to definition of the duties, authorization, and responsibilities of individual units in the central and provincial organizations of the revenue administration remained equivocal in most parts causing confusion and overlapping in practice. For instance, even though the General Directorate of Revenue was made up of heads of department organized in view of different kinds of taxes, tax offices themselves were organized according to taxation procedures. This situation proved to be unsatisfactory preventing both the central and provincial organizations from discharging their fundamental duties properly (Gerçek 2007, p. 62.). Yet another problem arose from the revenue administration's inability to follow the procedures in a complete manner at all stages of taxation ranging from the imposition of taxpayers' obligation to determination of whether taxpayers had paid their taxes on time. The main reason for this flaw was apparently two-fold that the authority of tax offices was kept quite wide in scope. Moreover, tax office staffs were overwhelmed with an intense flow of paperwork and circulation owing to excessive regulation which left them unable to fulfill their more fundamental duties properly such as planning, coordination, and observation (Bureau of Tax Auditors 2002, p. 29).

The Revenue Administration suffered a lack of leadership and adequate training to form a sense of self-scrutiny or internal checks. Failing to create a corporate culture and mentality of internal check created an ownership problem, mostly discouraging management using own initiative and thus preventing the staff from taking on responsibility. This situation became prevalent with the consequences of operational problems not being solved on-site and on time. Because of the fact that both the provincial and central organizations undertook the same duty in many overlapping fields, the unnecessary workload of the central organization increased exponentially causing a waste of time, manpower, and money (DPT 2001, p. 28). A notable shortcoming was that the General Directorate of Revenue did not have a stated mission or vision. Nor did it have strategic plans or goals concerning the future. Not only did their absence make it impossible for the revenue administration to conduct a performance review, but it also made inspection a difficult task to achieve.

From the outset, the revenue administration was organized on the basis of the hierarchy within the civil service, but the simple hierarchic structure was by no means enough for effective management of the organization. Although employment rights of the staff in the central and provincial organizations of the Revenue Administration were by law subject to the merit system, the lack of objective and transparent criteria applicable to appointment, promotion, change of location, and personal rights of the staff affected their long-term effectiveness and productivity negatively (DPT 2001, p. 29).

The Revenue Administration in Turkey did not possess the right equipment for the latest technological developments existed in the developed countries to allow it to follow modern developments and keep up with them. Slow technological progress delayed appropriate changes to meet the necessities of evolving economical and social life, causing inability to deliver effective service to taxpayers (Acar et al. 2003, p. 8).

In brief, the pre-2005 Turkish Revenue Administration was criticized on the grounds that the organizational structure was insufficient and inward-oriented, the provincial units were not directly connected to the center, direct and fast communication could not be realized among units, the processes of assignment and function were disconnected from each other, resources could not be used productively and efficiently enough by reason of inadequate technological infrastructure, qualified staff could not be retained, and the participatory and transparent mindset of administration was not sufficiently settled at all levels mainly due to poor quality in the delivery of services to taxpayers, the insufficiency of qualified labor and their lack of motivation as well as other structural problems stemming from ineffective administrative structure (Arıoğlu 2005, p. 70). Added to these was unsettled and ambiguous tax policies for processes to facilitate effective and quality service to taxpayers (Öner 2005b, p. 38), and to devise an objective performance assessment system that would increase efficiency and productivity in the revenue administration (Sarılı 2003, p. 212) were criticized.

2.2.2 *The Post-2005*

A tax strategy was developed to tackle rising tax administration issues of institutional improvements, automation, transparency, compliance, taxpayer services and tax audit. To reform the ailing structure of the revenue administration, a new law was enacted on the organization and duties of the Directorate of Revenue Administration (DRA) on May 16, 2005. The objective of the Law is to lay down the necessary legal ground to ensure that DRA will operate on the principles of transparency, accountability, participation, efficiency, and effectiveness. A taxpayer-oriented approach is adopted to implement the revenue policy. Fairness and impartiality are emphasized in tax collection to ensure voluntary compliance, to take necessary measures so as to help taxpayers to easily meet their liabilities by providing high-quality services with a consideration of taxpayer rights, all of which is thought to lead to the most cost-efficient way possible. The main institutional and organizational change in the law of 2005 is the establishment of a semi-autonomous tax administration operating on a functional basis. The Directorate of Revenue Administration is empowered to make plans on how to perform its tax responsibilities to address the need to minimize the tax burden on taxpayers by simplifying the tax system and providing the necessary assistance to taxpayer. In order to achieve its mission to increase the level of voluntary compliance with tax laws and combat against the black economy, the administration has established the following strategic objectives for improvement during the period between 2004 and 2006:

- Improve the efficiency and effectiveness of tax administration,
- Establish a modern integrated information technology support system, and
- Rationalize and simplify the tax system.

This process also implies a functional reorganization of the General Directorate of Revenue (GDR) from 2004 onwards. The tax policy department of the Ministry of Finance is upgraded while the tax audit management capacity is strengthened. A new strategy for taxpayer service as well as for improvements in the relations between taxpayers and the General Directorate of Revenue is also developed. With regard to the main organizational change, some entirely new functions were assigned to the Presidency of Revenue Administration as part of the restructuring process for expansion of services. For the first time, the functions such as taxpayer services, audit, and strategic planning were introduced and organized both at the headquarters and the local level. As a complementary component of the strategic planning function, a new performance management system based on the best international practices is also established. This system is to be supported by the use of IT and management information system in performance measurement (OECD 2006, p. 6).

With Law no 5345, adopted in 2005, the General Directorate of Revenue was abolished and replaced by the Presidency of Revenue Administration as part of the Ministry of Finance. In other words, from June 16, 2005 onwards revenue units were brought under the General Directorate of Revenue within the Ministry of Finance, central organization and financial offices and fiscal directorates in districts and provinces were all but abolished. An autonomous organizational structure under the new Revenue Administration was directly linked to the Ministry of Finance in the place of the abolished structure (Tuncer 2005, p. 10; Erol 2005, p. 23).

The visions of the Presidency of Revenue Administration are listed as

- Applying revenue policies on the basis of fairness and objectiveness
- Collecting tax and other revenues at the minimum cost
- Ensuring voluntary compliance of taxpayers
- Respecting taxpayer rights
- Supplying high-quality services to taxpayers (Tekin and Çelikkaya 2018, p. 252).

The new revenue administration was organized in two units: the central organization and the provincial organization. The organization of the headquarter consists of main services and numerous units of consultation and facilitation. In this concept, the Main Service Units are the Department of Revenue Management, the Department of Taxpayer Services, the Department of Implementation and Data Management, the Department of Collection and Disputed Cases, the Department of Audit and Compliance Management, and the Department of EU and Foreign Affairs. On the other hand Consulting Units are arranged as the Department of Strategy Development, the Department of Legal Consultancy, and the Department of Consultancy on Media and Public Relations, while Facilitation Services are delivered by the Department of Human Resources, the Department of Support Services. Pursuant to Article 8 of Law no. 5345, duties assigned to the main service units could be carried out by more than one head of department if and when deemed necessary (Fig. 2.3).

Article 4 of the same law lays down the duties of the Revenue Administration as follows: (GİB 2006, pp. 10–11).

(a) to implement the state revenue policy to be determined by the Ministry,
(b) to facilitate taxpayers' adaptation to the new tax regime and services,
(c) to take necessary measures in order to protect taxpayers' rights and relations based on mutual confidence between Ministry and taxpayers,
(d) to inform taxpayers about their rights and obligations arising from tax laws,
(e) to participate in the decision-making process and by-law workings related to the state revenues policy,

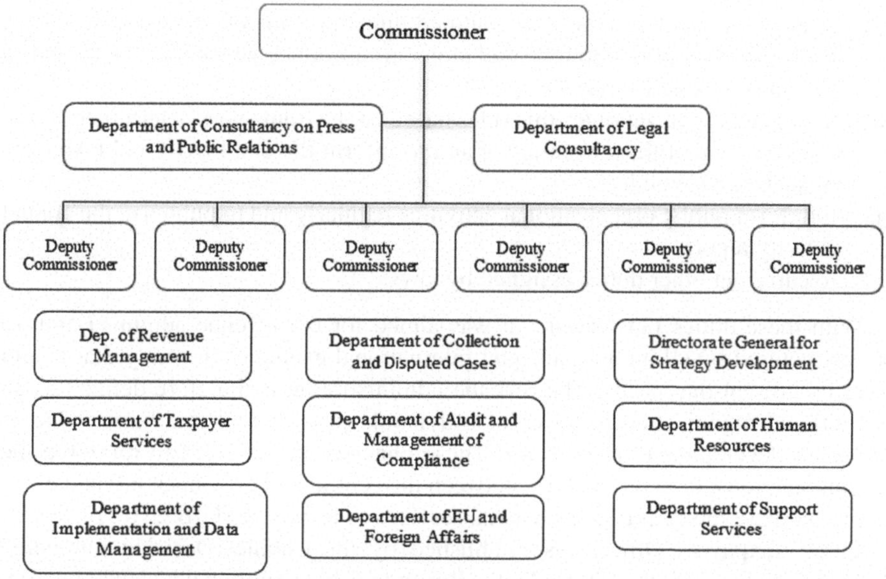

Fig. 2.3 Post-2005 central organization of directorates of tax administration

(f) to ensure the collecting of the governmental claims and to take necessary measures to this end,
(g) to take necessary measures to reduce disputes to the minimum level possible and to provide alternative dispute settlement,
(h) to collect information about taxation and to implement data processing activities,
(i) to measure the costs of all exceptions, exemption, and discounts in the tax laws or other fiscal laws, and to analyze their economic and social effects,
(j) to carry out tax inspection and audit at the direction of main policies and strategies determined by the Ministry and to take necessary measures in order to prevent tax loss and evasion,
(k) to take measures to ensure that the implementation of the local administration revenues policy is in compliance with the state revenues policy,
(l) to review all proposals of legislation and drafts of laws affecting revenues and to report its views on these regulations,
(m) to cooperate with other institutions and organizations on the implementation of revenue laws and regulations and to carry out data trade for this purpose,
(n) to follow international developments in the area of interest and to cooperate with the EU, international organizations, and other states,
(o) In accordance with the laws and regulations, to carry out operations for the deletion of tax dues and other governmental claims beyond the statutory limits,

(p) to ensure the enhancement of qualified human resources, to design strategies for improvement in employee relations, to introduce new career plans and to measure staff performance,
(q) to prepare organizational ethic rules based on the framework determined by the Civil Servants Ethics Committee and to inform the employees and taxpayers of such service ethics,
(r) to inform public organizational activities regularly and to publicize the annual activity report,
(s) to carry out other duties assigned by laws.

With these duties put forward, it was aimed for the revenue administration to be restructured by taking into account international examples in a way that would meet its present-day needs. The revenue administration is therefore defined as an institutional organization in terms of a dynamic process with the basic value of "constant development" at its heart. These changes are intended to reinforce the communication and functional ties between the central and provincial organizations and to increase the quality in provincial services to taxpayers (GIB 2018, p. 28).

Large Taxpayers Office was established by the Cabinet Decision numbered 2006/10788 dated 15.08.2006 under the Revenue Administration which was restructured with the Law No. 5345. The aims of establishing Large Taxpayers Office are to serve limited number of taxpayers who account for majority of tax revenues; to monitor and control these taxpayers closely; to determine problems occurred and take precautions; to eliminate uncertainties concerning interpretation of legislation and rules and to provide voluntary compliance (BMVDB 2019a, b, Large Taxpayers Office Activity Report-2013 http://www.bmvdb.gov.tr/lto_english/Activity%20Report.pdf).

Large Taxpayers is serving to 835 of the largest taxpayers of Turkey. The taxpayers are determined by some criteria such as turnover, total tax paid, assets and number of employees. Currently, 835 taxpayers of Large Taxpayers Office produce around 20% of total tax revenues of Turkish economy (BMVDB 2019a, b, Large Taxpaer Office http://www.bmvdb.gov.tr/lto_english/index.html)

Purpose and goals of Large Taxpayers Office are to increase voluntary compliance, to improve all kinds of economic activities, to improve service quality, and to become a participant and productive institution globally.

In view of the local organization of Revenue Administration under Law no. 5345, local administration consists of 30 Tax Office Directorates in 29 cities and 52 provincial offices. Tax Office directorates include group directorates, subdirectorates, sub-units, tax offices, and commissions. The structure of the Local Revenue Administration is illustrated in Fig. 2.4.

The provincial organization is thus made up of directorates of tax administration directly affiliated to the center, tax offices with the same responsibilities and authorization in places where directorates of tax administration were founded and directorates of revenue were affiliated to financial offices (Öner 2005b, pp. 36–39). The Directorates of tax administration are chambers that identify taxpayer in their

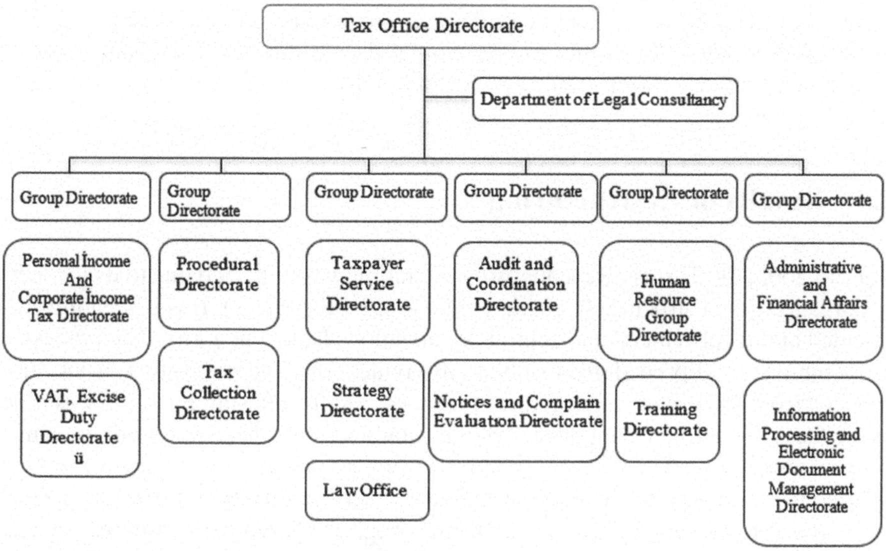

Fig. 2.4 Local revenue administration after 2005

scope of authority, carry out procedures of imposition, assessment, notification, collection, cancellation, deferment, return, payment, accountancy of taxes, and other similar tax activities and financial liabilities. They are authorized to make tax claims and respond to tax disputes before the judicial authorities arising out of legal procedures, objection to tax demand, appeals and declarative verdicts when necessary, and execute judicial decisions. They also develop and improve tax practices, express views to taxpayers about the implementation of laws, inform taxpayers about their rights and liabilities and observe the rights of taxpayers in practice. Among its duties are to carry out taxpayer services, data processing, statistics, collection of data, human resources management, buying, hiring, tax audit and inspection, cooperation, judgment so on and so forth. The Directorates of tax administration are made up of group managements, sub-managements affiliated with them, branches, tax offices and commissions. Tax offices are too chambers that identify taxpayers within their operational area to impose, assess, and collect taxes.

Directorates of revenue, designed to be affiliated to the financial offices, are provincial units responsible for answering tax queries on behalf of the provincial treasurer, preparing responses to requests and issues raised during inspections conducted on behalf of the provincial treasurers, compiling statistical data collected from provincial tax offices and sending them to the Directorate of Revenue Administration, as well as carrying out procedures concerning the cancellation of public receivables that need writing off (GİB 2018, p. 2) Currently the provincial organization of the Directorate of Revenue Administration comprises 30 directorates of tax administration (29 directorates of tax administration and 1 large taxpayer office) and 456 tax offices.

In July 2018, Turkey exchanged its 95-year-old parliamentary system for the new presidential system. According to presidential decree number 4, the status quo is maintained (Official Gazette: July 15, 2018: 30478).

2.3 Results of Restructuring

Prior to 2005, the Turkish Revenue Administration was criticized due to its incoherent organizational structure (General Directorate of Revenues). It was seen inward-oriented and its provincial and central organizations lacked integrity. The processes of assignment and procedures exhibited disconnection. The motivation of the staff suffered from inadequate management practices. As a result, staff retention was poor particularly in qualified manpower. Regular dataflow from other institutions remained inconsistent at best. The technological infrastructure was in its early stages, lacking in effectiveness and efficiency to the degree that service quality to taxpayers needed improvement and called for a new understanding, one based on a participatory and transparent administrative mentality. Such criticisms were addressed by Law no. 5345 of 2005 which intended to reorganize the entire system of Turkish Revenue Administration. It has brought about a radical restructuring whose results can be outlined as follows:

Firstly, the organizational structure of the revenue administration was separated from the central and provincial organizations of the Ministry of Finance after 2005. Instead, it was reorganized as a distinct organization directly responsible to the Minister in charge making it a semi-autonomous body. While previously, the General Director of Revenues ranked below the deputy secretary, the undersecretary and the minister, the new regulation placed the director as the highest ranking officer in the Directorate of Revenue Administration. Thus, the Directorate was excluded from the hierarchy of the deputy secretaries and the undersecretary. Red tape in the processes of decision-making and assignment were somewhat reduced.

In the pre-2005 structure, the central organization of the General Directorate of Revenues was organized according to tax types. The post-2005 legislation reorganized tax offices, which are provincial organizations, on the basis of the types of procedures. Moreover, tax office managers and staff had difficult and often complex duties such as knowing the taxation processes, accounting records and compulsory observance of all taxes, determining and supervising taxpayers. In the post-2005 period, an organizational model adopted in the center and the provincial organizations is function-based and focused on taxpayers. Thus, the newly-formed provincial organization now mirrors functional units projected as in the center. Accordingly, the new provincial organization now contains group directorates for taxpayer services, taxation, collection procedures and jurisdiction, accountancy, inspection and harmony management, human resources and support services as well as other directorates and branches linked thereto (Öner 2005b, p. 38).

With the new regulation, revenue units comprising the provincial organization of the General Directorate of Revenues are detached from the financial offices, which were the provincial organizations of the Ministry. The provincial organization of the Revenue Administration is reorganized in a directly affiliated way to the Administration. However, in the provinces where a directorate of tax administration does not exist, units affiliated to the administration will continue to operate in the body of financial offices. In doing so, the administration now has an opportunity to directly correspond with the provincial organizations without governors and district governors intervening.

While duties such as creating taxation policies, preparing and applying draft laws were previously carried out by the General Directorate of Revenues and provincial organizations, in the aftermath of 2005, these duties were divided between the Ministry of Finance and the newly founded Revenue Administration (Öner 2005a, p. 152). In the new organizational structure, the duties of preparing revenue policies and draft law proposals, and a state revenue budget are transferred to the Ministry of Finance, while the duties such as the application of tax laws, tax supervision, and realization of tax harmony are given to the Revenue Administration. Thus, the effective implementation of tax policies is ensured through a powerful Revenue Administration.

However, a greater challenge was to define duties, determine authorization and establish pertinent procedures and processes in the operation mechanism and more importantly, to achieve adaptation to the change and create a mindset to put it in practice. For instance, the new organizational structure in the post-2005 enabled the Revenue Administration to gain administrative integrity in its central and provincial organizations, which became noticeable in the procedures for appointment and assignment of the staff throughout. Many other procedures have since been successfully applied first hand (Öner 2005b, p. 38). Previously the Ministry of Finance held the exclusive authority in staff appointments. The new system now accords such authority to the Director of Revenue Administration.

Bringing departments like human resources, taxpayer services and the European Union within the body the Directorate of Revenue Administration is consistent with the goals of increasing the quality and productivity of services, creating a new mentality of administration based on performance, and creating a functional revenue administration focused on taxpayers (Saraçoğlu and Arslan 2007, p. 30; Gerçek 2009, p. 31).

Law no. 5345 centralizes delivery of the mutual services of tax offices such as accountancy and executive acts under a single authority of the presidency of each directorate of tax administration. In this way, it is ensured that tax offices are only responsible for taxation procedures, thereby fostering a closer contact with taxpayers. Concentration in operations means that the workload of regional tax offices is profoundly decreased, as they are saved from dealing with cumbersome internal procedures allowing them more time for taxpayer services such as declaration, registration, and supervision as core duties.

Although the automation and digital transformation of the Revenue Administration started in the 1990s, the process of automation and digitalization gained momentum only after the restructuring. Following the success of early pilot schemes, the first stage of Tax Office Automation Project called VEDOP-1 began to roll out in 1998. In the first stage of the project, 155 tax offices comprising 22 provinces were included in the scope of the projected automation system. Through this implementation, procedures such as registry, assessment, collection, vehicle registration, accountancy, and personnel affairs were implemented for the first time in an integrated manner in the computer-aided environment. The second stage of project (VEDOP-2) marked an important step between 2004 and 2006 in the fight against the black economy. The aim was to offer taxpayer services faster and in a better quality. Project VEDOP-2 allowed 283 tax offices to be included in the scope of automation. Added to these were group directorates and units of tax auditors. The new system of e-declaration, the Data Warehouse Project (VERIA) and call centers were created. The automation of tax offices responsible for collecting motor vehicle tax and the infrastructure of central servers was strengthened to match the widening capacity. The transition process to Web-Based Automated Tax Offices (e-VDO) is heralded as an important milestone in modernization of the revenue administration (GIB 2018, p. 4).

The third stage of VEDOP project (VEDOP-3) went on live in 2007 with a goal to extend e-VDO implementations to 301 tax offices, incorporating revenue services of 585 fiscal directorates. By 2008, e-VDO transformation of 507 revenue units and 123 tax offices were successfully completed (GİB 2018, p. 4).

By 2018, 447 all directorates of tax administration, large taxpayer offices and 581 fiscal directorates are included in the automation (GİB 2018, p. 4).

Furthermore, 2004 saw completion of a full transition to the system of "electronic declaration" within the scope of automation pursuant to Law no. 5228. New regulations within the process of restructuring the revenue administration ensured that by 2009; declarations received in the electronic environment remarkably constituted 99% of the total declarations submitted (GIB 2013, p. 43).

Notably, a new initiative to build a data warehouse aiming to determine tax-related issues falling outside declarations, to check the truthfulness of declarations and provide an informative support to control units has commenced within the scope of Data Warehouse Project (VERIA) (Tekin and Çelikkaya 2018, p. 261).

Turkish Revenue Administration has now reached a highly automated, technologically advanced e-services system including a complete e-tax office system with which a taxpayer can easily conduct almost anything he could finalize by getting to a tax office.

2.4 Conclusion

When the historical development of the Turkish Revenue Administration is examined, 2005 represents an important turning point in terms of radical changes in its organizational structure and working method. Prior to 2005, the tax administration was stiff, outdated and, unresponsive to ever-increasing demands placed on it; transformation into a flexible and agile structure shifted the focus on taxpayers who expect quick and effective decisions. International developments in taxation have played an important part in bringing about this process of change.

The Revenue Administration before 2005 did not have the organizational capacity to follow international developments closely and act on them. It lacked adaptation skills to make necessary changes to confront new challenges of economical and social life in a relatively short time. Not only did this situation impair its efficacy to devise quality service to taxpayers, but also its effectiveness and efficiency came under scrutiny, failing to rise to the challenges posed by modern economy and its ever-growing volume. By the same token, tax compliance ability was too affected. The classical organizational structure of the revenue administration suffered the predicted sysmptoms of insufficiency and complete inward-orientedness. The lack of coordination between central and provincial organizations resulted from the fact that provincial units were not directly affiliated with the center and that quality problems arose from the poor services of assignment and taxpayers, because of the inability to use resources efficiently and productively. The ensuing demoralization and lack of motivation among staff in turn gave rise to retention problems. Neither transparency nor participation was fully demonstrated in the administrative thinking at any levels, naturally causing weaknesses in the process of tax creation, imposition, and compliance. Law No. 5345 is geared toward addressing all these problems in such a way as to realize complete coordination and communication between the central and provincial organizations, increase quality in taxpayer services, and have the ability to use resources productively and efficiently. In the new legal regime, the central and provincial organizational structure of the revenue administration and its working principles were restructured in view of international developments.

These efforts at restructuring of the Turkish Revenue Administration have a dynamic character which has transformed it into a flexible organization with an ability to adapt to the needs and demands of the modern society. Economic necessities pose new challenges and newly created Turkish Revenue Administration is designed to tackle these difficult problems from a holistic approach, with the purpose of making the whole tax system more responsive, efficient and productive in line with international developments.

Acknowledgements We would like to thank Dr. Mete Erdem for his constructive comments and valuable contribution on an earlier version of this paper. However, we remain solely responsible for any errors and omissions.

References

Acar, F., Zeynel, M.G., Gökmen, S. (2003). "Türk Vergi Sistemindeki Sorunlar Ve Çözüm Önerileri", *Vergi Sorunları Dergisi*, 173: 3–109.

Arıoğlu, O. (2005). "Gelir İdaresi Başkanlığı". *Vergi Dünyası Dergisi*, 286: 68–72.

BMVDB, (2019). "Large Taxpayers Office Activity Report-2013" http://Www.Bmvdb.Gov.Tr/Lto_English/Activity%20Report.Pdf (Accessed on March 15th, 2019).

BMVDB, (2019). "Large Taxpayer Office", http://www.bmvdb.Gov.Tr/Lto_English/Index.Html (Accessed on June 4th, 2019).

DPT (Devlet Planlama Teşkilatı) (2001). *Sekizinci Beş Yıllık Kalkınma Planı, Vergi Özel İhtisas Komisyonu Raporu, Ankara.*

DPT (Devlet Planlama Teşkilatı). (1996). *Yedinci Beş Yıllık Kalkınma Planı, Vergi Özel İhtisas Komisyonu Raporu*, Ankara.

Erol, A. (2005). "Gelir İdaresinin Başkanlık Şeklinde Yeniden Yapılandırılması", Lebip Yalkın Mevzuat Dergisi, 23.

Gelir İdaresi Başkanlığı (The Presidency Of Revenue Administration). (2006). *Taxation In Turkey* 2006, The Presidency Of Revenue Administration Department Of Taxpayer Services, Publication No: 21, Ankara.

Gelir İdaresi Başkanlığı (The Presidency Of Revenue Administration). (2010). *Faaliyet Raporu 2009,* Gelir İdaresi Başkanlığı Strateji Geliştirme Daire Bakanlığı Yayını, Yayın No: 112. Ankara.

Gelir İdaresi Başkanlığı (The Presidency Of Revenue Administration). (2013) *2013 Yılı Performans Programı*, Gelir İdaresi Başkanlığı Strateji Geliştirme Daire Bakanlığı Yayını, Yayın No: 156. Ankara.

Gelir İdaresi Başkanlığı (The Presidency Of Revenue Administration). (2018) 2018 Yılı Performans Programı, Gelir İdaresi Başkanlığı Strateji Geliştirme Daire Bakanlığı Yayını, Yayın No: 254. Ankara.

Gerçek, A. (2007). Çağdaş Eğilimler Çerçevesinde Türkiye'de Vergi İdaresinin Modernizasyonuna Yönelik Çalışmaların Değerlendirilmesi. *ISGUC The Journal Of Industrial Relations And Human Resources*, *5* (2).

Gerçek, A. (2009). "Gelir İdaresi Ve Vergi Denetiminin Yeniden Yapılandırılması: Dünü, Bugünü Ve Yarını". *Vergi Sorunları Dergisi,* 254:1–52.

Gerçek, A., Sarılı M.A., Tezcan, K. (2006). *5345 Sayılı Kanun Çerçevesinde Gelir İdaresi Ile Vergi Denetiminin Yeniden Yapılandırılmasının Değerlendirilmesi Ve Öneriler*. Gelirler Kontrolörleri Derneği, Ankara.

Güzelsarı, S. (2007). "Küresel Kapitalizm Ve Devletin Dönüşümü Türkiye'de Mali İdarede Yeniden Yapılanma". Yayımlanmamış Doktora Tezi, Ankara Üniversitesi Sosyal Bilimler Enstitüsü Siyaset Bilimi Ve Kamu Yönetimi Anabilim Dalı, Ankara.

Karayılan, İ. Alantar, D., (2003)." Gelir İdaresinin Yeniden Yapılandırılması" *Yaklaşım*, 127: 74–83.

Kırım, A. (2001). *Türk Gelir Yönetiminin Organizasyon Yapısı Ve Gelir Yönetiminin Yeniden Yapılandırılması,* TODAE Kamu Yönetimi Uzmanlık Tezi, Türkiye Ve Orta Doğu Amme İdaresi Enstitüsü, Ankara.

Milliyet (1991). Vergi daireleri bağımsız olmalı, Panel: Türk Gelir İdaresinin Yeniden Yapılanması, Marmara Üniversitesi Maliye Araştırma ve Uygulama Merkezi, http://Gazetearsivi.Milliyet.Com.Tr/Arsiv/1991/01/26, (Accessed on July 7th, 2019).

OECD (2006). "Tax Policy Reforms in Turkey", Center for Tax Policy and Administration, https://Www.Oecd.Org/Tax/Tax-Policy/37154710.Pdf (Accessed on March 4th, 2019).

Öner, E. (2005a). "5345 Sayılı Kanunla Gelir İdaresinde Öngörülen Düzenlemeler Ve Değerlendirilmesi-I". *Yaklaşım,* 152: 36–39.

Öner, E. (2005b). "5345 Sayılı Kanunla Gelir İdaresinde Öngörülen Düzenlemeler Ve Değerlendirilmesi-II". *Yaklaşım* 153: 38–44.

Öz, E., Karakurt B. (2007). "Türk Gelir İdaresinde Yeniden Yapılanma Ve Gelinen Nokta". *Finans Politik & Ekonomik Yorumlar* 44 (510): 80–90.

Saraçoğlu, F., Arslan, C.B. (2007). "Gelir İdaresinde Yeniden Yapılanma". *Mali Hukuk Dergisi* 132: 29–33.

Sarılı, M.A. (2003). "Türkiye'de Vergi Tahsilatında Etkinliğin Sağlanabilmesi İçin Gelir İdaresi Nasıl Yapılandırılmalıdır?" *Vergi Dünyası Dergisi,* 262: 201–222.

Şevik, M.E. (2006). "Yeniden Yapılandırma Sürecinde Gelir İdaresinin Analizi". Yayımlanmamış Yüksek Lisans Tezi, T.C. Sakarya Üniversitesi Sosyal Bilimler Enstitüsü Maliye Anabilim Dalı, Sakarya.

Tekin, F., Çelikkaya, A. (2018). *Vergi Denetimi*. 8. Baskı Seçkin Yayıncılık.

Tezcan, K. (2003). "Türk Vergi İdaresinin Tarihsel Gelişimi Ve Bu Süreçte Geçirdiği Aşamaların Etkinlik Açısından Değerlendirilmesi", *Çukurova Üniversitesi Sosyal Bilimler Enstitüsü Dergisi*, 12 (12): 125–146.

Tuncer, S. (2005). "Gelir İdaresi Başkanlığı", *Yaklaşım Dergisi*, 152.

Ünal, E.K. (2014). "Türkiye'de Kayıt Dışı Ekonomi Ve Vergi Denetimi". Yayımlanmamış Yüksek Lisans Tezi, Süleyman Demirel Üniversitesi Sosyal Bilimler Enstitüsü İktisat Anabilim Dalı, Isparta.

Vergi Denetmenleri Derneği (2002). Türk Gelir İdaresinin Yeniden Yapılanması Hakkında Rapor, Ankara.

Tamer Budak is a Professor in the Department of Fiscal Law at the Inonu University Law Faculty. He has taught Turkish tax law and international tax law for more than ten years at different universities in Turkey. He has also held visiting positions at two universities overseas including the University of Florida, Levin College of Law in 2012 and the University of Exeter in 2013–2014 He holds an MBA as well as Master degree in Economics, and also Ph.D. in Tax Law. He has published over 50 research papers and his 2 books include Constitutional Criteria in Turkish Tax Law: Ability to Pay in Turkish in 2011 and The End of The Tax Liability to The Turkish Tax Law in 2012 both of them published by XII Sheets Publishing in Turkey.

Serkan Benk is a Professor at Inonu University Department of Public Finance. He received a B.S. degree in Public Finance (1999) and an M.S. degree in Public Finance at Karadeniz Technical University (2002). Benk completed his Ph.D. at Uludag University (2007). His research interests in public finance are the theory of taxation, public economics, tax compliance and taxpayer behavior. In recent years, he has focused on ethics of tax evasion. He has collaborated actively with researchers in several other disciplines of social science, particularly psychology, business, theology and law. Prof. Benk has authored and contributed to numerous books, book chapters and articles on tax compliance and tax evasion.

Chapter 3
Tax Audit Reform in Turkey

Neslihan Karataş Durmuş and İmran Arıtı Erdem

3.1 Tax Audit

The audit, which can be expressed in different ways for each discipline, can be defined as the activity of evaluating the compatibility of an activity or transaction according to predetermined rules and the assessment of the actual situation of the activity or transaction in question (Tekin and Çelikkaya 2018: 26–27). According to the OECD (2006: 9), tax audit is an examination of whether a taxpayer has correctly assessed and recorded their liabilities and fulfilled other obligations.

An obvious definition of tax audit is not found in our legislation; instead, types of tax audit are explained. Investigating and determining the accuracy of taxpayers' declarations and ensuring the correct declaration as well as the audit of the central and provincial organization of the tax administration are the subjects to tax audit (Saraçoğlu and Pürsünlerli Çakar 2016: 150). However, internal audit, which means that the tax administration audits its own officials, is not involved within the scope of our study; only the audit of taxpayers which is performed by the administration is examined.

Several definitions of tax audit can be found in the literature. The starting point of those definitions is the purpose of the administration in tax audit or types of audit or the qualification of the official who performs the audit. With the effect of all those definitions, the concept of tax audit can be defined as follows: tax audit is the sum of ways and methods used to investigate and to determine through its officials whether the person responsible for the tax (taxpayer and tax responsible) has duly and completely fulfilled duties derived from laws in due time. However, tax audit

N. K. Durmuş (✉)
Educational Consultant, Republic of Turkey Ministry of National Education, Brussels, Belgium
e-mail: neslihankaratas@hotmail.com

İ. A. Erdem
Faculty of Political Sciences, Yıldırım Beyazıt University, Ankara, Turkey
e-mail: aritimran@hotmail.com

H. Kıral and T. Akdemir (eds.), *Public Financial Management Reforms in Turkey: Progress and Challenges, Volume 1*, Accounting, Finance, Sustainability, Governance & Fraud: Theory and Application, https://doi.org/10.1007/978-981-15-1914-7_3

includes not only the investigation and determination process, but also it ensures the person responsible for the tax to fulfill the duties in compliance with the legal procedure.

In the declaration basis which is predicated on reliance on taxpayers (Akdoğan 2017: 107), taxpayers are obliged to inform the administration with regard to their income, in accordance with the laws and secondary regulations. In this system which starts from the idea that the taxpayer knows his/her situation himself/herself best (Önen 2017: 101), the information declared by the taxpayer is considered correct until the administration proves the contrary, pursuant to the presumption of first appearance (*présompsion de sincérité de la déclaration*) as in many other countries (Bienvenue and Lambert 2010: 122; Saban 2015: 556; Karataş Durmuş 2016: 67). Although this presumption is for the benefit of the taxpayers, the administration may prove the contrary of the information and documents through information it has obtained and the audits it has performed. This situation enables the taxpayers to make their declarations as close to the real situation. However, it should be stated obviously that performing tax audits efficiently has a great share in providing the accuracy of taxpayers' declarations. As stated in the following parts of this study, multiple factors come into play in performing an effective tax audit. Legislation, the administrative organization, tax awareness, and the presence of well-trained officials can be pointed as some of those factors.

The tax audit has the purpose of directing the administration to act in compliance with the legislation and also to lead the taxpayers to provide accurate declarations (Organ 2008: 39). In addition to these purposes, tax audit has fiscal, economic, social, and legal purposes.

The fiscal purpose of tax audit means directing the taxpayers to provide an accurate declaration and ensuring the duly payment of taxes in due time and thus preventing the loss of revenue of the state. While the government, which is the creditor in the taxation relationship, aims to collect taxes on due time and completely, the taxpayers make an effort to pay less tax as far as possible. As a result of taxpayers‘ attitudes which emerge as tax avoidance or tax evasion, there is a tax loss in a fiscal manner in any case. However, tax administration can prevent solely tax evasion through tax audits. Since tax avoidance is a legal practice, there is no option for tax administration against this. There are several causes of tax evasion evaluated in the literature (Tekin and Çelikkaya 2018: 52; Özkök Çubukçu and Pınar 2009: 475-476; Karakoç 2004). The question which needs to be answered here is not "why taxes are evaded?", but it is "what should be done to prevent evasion?". Tax audit is one of the most efficient tools to prevent tax evasion. In this way, tax administration may have prevented existing or future tax losses and evasions. Thus, the government generates revenue from collected taxes and their administrative fines.

In the event that public revenues do not meet public expenditures, the implementation of different solutions by the government may adversely affect the country economically. Since the imbalance of income and expenditure affects economy negatively, the government should collect taxes without any loss and evasion (Beşel 2017: 14). However, by means of effective and widespread audits, evaded or unrecorded incomes of taxpayers can be detected. Thus, a reduction in the number of unrecorded transactions can be experienced and on the other hand, an improvement in economy can be observed by virtue of the money which gets into the market. Hence, thanks to tax audits, the economy will be affected positively.

The social purpose of tax administration means the fair and equitable distribution of income in society. The improvement of the income level of society and the fair distribution of income are one of the aims which are desired to be achieved by the government. At the same time, this social purpose means an obligation of the government which is provided by Article 73 of Turkish Constitution. This purpose can be fulfilled through the distribution of income, which is obtained from elimination or reduction of tax losses or evasions, to low-income group. Tax audit plays a role through the prevention of tax evasion in increasing the quality of life of people, enabling everyone to reach a quality of life which is compatible with human dignity and also increasing the public welfare. Tax audit contributes to the collection of taxes, as well as the creation of awareness toward paying taxes and avoiding tax evasion.

Another purpose of tax audit is the legal purpose. As a result of the sovereignty of the state, tax administration collects taxes compulsorily from taxpayers in compliance with the legislation. Taxpayers who cause tax losses or evasions are also detected and subject to a penalty within the framework of the authority given by the legislation. This detection can be performed by means of tax audits. In the audit process, tax administration should act in compliance with legislation. Otherwise, an annulment action against courts for cancellation of the tax treatment as an administrative act can be brought due to improper audit and this leads to loss of income.

Investigation and determination of the accuracy of taxes which should be paid indicate the functions of tax audit (Organ 2008: 43). Tax audit has four main functions which are *investigation, correction, prevention,* and *educating*. First of all, tax administration should *investigate* information and documents which are declared by taxpayers. The *investigation* function is the most important function of tax audit. Tax officials report the case when they determine that there are some deficiencies. Then they correct these deficiencies and implement the penalty in compliance with the legislation. Therefore, the person responsible for the tax learns the response of activities and transactions which are carried out knowingly or unknowingly by them and they take measures to *prevent* such situations in the future. In order for such a prevention function of tax audit to be effective, audits must be carried out at regular intervals. With other words, the person responsible for the tax inclines to act carefully in the activities and transactions due to the risk of auditing at any moment. Because tax officials do not treat taxpayers as potential criminals and provide information exchange during the audit process, and taxpayers also may be informed about several issues. Thus, those tax officials, who inform and warn taxpayers in case of need, serve the *educational* function of tax audit. Therefore, tax audit does not only serve to detect losses and evasions but it also carries out the *educational* function.

In order for tax audit to carry out its purpose and its functions to be effective, audits must have certain characteristics. In other words, tax audit should have a legal, objective, and comprehensive character and also it should contain sanctions. Tax audits, which do not have a legal basis or are not based on a legal authority and are not in compliance with the legislation, could not have a legal validity; thus, if the administration carries out an administrative act based on such a tax audit, administrative courts may annul this act. In taxation relationship, since there is an intervention to property rights of taxpayers, audits should be carried out in accordance with laws and other binding sources in order to protect rights of both the administration and taxpayers. Tax officials should carry out tax audits objectively (Beşel 2017: 47). They should not make an effort to reach a result on behalf of the administration or the taxpayer, during the audit process. It should be important that the process should be conducted objectively and based on the true conditions. If it is performed in this manner, then it should be evaluated that whether a sanction should be imposed or not. As it is mentioned before, taxpayers know that they would be faced with a sanction, when they carried out inaccurate or faulty activities or transactions. Because besides investigations and determinations, tax audits include sanctions when required. Tax audit, which is carried out by tax officials on books and documents of taxpayers, contains every kind of activities and transactions of taxpayers. Although the scope of the audit changes according to the type of the audit, tax officials should carry out the audit comprehensively within the framework of their authority given by laws.

As it can be understood, the success of tax audit depends on the audit to be carried out effectively in terms of its functions. In systems based on the declaration basis, in order to increase the level of voluntary compliance of taxpayers and provide declarations of the closest situations to reality, the existence of an effective tax administration as well as tax awareness (Beşel 2017: 145–147), tax morale (Aktan 2012: 15), and tax education are important factors. However, these concepts are interwoven concepts. Thus, an effective tax audit conduces to increases in the level of voluntary compliance of taxpayers, and also it contributes to the development of tax awareness. For instance, tax audit plays a wider role in supporting tax compliance and deterring non-compliance as well as enhancing the trust of taxpayers in the fairness and effectiveness of the tax system (OECD 2017: 57). It should be added at this point that a study indicates that there is a positive relationship between tax audit and voluntary compliance (Niu 2011: 248). Thus, it can be concluded that tax audit has a significant role not only to verify the correct compliance with tax laws but also to stimulate a shift in taxpayer behaviors toward a more compliant attitude (DeAgosto et al. 2018: 32).

The effectiveness of tax audit means whether the purpose of it is fulfilled or not (Beşel 2017: 116). In an effective tax audit, avoiding from the payment obligation should not be an attractive option for taxpayers (Seer and Roman 2010: 442). In terms of the effectiveness, the structure of the administration, the competence of tax officials, and the existence of adequate legislation are particular factors. If all of those factors reach the sufficient level, then the effective audit can be observed. There are two conditions in evaluating the effectiveness of audit; the first one is the economical effectiveness and the latter is the legal effectiveness. In the literature, different factors are mentioned for the measurement of the economical effectiveness such as audit rates, the number of taxpayers per inspector, tax bases subject to audit, the amount of taxes paid after audit, taxes collected at end of audit/the amount collected from sanctions (Beşel 2017: 117). From the perspective of the legal effectiveness, the basis of the legislation, the administrative organization, and an effective judicial body are of significance. It is important that the legislation should be clear and understandable for both practitioners and taxpayers. Also the legislation should not change frequently pursuant to the principle of legal certainty. Otherwise, taxpayers cannot know which procedural provisions that they can be faced with or how sanctions are implemented in case of any deficiency or fault. In addition, it should be noted that there are also some duties for legislature in terms of the effectiveness of tax audit, except the duties of the administration. The fact that legislature imposes tax amnesties frequently leads to taxpayers not to pay taxes or not to comply with tax procedure provisions. Although the scope of tax amnesty laws may be different, some laws include provisions which state that taxpayers who benefit from the amnesty cannot be audited. Such provisions affect the effectiveness of tax audit in a negative way.

3.2 Types of Tax Audit

In Turkish tax system, types of tax audit are regulated in Sect. 7 of Tax Procedure Law No. 213 (TPL). Although the title of the section is "physical enquiry and audit," inquiry and gathering information also take place in third and fourth chapters. As it can be understood from the systematics of TPL, fundamental types of tax audit are physical enquiry and tax inspection but inquiry and gathering information are also legal tools to assist other types of audit and to increase the effectiveness of tax audit (Soydan 2015: 175; Beşel 2017: 37).

3.2.1 Physical Enquiry

Physical enquiry has a particular place in tax audit. Especially in systems based on the declaration basis, considering the fact that taxpayers may hide some information (Tekin and Çelikkaya 2018: 134), physical enquiry helps to uncover undeclared issues and to determine the matter of fact. Physical enquiry can be described as an operation which includes the physical inspection of facts which should be determined on the spot for the implementation of tax laws (Somuncu 2014: 142). Thus, physical enquiry involves, for instance, the inspection and examination of goods in stock, premises, etc. (OECD 2006: 9).

The definition of physical enquiry does not appear in TPL. However, it can be noted that legislator determines what should be understood from the concept of physical enquiry and a definition can be deduced from this point of view. The purpose of physical enquiry is regulated between Articles 117 and 123 of the Tax Procedural Law No. 5432 dated 1949. Pursuant to these provisions, physical enquiry purposes "*to inspect and determine the facts and cases related to taxpayer and tax liability.*" TPL No. 213, which abolishes this law, includes records in the scope of physical enquiry. Therefore, physical enquiry involves the control of books and documents which should be kept or generated by taxpayers, as well as the inspection of taxpayers.

Within the process of physical enquiry, not only taxpayers but also persons, who do not register as a taxpayer while they should register, can be detected. After then, sanctions regulated in the legislation can be implemented to the detriment of related taxpayers. Except this, tax officials who are authorized for physical enquiry have also some authorities in respect of implementation of tax laws (Akdoğan 2017: 108). A detailed explanation on how some of those authorities can be performed can be found in the General Communiqué of TPL No. 168.

In literature, starting from the fact that inspections which are included in physical enquiry require special authorities, some authors accept that there is also a concept "widespread and intensive tax audit," except physical enquiry (Tekin and Çelikkaya 2018: 145–172; Somuncu 2014: 148–166). However, legislator has not introduced a separate regulation on this matter. Turkish Revenue Administration uses this term (Somuncu 2014: 142). In this study, authorities regulated in the legislation are wholly and briefly explained from the perspective of the systematics of TPL. Within this context, provided that a particular authority is given, auditors can use those authorities such as determination of daily receipts, control the use of cash register and determination of their daily receipts, auditing books which should be kept and documents which should be prepared, control whether the obligation of keep tax registration certificate is met or not, inspecting means of transport in terms of control the required documents or taking inventory on goods.

Although the authorities related to physical enquiry are regulated in TPL, the administration can charge officials, who have the authority for physical enquiry to perform other duties. For instance, such officials usually take part in the denouncement process (Somuncu 2014: 143). However, physical enquiry can be conducted so as to detecting persons who did not register as a taxpayer but should pay tax. It is important to identify those who do not have a taxpayer registration in the fight against the informal economy.

Tax officials who have the authority for physical enquiry are regulated in Article 128 of TPL. Pursuant to this article, these officials are physical enquiry officials, managers of tax offices, officials who are authorized for physical enquiry by legal authorities, and revenue specialists. In practice, both tax inspectors and tax office managers do not carry out too many enquiries due to their workloads (Beşel 2017: 41). Physical enquiry, which constitutes one of the important pillars of tax audit, is generally carried out by personnel who are authorized by tax offices. In the literature, the inadequacy of the qualification of the personnel who are charged with physical enquiry which constitutes one of the most important components of the audit is criticized (Beşel 2017: 43).

Physical enquiry can be carried out at all times without any necessity to inform taxpayers formerly (Article 130 of TPL). However, the term "all times" in here means all times within the working hours in relation to the type of activity. An exception to that is the control of means of transport; thus, physical enquiry can be carried out even in the night provided that the process of transportation is maintained.

Tax officials, who are authorized to carry out physical enquiry, should comply with procedural rules while exercising this power. A few of the procedural rules are showing the identification in the beginning of physical enquiry (Article 129 of TPL), recording matters identified with physical enquiry to the minutes of physical enquiry in accordance with the procedure (Article 131 of TPL), submitting or posting a copy of the minute of physical enquiry to the taxpayer and submitting the other copy to the relevant tax office.

With the development of technology and the transition to the electronic system in keeping records (electronic declarations, electronic invoices, electronic archive, the electronic notification, electronic tickets), developments in the audit mechanism have been experienced accordingly. Pursuant to Article 132/A of TPL, which is added by Article 6 of Law No. 6637, the method of electronic physical enquiry has been introduced to the system. With this method, which is significant in fighting with informal economy, the entire process of physical enquiry is conducted under the electronic system and at the end of the process, the minute of physical enquiry is prepared in an electronic form. Details of the implementation of these methods are regulated in the General Communiqué of TPL No. 453. As also indicated in this General Communiqué, if physical enquiry cannot be conducted electronically in case of technical impossibility or due to the nature of the activity, then the standard general provisions are applied to the process of physical enquiry and the preparation of the minute of physical enquiry. In 2018, electronic physical enquiry is carried out in 2.118.528 cases (GİB 2019: 95).

3.2.2 *Tax Inspection*

Tax inspection, which is often used as a synonym for tax audit (Organ 2008: 126), is first introduced with Article 124 of former Tax Procedure Law No. 5432. The definition of tax inspection is found neither in former TPL No. 5432 nor in current TPL No. 213. In former TPL No. 5432, what is meant by using the term tax inspection was stated as follows "investigating, determining and providing the accuracy of the amount of taxes to be paid according to books and accounts." In TPL No. 213, the terms "according to books and accounts" are excluded and the other parts of the abovementioned statement are included as the same. Although the terms "according to books and accounts" are removed, it can be expressed that the most comprehensive method in tax audit is tax inspection (Tekin and Çelikkaya 2018: 172). In literature, there are different definitions of tax inspection, which is regulated in between Articles 134 and 141 of TPL. However, the starting point of all of those definitions is "investigating, determining and providing the accuracy of the amount of taxes to be paid." From this point of view, tax inspection has the function of investigating the taxes to be paid, the function of preventing taxpayers and tax responsible from doing faults or fraud, and, finally, the function of educating taxpayers on the matters needed during the inspection process. All of those functions are important in generating revenue for the government, as well they are effective in providing voluntary compliance of taxpayers.

The objective of tax inspection is regulated in a comprehensive way by legislator and it has been given the opportunity to make all kinds of investigation related to the taxes to be paid (Akdoğan 2017: 111–112). Within this framework, tax administration, on one hand, can investigate books, documents, and records of taxpayers, as well as other parties of transactions which are subject to tax; on the other hand, it can also determine the real transaction or the real amount of tax liability.

The scope of tax inspection includes revenues from all taxes, fees, duties, and other such financial obligations related with general budget, special provincial administrations, and municipalities (Article 1 of TPL) except revenues from customs duties (Article 2 of TPL). The addressees of tax inspection are natural and legal persons who are obliged to issue, keep and submit books and documents, since tax inspection is carried upon these books, records, and documents (Article 137 of TPL). Taxpayers, who do not have the obligation to keep books and documents pursuant to tax laws, such as taxpayers who generate income from wages, immovable property and rights, or capital investment, are not frequently subject to tax inspection. If such taxpayers cause tax losses, then tax administration may apply complementary or ex-officio tax assessment.

Tax inspectors, assistant tax inspectors, fiscal director of the district, and tax office managers are entitled to carry out tax inspections (Article 135 of TPL). In addition to them, managers who take place in the central and provincial administration of Turkish Revenue Administration can perform tax inspections under all conditions.

Tax inspection can be carried out within 5 years after the first day of the calendar following the date of occurrence of the taxable event, including the current fiscal year (the lapse of time for assessment) (Article 138 of TPL) (Artun et al. 2019: 210). The fact that a previous tax inspection or ex-officio tax assessment was carried out for the same taxpayer does not constitute an obstacle to be carried out again a tax inspection on the same taxpayer and for the same period. However, in order to perform tax inspection once again, a difference in tax assessment must be observed which is applied based on different taxes from previous ones. On the other hand, tax officials can carry out tax inspections without any necessity to inform taxpayers formerly (Article 138 of TPL). They have discretion on this matter.

Tax inspection can be divided into two types: full and limited inspection. Definitions of these types of inspection are not found in TPL; only duration of these processes is mentioned. Pursuant to The Regulation on Procedures and Principles to be Applied On Tax Inspections, full tax inspection is the inspection which is carried out in a way to include components of the tax assessment for all kinds of activities and transactions related to one or more than one taxation periods in respect to one or more than one kinds of taxes. Tax inspections except this can be defined as limited tax inspections. Full tax inspections must be completed within 1 year, while limited tax inspections must be completed within 6 months. If the subject of tax inspection is tax refund for value-added tax, it must be finished within 3 months. Tax officials can request extra time from tax administration for tax inspection in case of a necessity.

In principle, tax inspection is carried out at the workplace of the taxpayer who is subject to this inspection. However, if tax inspection cannot be performed in the workplace due to the impossibility stemming from the unavailability of the workplace or abandonment of work and death, or due to the request of taxpayer or tax responsible, this inspection can be carried out at tax office. In these cases, all books and documents must be brought to tax office. Although there is no explanation in legislation, in the process of tax inspections which are performed in tax offices, tax officials must get information on the nature, qualification, and the scope of the activity, by going to that workplace.

As it is explained in detail in Article 140 of TPL and the abovementioned Regulation, there are some obligations to both taxpayers and tax inspection personnel in the inspection process. In order to prevent the annulment of the action, all procedural rules must be observed. In practice, errors in the procedure may occur in terms of the place in which the inspection is performed, the preparation of official reports, or the breach of the time limit provided for finishing the inspection.

If tax inspection concludes in favor of the taxpayer, then "tax inspection report on acceptance" is prepared; if it concludes to the detriment of the taxpayer, then "tax inspection report" is prepared. If it is detected that the taxpayer issued or used forged documents, then "tax crime report" is prepared in addition to "tax inspection technical report" and they are submitted to the public prosecutor in order to ensure the investigation or prosecution. Since tax inspection reports do not have an executive character, they could not be subject to any actions before courts. However, they can be subject to actions together with acts of tax assessment which depend on that tax inspection report (Tekin and Çelikkaya 2018: 203).

3.2.3 Inquiry (Inspection with Inquiry)

Although inquiry itself is not a single type of audit (Şenyüz et al. 2017: 161), it can be expressed as an audit mechanism which is performed against the possibility of hiding some books and documents by persons who are relevant with the taxable event or the taxpayer before the tax inspection starts. Inquiry, which may be seen as a type of tax inspection, can be named as "inspection with inquiry." It can be implemented at workplaces or on taxpayers's own who are determined in Article 142 of TPL, as well as it can be performed in case there are signs of tax evasion. Since inquiry is closely related to taxpayers' rights and freedoms, it should be implemented in a sensitive way.

Inquiry can only be conducted in case officials, who are entitled to carry out physical enquiry, find it necessary and the judge in criminal courts of peace decides on that. In here, the aim is to provide accurate information about taxpayers and related persons by obtaining the books and documents quickly. When inquiry is needed based on a denouncement, again, the decision of judge in criminal courts of peace is required. However, in case of a groundless denouncement, tax administration must give the name of the informant in regard to the request of the taxpayer who is subject to inquiry.

Officials, who are entitled to carry out tax inspection, are also entitled to perform inquiry. However, security forces may participate in inquiry along with those officials based on the nature of the activity. Pursuant to Article 18 of Turkish Criminal Procedure Law, inquiry cannot be performed at night and it is also applied in tax inspection process, due to the reference to the general provisions for procedural rules to be followed in inquiry. Inquiries, which are started but not concluded, are continued till the end of working hours.

Information and documents which are obtained during inquiry are recorded with an official report and kept in boxes. Administration must compensate the damage caused by the failure to keeping them well (Article 143 of TPL).

Inspection with inquiry should be concluded as soon as possible due to its close relation with individual rights and freedoms; thus, it should be completed at least within 3 months. Judge in criminal courts of peace can extend the finishing time with three more months.

3.2.4 Gathering Information

One of the methods, which help tax inspection to confirm the accuracy of information declared by taxpayers, is gathering information. It helps tax administration to collect information about both matters related with tax liability and the amount of tax which is subject to tax loss, and thus it is an essential method with respect to the effectiveness of tax audit. It is not a single type of tax audit by itself but it can be seen as a complementary method to other types of audit (Organ 2008: 146). The fact that taxpayers know that the administration can easily access information about themselves ensures that they are more careful in their activities and transactions and it also increases their voluntary compliance. There are two main components in gathering information; the first one is that information should be collected in compliance with laws and the second one is that information should be requested in a written or an oral form (Article 148 of TPL).

Pursuant to Article 148 of TPL, public administrations and authorities must give requested information about taxpayers and related persons. Those information can be given upon request or permanently. Article 151 of TPL explicitly states that it cannot be avoided to provide information other than in exceptional circumstances. Administration is obliged to keep obtained information in intelligence archives. The Ministry of Treasury and Finance decides on who will use this information. The application of intelligence archives has been implemented since 1989 (Tekin and Çelikkaya 2018: 126).

3.3 Reform Process

In order to provide a sound information on the process of tax audit reform, first of all the main line of reform should be identified. The reform process can be divided into two main periods depending on the significant steps which took in this process. The first period contains the duration till 2011 and the second period begins with 2011 and reaches out today. Thus, this differentiation can be regarded as a bird's-eye view of the process.

3.3.1 Tax Audit Units Prior to 2011

Tax audit was also performed in Turkey in the pre-Republican period. Although the fiscal audit system had its origins in *Basbaki Kullugu* (dated 1579) which was a part of financial organization of Ottoman Empire (Tabakoğlu and Taşdirek 2015: 93), a modern fiscal audit system was established on July 25, 1879 with the establishment of Inspection Committee of Finance which was the antecedent of Inspection Board of Finance (Yılmaz 2019: 19–20). Inspection Law, which included 17 procedural provisions in relation with execution of inspection, was issued on September 8, 1879. These regulations were prepared based on the French financial audit system (Tabakoğlu and Taşdirek 2015: 107).

Although it has undergone different changes over time, the most significant changes in this process were made Statutory Decree on the Structures and Duties of Ministry of Finance No.178 of 1983; however, this statutory decree was repealed by Statutory Decree No. 703 of 2018. Another significant change in the organization of tax administration was made with Law No. 5345 dated May 16, 2005. In this area, revenue controllers and tax auditors carried out tax audit. They constituted 90% of the officials who had the authority for audits. The remaining 10% were constituted by finance inspectors and account specialist. Finance inspectors also performed internal audit of Ministry of Finance and tax inspection was not their main duty (Ozansoy 2011: 56). In addition, revenue controllers had also the authority for internal audit of tax offices.

In order to provide harmony in tax audit units, Tax Inspection and Audit Coordination Board was established with the Law No. 6009 of August 1, 2010. This board, which was established for the purpose of coordinating the tax inspection, was abolished by the Statutory Decree No. 646 1 year after its establishment.

Prior to Statutory Decree No. 646, there were different methods in selecting taxpayers to be subject to tax audit. Tax administration has often selected taxpayers based on plans and programs for 1 year and taxpayers could be selected with a sample of regions, business, work groups, and taxpayers who exceed a certain amount of tax base (Tekin and Çelikkaya 2018: 177). In addition, denouncement to tax administration also has played a role as a source in starting tax inspections. However, it should be noted that there were significant points to pay attention regarding assessments of those denouncements.

3.3.2 *Tax Audit Units After 2011*

As it is mentioned, tax units comprised of Inspection Board of Finance and Board of Account Specialists which directly rested on Ministry of Finance, as well as revenue controllers which were rested on Turkish Revenue Administration which was one of the connected establishments of Ministry of Finance and tax auditors which constituted provincial organization in the period prior to 2011. In 2011, this structure has changed and a new structure has been constituted by means of combining those units. Thus, this change in the structure can be regarded as one of the two components of the tax audit reform.

Tax Inspection Board (TIB) has been established under Statutory Decree No. 646 published in the Official Gazette No. 27990 of July 10, 2011 and pursuant to this statutory decree, all of abovementioned tax audit units were gathered under a single roof named "Tax Inspector." In addition, the duties and authorities of TIB are regulated in detail in mentioned statutory decree and heads of groups are determined based on qualifications of taxpayers, rather than geographical areas pursuant to the same statutory decree (Figs. 3.1 and 3.2).

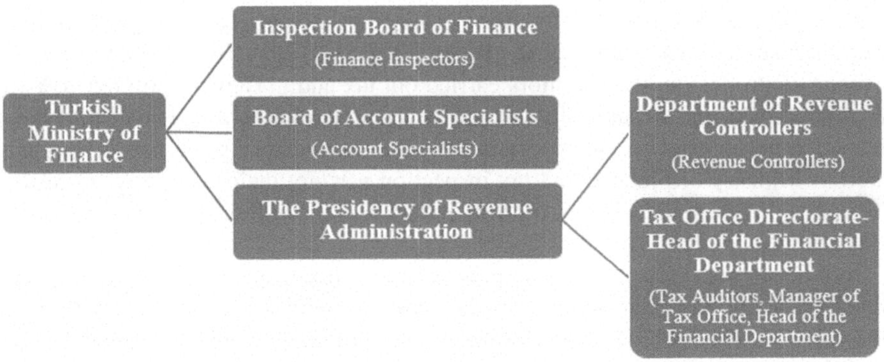

Fig. 3.1 Tax Audit Units Prior to 2011

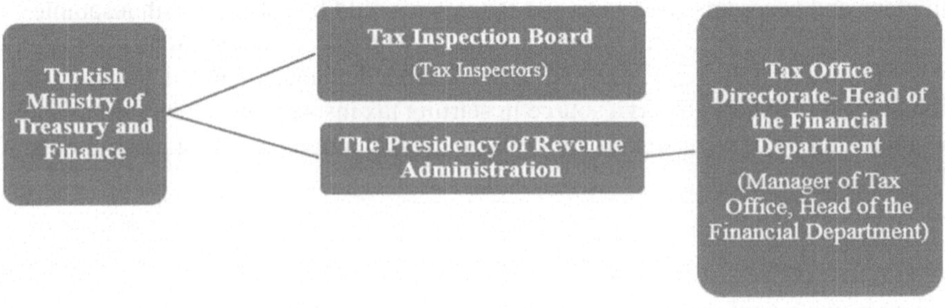

Fig. 3.2 Tax Audit Units After 2011

As it can be seen, after 2011, tax administration consists of, in central administration, TIB and the Presidency of Revenue Administration (RA) which is a connected establishment of Turkish Ministry of Treasury and Finance and, in provincial administration, Tax Office Directorates which rest upon RA and, in areas which Tax Office Directorates was not established, Managers of Tax Office and Head of the Financial Department (Söyler and Çolak 2013: 220). Within this framework, TIB consists of the president, vice presidents, heads of groups, and tax inspectors (Işık, Gelen and Sonsuzoğlu 2017: 46) and all of those rest upon the Minister. Tax inspectors include senior tax inspectors, tax inspectors, and assistant tax inspectors. Officials with the titles of senior finance inspector, senior account specialist, and senior revenue controller are transformed into the title of senior tax inspector, while the titles of finance inspector, account specialist, revenue controller, and tax auditor are transformed into tax inspector and their assistants become being assistant tax inspectors (Işık, Gelen and Sonsuzoğlu 2017: 46).

With the regulations made in 2011, four groups are established in order to provide specialization and cooperation in TIB and those are (a) Group of Small and Medium-Scale Taxpayers, (b) Group of Large-Scale Taxpayers, (c) Group of Combating Organized Tax Evasion, and (ç) Group of Thin Capitalization, Transfer Pricing and Foreign Incomes (Işık, Gelen and Sonsuzoğlu 2017: 47). Officials who were senior finance inspectors, senior account specialists, and senior revenue controllers prior to 2011 are employed in group presidencies of (b), (c), and (ç); while tax auditors and assistant tax auditors are employed in group presidency of (a) (Aydoğmuş 2011: 104). Also the performance assessment method begins to apply to transitions from the position of assistant tax inspector to tax inspector, as well as from the position of tax inspector to senior tax inspector (Aydoğmuş 2011: 104). In addition, 25% of the assistant tax inspectors, who are the most successful according to the written and oral exam which is carried out for 20% of the most successful and 3-month training participants who are assigned as assistant tax inspectors, work in the group presidencies of (b), (c), and (ç) (Gerçek 2011: 33).

It should be noted that although tax audit reform is carried out by establishing TIB and gathering tax audit units under a single roof named TIB, some new practices in terms of tax audit can also be regarded as the pioneers of reform. One point that needs to be addressed in this context is the establishment of Report Evaluation Commissions. Pursuant to the amendment to Article 140 of TPL, which is made by Law No. 6009 of 2010, commission to evaluate tax audit reports have been established. Within this context, tax inspection reports, which are prepared in the areas of provincial administrations or for inspections relating to tax bases over certain scales, are evaluated in report evaluation commissions placed in central administration (Yücedoğru, Sarıaslan and Kuştepe 2019: 318). Those commissions evaluate the conformity of tax audit reports with primary and secondary legislation (Gelen 2015: 35). In addition, the duration of tax inspections is limited with the same law; thus, full inspections should be concluded within 1 year and limited inspections should be concluded within 6 months. This change is important in terms of the acceleration of the investigation.

3.4 Risk Analysis Based Tax Audit

The second step, which is taken through tax audit reform in Turkey, consists of the adoption of a substantial risk analysis based tax audit approach. The development of information technologies along with the technological progress and the boost in the tendency toward using information technologies in the world in terms of tax audit lead Turkey to give weight to information technologies increasingly within the process of tax audit.

Risk analysis based tax audit is a system which provides substantial analysis of data obtained from taxpayer's own or from various public or private sector institutions in order to assess whether taxpayers are at a risky situation or not in terms of tax audit and this system allows the audit to focus on the taxpayers who can be determined as risky taxpayers as a result of the analysis. Thus, available sources of tax administration such as time can be allocated according to a priority risk order and then tax audit provides more revenue for the government by means of an efficient and effective tax audit (Lethbridge 2013: 181). In addition, computer and information technologies are being used in this system and an objective and fair tax audit is performed due to the selection of taxpayers by mathematical and statistical methods.

This strategy, which is implemented by many countries in the world, is based on risk scores of the taxpayers. Calculation of risk scores of taxpayers is performed through risk-scoring algorithm (Lethbridge 2013: 181). These scores are determined based on certain attributes such as the size, industry, or compliance history of taxpayers and the knowledge acquired during previous audits and those risk scores enable the tax administration to build several "profiles" of taxpayers and hence to identify those most likely not to comply with legislation (Vellutini 2011a: 20).

Methods such as data matching and data mining are conducted in order to determine risky taxpayers. In data matching method, data obtained from taxpayers' declarations and data obtained from customs administration, banks, insurance companies, or other taxpayers' declarations are matched, whereas data mining consists of automatically exploring and analyzing large quantities of data to uncover meaningful patterns and rules (Vellutini 2011b: 23–25). Data matching is preferred and widely used in most OECD countries (Vellutini 2011c: 60). For instance, in USA, declarations of taxpayers are evaluated by means of matching third-party declarations using a program named Automated Underreporter Program (Madison 2019: 389). Thus, potentially underreported income or unwarranted deductions or tax credits can be identified (Rettig 2016: 26). In addition to data matching or data mining, different methods such as parametric methods may be applied. For instance, in Britain, in order to profiling returns and predicting the likely risk in regards to build profiles of taxpayers, data matching and intelligence gathering are both used and a national ranking is created based on these methods (Hainey 2011: 66).

It should be noted that risk-based tax audit contains analyzing a wide range of data and using effectively information technologies. Tax administrations of most of the developed countries apply audit selection strategies based on risk-scoring techniques

(Vellutini 2011a: 20). However, this strategy can be costly in terms of data and information technology systems; thus, establishing such systems may be challenging in poorly equipped, data-poor developing countries, and transition economies, although these systems are suggested by international organizations. Determining risk scores of taxpayers requires a certain level of computerization and automation, so inability in access to electronic information in terms of developing countries makes this method difficult to implement risk-based strategies (Lethbridge 2013: 14).

Turkey is indicated as one of the countries which apply risk-based tax audit strategy. Prior to the adoption of such strategy, the first step to computerization has been taken in 1998 by means of the establishment of Tax Office Automation System Project (Bakar and Gerçek 2016: 182). The objective of this project was to reduce the workload of tax administrations by automating all of the tax office operations with information technologies, to boost the effectiveness and efficiency in tax office and to create a reliable decision support and management information system from the information gathered in the computer environment (GİB 2004: 75).

Following the implementation of VEDOP, the VEDOP-2, which is the continuation of VEDOP, and the data warehouse, which aims to comprehend the informal economy, have been started to be developed in order for the tax administration to benefit from the opportunities of computer technology. Within this framework, e-declaration has been started to be applied with VEDOP-2 (GİB 2010: 12). Subsequently the data warehouse was put into practice in 2009 and it was aimed to fight with the informal economy and tax evasion by the RA by means of processing data obtained from internal and external sources through data obtained from other public institutions and private sector organizations (GİB 2010: 14).

A pillar of the development and implementation of information technology and automation systems is the risk-based tax audit strategy which is related to the abovementioned computer systems. This strategy has been developed so as to give priority to the taxpayers who are considered risky in terms of tax compliance and designed to be implemented by using computer systems. In fact, much as risk analysis based tax audit in today's context has started to be implemented with the reform of 2011, some samples of this kind of audit have been seen in the past. Within this framework, the Computer-Aided Audit (Increasing the Capacity of the Tax Administration) Project has been started to be applied in 2005. The objective of this project was defined as "to establish information systems and to apply computer-aided audit techniques so as to allow for an effective risk analysis system and selection of taxpayers" (MB 2007: 67–68). With the effect of the implementation of VEDOP and e-declaration, the Audit Information System (MTK-DEBIS) of the former Finance Inspection Board can be mentioned as a similar application. One of the issues that it focuses on is "the detection of risky taxpayers who have high probability to evade taxes or to prepare fake or misleading documents" and this system has been implemented intensively later than 2007 (Kapanoğlu et al. 2012: 238).

It should be noted that using risk analysis in tax audit system was just one of the objectives of those mentioned samples. On the other hand, there have also been attempts to use the risk analysis strategy basically in tax audit. Such applications have focused on only risk-based tax audit. Within this context, firstly, the Central

Risk Analysis and Stratifying Model was created which was started to be developed in 2009 and aimed to select taxpayers for audit based on an objective risk analysis (GİB 2011). In 2010, the Value-Added Tax (VAT) Refund Risk Analysis System was created, and thus risk-based audit was started to be applied in VAT returns.

The next and the most important step of these movements, which can be considered together with the establishment of TIB, was prescribing risk-based tax audit as one of the duties of TIB. The main step in positioning the risk analysis to the focus of tax audit, which constitutes one pillar of tax audit reform, was taken in 2011. Within this framework, pursuant to the Regulation on Tax Inspection Board, duties of TIB related with the risk analysis are as follows: "to analyze the activities of taxpayers in terms of groups and sectors, to make comparisons and to identify risk areas through the Risk Analysis System which is formed by gathering all kinds of information, data and statistics."

With respect to the implementation of a tax audit strategy that focuses on risk analysis within the scope of TIB, studies were conducted in 2012 within the Risk Analysis Branch Office. In Risk Analysis Center, evaluations have been made based on sectors, subjects, and taxpayers by means of determining risky taxpayers with using Risk Analysis System (VDK-RAS) (VDK 2012: 42). Within this context, programs applied in risk analysis are also important. One of the steps taken in this process is to create Central Electronic Risk Analysis and Selection of Taxpayers Program. It is aimed with this program to determining risk areas and analyzing activities of taxpayers by using all kinds of information, data, and statistics (VDK 2015: 29).

As a result of risk analyses, 26.972 taxpayers were subjected to tax inspection in 2015 (VDK 2015: 29). In 2017, 26.006 taxpayers, which were determined through risk analyses, were subjected to tax inspection (VDK 2017: 63). This number reached 22.664 in 2018 (VDK 2018: 56).

It should be indicated that in the current Risk Analysis Model, information is collected from public institutions such as Social Security Institution and the General Directorate of Land Registry and Cadastre and private sector organizations such as banks or various financial institutions and third parties who are related with taxpayers regarding economical activities of taxpayers and all of these data are analyzed (Uğur 2016: 134). The significant point in analyses is dividing taxpayers as ranges and layers. Ranges are determined based on regions and/or sectors in which taxpayers operate, whereas layers are determined based on the scale of taxpayers. Data such as e-declaration, balance sheets, and income statements are considered in determining layers. Tax administration takes into account several criteria when evaluating those data. The criterion for e-declarations is diverging from the sector average, whereas balance sheets and income statements are evaluated based on sales-based analysis criteria (Merter 2016: 58). In addition to these, data obtained from the data warehouse such as registries of taxpayers, customs declarations, information on taxpayers' wealth, and results of previous inspections are also used in analyses. Several criteria are considered in the evaluation of those data, such as expense surplus, forged or misleading declarations, and information on tax penalties (Uğur 2016: 136). On the other hand, taxpayers' behaviors are also evaluated. In this context, it is examined whether there are any issues such as delayed payments, frequent change of address, not issuing VAT declaration (Dogan 2011: 74).

Taxpayers are divided into ranges and layers and each of the taxpayers is subjected to analysis only within their ranges and layers (Bakar and Gerçek 2016: 184). As a result of those analyses, which are carried out with purely mathematical and statistical methods, risk scores of taxpayers, which show their divergencies from the average of their ranges or layers, are determined (Uğur 2016: 134–135). For instance, taxpayers are considered as risky taxpayers in cases where the taxpayer continuously declares loss by years or borrows from shareholders high amounts of debt, the profitability ratio of the taxpayer is different from the average of the sector (Uğur 2016: 137–138).

This method is more likely to find actual tax evasion than if cases were picked up at random (Awasthi 2011: 121). In this respect, risk-based tax audit ensures that administrative costs are reduced, as well as limited time and resources are used effectively, and efficiency of audit is increased (Bakar and Gerçek 2016: 170). In addition, since risk-based tax audit reduces the necessity of the one-to-one relationship between the taxpayer and tax administration, it increases the implementation power of tax administration and voluntary compliance of taxpayers, whereas it reduces the risk of corruption and compliance costs of taxpayers (Awasthi 2011: 121). Performing tax audit within certain principles and standards contributes to providing a fair system. Tax audits can be concluded in a shorter process with the effect of computerization, and therefore unfair competition, which can exist between honest taxpayers and taxpayers who do not declare their liabilities or pay taxes on due time, can be prevented (Uğur 2016: 138).

It should be noted that the risk-based tax audit strategy is the preferred method by the tax authorities of developed countries. In this respect, the risk-based tax audit, which was previously developed by different units such as the Finance Inspection Board, the Board of Account Specialists and the RA and considered as an additional objective among other objectives, had the opportunity to be applied under a single roof and in a completely independent level with the establishment of TIB. Thus, both the development of information technologies and systems to be used in risk-based tax audit and the specialization of the personnel on this matter can be carried out in a more uniform reliable way.

3.5 Conclusion

The most significant reform in regards to tax audit system, which has undergone different changes over time, has been implemented in 2011 pursuant to the Statutory Decree No. 646. As a result of this reform, the administrative organization of tax audit has been completely changed and a separate presidency (TIB) has been established, as well as the names of the tax audit personnel have been changed. Depending on whether the tax inspection is full or limited, this reform brought a time limit to the tax inspection process.

From this point of view, it has been a positive development that tax audit is administered from a single center, since this increases the planning and coordination in the audit. Although tax audit seems now to be administered from a single center, the fact that the head of the financial department and tax office managers are authorized to carry out tax inspection indicates that tax audit is not exactly administered from a single center. At the same time, the fact that physical enquiry, which has a significant role in tax audit and constitutes a base for numerous acts, can be performed by personnel who serve under the RA, also shows the same. When viewed from this aspect, it is important to ensure the coordination between institutions (TIB-the RA) in an effective audit.

Risk analysis based tax audit constitutes the other pillar of the reform. In this model, data in relation to taxpayers are analyzed objectively and taxpayers who are determined as risky taxpayers based on those analyses are subject to tax inspections. This leads to a more objective standard in the selection of taxpayers. In our country, methods such as data matching or mining apply and within this context, tax administration benefits largely from information and computer technologies. These systems, which are further developed in time, are carried out in parallel with many developed countries in the world. In this regard, it can be said that Turkey has a position which is conforming to standards in the world in terms of the implementation of risk analysis based tax audit.

Increasing the effectiveness of the scope and the functioning of tax audit, which is mentioned in this study in general terms, and preventing unlawfulness in the tax audit process are significant matters. In addition to the many positive changes currently in place, it is thought that the effectiveness of tax audit will increase and the functions expected from it will be better performed, if the following points are considered:

1. Today, artificial intelligence is used in every field. Thus, tax administration can benefit from it in many areas from the selection of taxpayers for the audit to the audit process itself, as well as in the risk-based analysis. Considering that taxes will be calculated with using artificial intelligence in the following years (Webtekno 2019), the technical infrastructure can be prepared in order to carry out tax audit in this way.
2. The transition to electronic tax inspection is important, after the transition to electronic physical enquiry is done. In addition to many electronic applications carried out in parallel with the development of technology, the establishment of technical infrastructure for tax inspections in electronic methods has an important role. Such tax inspections can be performed by obtaining data from electronic invoices, books, documents, purchases, sales, etc. It provides an opportunity to both save time and have fewer errors in terms of results.
3. The preparation of a guideline, which aims to minimize procedural faults in the tax audit process, will be a beneficial method. A guideline, which is sent to taxpayers together with the first notification of the tax inspection, such as "*La charte des droits et obligations du contribuable verifié*" which applies in French system can be beneficial in order to inform taxpayers about the procedure and the process of tax inspection, also so as to prevent the tax administration from

procedural faults. In this guideline, information on both the context of taxpayer rights and the administrative acts conducted in the inspection process will be provided. Such a guideline has an important role to be fulfilled the educating function of tax audit.

References

Akdoğan, A. (2017). *Vergi Hukuku ve Türk Vergi Sistemi* (13rd ed.). Ankara, Turkey: Gazi Kitabevi.

Aktan, C.C. (2012). Vergi Psikolojisinin Temelleri ve Vergi Ahlakı. *Çimento İşveren Dergisi. 1*(26), 14–22.

Artun, E.S., Geçer, A.E. & Kalyon, A. (2019). Turkish General Tax Law. In: M.R. Korkusuz & F. İpekel Kayalı (Eds), *Turkish Public Law* (2nd ed.) (pp. 203–234). Ankara, Turkey: Seçkin Yayıncılık.

Awasthi, R. (2011). Conclusion: Lessons for Reforms. In: M.S. Khwaja, R. Awasthi & J. Loeprick (Eds), *Risk-Based Tax Audits, Approaches and Country Experiences* (pp. 119–126). Washington DC, USA: The World Bank. https://doi.org/10.1596/978-0-8213-8754-2.

Aydoğmuş, M. (2011). Vergi Denetiminde Yeni Dönem. *Vergi Sorunları Dergisi, 34*(276), 102–109.

Bakar, F. & Gerçek, A. (2016). Vergi Denetiminde Risk Analizinin Yeri: Bazı Ülke Uygulamaları ve Türkiye İçin Bir Değerlendirme. *International Journal of Public Finance, 1*(2), 168–193. https://doi.org/10.30927/ijpf.319894.

Beşel, F. (2017). Türkiye'de Vergi Denetiminin Ekonomik ve Hukuki Etkinliği, Unpublished Doctoral Dissertation. Sakarya Üniversitesi Sosyal Bilimler Enstitüsü, Sakarya, Turkey.

Bienvenue, J.J. & Lambert, T. (2010). *Droit Fiscal*, (4th ed.). Paris, France: PUF.

DeAgosto, E., Manzo, M., Pisani, S., & D'Arcangelo, F.M. (2018). The Effect of Audit Activity on Tax Declaration: Evidence on Small Businesses in Italy. *Public Finance Review, 46*(1), 29–57. https://doi.org/10.1177/1091142117698035.

Dogan, U. (2011). Data Warehouse and Data-Mining Tools for Risk Management: The Case of Turkey. In: M.S. Khwaja, R. Awasthi & J. Loeprick (Eds), *Risk-Based Tax Audits, Approaches and Country Experiences* (pp. 71–76). Washington DC, USA: The World Bank. https://doi.org/10.1596/978-0-8213-8754-2.

Gelen, Ş. (2015). *Vergi Denetiminde Yapısal Dönüşüm: Vergi Denetim Kurulu*. Unpublished Master's Thesis. İstanbul Aydın Üniversitesi Sosyal Bilimler Enstitüsü, İstanbul, Turkey.

GİB (2004). *2004 Yılı Faaliyet Raporu*. Ankara, Turkey: T.C. Maliye Bakanlığı Gelirler Genel Müdürlüğü Organizasyon Metod Şubesi Müdürlüğü.

GİB (2010). *2009 Yılı Faaliyet Raporu*. Ankara, Turkey: T.C. Maliye Bakanlığı Gelir İdaresi Başkanlığı Strateji Geliştirme Daire Başkanlığı.

GİB (2011). *2010 Yılı Faaliyet Raporu*. Ankara, Turkey: T.C. Maliye Bakanlığı Gelir İdaresi Başkanlığı Strateji Geliştirme Daire Başkanlığı.

Gerçek, A. (2011). Vergi Denetim Birimlerinin Birleştirilmesi ve Sonuçları. *Yaklaşım, 19*(224), 31–36.

Hainey, M. (2011). Building and Integrating Databases for Risk Profiles in the United Kingdom. In: M.S. Khwaja, R. Awasthi & J. Loeprick (Eds), *Risk-Based Tax Audits, Approaches and Country Experiences* (pp. 65–70). Washington DC, USA: The World Bank. https://doi.org/10.1596/978-0-8213-8754-2.

Işık, H., Gelen, Ş. & Sonsuzoğlu, E. (2017). Restructuring of Turkey Tax Audit Units. In: M. Khosrow-Pour (Ed.), *Handbook of Research on Global Enterprise Operations and Opportunities* (pp. 36–60). Hershey PA, USA: IGI Global.

Kapanoğlu, A., Sökmen, B. & Aykın, H. (2012). Kayıtdışı Ekonomi ve Yolsuzlukla Mücadele Açısından Maliye Teftiş Kurulu Elektronik Denetim Uygulaması. In: O.E. Arslan, N. Savaşkan

Akdoğan, B. Tangör, H. Mimaroğlu Özgen & A. Altunoğlu (Eds.), *Kamu Yönetimi ve Teknoloji* (pp. 435–455). Ankara, Turkey: Türkiye ve Orta Doğu Amme İdaresi Enstitüsü.
Karakoç, Y. (2004). Hukuki Nedenlerden Kaynaklanan Vergi Kayıp ve Kaçakları (Düzenleme-Uygulama-Yargılama). 19. Türkiye Maliye Sempozyumu "Türkiye'de Vergi Kayıp Ve Kaçakları, Önlenmesi Yolları", Ankara, Turkey, 99–126.
Karataş Durmuş, N. (2016). La Fonction Economique de l'impôt. *Law&Justice Review, 7*(13), 64–79.
Lethbridge, C. (2013). Audit. In: *Detailed Guidelines for Improved Tax Administration in Latin America and the Caribbean* (pp. 174–200). Paris, France: U.S. Agency for International Development.
Madison, A. D. (2019). *Fundamentals of Federal Tax Procedure and Enforcement*. New York, USA: Wolters Kluwer.
MB (2007). *2007 Yılı Faaliyet Raporu*. Ankara, Turkey: T.C. Maliye Bakanlığı.
Merter, M.E. (2016). Ülkemizde E-Beyanname Uygulamasının Vergi Denetiminin Etkinliği Üzerindeki Etkisi. *Celal Bayar Üniversitesi Sosyal Bilimler Dergisi, 14*(2), 51–74. https://doi.org/10.18026/cbusos.63563.
Niu, Y. (2011). Tax Audit Impact on Voluntary Compliance. *Journal of Economic and Social Measurement, 36*, 237–251. https://doi.org/10.3233/jem-2011-0346.
OECD (2006). *Strengthening Tax Audit Capabilities: General Principles and Approaches*. Information Note Prepared by Forum on Tax Administration's Compliance Sub-group of OECD. Retrieved from http://www.oecd.org/tax/administration/37589900.pdf.
OECD (2017). *The Changing Tax Compliance Environment and the Role of Tax Audit*. Paris, France: OECD Publishing. DOI:https://dx.doi.org/10.1787/9789264282186-en.
Organ, İ. (2008). *Vergi Denetimi ve Türkiye Uygulaması*. Ankara, Turkey: Gazi Kitabevi.
Ozansoy, A. (2011). Vergi Denetim Kurulu Eksik Kuruldu. *Yaklaşım Dergisi, 19*(224), 55–59.
Önen, Z.S. (2017). *Genel Vergi Hukuku*. Ankara, Turkey: Detay Yayıncılık.
Özkök Çubukçu, D. & Pınar, A. (2009). Vergilendirme Süreçlerinde Vergi Kaçakçılığının Önlenmesi: Uluslararası Deneyimlerden Seçmeler. In: *Mualla Öncel'e Armağan*, Volume I (pp. 473–492). Ankara, Turkey: Ankara Üniversitesi Yayınları.
Rettig, C. P. (2016). IRS Audit Selection and Classification Processes. *Journal of Tax Practice and Procedure, 18*(1), 25–32.
Saban, N. (2015). *Vergi Hukuku* (7th ed.). İstanbul, Turkey: Beta Yayınları.
Saraçoğlu, F. & Pürsünlerli Çakar, E. (2016). Vergi Hukuku. Ankara, Turkey: Gazi Kitabevi.
Seer, Roman (2010). Vergi Denetiminde Etkinlik Sorununun Nedenleri ve Çözüm Yolları. In: B. Ozturk & F. Başaran Yavaşlar (Eds.), *Vergi Hukuku Örneğinde Hukuka Uygun ve Etkin Kamu Denetimi Sempozyum Kitabı* (pp. 439–461). Ankara, Turkey: Seçkin Yayıncılık.
Somuncu, A. (2014). Yaygın ve Yoğun Vergi Denetimi: Hukuki Yapı ve Uygulamanın Değerlendirilmesi. *Erciyes Üniversitesi İktisadi ve İdari Bilimler Fakültesi Dergisi, 43*, 133–173.
Soydan, B. (2015). *Türk Vergi Hukukunda Vergi İncelemesi*. İstanbul, Turkey: On İki Levha Yayıncılık.
Söyler, İ. & Çolak, M. (2013). Nasıl Bir Vergi Reformu?. *Dumlupınar Üniversitesi Sosyal Bilimler Dergisi, 35*, 215–222.
Şenyüz, D., Yüce, M. & Gerçek, A. (2017). *Vergi Hukuku Genel Hükümler*. Bursa, Turkey: Ekin Yayınevi.
Tabakoğlu, A. & Taşdirek, O.Ç. (2015). Osmanlıda Mali Denetimin Kurumsal Gelişimi-Maliye Heyetini Kuruluşu. *Yönetim ve Ekonomi Araştırmaları Dergisi, 13*(2), 91–113.
Tekin, A. (2010). OECD Ülkelerinde Yapılan Vergi Reformlarının Değerlendirilmesi. *Dumlupınar Üniversitesi Sosyal Bilimler Dergisi, 26*, 54–70.
Tekin, F. & Çelikkaya, A. (2018). *Vergi Denetimi* (8th ed.). Ankara, Turkey: Seçkin Yayınları.
Uğur, A.A. (2016). Vergi Denetimi Etkinliğinde Risk Analizi Sisteminin Uygulanabilirliği (Gaziantep Halı Sektörü Üzerine Örnek Bir Uygulama). *International Journal of Public Finance, 1*(2), 122–145. https://doi.org/10.30927/ijpf.319881.

Vellutini, C. (2011a). Key Principles of Risk-Based Audits. In: M.S. Khwaja, R. Awasthi & J. Loeprick (Eds), *Risk-Based Tax Audits, Approaches and Country Experiences* (pp. 13–21). Washington DC, USA: The World Bank. https://doi.org/10.1596/978-0-8213-8754-2.

Vellutini, C. (2011b). Risk-Based Audits: Assessing the Risks. In: M.S. Khwaja, R. Awasthi & J. Loeprick (Eds), *Risk-Based Tax Audits, Approaches and Country Experiences* (pp. 23–35). Washington DC, USA: The World Bank. https://doi.org/10.1596/978-0-8213-8754-2.

Vellutini, C. (2011c). Database and IT Framework for Risk Analysis. In: M.S. Khwaja, R. Awasthi & J. Loeprick (Eds), *Risk-Based Tax Audits, Approaches and Country Experiences* (pp. 57–64). Washington DC, USA: The World Bank. https://doi.org/10.1596/978-0-8213-8754-2.

VDK (2012). *2012 Yılı Faaliyet Raporu*. Ankara, Turkey: Vergi Denetim Kurulu Başkanlığı Strateji ve Dış İlişkiler Şube Müdürlüğü.

VDK (2015). *2015 Yılı Faaliyet Raporu*. Ankara, Turkey: Vergi Denetim Kurulu Başkanlığı Strateji ve Dış İlişkiler Şube Müdürlüğü.

VDK (2017). *2017 Yılı Faaliyet Raporu*. Ankara, Turkey: Vergi Denetim Kurulu Başkanlığı Strateji, İş Geliştirme ve Kontrol Şube Müdürlüğü.

VDK (2018). *2018 Yılı Faaliyet Raporu*. Ankara, Turkey: Vergi Denetim Kurulu Başkanlığı Strateji, İş Geliştirme ve Kontrol Şube Müdürlüğü

Webtekno (2019). Yeni Dönemde Vergiler Yapay Zeka ile Hesaplanacak. Retrived from https://www.webtekno.com/yeni-donemde-vergiler-yapay-zeka-ile-hesaplanacak-h63972.html (Accessed on May 16th, 2019).

Yılmaz, Y. (2019). Osmanlı Devleti'nde Vergi Sistemi ve Vergi Denetimi, *Vergi Raporu*, *232*, 11–22.

Yücedoğru, R., Sarıaslan, O. & Kuştepe, A. (2019). Türk Vergi Denetimini Üç Boyutu ile Tartışmak: Teori, Uygulama ve Yargı. *Vergi Raporu*, *232*, 312–331.

Neslihan Karataş Durmuş worked as an Associate Professor of Fiscal Law at the Ankara Yildirim Beyazit University, Faculty of Law. She is currently the Educational Consultant of Republic of Turkey Ministry of National Education in Brussels, Belgium. She was a member of Legislation Commission at Council of Higher Education of Turkey and also a member of Quality Commission at Ankara Yildirim Beyazit University. Dr. Karatas Durmus completed her LLM (Tax Law) in Paris 1 Pantheon Sorbonne University and she holds her Ph.D. (Tax Law) from Paris 1 Pantheon Sorbonne University with highest honor. Dr. Karatas Durmus has authored two boks and contributed to a book chapter. She has also authored numerous articles. She was the editor of Yildirim Beyazit Law Review. Her research interests focus on fiscal law, tax law, international tax law, tax disputes and resolution methods.

İmran Arıtı Erdem is an Research Assistant of Public Finance at Ankara Yıldırım Beyazıt University, Faculty of Political Sciences. She completed her MSc (Public Finance) at Ankara Yildirim Beyazit University in 2018. She continues her Ph.D. (Public Law) at the same university. Her research interests focus on fiscal law, tax law and international tax law.

Part II
Public Expenditure Management

Chapter 4
The Experience of a Medium-Term Expenditure Framework in Turkey

Tolga Demirbaş

4.1 Introduction

Modern public expenditure management (PEM) is a new budgeting approach that takes into account the preferences and behaviors of the actors in the budgeting process. In this approach, three important budgetary outcomes are desired: aggregate fiscal discipline, allocation of public resources in line with strategic priorities, and effective provision of public services. The main argument of PEM is that changes should be made in the rules of the game in budgeting to gain these outcomes effectively. According to PEM, poor outcomes are unavoidable if the budgetary tools do not produce sufficient information or incentives for the actors in budgeting (Campos and Pradhan 1996; Schick 1999; World Bank 1998).

Medium-term expenditure frameworks (MTEFs) are currently the main component of institutional arrangements for better budgetary outcomes. Broadly, MTEFs symbolize a transition from focusing on a single year in budgeting to a medium-term period (Holmes and Evans 2003). However, the concept is far beyond simply preparing the budget in terms of multiple years. MTEFs may include many important elements for achieving good budgetary outcomes, such as macroeconomic projections, fiscal rules, top-down budgeting, organizational strategic planning, outcome-based budgeting, accrual accounting, and fiscal transparency. Thus, multiyear budget estimates are only one part of MTEFs.

MTEFs are not a new phenomenon, but it is only relatively recently that have they spread all over the world (World Bank 2013). In the 1970 and 1980s, disappointments in multiyear expenditure planning in developed countries such as the United Kingdom, Australia, and Canada were important steps in the development of MTEFs (Asian Development Bank 2000; OECD 2001). The Australian "forward estimates" approach pioneered an MTEF integrated with institutional arrangements

T. Demirbaş (✉)
Department of Public Finance, Bursa Uludag University, Bursa, Turkey
e-mail: tolga@uludag.edu.tr

H. Kıral and T. Akdemir (eds.), *Public Financial Management Reforms in Turkey: Progress and Challenges, Volume 1*, Accounting, Finance, Sustainability, Governance & Fraud: Theory and Application, https://doi.org/10.1007/978-981-15-1914-7_4

and achieved success in the 1980s (Campos and Pradhan 1996). A few advanced countries followed Australia in the 1980s and early 1990s (Denmark, New Zealand, the Netherlands, and Norway). MTEFs have started to rapidly spread with the support of the World Bank since the end of the 1990s. While implemented in 11 countries in 1990, it had spread to 132 countries as of 2008. In this period, the World Bank was directly involved with MTEFs in 109 developing countries, including Turkey (World Bank 2013).

Turkey had two major economic crises in the 2000s and has made important structural reforms. Particularly the projects carried out jointly with the International Monetary Fund (IMF) and the World Bank have been an important driving force for these efforts. Turkey's efforts to be a member of the European Union has led to accelerating structural reforms. In this context, Turkey started to implement an MTEF in 2006 as part of public financial management reform. This study examines the main processes of the MTEF in Turkey and assesses its implementation over a period of nearly 15 years.

4.2 What Is an MTEF?

4.2.1 Conceptual Framework

An MTEF is commonly known in government budgeting literature as a multiyear expenditure or budget-planning approach (Allan 1996; OECD 2001; Premchand 1984). Broadly, it can be defined as an institutional arrangement that addresses the inability of traditional annual budgeting to achieve effective budgetary results (World Bank 2013). Annual budgeting does have many disadvantages for good budgetary outcomes (Blöndal 2005; Due and Friedlaender 1977; Wildavsky 1986; World Bank 1998).

For example, it only focuses on the budget expenditures of the next year and does not take into account the costs of current and new policy decisions in future budgets. Therefore, in annual budgeting, policy decisions are made distinct from the government's availability of resources. This short-sightedness can lead to unsustainable policies, out-of-control spending, and chronic budget deficits.

In the traditional approach, the budget is formulated from the bottom-up, and spending agencies formulate expenditure proposals without any spending limits. Thus, the budget formulation is like a game for actors. All actors know that the departments' proposals submitted to the Ministry of Finance (MoF) are not realistic. Any agency can receive more allocation than what it requires at the end of negotiations with the MoF. Therefore, budgetary allocations are generally not convenient for the strategic priorities of the government.

Annual budgeting has mostly an incremental nature. Current programs and their annual costs are not reviewed in depth every year. Therefore, each spending agency demands additional resources from the MoF for new programs or activities in budgeting processes. Mostly, there is not any mechanism for reallocation within departments and any incentive for the effective provision of public services.

An MTEF is an instrument designed to overcome these shortcomings firstly by extending the time horizon of budgeting from one year to three years or more. MTEFs produce estimates of government expenditures (policy costs) and revenues for both the annual budget year (t) and beyond mostly two (t + 2) or three additional years (t + 3). However, an MTEF is not simply a paper that includes only forward estimates. Instead, it is a process through which "annual budget decisions are made in terms of aggregate or sectoral limits on expenditures for each of the next three to five years." (Schick 2003, p. 11).

4.2.2 Main Stages and Types of MTEFs

An MTEF is composed of three main phases. First, the government makes a medium-term resource envelope with a top-down approach that is in line with macroeconomic conditions. Second, the medium-term costs of government policies are estimated through a bottom-up approach. Finally, policy costs and available resources are matched in the annual budget process (World Bank 1998). Table 4.1 provides more detailed steps for a comprehensive MTEF at the government-wide level.

The starting point of an MTEF integrated with annual budget processes is developing or updating the medium-term macroeconomic framework (MTMF). MTMFs are generally based on macroeconomic models that produce multiyear projections of economic variables such as growth, the balance of payments, inflation, credit growth, unemployment, and public sector accounts (OECD 2001).

Table 4.1 Stages of a comprehensive MTEF

1	Developing/updating macroeconomic framework (by MoF)
2	Developing/updating medium-term fiscal framework and setting general resource envelope (by MoF)
3	Setting out national and sectoral strategic priorities (by Cabinet and line ministries), and costing current and new programs (by spending agencies)
4	Preparing medium-term budget strategy paper (by MoF) including sectoral expenditure ceilings and Cabinet approval
5	Medium-term budget proposals of spending agencies based on sectoral policies, program costs, and expenditure ceilings
6	MoF reviews of budget submissions of agencies and holding of hearings with spending agencies
7	Updating fiscal framework and ceilings, and presentation of final budget estimates to Cabinet and legislature

Source Di Francesco, Michael Barroso 2014; World Bank 1998, 2013

The second phase of an MTEF is developing a medium-term fiscal framework (MTFF) that links macroeconomic projections with fiscal policy objectives or rules and determines the aggregate resource envelope (expenditure ceiling) for the general government. In this stage, the MoF estimates the expenditure baseline under the assumption that the current governmental policies will not change in the future. If the resource envelope is higher than the baseline, it means there is fiscal space for new policies. Otherwise, there is no space for additional government expenditures, and the government will need to cut the current expenditure level to reach fiscal targets (Rosalky 2012; World Bank 1998).

The third stage involves setting strategic priorities at both the national and sectoral levels. The aim of an MTEF is not only to enhance fiscal sustainability but also to promote efficient resource allocation between programs or sectors. Therefore, the government should make real policy decisions based on both societal preferences and overall fiscal constraints (Holmes and Evans 2003). Governments may use various mechanisms such as forums, strategic plans, and sectoral expenditure reviews to formulate sound national or sectoral expenditure priorities (Harris, Hughes, Ljungman, and Sateriale 2013). After setting strategic priorities, spending agencies cost their existing and (if there is fiscal space) new policies consistently with national and sectoral strategic priorities. Policy proposals and their costs are discussed within government centers, and policy decisions on sectoral resource allocation are made by the Cabinet (van Eden, Khemani, and Emery 2013; World Bank 2013). These allocations comprise the medium-term expenditure ceilings for sectors, programs or ministries at the same time.

The fourth stage covers the preparation of a medium-term budget strategy paper (MTBSP) by the MoF. The MTBSP is actually an output of the previous stages and is a supportive document for the strategic phase of budgeting. The MTBSP contains the government's medium-term fiscal policy, sectoral policies, priorities, and medium-term expenditure ceilings (Holmes and Evans 2003).

In stage five, spending agencies prepare their multiyear budget submissions (annual budget and additional two- or three-year budgets) in accordance with sector strategies, program costs, and expenditure ceilings. In the sixth stage, the MoF reviews the individual submissions and organizes hearings with spending agencies to resolve technical differences. In the last stage, the MoF updates the macro-fiscal framework and ceilings and submits the final budget estimates to the Cabinet for approval (World Bank 2013).

An MTEF can be designed for three main budgetary objectives: financial discipline, allocative efficiency, and technical efficiency. However, an MTEF that actively works for these three outcomes requires a powerful background. Countries can develop three types of frameworks to achieve the desired budgetary outcomes:

- *Medium-term fiscal frameworks (MTFFs)* present macro-fiscal targets such as government expenditures, fiscal balance, and debt level. An MTFF as a basis for providing financial discipline may also include medium-term expenditures at the broad economic category level (Tommasi 2009).

- *Medium-term budgetary framework (MTBF)* is a type of MTEF that allows for the production of multiyear expenditure estimates for individual agencies. Such a framework can help to enhance resource allocation between sectors, programs, or agencies, along with financial discipline. Two types of MTBFs can be specified: a "forecasting MTEF" and a "programmatic MTEF." In a forecasting MTEF, multiyear estimates based on expenditure ceilings are determined mostly mechanically by the MoF through a top-down process. Since spending agencies submit budget requests to the MoF without dividing them into current and new policies, a forecasting MTEF does not have enough power to provide efficient resource allocation. In a programmatic MTEF, the fiscal space is filled with bottom-up policy-based proposals from the spending agencies. Therefore, it requires the implementation of a program-based expenditure classification. With supportive instruments, a programmatic MTEF can work for efficient resource allocation (Schiavo-Campo 2009; Tommasi 2009; World Bank 2013).
- *Medium-term performance framework (MTPF)* is called "a full-fledged MTEF" because it requires a change in budgeting from inputs to outputs and outcomes, as well as linking performance levels to resource allocations. Therefore, an MTPF provides incentives for spending agencies to provide better public services (e.g., for technical efficiency) (World Bank 2013). Consequently, as the most advanced type of MTEF, an MTPF can be useful for enhancing all three budgetary outcomes.

According to the World Bank database, there were 71 MTFFs, 42 MTBFs, and only 19 MTPFs in 132 countries as of 2008 (World Bank 2013, p. 27).

4.2.3 Requirements for an Effective MTEF

The approach to building an MTEF depends on the conditions in a particular country (World Bank 1998). Experience shows that "the MTEF is not a panacea." Therefore, "a successful MTEF must be diagnostic, rather than formulaic" (Oxford Policy Management 2000, p. 3). Nevertheless, some advice for an effective MTEF can be given:

- Political leaders should use the MTEF as a tool for fiscal policy making and spending priorities. Without political support, an MTEF cannot go beyond a technical application (Downes 2013). In particular, the involvement of the Cabinet in the MTEF at the beginning of the budget preparation process is very important for the credibility of the expenditure ceilings (de Renzio and Smith 2005).
- Realistic and honest estimates are one of the key success factors in the MTEF. For example, expenditure baselines of the MTEF should be based on sound economic data. Political manipulation of baselines will have negative effects on budgetary outcomes (Holmes and Evans 2003; Rosalky 2012).
- An MTEF is not a substitute for the annual budgetary principle and needs to be fully integrated into the annual budget process (Downes 2013).

- A strong MoF is needed to coordinate fiscal aggregates and strategic priorities (Downes 2013).
- Changes in economic and financial conditions require updating the MTEF and budget estimates. Routine updating of parametric estimates is relatively easy. It may be more difficult to take into account program or policy changes such as greater use of unemployment benefits. Consequently, the government should have the capacity to measure the future fiscal effects of its policy decisions or changes (Rosalky 2012).
- An MTEF needs transparency for better credibility. For example, updating of the procedure of the MTEF baseline projections should be clear for all actors. An MTEF can be supported with accrual-based accounting that produces sound cost information and improves fiscal transparency for policy making.
- The duties and responsibilities of the MTEF actors must be clear for success in linking budgetary outcomes with policy objectives. If there are no effective accountability mechanisms for actors, the MTEF is likely to fail (Oxford Policy Management 2000).
- Top-down and bottom-up approaches must work together to ensure that resource allocations are consistent with strategic priorities. Therefore, sectoral resource allocation decisions should be the result of a reconciliation process between the spending agencies and the central government (World Bank 2013).
- For an effective MTEF, it makes sense to include some programmatic elements in the budgeting system. However, this should not be perceived as a complete transition to the program budget (Schiavo-Campo 2009). As stated by Di Francesco, Michael Barroso (2014, p. 54), "In principle, an MTEF has greatest technical efficacy when it constructs estimates based on spending ministry informed costing of programs, rather than finance ministry extrapolation of historical funding levels."

4.2.4 Potential Benefits

MTEFs could provide many benefits if they work effectively:

- The main reason why good budgetary results cannot be achieved, especially in developing countries, is that policy, planning, and budgeting are independent and fragmented. In particular, MTEFs have the potential to strengthen the links between these three factors (World Bank 1998).
- In the traditional approach, spending agencies are unaware of the total resource availability when they are making budget proposals to MoF during the budget formulation processes. In this process, the total expenditure proposals are generally higher than the resource available, and therefore, the MoF has difficulty in rejecting or cutting the proposals. There is often a tension between the organizations defending their proposals (i.e., needs) and the MoF defending fiscal discipline (i.e., the availability of resources). Given that an MTEF calls for policy decisions

to be made while considering budget realities, it can reduce the tension between the "needs" and "availabilities" (World Bank 1998).

- An MTEF can prevent the tendency of policy makers to overuse public resources (that is, the common pool problem) (World Bank 2013).
- An MTEF provides information on the medium-term impact of decisions. In other words, it is a preventive tool in the budget formulation as it enables a comparison of the costs of policy proposals with fiscal targets. However, an MTEF is not a substitute tool for politicians. (OECD 1997; Rosalky 2012).
- An MTEF allows the government to determine policies by assessing financial risks such as possible shocks, government guarantees, and natural disasters (Rosalky 2012; World Bank 2013).
- An MTEF strengthens the transparency of medium-term fiscal-budgetary objectives and improves time consistency in fiscal policy (Sherwood 2015).
- An MTEF can be an important tool for expenditure prioritization. Under hard spending ceilings, resources can be reallocated from wasteful programs, projects, and activities (e.g., white elephants) to high-priority policy areas (e.g., human development) (World Bank 2013).
- An important benefit of MTEFs is providing predictability about the flow of resources to spending agencies. They may see funds to be received in the coming years under economic stability. In addition, they can estimate that they can receive more funding if they work toward government priorities (World Bank 1998).

The World Bank's econometric analysis has also shown that in practice, an MTEF can make significant contributions to the three main budgetary outcomes (World Bank 2013): A comparison with the years without an MTEF analysis based on 72 MTEFs showed that the positive contribution to the fiscal discipline (as a percentage of GDP) was 0.9% for MTFFs, 1.0% for MTBFs, and 2.8% for MTPFs. In terms of allocative efficiency, MTEFs were also associated with declines in both total and health expenditure volatility, as well as increases in the share of health expenditure within total government expenditure. However, the positive effect of MTEFs for technical efficiency is less clear.

4.3 The Adoption of the MTEF in Turkey

4.3.1 Transition Processes to MTEF: From Past to Present

Founded Medium-Term Expenditure Framework (MTEF) in 1923, the Republic of Turkey is a unitary state. It has a Continental European tradition in terms of public finances and state administration, and the government is largely centralized. Turkey has followed policies for opening up to the world and liberalization of the economy since the 1980s but could not capture the high growth rates seen in emerging market economies. Despite its young population and strategic location, Turkey's annual growth rate has remained below its potential (5% on average in the 1980s and 4%

in the 1990s). The country's economy has grown unevenly with high inflation and was shaken by three major crises that occurred in April 1994, November 2000, and February 2001. Therefore, the GDP contracted by 4.7–7.5%. Turkey was the only economy with a 30% rate of inflation among big economies throughout the world in 2003 (World Bank 2003). Failures to follow a sustainable fiscal policy played a major role in these economic crises, and many problems that negatively affected budgetary results dominated public finance in the 1990s (see Box 4.1).

Box 4.1: Basic Problems of Turkish Public Finance in the 1990s

Very narrow budget coverage, high extra-budgetary spending areas
Noncompliance with international standards in fiscal aggregates
Lack of fiscal transparency
Fragmented organizational structure in fiscal policy making
Poor linking between planning, policy making, and budgeting.
Budget processes not based on an effective macroeconomic framework
Bottom-up budget preparation process
Short-term budget and fiscal policies
Traditional input-oriented budgeting (even though it is called program budgeting)
Lack of ownership and credibility of development plans
Failure to calculate costs of policies and measures specified in annual programs
Lack of medium-term planning at the agency level
Modified cash-based accounting system
Broad powers of the executive authority to disrupt budgetary discipline
High share of debt interest in the budget and inefficiency in allocation
Unnecessary use of budgetary allowances towards the end of the year (December fever)
Lack of effective accountability mechanisms in public sector management
Prevalence of legal compliance auditing in the public sector.
Source: Demirbaş (2006)

A delegation headed by S. Schiavo-Campo and D. Pannier from the World Bank came to Turkey in September 1994, and they made some recommendations such as ensuring budgetary unity, updating the accounting and technical systems, and strengthening the budget preparation process, which had suffered a loss of credibility. The delegation stated that the expenditure ceiling model in France could be implemented for the budget formulation process of the government in Turkey. Moreover, they recommended that the government present its annual budget together with estimates for two additional years to Parliament (World Bank 1994). However, most of these recommendations did not receive sufficient support from the government at the time (Kesik 2000).

The economic crises in 2000 and 2001 in particular, had a driving role in the transition to the medium-term expenditure programming in Turkey. Turkey's increased relations with the IMF and the World Bank after the crises made public expenditure reform compulsory. Another important driving force for Turkey to make structural reforms was gaining a candidate country status for the EU in 1999. We should also note that there were many bureaucrats willing to make expenditure reforms in the relevant period, and their reports made significant contributions to the reform processes.

Box 4.2: Key historical steps towards the progress of the MTEF in Turkey

1999 IMF standby arrangement and adopting structural reforms
1999 Declaration of Turkey as a candidate country for EU in Helsinki summit.
2000 National Report of Ad Hoc Committee on Restructuring of Public Finance Management and Fiscal Transparency (under the eighth development plan)
2000 First Turkey Report of IMF on the Observance of Standards and Codes
2001 World Bank Public Expenditure and Institutional Review Report
2001 Eliminating extra-budgetary funds.
2001 Web-based Accounting Office Automation Project (Say2000i)
2002 Macroeconomic framework and first annual expenditure ceilings for the FY 2003
2002 Preliminary testing of performance-based budgeting (PBB) system in piloted agencies
2003 Adoption of Public Financial Management and Control (PFMC) Law
2003 Formulation of the government budget based on GFS for the FY 2004
2004 Transition to accrual-based accounting
2004 Strengthening the Budget Process Project (MATRA)
2005 Guidance of new budgeting under fiscal reforms (MoF)
2005 Preparation of the first MTEF for 2006–2008
2011 Modification of government budget formulation calender with PFMC Law amendment.
2015 Action plan for the program of rationalization of public expenditures (under the tenth development plan)
2018 Transition to presidential government system and reorganization of government agencies.
Source: Demirbaş 2006; MoF, Budget Justifications.

The legal infrastructure of the MTEF in Turkey is the Public Financial and Management (PFMC) Law (2003), which was adopted by Parliament in December 2003 (Articles 13, 15, 16, 17, 18). Since the provisions of the MTEF laws entered into force in 2005, the first MTEF started in the period of 2006–2008. Nevertheless, the implementation of the expenditure ceiling based on a macroeconomic framework in the budget formulation process started for the first time in 2002 (albeit for only the next year) with a decision of the High Planning Council. Key steps in the progress of the MTEF in Turkey are summarized in Box 2.

In May 2004, the MoFs of the Netherlands and Turkey jointly launched the "Strengthening the Budget Process Project (MATRA Project)," which has been an important contribution to the design of the MTEF. The MoF has also examined the MTEF models of Sweden, Australia, New Zealand, UK, South Africa, and Germany with the Netherlands (Alantar 2009).

4.3.2 The Aims and Features of the MTEF

The main objectives of the MTEF in Turkey were expressed as follows in the Budget Justification for FY2006 (Ministry of Finance 2005):

- Improving macroeconomic balance by developing a realistic and coherent public resource framework.
- Determining the priority areas where public resources will be allocated within the fiscal discipline principle and presenting them to the relevant institutions, public, and markets.
- Increasing predictability in public financial management system and ensuring stability in budgeting.
- The allocation of resources according to strategic priorities between institutions, thus ensuring harmonization between policy-making, planning, and budgeting.
- Encouraging government agencies to use public resources effectively and efficiently.
- Providing institutions and practitioners with the opportunity to make long-term plans and programs and improving the institutional culture in this direction.
- Giving necessary information to political decision-makers about the costs of revenue and expenditure policy changes.

MTEF in Turkey is often called to as "a multiyear budgeting approach" at official documents. The general characteristics of current MTEF are as follows:

- The MTEF estimates cover the coming budget year and two additional years (i.e., a three-year horizon). The budget year (also known as the fiscal year) is equivalent to the calendar year (i.e., January 1–December 31).
- The main actors responsible for the MTEF are the Presidency of Strategy and Budget (PSB) and the Ministry of Treasury and Finance. As will be mentioned later, many MTEF documents are produced in collaboration with these two actors.
- The MTEF defines medium-term fiscal targets for both the central and general government. The targets on the general government debt and deficit as percentages of the GDP are set in MTEF documents. Given that there are no legally binding numerical fiscal rules, these targets can be described as the political commitment of the executive body.
- The expenditure ceilings of the MTEF cover only the central government (excluding independent administrative authorities). Ceilings do not have a binding structure; It is indicative of the agencies. These ceilings are expressed in nominal terms and revised each year.

• The MTEF targets and ceilings are set each year for a three-year period. Therefore, the MTEF is a rolling-based framework. Each year, the first year of the MTEF falls, and a new out year is added to its end (Downes 2013).

• All agencies in the general government of Turkey prepare multiyear budget estimates based on a detailed line-item budget classification.

• Institutional strategic planning and performance-based budgeting are parts of the MTEF.

4.4 The Main Stages of the MTEF in Turkey

In Turkey, the Central Government Budget is prepared by the president. According to the Turkish Constitution, the president has to submit a budget law proposal to Parliament at least 75 days before the beginning of the fiscal year (The Constitution of the Republic of Turkey 1982). This proposal includes multiyear estimates for government agencies (which is an output of the MTEF). The production process of the MTEF estimates can be described in three stages:

4.4.1 The Top-Down Stage of the MTEF

In accordance with the Constitution of the Republic of Turkey, development plans are prepared to provide economic, social, and cultural development (Article 166). Therefore, development plans are a binding policy document for all government agencies by the constitution. Additionally, there are many other policy documents at the macro level in Turkey, such as the presidential annual program, as well as sectoral and regional plans (see Fig. 4.1). The first document of the MTEF in the top-down stage is the Medium-Term Program (MTP), which must be prepared in accordance with the aforementioned policy documents.

With a three-year horizon, the MTP includes macroeconomic projections on growth, inflation, employment, and foreign trade. The MTP also displays revenue, expenditure, and balance estimates for three groups: the public sector, general government, and central government. As stated before, the general government deficit and debt relative to GDP (two fiscal criteria of the Maastricht Treaty) are the important parts of the fiscal targets in the MTP. The MTP is not merely a technical document but also lists policies and measures to be adopted in the public sector in the medium-term. The MTP is jointly prepared by the PSB and the Ministry of Treasury and Finance by considering the opinions of the Policy Boards within the Presidency. After approval by the President, the program is published in the Official Gazette by the end of the first week of September at the latest (PFMC Law 2003, Article 16; Presidency of the Republic of Turkey 2018a).

The second document of the MTEF in the top-down stage is the Medium-Term Fiscal Plan (MTFP). This plan is a fiscal policy statement for the central government.

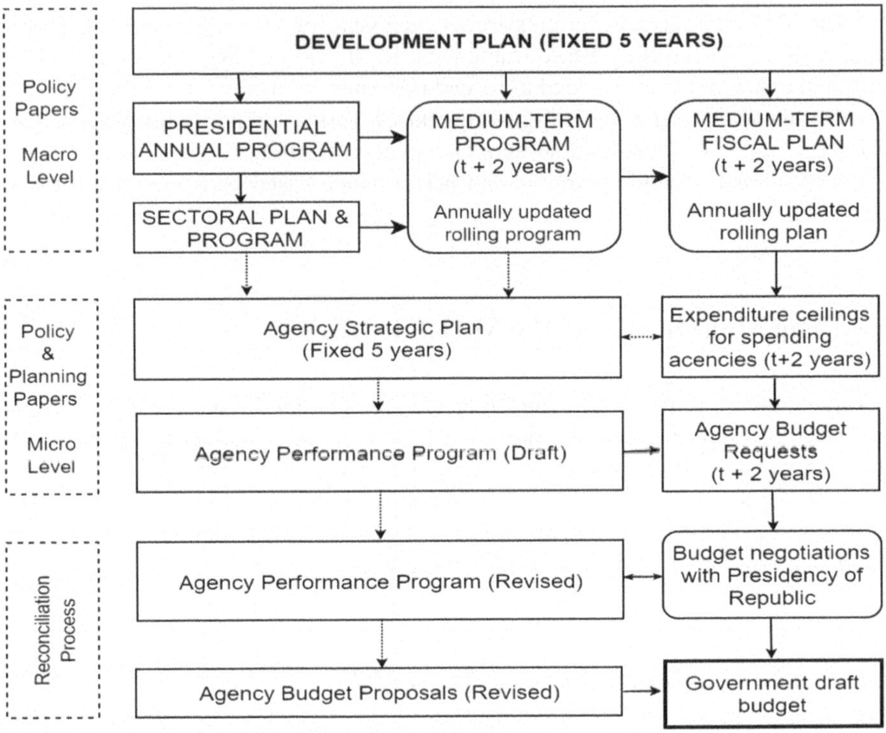

Fig. 4.1 Stages of the MTEF in Turkey. *Source* Prepared by the author based on PFMC Law

Together with policy measures, the MTFP includes three-year fiscal targets (based on economic classification) for central government revenues, expenditures, and budget balance. The MTFP also announces expenditure ceilings (called appropriation proposal ceilings) based on the institutional and economic classifications for central government agencies (excluding independent administrative authorities).

Like the MTP, the MTFP is prepared jointly by the PSB and the Ministry of Treasury and Finance by considering the opinions of the Policy Boards within the Presidency. After approval by the President, the MTFP is published in the Official Gazette by September 15 at the latest (PFMC Law, Article 16; Presidency of the Republic of Turkey 2018b).

4.4.2 *The Bottom-up Stage of the MTEF*

Turkey has moved to a performance-based budgeting (PBB) system with PFMC Law (Article 9). Therefore, at the microlevel, public agencies have five-year strategic plans that demonstrate their mission, vision, strategic goals, and objectives. Each year, the agencies prepare a performance program in line with their strategic plans. This program includes the annual performance targets and performance indicators of the agency. With the PBB system logic, the agencies should base their budget estimates on their own performance programs. It is clear that the agencies should prepare their multiyear budget proposals in accordance with the expenditure ceilings announced by the MTFP (see Fig. 4.1).

4.4.3 Reconciliation Stage of the MTEF

Since the expenditure ceilings in the MTFP are indicative, agencies can propose expenses that exceed the ceiling by specifying their justification. After the multiyear budget proposals are submitted to the presidency, formal negotiations are conducted with the agencies about their budget proposals. After the negotiations, the budget aggregates are finalized by the presidency, and then agencies revise their performance programs and budgets. Ultimately, the president submits the central government budget proposal to the Parliament by October 17 at the latest.

Table 4.2 shows the compliance of the MTEF with the annual budget formulation calendar. As stated before, the budget year is the same as the calendar year in Turkey. The budget preparation phase lasts for approximately four months from mid-June to mid-October. Expenditure ceilings of the previous year are not updated at the beginning of the budget preparation process in Turkey. For this reason, spending agencies prepare their first budget proposals while considering the ceilings published in mid-September of the previous year. However, as mentioned, these ceilings are indicative of the agencies, and they can make proposals that exceed the ceilings. The final expenditure ceilings of the agencies are determined with the publication of the new MTFP.

As will be discussed later, inflation forecasts are generally optimistic in Turkey. Thus, it can be claimed that the implementation of expenditure ceilings is oriented toward achieving fiscal discipline. Aside from its negative effects on the economy, high inflation rates can help the main actors to suppress the level of real spending.

4.5 Evaluation of MTEF in Terms of Budgetary Outcomes

MTEF has been implemented in Turkey since 2006. This period seems sufficient to make some qualitative and quantitative evaluations. Therefore, we will first make an assessment in terms of three main budgetary outcomes. In the next section, we will proceed to qualitative evaluations.

Table 4.2 Budget formulation timetable for central government in Turkey (for 2019 as the current year)

Mid-June	Beginning of the budget preparation process for the period of 2020–2022 with the budget circular of the Presidency of Strategy and Budget (PSB) Agencies start to prepare their own budgets according to the previous Medium-Term Program (2019–2021) and to the indicated expenditure ceilings in the previous Medium-Term Fiscal Plan (2019–2021)
Mid-July	Preparation of agency performance program draft (2020) Entering multiyear budget proposals (2020–2022) into the PSB's e-budget module by agencies
August	Negotiations between agencies and PSB specialists on budget proposals
First week of September	Publication of the Medium-Term Program (2020–2022) in the official gazette
Mid-September	Publication of the Medium-Term Fiscal Plan (2020–2022) including new expenditure ceilings with nominal terms in the official gazette Publication of the Budget Call and Budget Preparation Guide (2020–2022) in the official gazette Publication of the Investment Call and Investment Program Preparation Guide (2020–2022) in the official gazette
Mid-October	Agencies revise their multiyear budget proposals (2020–2022) according to the new expenditure ceilings in the MTFP (2020–2022) Agencies revise their performance programs (2020)
October 17 (75 days before the beginning of the new FY)	The president submits the Central Government Budget Proposal to Parliament

Source Prepared by the author based on relevant legislation and information from interviews with practitioners

4.5.1 Fiscal Discipline

Fiscal discipline is one of the fundamental principles of public financial management in Turkey. PFMC Law emphasizes that the principles of macroeconomic stability, fiscal discipline, sustainable development, and budget balance should be followed by actors throughout the budgeting process (Articles, 5, 13). Figures 4.2, 4.3, 4.4 and

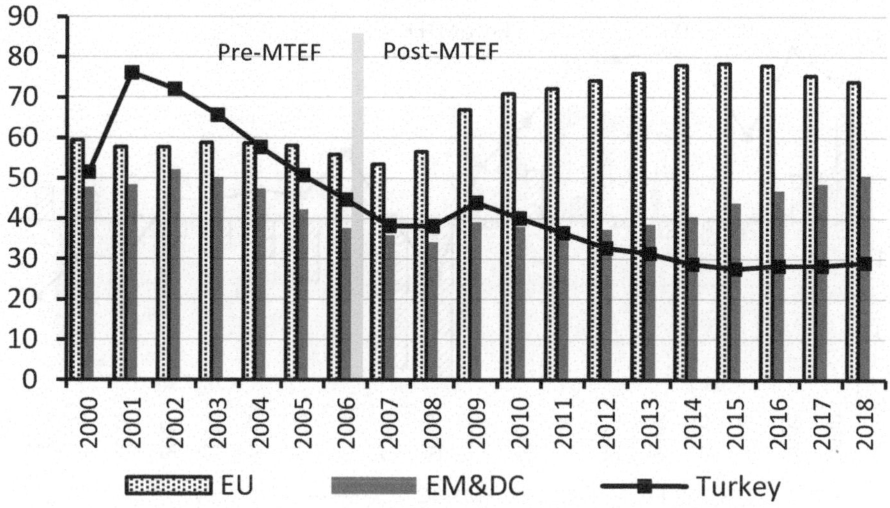

Fig. 4.2 General government gross debt (% of GDP). *Source* Based on IMF 2019

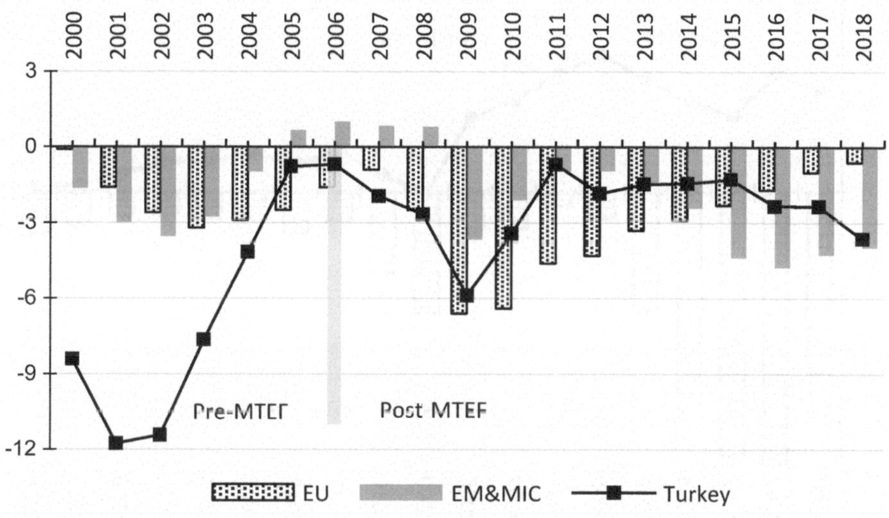

Fig. 4.3 General government balance (% of GDP). *Source* Based on IMF (2019), EUROSTAT (2019)

4.5 illustrate the two important parameters of fiscal discipline: government debt and balance to GDP.

Turkey has demonstrated successful performance in terms of the general government debt since the 2001 crisis. Rising to 76.1% during the crisis, the debt to GDP ratio was reduced to 29.1% in 2018. At present, Turkey is among the best in the EU and emerging markets and developing countries (EM&DC).

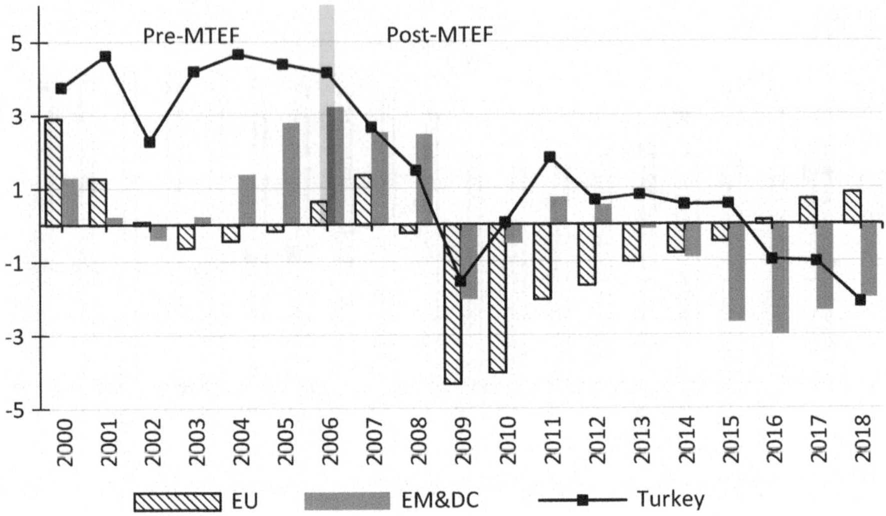

Fig. 4.4 General government primary balance (% of GDP). *Source* Based on IMF (2019)

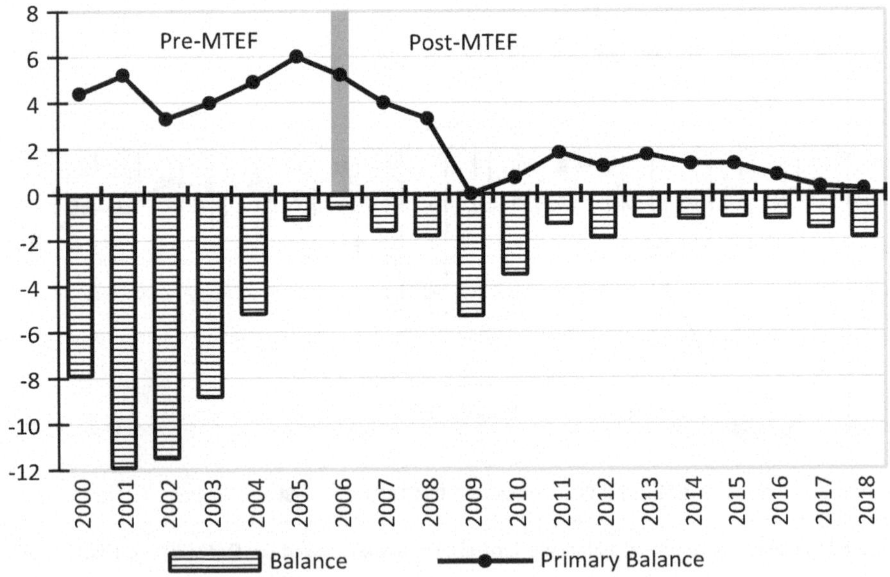

Fig. 4.5 Central government balance (% of GDP). *Source* Ministry of Treasury and Finance (2019)

The general government's overall balance rates show that the post-MTEF period is generally successful (see Fig. 4.3). Except for the period of global crises in 2008–2009, post-MTEF deficit figures slightly exceeded the Maastricht criteria (3%) in 2018 only. Primary balance ratios indicate deterioration in 2016–2018, which is in line with EM&DC (see Fig. 4.4).

4.5.2 Allocative Efficiency

As stated, the MTFP in Turkey explains the expenditure ceilings based on the institutional and economic classification of the central government. The following figures 4.6 and 4.7 show the trends of expenditures in four main components of the economic classification of expenses. The figures show that the share of interest expenditures has decreased and current transfers have increased remarkably. For capital expenditures, there has been a partial improvement.

The main indicator of efficiency in allocation is the improvement in sectoral resource allocation. This means an increase in the share of education and health expenditures in the budget and GDP. Figures 4.8 and 4.9 illustrate the distribution of health, education, and defense expenditures. During the MTEF implementation period, there was no significant increase in the share of health expenditures. However, it is noteworthy that the share of defense expenditures decreased slightly. The share of education expenditures in the budget and GDP has increased significantly.

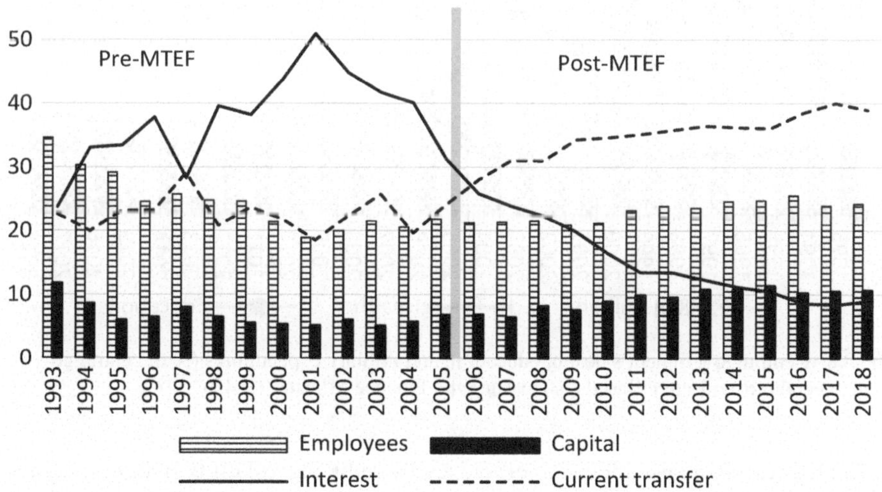

Fig. 4.6 The composition of central government expenditures by economic classification (% of central government expenditures). *Source* Based on Treasury and Finance Ministry (2019)

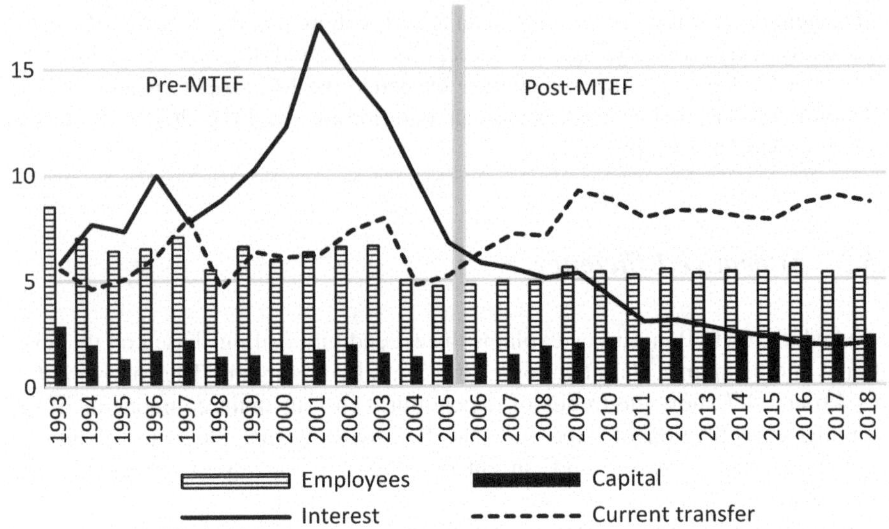

Fig. 4.7 The composition of central government expenditures by economic classification, (% of GDP). *Source* Based on Treasury and Finance Ministry (2019)

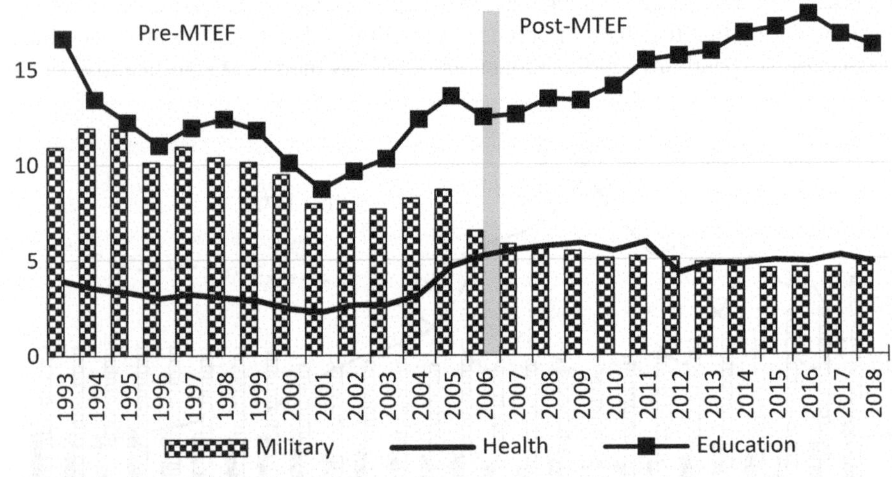

Fig. 4.8 Central government's health, education, and military expenditures (% of central government expenditures). *Source* Based on Treasury and Finance Ministry (2019)

MTEFs can increase allocative efficiency by reducing volatility in both total and productive expenditures. Figures 4.10, 4.11, 4.12 and 4.13 compare the expenditure volatilities between pre-MTEF (1993–2005) and post-MTEF (2006–2018) periods. MTEF significantly reduced the total spending volatility of central government in Turkey (see Fig. 4.10). The mean volatility score of 3.2 in the pre-MTEF period

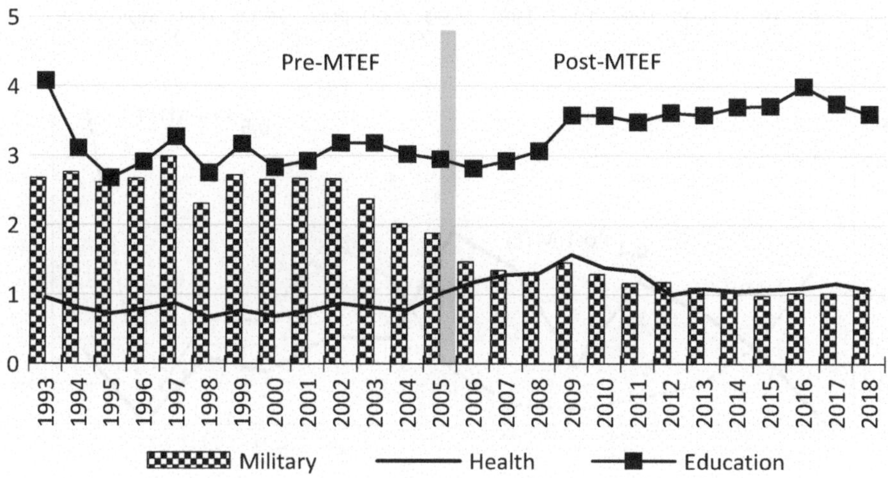

Fig. 4.9 Central government's health, education, and military expenditures (% of GDP). *Source* Based on Treasury and Finance Ministry (2019)

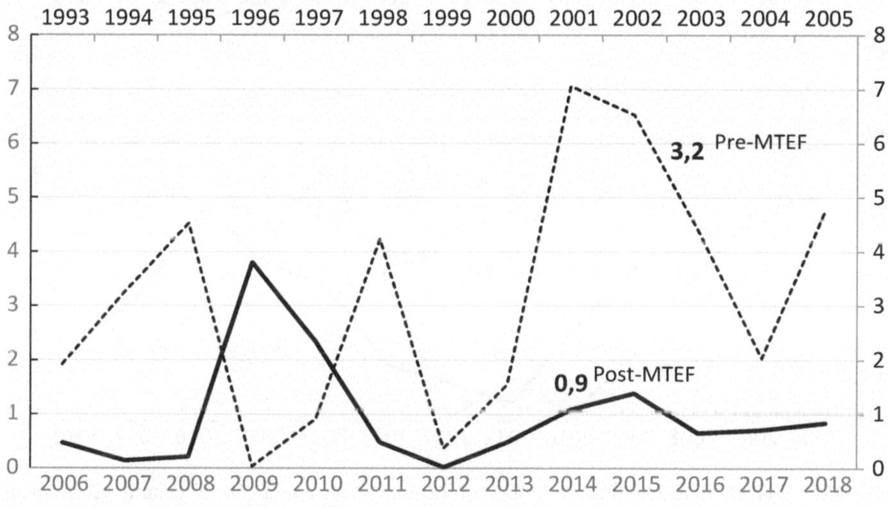

Fig. 4.10 Total expenditure volatility of central government (% of GDP). *Source* Based on Treasury and Finance Ministry (2019)

decreased to 0.9 in the post-MTEF period. Similarly, MTEF reduces the volatility in defense expenditures from 1.3 to 0.4 (see Fig. 4.13). On the other hand, MTEF does not seem to have a sufficient effect on reducing volatility in education and health expenditures (see Figs. 4.11, 4.12).

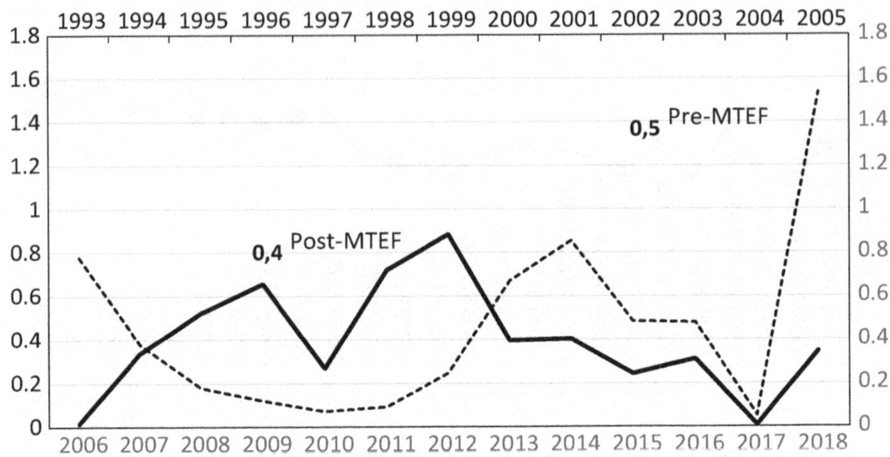

Fig. 4.11 Health expenditure volatility of central government (% of central government expenditures). *Source* Based on Treasury and Finance Ministry (2019)

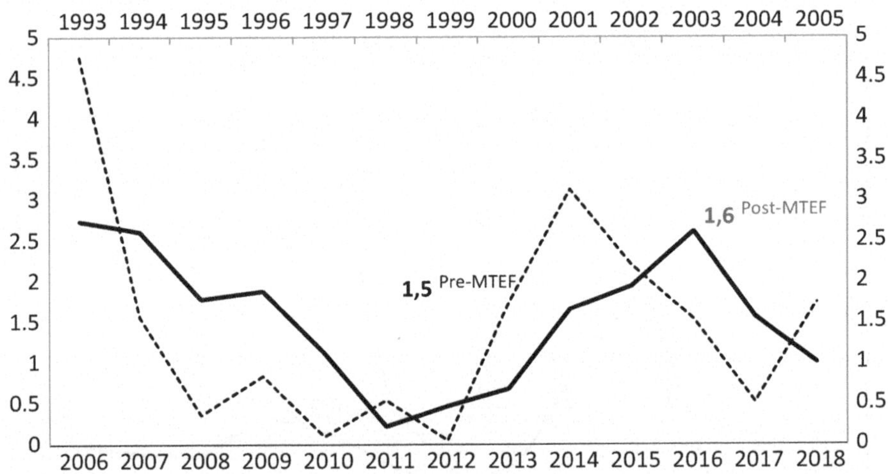

Fig. 4.12 Education expenditure volatility of central government (% of central government expenditures). *Source* Based on Treasury and Finance Ministry (2019)

4.5.3 Technical Efficiency

Efficiency in service delivery is based on the relationship between inputs, outputs, and outcomes. In the public sector, it is not easy to clearly define the outputs and outcomes of expenditure programs. Generally, expenditure programs work toward achieving economic and social outcomes such as stable growth, poverty reduction, and social protection. However, outcomes are influenced by many factors other than government

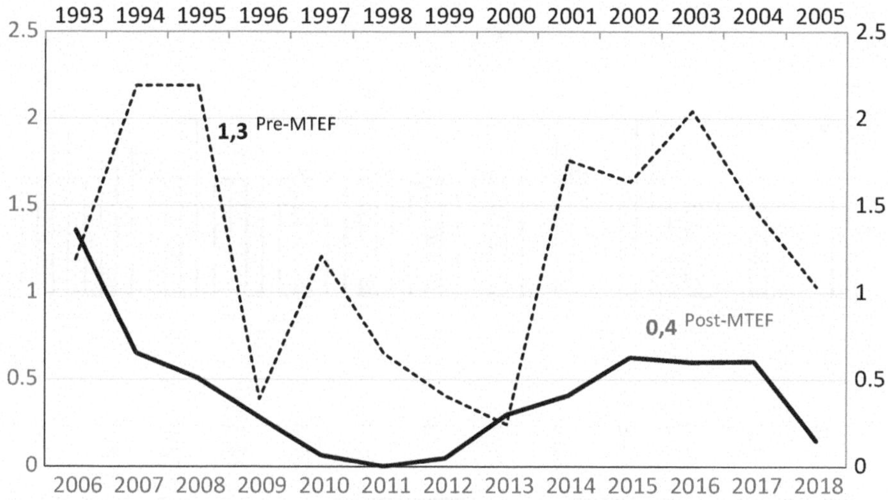

Fig. 4.13 Military expenditure volatility of central government (% of central government expenditures). *Source* Based on Treasury and Finance Ministry (2019)

expenditures (World Bank 2013). Thus, measuring technical efficiency is difficult and is beyond the scope of this study. Nevertheless, we tried to examine the correlations between central government health expenditures, average life expectancy, and citizen satisfaction (TurkStat 2019a, b). As a result, we obtained a significant and positive correlation between central government health spending per capita and average life expectancy at birth for the period of 2006–2017 in Turkey (r_s= 0,958, p = 0,000). However, we could not find a meaningful relationship between health spending and citizen satisfaction with government health services (see Table 4.3).

Table 4.3 The correlation table on health expenditures in Turkey (2006–2017)

	Life expectation at birth	Citizen satisfaction with public health services
Health expenditure of central government (Per capital)	0.958**	0.524

**p < 0.01

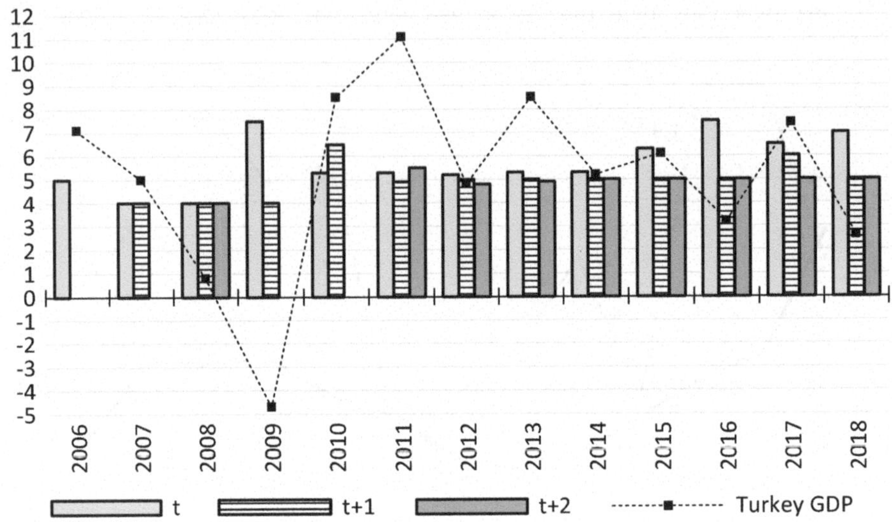

Fig. 4.14 Real GDP forecasts of MTP* and outturns, 2006–2018 (%)* Not available forecasts in some out-years of MTPs. *Source* Based on MTPs and the Turkish Central Bank Database

4.6 Evaluation of Processes and Design of MTEF

4.6.1 Forecasting Errors in Macroeconomic Variables

The MTEF in Turkey has had some challenges that may negatively affect budgetary outcomes. One of the important conditions of fiscal discipline is the success of macroeconomic forecasting. Since MTEF forecasts are made one year (t-1) before the fiscal year, deviations from the forecasts can be expected to increase in out-years. Figure 4.14 shows the GDP forecasts of MTP and actual GDP growth rates for the period of 2006–2018. A growth rate of around 5% was estimated throughout this period, but actual growth rates varied between –4.7% (FY2009) and +11.1% (FY2011). Figure 4.15 compares the gap between multiyear forecasts and outturns for another macroeconomic variable: inflation. The figure shows that inflation forecasts were generally optimistic. In sum, there were significant forecast errors in real GDP and inflation variables during the MTEF period of Turkey.

4.6.2 A Multitude of Policy Documents

In Turkey, two policy documents, the MTP and MTFP, contain the policies to be followed in the future three-year horizon and are published in the budget preparation process. There are also other policy documents in various forms such as development

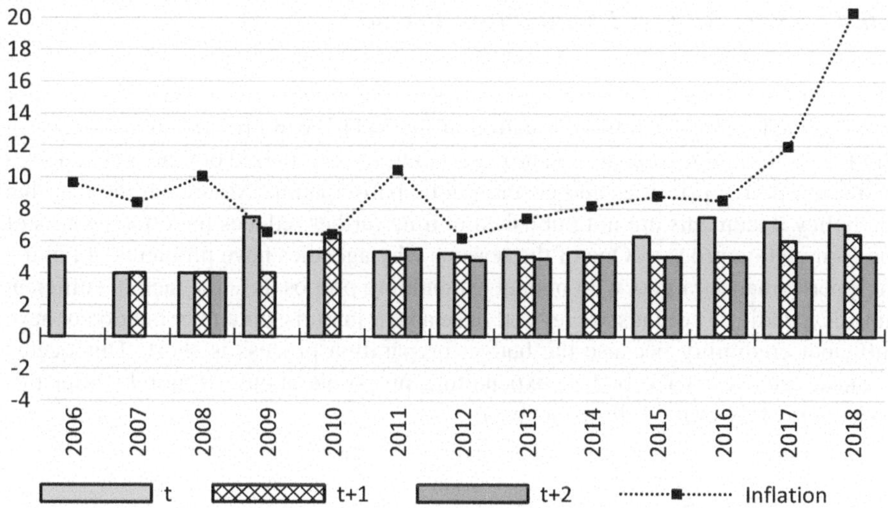

Fig. 4.15 Inflation forecasts of MTP* and outturns, 2006–2018 (%)* Not available forecasts in some out-years of MTPs. *Source* Based on MTPs and the Turkish Central Bank Database

plans, presidential annual programs, and sectoral plans. All of these documents are announced at different times and must be compatible with each other (Demirbaş 2006). The abundance of policy documents to be followed in the budget preparation process leads to transaction costs for budgetary actors. To sum up, the many policy documents mean a decrease in the power of guidance for the actors.

4.6.3 Weaknesses in Linking Policy, Planning, and Budgeting

A performance-based budgeting system is in force in Turkey. However, there are problems in establishing the links between the strategic plan, performance program, and budget at the microlevel. In practice, it has been observed that performance programs are prepared without establishing a sufficient relationship with the objectives and targets in the strategic plans. There are similar problems with the annual budget's compliance with the annual performance program. Additionally, performance programs do not receive enough attention from the actors during the reconciliation process in the budget formulation and budget debates in Parliament (Ministry of Development 2015). Problems in policy costing at the agency level make it difficult to establish the link between policy-planning and budgeting at the governmental level. Although medium-term policy documents contain policies and measures, they do not provide sufficient explanations about their costs. (Demirbaş 2006; Yılmaz and Biçer 2010).

4.6.4 Short Budget Formulation Period

The length of the central government budget preparation period in Turkey is just four months. Generally, the rolling structure of the MTEF can provide an advantage in shortening the budget preparation process. However, this period of time is not enough to discuss policy priorities and ensure public participation. Moreover, the fact that the policy documents are not published in time further reduces the effectiveness of the formulation process. One of the reasons why agencies have problems in linking their performance targets with budget expenditure proposals is the lack of sufficient time. Expenditure ceilings are revised once a year in mid-September but do not have sufficient credibility because the budget preparation process is short. This occurs because agencies make budget expenditure proposals about 10 months after this revision (in July of the following year).

4.6.5 Detailed Line-Item Budget Classification

The central government's budget preparation process in Turkey has built extensively on the line-item expenditure classification. Expenditure ceilings in the MTFP only apply to the type of economic classification for each agency. Such a classification is useful for controlling inputs, but not for effective policy-making and performance management. The functional classification of government expenditures that is compatible with COFOG is also used as a budget classification in Turkey. This classification shows the distribution of resources between sectors. However, it is intended to produce international comparative standardized statistical data; it is not actually a budget classification, and the aim is ex post reporting (Robinson 2013). Given that there is no program-based classification based on policy aims and outcomes, the MTEF does not have sufficient power to allocate resources in line with government policy priorities. However, there are studies on the transition to program-based classification.

4.6.6 Lack of Fiscal Transparency, Accountability, and Public Participation

Although many MTEF documents are produced in Turkey, they are usually not published on time. The publication of the top policy documents—the MTP and MTFP—extends to October. Furthermore, these documents do not include detailed explanations about the level of deviation from the forecasts, reasons for deviations, and fiscal risks. Therefore, it difficult to argue that both documents provide enough guidance to society about government policies.

Participation in policy-making is a natural right of citizens and nongovernmental actors. Public participation in fiscal policy is key to the MTEF (GIFT 2016). Unfortunately, Turkey could not provide sufficient progress in terms of public participation in the central government budget. In recent years, the Ministry of Treasury and Finance has started to publish a citizen budget. However, this initiative is only a small step towards active participation.

4.7 Conclusion

The MTEF that came into force in 2006 can be considered as successful in terms of providing financial discipline in Turkey. However, Turkey has implemented three stand-by arrangements between 1999 and 2008 (Kaya and Yilar 2011). The MTEF was an implementation tool of the IMF-supported program for a while. Therefore, more years without the IMF are needed to obtain stronger evidence on this issue.

The MTEF in Turkey is a forecasting MTEF, and the next step is the transition to a programmatic MTEF. It could be said that Turkey has some advantages because of the infrastructure of performance-based budgeting and accrual-based accounting. Nevertheless, it is important to note that MTEFs should not be seen as only a technical tool. If the transition to a programmatic MTEF remains only the adaptation of the program classification to the budget, the desired benefits will not be obtained. The greater involvement of spending agencies, civil society and, of course, Parliament in the MTEF processes will be a key factor in success. In addition, evaluating the social and economic consequences of public expenditures will also strengthen the processes.

Some suggestions to improve the MTEF in Turkey are as follows:

- To reduce estimation errors, macroeconomic projections could be submitted to a panel of independent experts or the Court of Turkish Auditors. The evaluations of these actors could increase the credibility of the projections (OECD 2001).
- The number of policy documents could be reduced. At least, the MTP and MTFP could be merged in a single document.
- The budget preparation process must be at least six months long. In addition, an economic and financial update report should be issued by the government every six months.
- A distinction should be made between current and new policies to focus the budget formulation process on policy changes and policy costs.
- Including the agency performance program and budget preparation in a single document could strengthen the target–cost relationship at the microlevel (Çatak and Çilingir 2010).
- Reducing the detail in budget classification may lead to further debates by budgetary actors about program outcomes and technical efficiency (Kraan, Bergvall, and Hawkesworth 2007).

- Turkey uses the MTEF like most other OECD countries. However, fiscal policies require not only a medium-term perspective but also long-term planning (Robinson 2016). Therefore, long-term financial projections and analysis should also be done in Turkey.

References

Alantar, D. (2009). Medium Term Expenditure Framework Reform in Turkey. Retrieved June 24, 2019, from https://www.pempal.org/sites/pempal/files/attachments/mtef-turkey_eng.pdf

Allan, W. (1996). Public Expenditure Planning and Forecasting. In N. Caiden (Ed.), *Public Budgeting and Financial Administration in Developing Countries* (pp. 93–113). London: JAI Press Inc.

Asian Development Bank. (2000). *Managing Government Expenditure*. Retrieved from https://think-asia.org/handle/11540/2586

Blöndal, J. (2005). *The Reform of Public Expenditure Management Systems in OECD Countries. SSRN*. https://doi.org/10.2139/ssrn.2028366

Campos, E., & Pradhan, S. (1996). *Budgetary Institutions and Expenditure Outcomes: Binding Governments to Fiscal Performance* (No. 1646). *Policy Research Working Paper Series*.

Çatak, S., & Çilingir, C. (2010). Performance Budgeting in Turkey. *OECD Journal on Budgeting, 10*(3), 1–39. https://doi.org/10.1787/budget-10-5km4d794l142

de Renzio, P., & Smith, S. (2005). *Linking Policies and Budgets: Implementing Medium Term Expenditure Frameworks in a PRSP Context*. London. Retrieved from https://www.odi.org/publications/1368-linking-policies-and-budgets-implementing-medium-term-expenditure-frameworks-prsp-context

Demirbaş, T. (2006). *Kamu harcama yönetimi bağlamında orta vadeli harcama sistemi ve Türkiye açısından değerlendirilmesi*. Uludag University, Bursa, Turkey.

Di Francesco, Michael Barroso, R. (2014). *Review of International Practices for Determining Medium Term Resource Needs of Spending Agencies. World Bank Other Operational Studies*. The World Bank. Retrieved from https://ideas.repec.org/p/wbk/wboper/21812.html

Downes, R. (2013). Medium-Term Expenditure Frameworks (MTEF): Logic, Benefits, Limitations. Retrieved June 24, 2019, from https://wpqr4.adb.org/LotusQuickr/cop-mfdr/PageLibrary482571AE005630C2.nsf/0/4EE654D494FED26648257BD9007E641E/$file/4 MTEF - R Downes.pdf

Due, J. F., & Friedlaender, A. F. (1977). *Government Finance Economics of the Public Sector* (6th ed.). USA: Richard D. Irwin, Inc.

EUROSTAT. (2019). Government finance statistics. Retrieved June 24, 2019, from https://ec.europa.eu/eurostat/data/database

GIFT. (2016). *Principles of public participation in fiscal policy*. Retrieved from http://fiscaltransparency.net/PP_Approved_in_General_13Dec15.pdf

Harris, J., Hughes, R., Ljungman, G., & Sateriale, C. (2013). Medium-Term Budget Frameworks in Advanced Economies: Objectives, Design, and Performance. In M. Cangiano, T. Curristine, & M. Lazare (Eds.), *Public Financial Management and Its Emerging Architecture* (pp. 137–173). Washington, DC: International Monetary Fund.

Holmes, M., & Evans, A. (2003). *A Review of Experience in Implementing Medium Term Expenditure Frameworks in a PRSP Context : A Synthesis of Eight Country Studies. Centre for Aid & Public Expenditure*. London.

IMF. (2019). World Economic Outlook Database April 2019. Retrieved June 24, 2019, from https://www.imf.org/external/pubs/ft/weo/2019/01/weodata/index.aspx

Kaya, F., & Yilar, S. (2011). Fiscal Transformation in Turkey over the Last Two Decades. *OECD Journal on Budgeting, 1*, 59–74. https://doi.org/10.1787/budget-11-5kggc0zr42g6
Kesik, A. (2000). Türk Mali Yönetiminin İşleyiş Yönünden Yeniden Yapılandırılmasına Yönelik Çabaların Yönü ve Bu Çabaların Değerlendirilmesi. In *Türk Kamu Mali Yönetiminin Yeniden Yapılandırılması ve Bu Yapılanmada Performans Yönetimi ve Denetiminin Yeri* (pp. 139–168). Antalya: Akdeniz Üniversitesi.
Kraan, D.-J., Bergvall, D., & Hawkesworth, I. (2007). Budgeting in Turkey. *OECD Journal on Budgeting, 7*(2), 7–58. https://doi.org/10.1787/budget-v7-art8-en
Ministry of Development. (2015). *Kamuda stratejik yönetim çalışma grubu raporu* (No. 2942). Ankara, Turkey.
Ministry of Finance. (2005). *2006 Yılı Bütçe Gerekçesi*. Ankara, Turkey.
Ministry of Treasury and Finance. (2019). Statistical Databases. Retrieved from www.hmb.gov.tr
OECD. (1997). *Budgeting for the Future* (No. OCDE/GD(97)178). Paris.
OECD. (2001). *Managing Public Expenditure*. (R. Allen & D. Tommasi, Eds.). France: OECD.
Oxford Policy Management. (2000). Medium Term Expenditure Frameworks - Panacea or Dangerous Distraction? Retrieved June 23, 2019, from http://www1.worldbank.org/publicsector/pe/OPMMTEFReview.pdf
Premchand, A. (1984). *Government Budgeting and Expenditure Controls: Theory and Practice* (2nd ed.). Washington, DC: IMF.
Presidency of the Republic of Turkey. Decree on the organization of Presidency of Strategy and Budget, Pub. L. No. 13, 30488 (2018a). Official Gazette. Retrieved from http://www.mevzuat.gov.tr/MevzuatMetin/19.5.13.pdf
Presidency of the Republic of Turkey. Decree on the organization of the Presidency of the Republic of Turkey, Pub. L. No. 1, 30474 (2018b). Official Gazette. Retrieved from http://www.mevzuat.gov.tr/MevzuatMetin/19.5.1.pdf
Public Financial and Management Law, Pub. L. No. 5018 (2003). Turkey. Retrieved from http://www.mevzuat.gov.tr/MevzuatMetin/1.5.5018.pdf
Robinson, M. (2013). *Program Classification for Performance-Based Budgeting: How to Structure Budgets to Enable the Use of Evidence*. Washington, DC. Retrieved from http://documents.worldbank.org/curated/en/627581468322141749/pdf/959380PUB0perf00Box391429B00PUBLIC0.pdf
Robinson, M. (2016). Budget reform before and after the global financial crisis. *OECD Journal on Budgeting, 16*(1), 29–63. https://doi.org/10.1787/budget-16-5jlvc85w7nkf
Rosalky, D. (2012). Budget Process and Medium Term Expenditure Framework. Retrieved June 23, 2019, from https://wpqr4.adb.org/lotusquickr/cop-mfdr/PageLibrary482571AE005630C2.nsf/0/DE4711BA26950ECF48257AAF002837E9/$file/Dr. David Rosalky-S2 BUDGET PROCESS AND MTEF.pdf
Schiavo-Campo, S. (2009). Potemkin Villages: "The" Medium-Term Expenditure Framework in Developing Countries. *Public Budgeting & Finance, 29*(2), 1–26. https://doi.org/10.1111/j.1540-5850.2009.00926.x
Schick, A. (1999). *A Contemporary Approach to Public Expenditure Management*. World Bank Institute. Retrieved from http://documents.worldbank.org/curated/en/739061468323718599/pdf/351160REV0Contemporary0PEM1book.pdf
Schick, A. (2003). Does budgeting have a future? *OECD Journal on Budgeting, 2*(2), 7–48. https://doi.org/10.1787/budget-v2-art8-en
Sherwood, M. (2015). *Medium-Term Budgetary Frameworks in the EU Member States* (No. 21). European Union. https://doi.org/10.2765/905635
The Constitution of the Republic of Turkey, Pub. L. No. 2709 (1982). Turkey. Retrieved from http://www.mevzuat.gov.tr/MevzuatMetin/1.5.2709.pdf
Tommasi, D. (2009). Strengthening Public Expenditure Management in Developing Countries: Sequencing Issues. Retrieved June 23, 2019, from https://europa.eu/capacity4dev/public-pub.sector-reform-decentralisation/document/tommassi-2009-strengthening-public-expenditure-management-developing-countries-sequencing-i

TurkStat. (2019a). Expectation of life at birth. Retrieved from www.tuik.gov.tr
TurkStat. (2019b). Satisfaction from public services in general, 2003–2018. Retrieved from www.tuik.gov.tr
van Eden, H., Khemani, P., & Emery, R. P. J. (2013). Developing Legal Frameworks to Promote Fiscal Responsibility: Design Matters. In M. Cangiano, T. Curristine, & M. Lazare (Eds.), *Public Financial Management and Its Emerging Architecture* (pp. 79–105). Washington, DC: International Monetary Fund.
Wildavsky, A. (1986). *Budgeting: A Comparative Theory of Budgetary Processes* (2nd ed.). New Brunswick: Transaction Publishers.
World Bank. (1994). *Kamu Harcamaları ve Personel Yönetimi İçin Kurumsal ve Teknik Çerçevenin Modernleştirilmesi Ön Değerlendirme Heyeti Raporu*. Ankara.
World Bank. (1998). *Public Expenditure Management Handbook* (No. 186168). Washington, DC: World Bank.
World Bank. (2003). *Turkey - Country economic memorandum : towards macroeconomic stability and sustained growth : Summary Report (English)*. Washington, DC. Retrieved from http://documents.worldbank.org/curated/en/266271468761359775/Summary-Report
World Bank. (2013). *Beyond the Annual Budget*. Washington, DC: World Bank. https://doi.org/10.1596/978-0-8213-9625-4
Yılmaz, H. H., & Biçer, M. (2010). Türkiye'de mali reformlar sonrası değişen politika oluşturma, planlama, bütçeleme süreci ve orta vadeli harcama sisteminin uygulanabilirliği. *İktisat İşletme ve Finans*, *25*(287), 33–68. https://doi.org/10.3848/iif.2010.287.2539

Tolga Demirbaş is an associate professor at Bursa Uludag University, Faculty of Economics and Administrative Sciences in Bursa, Turkey. He received his Ph.D. in public budgeting and fiscal planning from the Institute of Social Sciences, Bursa Uludag University in 2006. His dissertation title is Medium Term Expenditure Framework in the Context of Public Expenditure Management and the Evaluation of Turkish Case. The author's current research interests include public budgeting reforms, performance budgeting and auditing, fiscal transparency, accountability, and government accounting.

Chapter 5
An Assessment of the Public Procurement System in Turkey

Özhan Çetinkaya and Erdal Eroğlu

5.1 Introduction

Public administrations within the state organization are responsible for meeting social needs. The needs demanded by the society require public production and provision. In line with this requirement, administrations can both accomplish production and provision on their own and may also procure them from the market. The main reason behind this is that producers in the market economy can manage production and provision at lower costs compared to public producers. In this regard, producers in the public sector (public administrations) started to hold competitions (tenders) so as to choose the producer that can manage production and provision at the lowest cost. Public production and provision, which was also implemented in the period before 1980, became market-based in the post-1980 period with the "intensive free market economy understanding". In this scope, public sector producers initiate procurements to find the candidate that will carry out production and provision at the lowest cost for the public procurements they will make from the market.

One of the specially focused areas in the restructuring process of public finance management through good governance model is Public Procurement Law. Considering that a major part of the state budget is allocated for construction works and purchase of goods and services, the significance of procurement law is apparent for efficient and effective use of resources. Having a good procurement system increases

Ö. Çetinkaya (✉)
Faculty of Economics and Administrative Sciences, Department of Public Finance, Bursa Uludağ University, Bursa, Turkey
e-mail: ozhanc@uludag.edu.tr

E. Eroğlu
Faculty of Economics and Administrative Sciences, Department of Public Finance, Çanakkale Onsekiz Mart University, Çanakkale, Turkey
e-mail: erdaleroglu@comu.edu.tr

H. Kıral and T. Akdemir (eds.), *Public Financial Management Reforms in Turkey: Progress and Challenges, Volume 1*, Accounting, Finance, Sustainability, Governance & Fraud: Theory and Application, https://doi.org/10.1007/978-981-15-1914-7_5

the efficiency and performance of public finance management and reduces prodigality. A good procurement system functions by arranging each and every stage starting from the inclusion of appropriations required for the needs into the budget and determining the tender procedure, going out to tender, making, approving, and concluding the tender to signing the contract harmoniously in a competitive and transparent manner.

The main motivation of this study is to evaluate the efficiency of the public procurement system in Turkey in the light of the Public Procurement Law numbered 4734 in terms of the results of implementation within the perspective of the process in question and suggestions are made for the improvement of defective aspects. To this end, the study is designed in three sections. The first section focuses on the legal basis and content of the public procurement system. In the second section, practical operation of the public procurement system is examined. The final section evaluates the public procurement system based on the shortcomings and defects in the present implementation in terms of the procurement law and administration and authorities as well as offering suggestions.

5.2 Legal Aspect and Content of Public Procurements

Public procurement system starts with the inclusion of the appropriation required for the needs into the budget and goes on with the processes of determining the tender procedure, going out to tender, implementation, approval, and conclusion of the tender and signing the contract. This system is built upon three pillars which include the procurement law, administrative procurement department, and candidates. The system will be able to operate well on condition that these three pillars are synchronized. However, if the law is poor or the procurement department is inadequate, in fact, if one of these three pillars is weak, a sound system operation cannot be possible. This was explained by the Chinese reformist Wang An Shih, who lived between 1020 and 1086 A.C., with two main reasons (Uğur 2012: 306). These are "Bad Laws and Bad Men". If the law is designed poorly, the result is bad even if men implemented it well, if the law is designed well, but implemented badly by men, the result will be bad in the same way. The literature concerning public procurements includes a great many studies showing that badly designed procurement laws cause corruption, bureaucratic degeneration, inefficient use of resources, borrowing, and even financial crises, while well-designed procurement laws contribute to the development of competitive market, efficient use of resources, increase in quality services, economic growth, and welfare (Schapper et al. 2006; Bovis 2005; Caldwell et al. 2005; Klun and Setnikar 2013; Edler and Georghiou 2007; McCrudden 2004).

The main issue in the implementation of public procurements is to have a well-designed law on tendering. To this end, all countries have been trying to carry out procurements on a good legal basis. Therefore, the operation of the procurements to be made by public administrations is an issue that depends on a legal basis in every country. For example, having a significant role in the economy of the European Union (EU), public procurements are not included under a separate title in any of the European Union Treaties (Prime Ministry 2011). However, it can be understood that sufficient legal basis has been formed to harmonize the legislation to the field particularly from the articles of "*The Treaty on European Union and Treaty on the Functioning of the European Union*" concerning the free movement of labor, services, and capital as well as the freedom of establishment (Ünay 2004: 1). In this regard, it can be seen that regulations and main principles on public procurements are included in the "*EU directives*" within the EU legislation. Directives and regulations numbered 2004/17/EC and 2004/18/EC include the issues of tendering procedures as well as the procurement of goods and services and construction works. In the directive 2004/18 of the European Parliament and Council published in the Official Journal of the EU dated 30.4.2004, tendering procedures to be employed in public procurements are stated as open tendering procedure, tendering among certain preselected candidates (restricted procedure), negotiated procedure with or without notice and competitive dialogue, and it is also stated that procurements can be held under framework contracts. Procurements carried out as a softened form of these implementations apart from the tendering procedures included in the directives are addressed in the individual legal regulations of the member countries. These procurements are those carried out under threshold values or under a given limit (Strand et al. 2011: 5). Generally called direct procurements, these procurements vary in amount and the way they are carried out by country (Bianchi and Guidi 2010: 1–227). Procurements carried out in the form of direct procurements within the scope of negotiated or restricted tendering procedures are implemented in different ways. Thus, direct procurements appear as a practice implemented in negotiated procurements or those held among certain candidates. This practice may vary by country. For instance, among the procurements carried out this way, the share of procurements without notice in the total is 5% (Strand, et al. 2011: 16). It is similar for procurements among certain candidates, which is also around 5%.

As a nonmember country, Turkey formed the legal basis for public procurements with the "*Public Procurement Law numbered 4734 and dated 2002*". This law, at the same, depends on UNCITRAL (The United Nations Commission on International Trade Law, the model law of the World Bank. In order for the tenders made on the basis of this law to be completed, "*The Law on Public Procurement Contracts numbered 4735 and dated 2002*" was enacted. Hence, these two main laws set the legal infrastructure of public procurements. In the same way, regulations issued in accordance with these two laws support the legal infrastructure of tendering procedures. The regulations that were issued for procurement of goods, services, and construction works and are included in the scope of the procurement law are as follows: "*Framework Regulation on Procurement of Goods, Framework Regulation on Procurement of Services, Framework Regulation on Procurement of Work and Framework Regulation on Procurement of Consultancy Services.*" In addition to the Laws numbered 4734 and 4735 as well as the related regulations, communiqués issued are also important arrangements for the smooth functioning of the system. With the updates completed on it, "General Communiqué of Public Procurement" dated 2009 is the main communiqué in the system. Hence, in line with the content of their needs, public administrations carry out public procurements applying to the Public Procurement Law (PPL) and Law on Public Procurement contracts within the general frame and to the related regulations and communiqués announced as the secondary legislation in the sub-framework.

Main arrangements have been made concerning tenders in the content of Public Procurement Law which is included in the legal basis of public procurements. These main arrangements concern the coverage of administrations by the law, procurements excluded by the law, main principles, exceptions, tender procedures, rules on participation, procurement proceedings dossier, tender conditions and noticing principles, submission and conclusion of applications, and conclusion of the tender and complaint application.

5.3 Operation of the Public Procurement System

Public administrations are liable to carry out the procurements they need pursuant to the Public Procurement Law. Administrators cannot supply the procurement of goods and services and needs concerning construction works of their administrations from the market on their own will. Administrations are obliged to carry out procurements in accordance with the Public Procurement Law. The law brings together procurements from the lowest to the highest amount by separating them as with or without notice to form a system. Procurement departments of administrations can initiate their procurement proceedings by opening the procurement dossier in accordance with the appropriation allocated and depending on the content of goods, services, or works to be procured.

The law pays attention to the procurement procedures to be applied in procurements and specifies open and restricted procedures as the main procedures. In addition to the "*open procurement procedure*" and "*restricted procurement procedure*", "*negotiated procedure*" is included as the third and last procedure. Considering these procedures, open procedure appears to be the most competitive procurement when any tenderer is expected to submit a tender (PPL; a; 19). Since the use of the restricted procedure requires specific conditions, it also provides a competitive proceeding as those who fulfill the specified conditions submit tenders. As for the negotiated procedure, the last procurement procedure stated, procurement proceedings are carried out with or without notice in cases specified in the Law. Procurements carried out with this procedure have a less competitive characteristic in comparison with the other two procedures. This is because some of the procurements are ensured to be held without notice in the negotiated procedure. Apart from these procedures, there is another way of procurement included in the Law, but not stated as a tendering procedure, which is called "direct supply" method. the Law lays down the conditions for the purchases to be made through direct supply method. The most frequently used condition is that in procurements not exceeding a certain amount of a monetary limit for needs of contraction authorities within the boundaries of metropolitan municipalities and procurements not exceeding a certain amount of another monetary limit for needs of other contracting authorities can be made by direct supply method (PPL, a; 22/d). These amounts are updated annually by the Public Procurement Authority.

Setting aside which tender procedure to choose depending on the conditions for public procurements, the condition that adequate appropriation for the related procurement shall be allocated in the budget is among the significant conditions of the Law. Procurement proceedings with adequate appropriation which are determined according to the conditions laid down by the Procurement Law are fulfilled within the time limits stated by the Law. For instance, notices of procurements to be conducted by open procedure are published 40 (forty) days prior to the procurement date on the EPPP (Electronic Public Procurement Platform) and the procurement is held on the date and at the hour specified. Following the procurement, the contracting officer approves or cancels the tender decision within 5 (five) working days. In this example, it is assumed that the process continues uninterruptedly. Even assuming that all the stages of the procurement go on without any interruptions, completion of the procurement shall be realized within 60 (sixty) days. However, any possible problem to come up in the procurement process extends the time, which causes administrations to avoid procurements with notice. In this regard, direct supply procurements (PPL, a; 22) and those carried out in the negotiated procedure without notice (PPL, a; 21/b, c, f) are included in the procurement methods that can be defined as without notice in the law.

The contracting officer[1] is obliged to give the certificate of approval for the procurements needed for spending the appropriation allocated to him. Procurement proceedings are initiated upon the certificate of approval. The procurement department conducts market research for prices and ensures that the administration can specify the highest procurement price (estimated cost). The highest value that the administration wishes to purchase is found among market prices. Tender is submitted with this value which is called the estimated cost. Offers to be received must be as high as this value or lower. The candidate offering the minimum price wins the tender.

What is important in the operation of the procurement system is that administrations shall carry out procurement proceedings pursuant to Public Procurement Law. If administrations conduct procurement proceedings as stated by the Law, an important part of the system operation is fulfilled. The rest is concerned with the candidates. Ensuring that all tenderers have equal opportunities and conditions constitutes the other significant aspect of the system operation.

[1]Contracting Officer means authorized and liable persons or boards as well as those persons to whom the required authority and liability has been transferred properly in the contracting authority to spend and to carry out procurement proceedings.

5.4 Evaluation of the Public Procurement System

Public procurements shall be carried out in line with the principle of competition in choosing procurement procedures and preparing the procurement dossier as well as concluding the proceedings. By complying with this principle, it is assumed that the law makes procurements at the most economical prices and the procurement system functions well. As mentioned before, the content of the procurement law (good law) and the opinions and acts of candidates (good men) are two very important factors in attaining this functioning. In this regard (good law, good men), it is possible to evaluate the public procurement system in Turkey as follows.

(a) **Evaluation of the System in terms of the Procurement Law**

When evaluating the public procurement system, it is important to analyze whether the Public Procurement Law can be qualified as "good law". The Public Procurement Law is dated 2002. As of 2018, it can be seen that the Law has gone through amendments for many times over the past sixteen years. The Law has been amended nearly two hundred times in many of its articles with approximately fifty-five legal arrangements (see: PPL). While keeping laws up-to-date and making necessary amendments to this end is acceptable, such many changes on a sixteen-year-old law should be considered as a practice beyond the need for updating the law. When the amendments are examined, it is seen that they have been made in order to carry out proceedings faster rather than improving procurements or promoting competitiveness, and it is possible to state that they have brought about conditions which weaken competition, damage transparency, and impede equal treatment. The best example to be given concerning the issue is that about twenty of these amendments are on exceptions.

The fact that the law included five exceptions in the first year it was enacted while today there are twenty exceptional conditions; that is there are so many exceptions implies that there is a tendency to move related procurements beyond the law and conduct them freely. Some evaluations have been presented in the "*European Commission 2010 Progress Report of Turkey*" (Günal 2011: 108) and later in the "*European Commission 2016 Progress Report of Turkey*" which pointed out the increase in the amendments made on the Law from the time it was enacted up to today. According to the 2017 Procurement Monitoring Report, 19 billion (8%) TL of the total public procurements of 232 billion TL was made within the scope of exceptions. Exceptional procurements (12 billion TL) of municipal companies and state economic enterprises are particularly noticeable. Especially procurements by municipal companies from municipalities in the scope of exceptions impair competitiveness, equal treatment, and transparency with regard to market. After all, works to be conducted by municipal companies may as well be carried out by other companies on the market. This is specifically stated by the European Union Directives (2004/17 and 2004/18), which emphasize the importance of ensuring nondiscrimination among companies, equal treatment, and transparency[2]. We are in the opinion

[2]Directive 2014/24/Eu of the European Parliament and of the Council of 26 February 2014, On Public Procurement and Repealing Directive 2004/18/Ec.

that the figures pertaining to procurements given to publicly owned companies have reached a level that should be considered in terms of competition and equal treatment. In this regard, it is possible to assert that this law has moved away from being a "good law". What should be done concerning the problem is to downsize the scope of exceptions so that it is transformed back into the framework it had when the Law was first enacted.

Another issue concerning the evaluation of the Law is the ratio of the amount of direct supply procurements and negotiated procurements without notice which also include exceptions within the total procurements in order to ensure competition, transparency, and equal treatment. In the data of the Public Procurement Authority, it is seen that this ratio is rather high. For example, according to the figures pertaining to 2017, around 29% of the total procurements are comprised of procurements carried out through negotiated procedure without notice, direct supply, and exceptions (Public Procurement Monitoring Report 2017: 4). Although the practice of "Direct procurements", which is called "direct supply" in Turkey, is indispensable for European Union countries as well, it is important to ensure competition and transparency. In the European Union, this procurement procedure is employed when carrying out emergent, priority, and special works, and firms are provided with information flow (notice) and a satisfactory environment. While Germany, Spain, Denmark can be given as examples of countries where a competitive environment is established, Slovakia, Estonia, and Poland can be referred as those where competitiveness is poor (Strand et al. 2011: 96). In the decisions it makes, the Council of the European Union pays attention particularly to the core principles which can be defined as competition, transparency, equal treatment, and nondiscrimination (OECD 2011: 4). Attaching importance to these key principles in the tender procedures that member countries use in their procurements is considered critical to eliminate unlawful acts between member states and candidates.

As for the evaluation in the context of Turkey, in terms of competition and equal treatment principles, it is necessary to eliminate procurements held both through "direct supply" without notice and "negotiated procedure" without notice, to publish notices on the EPPP by shortening notice periods and not to conduct procurements without notice by reducing exceptions. Such actions to be taken to this end would enhance the good law characteristic of the Law.

Another point concerning the evaluation of the Law is about the valid time periods in the procurements particularly in open tenders and those among certain candidates (restricted tenders). Basically, these periods are close to those implemented by the European Union. However, in Turkey, both problems coming up in the preparation process for tenders and the fact that complaint applications are made quite frequently negatively affect administrations' conclusion of tender proceedings as well as causing them to turn to negotiated procedure or direct supply in the event that procurement is not realized. Concerning tendering periods the Law includes the provision that notices shall be published at least 40 (forty) days prior to the date of the tender for open procedures (it can be shortened 7 (seven) days if the notice is published via electronic media) (PPL, a; 13). Considering such time periods requiring that the tender decision shall be approved in 5 (five) days, the tenderers shall be acknowledged in 3 (three) days, the contract shall not be signed unless 10 (ten) days pass, responses shall be made in 10 (ten) days before signing the contract in case of a complaint, complainants shall apply to the Public Procurement Authority in 10 (ten days) for appealing complaints and the Authority shall make a decision in 20 (twenty) days, the Authority shall make a notification in 5 (five) days, and the concerning Administration shall implement the decision urgently upon notification; a tender shall be concluded in 2 (two) months without any complaints and in a period exceeding 3 (three) months in case of complaints. Such extended periods conflict with the understanding of running works faster held by the administrators in Turkey. Moreover, in the event that the tender is canceled at the end of the tender proceedings, administrations get into a problematic process particularly in service and construction works. This seems significant especially for municipalities. Since municipalities are the closest service units to the community, when a work fails to be tendered, they come up against the community. Hence, although notice periods are similar to those in the European Union, as the understanding of the management is to run works faster in Turkey, it should be considered that the periods are, to our opinion, long, preparation periods should be shortened seriously together with the EPPP and complaint and contract periods should be shortened similarly. Shortening notice periods for tenders would also move this Law closer to being a good law.

(b) **Evaluation of the System in terms of the Administration and Authorities**

It can be said that public procurements have a systematic operation and this systematic operation is well/badly affected by the good/bad design of the law as well as the good/bad acts of the administrations and authorities implementing this law. In this framework, administrations and authorities implementing Public Procurement Law may carry out procurement proceedings both by interpreting the articles of the Law in their personal way and by opposing to these articles. However, such acts violate competition, transparency, and equal treatment principles in public procurements and cause the system to be damaged. Therefore, as mentioned at the beginning of the present study, in addition to "good law", the acts of administrators and contracting officers for the functioning of the motto of "good men" are also important in order for the system to operate well. Concerning people's operating the Law correctly; it is possible to define the situations faced in Turkey and to assess the precautions to be taken in such situations as follows:

The first issue to be covered concerns the tender procedures employed in procurements. The law specifies the principal tender procedures as open procurements and procurements among certain candidates. When the implementation is concerned, data pertaining to the year 2017 show that procurements of 165 billion TL out of the total 232.8 billion TL were made using these procedures. The rest of them were carried out through direct supply (3.2 billion TL), negotiated procedure (45.3 billion TL) and in the scope of exceptions (19.3 billion TL). According to these figures, 70% of the procurements were made using main tender procedures, while negotiated procedure, direct supply, and the scope of exceptions were employed in the remaining 30%. Considering the fact that a majority of the tenders conducted with these procurement procedures are made without necessitating notices, it should be asserted that their preference by administrations violates competition and equality, which may in turn bring about the risk of corruption (Çetinkaya 2014: 103). It was also stated in the European Commission 2016 Progress Report of Turkey that the Procurement Law is open to corruptions from this aspect. Comparing the negotiated procedures implemented with and without notice, procurements made without notice constitute over 90% of the total negotiated procedure. The considerable extent of application to the article 22/d of the Law for direct supplies and 21/b for negotiated procedures (Public Procurement Monitoring Report 2017: 4–5) indicate how much competition and equality principles are violated. Court of Accounts reports indicate that administrations make procurements which are not included within the scope of the article 22/d (direct supply) of the Law referring to it particularly because they interpret the article in their own perspectives. Moreover, it is also included in the Court of Accounts reports that administrations do not comply with the provision that *"the annual total of expenses to be made within the monetary limits specified in the articles on negotiation (a: 21) and direct supply (a: 22) of this Law cannot exceed 10% of the appropriations to be allocated in administrations' budgets for this purpose."* The Law aims to state clearly that *"accordingly, the administration can make procurements from the persons they wish through direct supply up to 10% of the appropriations, but any amount exceeding this would not be in compliance with the competitive and equal treatment characteristics of the Law,"* which, however, is not considered by administrations. Approaching the issue from the administrations' side, they regard this fact as fulfilling works fast through facilitating procurements. However, bringing a competitive and equal treatment oriented understanding to tenders is favored by all parties. What should be done in this respect is to carry out any procurement, small or big, with notice and it should be seen as an important change to extend EPPP practices and to remove publishing newspaper notices from the legislation.

Another issue concerning administrations is the estimated cost. The Law states that estimated costs shall be determined by the administration and shall not be explained under any circumstances. During the tender process, the administration determines the estimated cost, candidates submit their offers, candidates' offers are compared to the administration's estimated cost, and the winner is announced. However, in this process, some non-visible situations may come up. For instance, the fact that the offers of some candidates are very close to each other in some tenders[3], some firms had been informed of the estimated cost or in some cases that offers remain much lower than the estimated cost and eliminated in the offer evaluation, but the offer of the winning firm is seen to be suitable may indicate that the estimated cost had been learnt or determined incorrectly. Hence, keeping estimated costs confidential is not beneficial to the administration, but it even brings about a disadvantageous situation for the administration. This may cause either extremely low valuation for

[3]In a decision made by PPL on the issue, it was stated that the incidence of two candidates submitting the same amounts of offer and the third candidate submitting an offer only different in the kuruş part is too low in the ordinary course of events and in the bounds of possibility and the tender was canceled.

tenderers or administrations' making procurements at high costs (Serdar 2010: 38). Confronting extremely low offers puts both the administration and the candidates into difficulty. Therefore, extremely low offers constitute a critical problem particularly in construction works (Eren 2010: 72–73). Incorrect determination and violation of confidentiality of estimated costs has been a noticeable result obtained from questionnaires conducted with administration personnel (Kömürcü 2006: 93–94).

The fact or the impression that the estimated cost was already known causes everybody to come under suspicion (Serdar 2010: 34). Hence, problems stated concerning the estimated cost appear to be practices that impair competition and equal treatment principles. In the Public Procurement Authority data concerning the far-fetched determination of estimated costs, it is seen that a 20% difference occurred in the open procurements for 2017 between estimated costs and the contract amounts in reality (Public Procurement Monitoring Report 2017: 8). It is a well-known fact that tender prices come out high as a result of the lack of qualified personnel in the administration and failure to conduct market research effectively, particularly in construction works (Doğanyiğit 2010: 98–99). This fact is also stated in the European Commission 2018 Progress Report of Turkey. The report expresses that preparation of procurement documents has some defects, methodological and organizational shortcomings, and that personnel change occurs frequently. Although there is an effort to observe the provision that estimated costs shall be kept confidential in the Law today, it has become possible for market actors to be able to predict these costs with no big differences considering that administrations determine pricing by asking market actors. In addition, since market actors know each other by the sector, they are able to predict the offer each may give. Therefore, the meaning of keeping the estimated cost confidential seems extremely important. If the estimated cost was determined and announced by the administration, it would mean the administration stated that "*We would like to purchase under this specific value*" and market actors would base their offers on this value. Such an arrangement would eliminate many troubles (extremely low offers, incorrect cost determination, malicious agreements of firms, etc.) within the system. Hence, tenders could be concluded in a fast and complaint-free way.

For a smooth operation of the procurement system, another important issue to be covered is the personnel responsible in system operation. The ordinary status of the officers working in the procurement departments of public administrations remains insufficient as far as the significance of the task they undertake. Moreover, although these officers get to know the work better in time, their position changes within the institution and the fact that they work with continuously changing managers affect the smooth sustainability of procurement proceedings negatively. In this respect, considering the material and nonmaterial responsibilities of the personnel conducting procurement proceedings within the framework of the provisions included in several laws (State Personnel Law, Public Procurement Law), it would be important to add the title "procurement personnel" to the related law (when the efficiency of spending public revenues also covers this point is taken into consideration). In the context of professionalization of the procurement department, physical opportunities and working conditions of the personnel should be provided at the highest level. It is extremely important to increase the quality and number of the personnel working in the procurement department. Persons to be recruited in the procurement department must be subjected to training on procurement legislation and it should be ensured that they receive continuous training to refresh themselves as well. In the European Commission 2015 Progress Report of Turkey, the issue is stated as "*The Public Procurement Authority should direct its educational and operational support onto institutions with more limited capacities such as municipalities*." In addition to the personnel carrying out regular procurement proceedings, it must be ensured that payments are made in the form of risk payment or daily allowances to the persons to be included in the tender commission (Karatoprak 2011: 422). Persons assigned to take part in the commission feel the commission membership as forced labor, so additional payments to be made to these individuals may lead to relieve their minds at least.

The emphasis that human factor is important in the operation of public procurements has been made at some points and the biggest step to be taken is to adopt an operational and professional understanding. In order to have a system that can be sustained in a professional understanding together with the managers and officers of administrations, it is important to establish a professional personnel network at the central level and to put effort for its maintenance at the rural level as well.

5.5 Conclusion

The present study focusing on a brief description and evaluation of the public procurement system in Turkey is based on the motto "good law, good men". Most of the time, many well-prepared and well-constructed laws have been deviated from their man goals and targets due to poor implementation. As a natural result of the rapid changes taking place today, amendments are inevitable. Such flexibility is also significant in terms of the efficiency of laws. However, it is essential that laws are designed well and the spirit of the law should not be violated by the amendments made thereafter. In addition, it is also necessary that the administrators implementing the law and related parties have good intentions and qualifications complying with the rules. In this regard, Public Procurement Law numbered 4734, which sets the basis for public procurements, has some defects in terms of sound operation and conclusion of procurements as also stated in the study. These defects concern the issues of exceptions, the choice of tender procedures, ways of procurement other than procurement procedures and estimated costs.

For an effective process in the public procurement system, establishing competition is rather critical in each and every step from determining tender procedures to preparing the procurement dossier to concluding the tender. This principle ensures effective and efficient use of the resources. Competition in the public procurement system defines a transparent process in all aspects and equal treatment. Examined as of 2018, the law dated 2002 appears to have gone through many amendments and a great number of exceptions have been included within the scope of the Law.

Making amendments is an ordinary practice considering the necessity for updating the Law. However, amendments seem to be made in order to carry out works in a faster pace rather than implementing public procurements in a more correct and sound manner or increasing competition. In this respect, it could be said that the Law has been through a change that weakens competition, impairs transparency, and impedes equal treatment. For instance, the share of procurements particularly made in the scope of exceptions within the total amount is 8% (19 billion TL) as stated in the evaluation section. Considering the fact that a majority of exceptions are included in the procurements made by municipal companies and state economic enterprises, how much market competition is negatively affected is observed. Another important point we have spotted concerns the time periods that are valid particularly in open procedures and procedures among certain candidates. Our opinion that tendering processes should be shortened is based on the necessity for the periods of preparation, complaint, and contract to be influent in procedure within the scope of the Law. Otherwise, bringing more exceptions for a faster procurement is against the nature of a competitive procurement. Another issue we addressed in the study is high costs. Inaccurate determination of estimated costs and violation of confidentiality are indicators that resources are not used effectively and efficiently in the first place. According to Procurement Monitoring Report values, there is a 20% difference between estimated costs and contract amounts. On the other hand, in procurements especially participated by municipality-owned enterprises, this difference is almost zero. These facts are concerning. Finally, the issue we see necessary for a good procurement system is about the personnel employed in the operation of the system. Our main suggestion in this respect is that administrators, like those in all other public institutions and organizations, should have sufficient expertise, technical competence, and experience regarding the cost of the work. In other words, it is the necessity for them to be professional. In this respect, as also mentioned in the evaluation section, the personnel conducting the procurement proceedings should be reassessed with the tile of "procurement personnel" by considering their material and nonmaterial responsibilities.

While they seem to be low in quantity considering the whole body of the Law, these aspects are very influential in terms of quality. The evaluations made concerning these aspects throughout the article may help the procurement law to be sounder. The issue of administrators and related officers, which is dealt with as another point in addition to the content of the Law, brings about results as significant as the Law itself. After all, in the case that these persons as the implementers of the Law have bad intentions, inefficient use of appropriations (resources) comes into question. As the final say; considering both in the context of Turkey and other countries, the motto "good law, good men" is a critical expression that can be accepted as a universal slogan.

References

Bianchi, T., & Guidi, V. (2010). The Comparative Survey on the National Public Procurement Systems across the PPN. Authority for the Supervision of Public Contracts, Department for the Co-ordination of European Union Policies, PPN Presidency.

Bovis, C. (2005). *Public Procurement in the European Union*. Houndmills, Basingstoke, Hampshire: Palgrave Macmıllan.

Caldwell, N., Walker, H., Harland, C., Knight, L., Zheng, J., & Wakeley, T. (2005). Promoting Competitive Markets: The Role of Public Procurement. *Journal of Purchasing and Supply Management*, 11(5–6), 242-251.

Çetinkaya, Ö (2014). "*Kamu İhale Kanunu ve Yolsuzluk Riskler*i". Bursa: Ekin Yayınevi.

Doğanyiğit, S. (2010). İhalenin Ruhu. Yaklaşık Maliyetin Gizliliği. *Dış Denetim Dergisi*, Ekim-Aralık 98–99.

Edler, J., and Georghiou, L. (2007). Public Procurement and Innovation-Resurrecting the Demand Side. *Research Policy*, 36(7); 949–963.

Eren, M., E. (2010). 4734 Sayılı Kamu İhale Kanunu ve Yeni Bir Kanun İhtiyacı, *Dış Denetim Dergisi*, Ekim-Aralık, 71–75.

Günal, C. (2011). "İdarelerin Mal ve Hizmet Edinme Usullerinden Biri Olarak Kamu İhaleleri". *İstanbul Üniversitesi Sosyal Bilimler Enstitüsü*. Yayınlanmamış Yüksek Lisans Tezi.

Karatoprak, E. (2011). Kamu İhalelerinde ve Sözleşme Yönetimi Süreçlerinde görevlendirilen Kamu Personelinin Sorumlulukları, *Maliye Dergisi*, 160; 411–422.

Klun, M., & Setnikar, C., S. (2013). Better Regulation and Public Procurement in Slovenian Municipalities. *Transylvanian Review of Administrative Sciences*, (38), 96–106.

Kömürcü, G. (2006). "4734 Sayılı Kamu İhale Kanununun Uygulamasında Karşılaşılan Sorunlar". *İstanbul Teknik Üniversitesi Fen bilimleri Enstitüsü*. Yayınlanmamış Yüksek Lisans Tezi.

McCrudden, C. (2004). Using Public Procurement to Achieve Social Outcomes. *Natural Resources Forum*, 28(4); 257–267.

OECD, (2011). *Public Procurement in the EU: Legislative Framework, Basic Principles and Institutions, Brief 1*, Retrieved from http://www.sigmaweb.org/publications/Public-Procurement-Policy-Brief-1-200117.pdf.

Olgun, B. (2006). "4734 Sayılı Kamu İhale Kanunu'nun Uygulanmasında Karşılaşılan Sorunlar İçin Çözüm Önerileri". *İstanbul Teknik Üniversitesi Fen Bilimleri Enstitüsü*, Yayımlanmamış Yüksek Lisans Tezi.

Schapper, J., Malta, N. J., and Gilbert, L. D. (2006). An Analytical Framework for the Management and Reform of Public Procurement. *Journal of Public Procurement*, 6(1/3); 1–26.

Serdar, A. (2010). Kamu İhale Mevzuatı Hakkında Genel Değerlendirme, *Dış Denetim Dergisi*, Ekim-Aralık, 34–43.

Strand, I., Ramada, P., Canton, E., Muller, P., Devnani, S., Bas, P. D., & Dvergsdal, K. (2011). Public procurement in Europe. Cost and effectiveness. Bruss. PwC Lond. Econ. Ecorys.

T.C. BAŞBAKANLIK Avrupa Birliği Genel Sekreterliği (2011), Avrupa Birliği Antlaşması ve Avrupa Birliği'nin İşleyişi Hakkında Antlaşma, Ankara, Retrieved from https://www.ab.gov.tr/files/pub/antlasmalar.pdf.

Uğur, H. (2012). Türkiye'nin Yolsuzlukla Mücadele Enstrümanları, *Türkiye Barolar Birliği Dergisi*, 98; 301–344.

Ünay, N. (2004). Türk Kamu İhaleleri Sisteminin Avrupa Birliği Kamu İhaleleri Sistemi İle Uyumlaştırılması, Retrieved from http://www.escrc.com/article/1449/turk-kamu-ihaleleri.

Internet References

Avrupa Komisyonu Türkiye 2010 Yılı İlerleme Raporu, Retrieved from https://www.ab.gov.tr/files/AB_Iliskileri/AdaylikSureci/IlerlemeRaporlari/turkiye_ilerleme_rap_2010.pdf.

Avrupa Komisyonu Türkiye 2016 Yılı İlerleme Raporu, Retrieved from https://Www.Ab.Gov.Tr/Files/Pub/2016_Ilerleme_Raporu_Tr.Pdf.

Avrupa Komisyonu Türkiye 2015 Yılı İlerleme Raporu Retrieved from https://www.ab.gov.tr/files/5%20Ekim/2015_ilerleme_raporu_tr.pdf.

Public Procurement Authority, Public Procurement Law numbered 4734, Retrieved from http://www2.ihale.gov.tr/english/4734_English.pdf.

Özhan Çetinkaya is a professor of Public Finance at the Faculty of Economics and Administrative Sciences, Bursa Uludağ University, Turkey. He is also the head of Public Finance Department. His research focuses on budgeting and financial management, strategic planning and management, public procurement and local government finance. Prof. Çetinkaya has authored and contributed to numerous books, book chapters, articles, and reports on public budgeting process, intergovernmental finance, public financial management, and municipalities. He took part in many projects especially on municipalities' service quality, participation and tax awareness. He also supervised municipal tenders and submitted reports.

Erdal Eroğlu is an assistant professor at the Department of Public Finance, Faculty of Economics and Administrative Sciences, Çanakkale Onsekiz Mart University, Turkey. He received his PhD in Public Budgeting and Fiscal Planning from the Institute of Social Sciences, Uludağ University in 2016. His research interests concern public budgeting, the political economy of budget, taxation, local governments, public procurement and fiscal transparency.

Chapter 6
Public-Private Partnership—The Case of Turkey

Bernur Açıkgöz

6.1 Literature Review

The literature scope regarding P3 has shown impressive growth over the past two decades. The P3 application has attracted considerable attention from many areas such as management, economic, and public administration (Spielman et al. 2007). Osborne (2000) claims that governments around the world are becoming almost dependent on P3 for the implementation of public policies. Concordantly, Teisman and Klijn (2002) show that governments need cooperation with various actors. In this respect, Hodge and Greve (2007) revealed that P3 is a cooperative institutional arrangement between the public and private sectors. Ross and Yan (2015) searched the optimality of the bundling of the various tasks and focused on how to design, operate, and maintain P3 projects.

Akintoye et al. (2001), Corbett and Smith (2006), Jefferies et al. (2002), Li et al. (2005), Zhang (2005) have revealed that project financing by the private sector is the main success factor in public infrastructure projects. P3 is no longer seen as a temporary requirement (Langford 2002; Rondinelli and Lacono 1996). Dahl and Lindblom (1953) predicted the relations getting closer gradually between the public and private sectors. P3 is clearly different from privatization. In addition, Middleton (2000), Hart and Moore (1990), Akintoye et al. (2006) claimed that with the application of P3, the public sector has created an alternative to privatization without losing power.

There are three main reasons for the P3 usage in public procurement;

1. P3 composes of multi-job contracts, the responsibility is shared, and the finance is remaining with the private sector (Bettignies and Ross 2004; Peters 1998; Akintoye et al. 2006; Bult-Spiering and Dewulf 2006).

B. Açıkgöz (✉)
İzmir Katip Çelebi University, İzmir, Turkey
e-mail: bernur.acikgoz@ikc.edu.tr

H. Kıral and T. Akdemir (eds.), *Public Financial Management Reforms in Turkey: Progress and Challenges, Volume 1*, Accounting, Finance, Sustainability, Governance & Fraud: Theory and Application, https://doi.org/10.1007/978-981-15-1914-7_6

2. An efficient strategy transfers the risks to the private sector (Thobani 1999; Hall 1998).
3. P3 opponents fear that the public interest is at stake because the private sector's profit motive conflicts with public values (Peters 1998; Rosenau 1999). However, many applications of P3 clearly showed that there is no loss in public benefits. However, since many PPP projects will be returned to host governments after the end of the concession period, problems with the subsequent management of PPP projects have not been fully studied yet (Jingfeng et al. 2015).

6.2 The Definitions of Public-Private Partnership

Although there is no consensus about how to define P3 (Marsilio et al. 2011), The Public–Private Partnership Knowledge Lab defines a *"public private partnership" (PPP) (P3) as "a long-term contract between a private party and a government entity, for providing a public asset or service, in which the private party bears significant risk and management responsibility, and remuneration is linked to performance."* There are various types of P3 and they are used in a variety of ways and in situations, so that we can define it in a variety of ways. It is not easy to combine the various definitions of P3, but some of the common concepts and assumptions could be defined. Some of the key features of P3 are as follows: First, P3 should be permanent cooperation, because this short-term contract is not a de facto P3. For this reason, it generally involves long-term cooperation (Girth 2014; Hodge and Greve 2007).

Secondly, the private sectors in the P3 project join the specific stages of the project, involving design, construction, operation, reparation. These stages usually include grand capital expenditures, which are worth more than hundreds of millions of dollars (Newman and Perl 2014). For this reason, a long-term agreement allows both partners to utilize cooperation (Silvestre and Araújo 2012). Thirdly, P3 enables sharing of important items such as risks, expenditures, benefits, sources, and responsibilities (Koppenjan 2005). Sharing is an indispensable element of P3 partnership. All costs will not be charged to the private sector partnership. Fourth, P3 projects are not simple projects (Ross and Yan 2015). Due to the character of the contract and the necessary multi-STAGE collaboration, the objectives of the P3 partners and the political environment can be dynamic. These factors reveal the need for partners to discuss and affect each other during the period of the collaboration. This potentially complicates the collaboration process in the P3 project. In addition, all the P3 partners have self-tactics/strategy and institutional history. This situation can complicate the decision-making process in P3 plans/projects (Klijn and Teisman 2003). Finally, P3 plans/projects have common goals. These common goals lead to do business between the public and private sectors and to establish partnerships (Wang et al. 2017).

P3 offers an opportunity between a state that individually undertakes the dual challenge of efficiency/productiveness and effectiveness in a multiplicity of fields of activity and a state that provides outsourcing to its representatives from the private sector (in Table 6.1) (Mazouz et al. 2008).

Table 6.1 P3s: an intermediate course of action

<table>
<tr><th>Public sector</th><th colspan="2">P3</th><th>Private sector</th></tr>
<tr><td rowspan="4">– The public sector does everything alone
– Political and ideological coherence of state intervention
– Problems of efficiency and effectiveness push toward boxes B and C of the matrix (elementary and symbiotic)</td><td colspan="2">Find a dual complementarity:
– resources
– performance criteria</td><td rowspan="4">– The public sector lets the private sector do everything
– Search for efficiency and effectiveness
– Problems of agency, control, opportunistic behavior. Public satisfaction push toward boxes A and D of the matrix (situational and forward-looking)</td></tr>
<tr><td colspan="2">Two perspectives</td></tr>
<tr><td>The public</td><td>The private</td></tr>
<tr><td>The “customer”
Logic of outsourcing or dependence
Withdrawal of the government or alternative to privatization</td><td>The “supplier”
Logic of cost of entry or of dominant position</td></tr>
</table>

Source Mazouz et al. (2008)

6.3 Public-Private Partnership Models

Many state agencies are exploring different P3 models as a means of sustaining updated substructures without having to make sizable investments under the limited financing and increasing restrictions. Such projects can be very useful however, the costs should be closely controlled to provide cost-effective solutions.

Public-private partnerships are recognized by many governments as the future of infrastructure projects because they offer solutions to investment problems in large projects without compromising of financing, job completion on time, and state financing. There are many different types P3 to suit various construction, operation, ownership, and revenue-generating scenarios (Table 6.2).

According to Mazouz and Belhocine (2002), the typology of P3 is affected by two major variables. The first variable is the closeness of the aim. It means that the

Table 6.2 A project-based management typology of public-private partnership projects

Capacity to generate projects	Proximity of target	
	Close	Distant
High	**Situational partnership** Dictated by imperatives of management, expertise, injection of private capital	**Elementary partnership** Search for savings, effectiveness, and efficiency
Low	**Symbiotic partnership** Resulting from a true community of practices, of convergences of values and interests	**Forward-looking partnership** Dictated by strategic issues at the scale of nations and governments

Source Mazouz et al. (2008, p. 101)

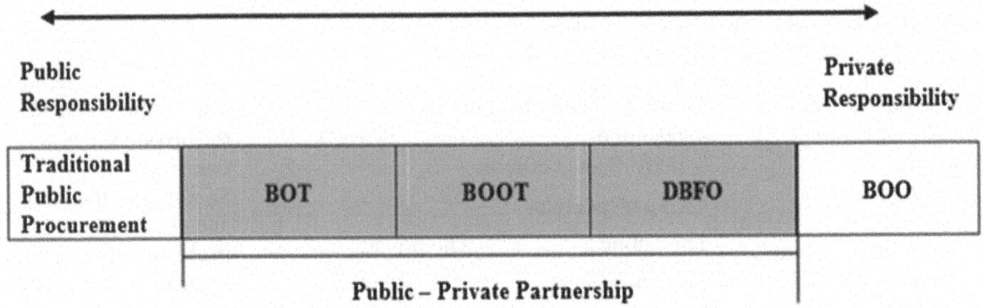

Fig. 6.1 Schematic scale of the public procurement classification. *Source* Akbiyikli and Eaton (2018)

distance/space between a public service provider and the consumers it serves. The second variable is the capacity to produce projects which means the ability of the vendor to transform a social demand into goods and services (see Fig. 6.1).

The public-private enterprises emerge in various types such as Build–Operate–Transfer (BOT), Build–Own–Operate–Transfer (BOOT), Build–Own–Operate (BOO), and Design–Build–Finance–Operate (DBFO). Because of the provision of substructure facilities, this situation provides governments the option to meet their substructure needs and demands in alternative ways. In general, such tools include a user-pays concept, which always can be applied by governments. But many governments have chosen to carry out the concept for the private sector to reduce their financial responsibilities (Confoy et al. 1999).

Figure 6.1 shows that various procurement paths, involving public-private partnership approaches in a spectrum. At the beginning of the spectrum, the public sector gets the whole responsibility of the financing, creation, operation, and maintenance of assets. It means that consists the responsibility to assume in related risk. Many of the public-private approaches remain in the middle of the spectrum. This location exists through the risks and responsibilities shared between the parties in line with their capabilities and strengths. At the end of the spectrum, the private sector takes over the whole responsibilities.

6.4 Public-Private Partnership Examples in the World

Throughout the world, P3 finds applications in a wide range of sectors. The transportation sector, whose first projects consist of models based on the "shadow toll" principle, is often at the forefront. In the applications, P3s in the transport sector include railway and city transportation. Other sectors that have a significant share in P3 are education, defense, water, health, and prisons (IFSL 2003). The main European countries that develop P3 models include Ireland, Portugal, Spain, Italy, Germany, Greece, and the Netherlands. In Central and Eastern Europe, many countries, including Czech Republic, Hungary, Poland, Bulgaria, and Lithuania, have initiated P3s due to the significant budgetary constraints with significant infrastructure requirements (IFSL 2003). Outside of Europe, the largest interest came from Australia, Japan, Canada and South Africa (Canadian Union of Public Employees 2006; National Treasury P3 Unit 2007). It would be correct to add Argentina, Brazil, Chile, Mexico, New Zealand, South Korea, Hong Kong, and Singapore to these countries.

In Hong Kong and Singapore, P3s are being developed together with the privatization program. Since 2000, many countries have established central government units to develop P3 programs (IFSL 2003). The US is the country with the longest history of the P3. In the US, the P3 was used as a tool to attract the private sector to regional economical development and urban infrastructure investments in the 1950s and 1960s (Stephenson 1991; Linder 1999; Moulton and Anheier 2001; Pongsiri 2002).

Throughout the 1980s, the P3 was increasingly shifting to privatization. In this context, with the assumption that private suppliers can offer goods and services with lower costs and higher quality, the work and responsibilities of the public sector are gradually reduced (UN 1993; Linder 1999; Bult-Spiering and Dewulf 2006; Hemming 2006). Other countries in Europe started to use P3 in the late 1980s. For example, in the Netherlands, the idea of P3 was clearly stated in the 1986 government policy statement. In Norway, P3 has been implemented especially in many infrastructure studies in recent years (Bult-Spiering and Dewulf 2006). The examples of P3 application are also available outside of Europe and America. For example, public-private partnerships were used in the renewal of infrastructures in the early 1990s in Australia. In the mid-1990s, the first projects took place relating to motorways, hospitals, water, and energy. In the late 1990s, airports, stadiums, and harbors were built with this method. In 2001, public defense, schools, and courts were added to this list. The Australian case has produced positive results such as cost-effective, early project delivery, and innovation (Barlow 2007).

The transfer of some projects and financing risks to the private sector and the availability and quality of services provided to citizens. Belgium, France, Germany, Greece, Ireland, Portugal, and Spain have comprehensive P3 laws. P3 units have been established at the central government level. One of the aims of these units is to organize the P3. Member States consider P3 as a necessary structure for the realization of infrastructure projects such as transport, public health, education, and national security (Bult-Spiering and Dewulf 2006). In 2014, the EU Commission has prepared three new Directives packages to reform public procurement in the Member States. These Directives are as follows:

- 2014/23/EU—on the award of concession contracts.
- 2014/24/EU—on the award of public contracts,
- 2014/25/EU—on the award of contracts by Utilities.

Concessions involving private partners are a special form of PPP. Although PPPs have never been defined in the EU Public Procurement Legislation, they are generally understood as a cooperation between the public authority and the private partner; in addition, it carries risks that are to be met by the public sector traditionally and generally contributes to the financing of the project. Some PPPs are structured as public contracts however, based on estimates of Commission services, more than 60% of all PPP contracts are compromised (The Concessions Directive 2018).

In terms of P3 applications, EU member countries can be examined in 3 groups: advanced adaptation to P3 countries such as England, in some respects France, Germany, Ireland, South Africa, Australia, Chile, and Italy; countries with moderate compliance to P3 such as Spain which have demonstrated extensive success in P3 (although not in all sectors yet); latecomers such as Luxembourg.

Mexico and Sweden, which are only at the beginning level in P3 applications (Renda and Schrefler 2006; Bult-Spiering and Dewulf 2006; Cuttaree 2008).

6.5 Public-Private Partnership in Turkey

Infrastructure investments need to be increased substantially in many developing countries like Turkey to boost the economic growth (Brux and Saussier 2018). P3 models have been implemented in Turkey, especially in the 90s, "BOT" and "BOO" type was applied in the areas of power generation, drinking water, etc. (Gümüştekin 1992).

However, with the concrete arrangements of the European Union regarding the provision of infrastructure services of the member states by the model referred to as P3 model, the political, economic, and legal infrastructure, political instability and the mistakes made in the design of the contract have brought serious negativities in terms of public and private sector cooperation, and the reliability of these models has been debated publicly.

In Turkey, "the concessions relating to public interest" law adopted in 1910, have created the legal basis of the first P3s. This law has continued to be one of the general legal grounds for the transfer of the services, which constitutes concession to the private sector after the establishment of the Republic of Turkey (Gümüştekin 1992; Tekin 2007). The developments in the Republican era date back to the 1980s. In 1984, with the BOT (Law No. 3096) and BOO (Law No. 4283) models, which were first enacted in the field of electricity generation; "The Transfer of Operating Rights" and BOO methods were put into practice (Gümüştekin 1992). With these methods, 30 power plants (8500 MW) have been put into operation, providing approximately one-fourth of the installed power plant (35 thousand MW) of the country (Yüzer 2007). 16 power plants, which constitute approximately 90% of their installed power, were installed through Treasury guarantees provided by the Undersecretariat of Treasury. In addition to this, with the Law No. 3465 issued in 1988, the possibility of highway construction and maintenance services under the responsibility of the General Directorate of Highways were made possible by the private sector. With the Law No. 3996 issued in 1994, the BOT model has been defined as a special financing model developed for use in the implementation of projects requiring advanced technology and high financial resources (Özdogan and Birgönül 2000).

Today, the legislative framework dealing with various models and sectors in Turkey cannot be consolidated under a single law. All P3 models, except for the

Intergovernmental Agreements-Host Government Agreements (IGA-HGA) model, are written in separate legislative pieces, the most important ones can be listed as follows:

- *Law No. 3996 on the Procurement of Certain Investments and Services under the BOT Law;*
- *Law No. 6428 on the Construction, Renovation and Purchase of Services by the Ministry of Health by way of the Public-Private Cooperation Model and Amendments to Certain Laws and Decrees with the Force of Law (BLT Law); and*
- *Law No. 4046 on Privatisation Practices (Privatisation Law).*

Although the UK has been modeled for P3 applications in Turkey, it is a known fact that there are some differences between the two countries. For example, unlike the UK system, in Turkey; in addition to the Ministry of Treasury and Finance, Presidency of Strategy and Budget, the Ministries and, in some cases, the municipalities appear as other organizations in the process. Depending on the type of P3 and the region where it is implemented, the participation rates of institutions and organizations in the process also vary. Despite Turkey is one of the leading countries that implemented P3s, the targeted development is unfortunately not yet achieved. P3s have always remained in the shadow of privatization activities in Turkey. Moreover, Turkey's three severe crises after 2000; macroeconomic conditions adversely affected the investment environment and became one of the obstacles of the development of the P3 model. However, in progress of time, Turkey has developed many different P3 models and projects in different sectors such as: build–operate–transfer (BOT) model for infrastructure projects such as highways, airports, and electricity generation facilities; build–lease–transfer (BLT) model for healthcare projects (and education facilities, under a separate piece of legislation yet to be implemented); transfer of operating rights (TOR) for ports and airports; and build–operate (BO) model for thermal electrical energy generation facilities. The current number of P3 projects in Turkey are as follows.

If we compare the sectors in terms of the number of projects with the latest data (Figs. 6.2 and 6.3); the energy sector has the highest number of P3 projects however, when it comes to the sector-based contract values, the energy sector is ranked second after airports projects.[1] P3s for Motorways ranked second in terms of the number of projects, while the contract values are in the third place.

If we compare the sectors in terms of the number of projects and contract values with the latest data (Figs. 6.4 and 6.5); The BOT model has the highest number of P3 projects and highest contract values in Turkey. The TOR model is ranked second after BOT model projects both in terms of the number of projects and contract values (Figs. 6.6 and 6.7).

[1]The reason for this is that the new airport in Istanbul is the airport with the highest passenger capacity in the world and the investment cost is very high.

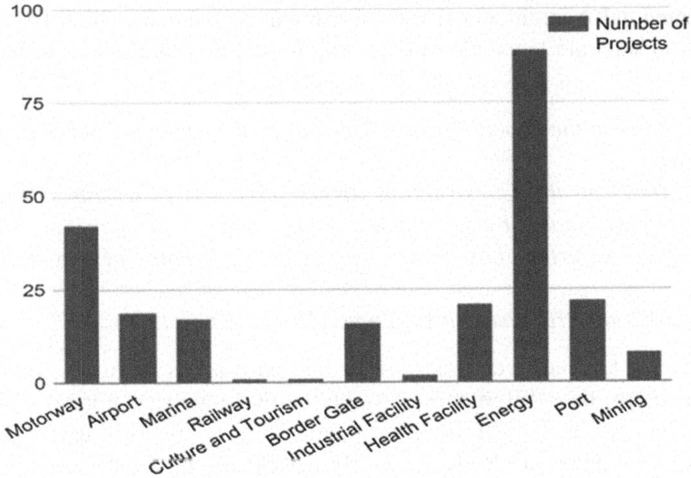

Fig. 6.2 Distribution of project numbers by sector. *Source* Presidency of The Republic of Turkey, Access date: 21.11.2018. https://koi.sbb.gov.tr/Main_EN.aspx

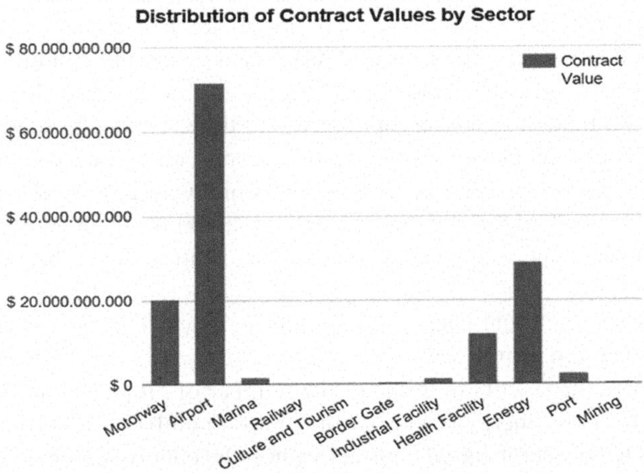

Fig. 6.3 Distribution of contract values by sector. *Source* Presidency of The Republic of Turkey, Access date: 21.11.2018. https://koi.sbb.gov.tr/Main_EN.aspx

When the data from 1986 to 2018 is analyzed, according to the project number and contract value, year 2012 has the highest number of projects and contract values in Turkey.

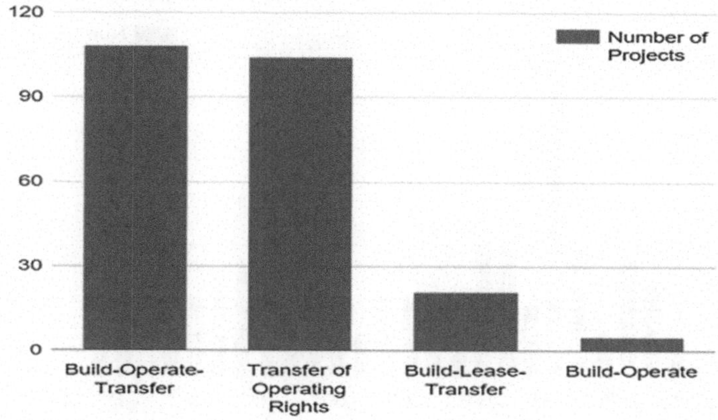

Fig. 6.4 Distribution of project numbers by model. *Source* Presidency of The Republic of Turkey, Access date: 21.11.2018. https://koi.sbb.gov.tr/Main_EN.aspx

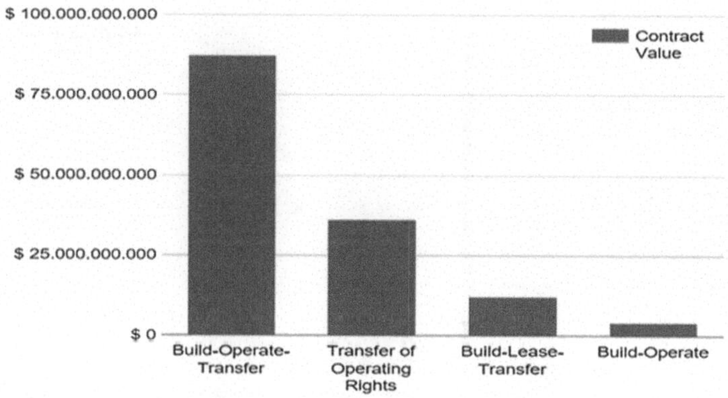

Fig. 6.5 Distribution of contract values by model. *Source* Presidency of The Republic of Turkey, Access date: 21.11.2018. https://koi.sbb.gov.tr/Main_EN.aspx

6.6 Result and Policy Suggestions

In the last four decades, countries under the influence of neo-liberalism have undergone serious changes in meeting the need for financing public goods and services. The P3 method has created an opportunity for short-term investments in various scales for countries that are exploring different alternative financing methods for large-scale investments that cannot be met with public budgets. P3 deals with the complex policies, projects, and public services. This is because P3 includes joint development and risk sharing among parties, which are areas where traditional procurement processes do not address. Risk sharing is an important feature that distinguishes P3 from traditional procurement projects.

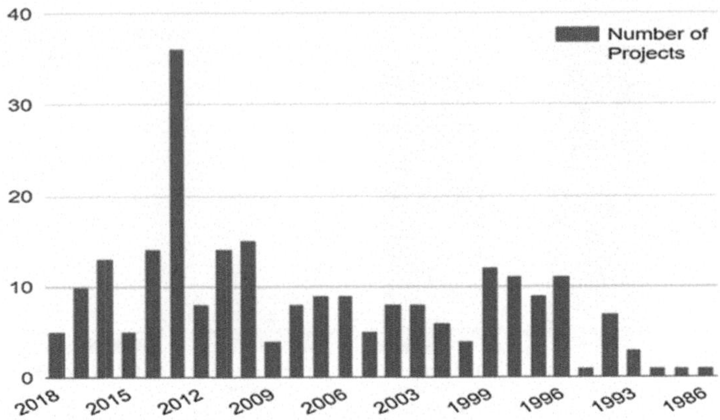

Fig. 6.6 Distribution of project numbers by year. *Source* Presidency of The Republic of Turkey, Access date: 21.11.2018. https://koi.sbb.gov.tr/Main_EN.aspx

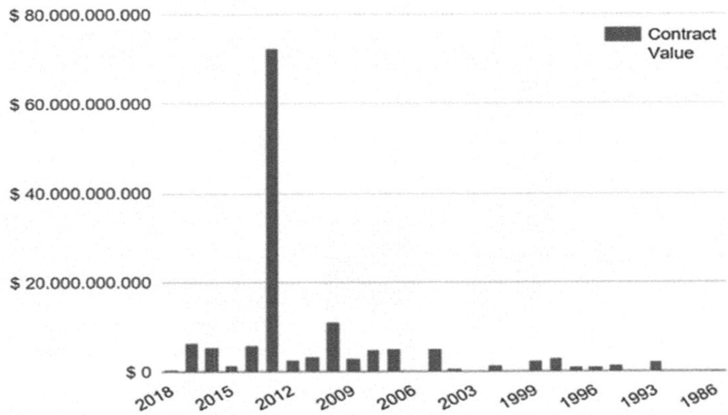

Fig. 6.7 Distribution of contract values by year. *Source* Presidency of The Republic of Turkey, Access date: 21.11.2018. https://koi.sbb.gov.tr/Main_EN.aspx

Worldwide, P3 finds applications in a wide range of sectors. The transportation sector, whose first projects consist of models based on the "shadow toll" principle, is often leading. In the applications, P3s in the transport sector include railway and city transportation. Other sectors that have a significant share in P3 are education, defense, water, health, and prisons (IFSL 2003). The main European countries that develop P3 models include Ireland, Netherlands, Spain, Italy, Germany, Portugal, and Greece.

In recent years, Turkey has an ambitious P3 portfolio (Emek 2015) and there are many large P3 projects that are among the highest valued P3 projects in the world (e.g., the third airport of Istanbul, the third bridge of Bosphorus, and the Eurasia highway tunnel project). In addition to the abovementioned P3 models, Turkey has also implemented certain P3 projects by partnership or agreement at government level, through use of intergovernmental agreements (IGAs) and host government agreements (HGA). The IGA-HGA models have been used for energy projects including nuclear power plants and oil pipelines. The most commonly used models in Turkish P3 projects (particularly greenfield projects) are the BOT and BLT models.

In Turkey, the P3 model has most actively been used in the transportation (especially highways and airports), healthcare and energy sectors. Municipality projects (water, geothermal, wastewater facilities and heating facilities) are normally projects falling under the jurisdiction of municipalities, and these projects may also be carried out under the BOT model together with the applicable municipality legislation. However, given the total number of municipalities in Turkey, we can say that volume-wise the BOT model is not generally used in municipal projects compared with transportation or healthcare projects that have been initiated at a national level.

As some suggestions;

- In the P3 contracts, the contractor should be able to offer the service in a quality manner.
- The contract price and/or fee must be determined in such a way that the contractor can obtain a return on investment and reasonable profit.
- In the stage of sharing the risks and determining the state supports to be given, the evaluations should be done in detail.
- As stated in 10th Development Plan, it should be ensured that the scattered PPP legislation is gathered under a framework law and the coordination of PPP policies and practices should be strengthened and an effective monitoring and evaluation system should be established to measure the risks and impacts of the projects on the budget.
- Since P3 projects are made for the establishment, operation or renewal of the infrastructure investments utilized in the provision of public services by the private sector, the authority of the public administration should be given an audit mandate, but the content, time, and frequency of this audit power need to be regulated.

References

Akbiyikli, & Eaton, (2018). "A Comparison of PFI, BOT, BOO, and BOOT Procurement Routes for Infrastructure Construction Projects", p. 506, Access date: 30.11.2018 https://www.irbnet.de/daten/iconda/CIB16757.pdf.

Akintoye, A., Beck, M., Hardcastle, C., Chinyio, E. & Asenova, D. (2001). "The financial structure of private finance initiative projects". Proceedings of the 17th ARCOM Annual Conference, Salford University, Manchester, p. 1361–9.

Akintoye, A., Beck, M., & Hardcastle, C. (2006). *Public-private partnerships: Managing risks and opportunities*. Oxford: Blackwell Science.

Barlow, J. (2007). "Redefining healthcare infrastructure: Integrating services and the built environment. Revaluing Construction 2007-Crossing Boundaries", Health and Care Infrastructure Research and Innovation Centre-HaCIRIC, Copenhagen.

Bettignies, J-E. & Ross, T. W. (2004). "The Economics of Public-Private Partnerships", Canadian Public Policy, Analyse De Politiques, Vol. XXX, No.2.

Brux, J. D., & Saussier, S. (2018). "Introduction: The Economics of Public–Private Partnerships". *The Economics of Public-Private Partnerships,* 1–13. https://doi.org/10.1007/978-3-319-68050-7_1
Bult-Spiering, M. & Dewulf, G. (2006). Strategic Issues in Public-Private Partnerships in International Perspective, Oxford: Blackwell Publishing.
Canadian Union of Public Employees (CUPE). (March 8, 2006). Britain having second thoughts about PFI hospitals., http://cupe.ca, 05.12.2018.
Confoy, B., Love, P.E.D., Wood, B.M, & Picken, D.H. (1999). "Build-Own-Operate – The Procurement of Correctional Services" in Profitable Partnering in Construction Procurement, CIB W92 & CIB TG 23 Joint Symposium, Edited by Stephen O. Ogunlana, E & FN Spon, London.
Corbett, P. & Smith, R. (2006). "An analysis of the success of the private finance initiative as the government's preferred procurement route", Proceedings of the Accelerating Excellence in the Built Environment Conference, Birmingham, UK, October 2–4.
Cuttaree V. (2008), "Successes and Failures of PPP Projects", The World Bank Europe & Central Asia Region, Warsaw – (June 17, 2008).
Dahl, R.A., & Lindblom, C.E. (1953). Politics, economics and welfare. New York: Harper & Brothers.
Emek, U., (2015). "Turkish experience with public private partnerships in infrastructure: Opportunities and challenges". Utilities Policy, http://dx.doi.org/10.1016/j.jup.2015.06.005
Girth, A. M. (2014). "What Drives the Partnership Decision? Examining Structural Factors Influencing Public–Private Partnerships for Municipal Wireless Broadband." International Public Management Journal 17 (3): 344–364. https://doi.org/10.1080/10967494.2014.935240
Gümüştekin, A. (1992). Build-Operate - Transfer Model for Investment Projects: A Comparison with Social Benefit-Cost Analysis. Thesis, METU, Ankara.
Hall, J. (1998). "Private Opportunity, Public Benefit", Fiscal Studies, 19(2).
Hart, O. & Moore, J. (1990). "Property Rights and the Nature of the Firm", The Journal of Political Economy, 98 (6), 1119–1158.
Hemming, R. (2006). Public-Private Partnerships, Government Guarantees, and Fiscal Risk. https://scholars.duke.edu/display/pub1027432, 05.12.2018.
Hodge, G. A., & C. Greve. (2007). "Public–Private Partnerships: An International Performance Review." Public Administration Review 67 (3): 545–558. https://doi.org/10.1111/j.1540-6210.2007.00736.x.
International Financial Services London (IFSL). (2003). Public Private Partnerships: UK Expertise for International Markets, International Financial Services, Trade Partners, UK, KPMG, Norton Rose, PriceWaterhouseCoopers, Partnerships UK.
Jefferies, M., Gameson, R. & Rowlinson, S. (2002), "Critical success factors of the BOOT procurement system: reflections from the stadium Australia case study", Engineering Construction and Architectural Management, Vol. 9 No. 4, p. 352.
Jingfeng, Y, Chan A. P. C., Xiong W., Skibniewski M. J., ASCE M.& Li O. (2015), "Perception of Residual Value Risk in Public Private Partnership Projects: Critical Review", Journal of Management in Engineering, Vol. 31 Issue 3.
Klijn, E.-H., & G. R. Teisman. (2003). "Institutional and Strategic Barriers to Public–Private Partnership: An Analysis of Dutch Cases." Public Money & Management 23 (3): 137–146. https://doi.org/10.1111/1467-9302.00361.
Koppenjan, J. (2005). "The Formation of Public–Private Partnerships: Lessons from Nine Transport Infrastructure Projects in the Netherlands." Public Administration 83 (1): 135–157. https://doi.org/10.1111/padm.2005.83.issue-1.
Langford, J. (2002). Contribution to discussion. In M. Edwards & J. Langford (Eds.), New players, partners and processes: A public sector without boundaries. Victoria, British Columbia: National Institute for Governance, University of Canberra, and Center for Public Sectors Studies, University of Victoria.
Linder, S.H. (1999). "Coming to terms with the public-private partnership, a grammar of multiple meanings". American Behavioral Scientist, 43, 35–51.

Li, B., Akintoye, A., Edwards, P.J. & Hardcastle, C. (2005). "Critical success factors for PPP/PFI projects in the UK construction industry", Construction Management and Economics, Vol. 23, pp. 459–71.

Marsilio, M., Cappellaro, G & Cuccurullo, C. (2011). "The Intellectual Structure of Research into PPPs", Public Management Review, Vol 13 (6), pp. 763–782.

Mazouz, B., & Belhocine, N. (2002). "Partenariats public-privé: Une équation à résoudre par la gestion de projets". Public-private partnerships: An equation to solve through project-based management.

Mazouz B., Facal J., Viola J.M. (2008). "Public-Private Partnership: Elements for a Project-Based Management Typology ", Project Management Journal, Vol. 39, No. 2, 98–110 © 2008 by the Project Management Institute Published online in Wiley InterScience (www.interscience.wiley.com) https://doi.org/10.1002/pmj.20040

Middleton, N. (2000). "Public Private Partnerships: A Natural Successor to Privatisations?". Available at: www.pwcglobal.com/uk/eng/about/svcs/pfp/ppp.html, Accessed May 2005.

Moulton, L. & Anheier, H. K. (2001). "Public-private partnerships in the United States: historical patterns and current trends". Civil Society Working Paper, 16, 14.

National Treasury PPP Unit (2007). Introducing Public-Private Partnerships in South Africa. http://www.ppp.gov.za/Documents/Final%20Intro%20to%20PPP%20in%20SA%2021%2009%2007, 05.12.2018.

Newman, J., & A. Perl. (2014). "Partnerships in Climate: Public–Private Partnerships and British Columbia's Capacity to Pursue Climate Policy Objective." Canadian Public Administration 57 (2): 217–233. https://doi.org/10.1111/capa.12051.

Osborne, S. P. (2000). Public–Private Partnerships: Theory and Practice in International Perspective. London: Routledge.

Özdogan, I.D. & Birgönül, M.T. (2000). "A decision support framework for project sponsors in the planning stage of build-operate-transfer (BOT) projects". Construction Management and Economics, 18, pp. 343–353.

Peters, B.G. (1998). With A Little Help from Our Friends: Public-Private Partnerships as Institutions and Instruments, in Pierre, J. (Eds), Partnerships in Urban Governance: European and American Experience, Macmillan Press, 11–33.

Pongsiri, N. (2002). Regulation and public-private partnerships. International Journal of Public Sector Management, 15(6), 487–495.

Presidency of The Republic of Turkey, Presidency of Strategy and Budget, Public-Private Partnership Projects in Turkey, Access date: 21.11.2018. https://koi.sbb.gov.tr/Main_EN.aspx

Renda, A. & Schrefler, L. (2006). Public Private Partnerships National Experiences in The European Union. European Parliament DG International Policies of The Union, Directorate A, Economic and Scientific Policy, Briefing note No. IP/A/IMCO/SC/2005-160.

Rondinelli, D., & Lacono, M. (1996). Policies and strategies for managing privatisation. Turin: BIT.

Rosenau, P. V. (1999). "The Strengths and Weaknesses of Public-Private Policy Partnerships", American Behavioral Scientist, 43 (1), 10–34.

Ross, T. W., & J. Yan. (2015). "Comparing Public–Private Partnerships and Traditional Public Procurement: Efficiency Vs. Flexibility." Journal of Comparative Policy Analysis 17 (5): 448–466. https://doi.org/10.1111/j.1467-9299.2010.01877.x.

Silvestre, H. C. & Araújo, J. F. (2012). "Public private partnership/private finance initiative in Portugal: theory, practice and results". Public Performance and Management Review, in press.

Spielman D, Hartwich F & von Grebmer K. (2007). "Sharing science, building bridges and enhancing impact: Public-private partnerships in the CGIAR". IFPRI Discussion paper 708. Washington, DC: International Food Policy Research Institute.

Stephenson, M.O. (1991). "Whither the public-private partnership: a critical Overview". Urban Affairs Quarterly, 1, 27, 109–136.

Teisman, G. R., & E. H. Klijn. (2002). "Partnership Arrangements: Governmental Rhetoric or Governance Scheme." Public Administration Review 62 (2): 189–198. https://doi.org/10.1111/00333352.00170.

Tekin, A.G. (2007). "Kamu-Özel Sektör İşbirlikleri- Kamu-Özel Ortaklıkları/Public Private Partnerships veya PPP Modelleri". İdarecinin Sesi Journal, 21, 122.
The Concessions Directive, (2018), "Information Note- The Concessions Directive", file:///C:/Users/Bernur/AppData/Local/Packages/Microsoft.MicrosoftEdge_8wekyb3d8bbwe /TempState/Downloads/Information-Note-on-the-Concessions-Directive-3%20(1).pdf
Thobani, M. (1999). "Private Infrastructure, Public Risk", The Newsletter of The International Project Finance Association, 1(1).
UN. (1993). Public-Private Partnerships in Enabling Shelter Strategies. United Nations Centre for Human Settlements (Habitat), Nairobi.
Wang, H., Xiong, W., Wu, G., & Zhu, D. (2017). "Public–private partnership in Public Administration discipline: a literature review". Public Management Review, 20(2), 293–316. https://doi.org/10.1080/14719037.2017.1313445.
Yüzer, M. (2007). "Enerji Sektöründe Yap İşlet Devret Modelinin Diğer Finans Modelleri ile Karşılaştırılması". Thesis, Gazi University Finance BD, Ankara.
Zhang, X.Q. (2005), "Critical success factors for public-private partnerships in infrastructure development", Journal of Construction Engineering and Management, Vol. 131 No. 1, pp. 3–14.

Professor Bernur Açıkgöz was born in 1979 in Ankara. After attending Ankara Finance School, she continued her undergraduate studies at Dokuz Eylül University, Department of Finance. She received her master's degree in Financial Law from Dokuz Eylül University. In 2006, she was awarded her Ph.D. degree from Dokuz Eylul University Department of Public Finance. Her Ph.D. thesis covered the topics of poverty and development. In 2006, she won the Harvard University Project fellowship and worked as a visiting professor at Harvard University for 3 months. In 2009, she won the Swiss Government Scholarship and completed her post-doctorate studies in economics at the University of Neuchatel in the French canton of Switzerland and taught for a two-year master's degree in both Neuchatel and Bern Universities. Then she started to work on experimental economics and game theory and worked as a visiting professor at Montpellier University in Montpellier, France for three consecutive months. She then went on to study at the Missouri University of Missouri, University of Indiana and the University of Arizona as a visiting professor and worked at the Economics Laboratories. She then worked as a visiting scholar at the University of East Anglia, University of Exeter, England, with a scholarship from Tubitak. Professor Dr. Bernur Açikgöz has books, articles and papers on foreign direct investments, economic growth, panel econometrics, experimental economics and game theory. She is currently the head of the Public Finance Department at Izmir Katip Çelebi University. In addition, Açıkgöz teaches at the Department of International Trade and Finance at Izmir University of Economics.

Chapter 7
Revisiting Conditional Cash Transfers: General Overview and Its Implementation in Turkey

Tekin Akdemir, Barış Alpaslan and Halis Kıral

7.1 Introduction

Since the second half of the 1990s, public expenditure reforms have been implemented in many countries around the world in attempting to solve the increasing resource scarcity, budget deficit, and public debt. The main objective of these reforms, however, is to allocate public expenditures according to strategic priorities and to ensure that public resources are efficiently allocated. Like developed countries that have become successful in public expenditure reforms, developing countries have also come up with alternative ways of using their national budget in a more efficient way. To that end, they have revised their strategy in a way that could help reduce poverty and improved their public expenditure reforms accordingly. In this respect, conditional cash transfers have been instrumental in our understanding of the issue of public expenditure reforms. This study first provides a general overview of conditional cash transfers and then reviews in detail the available information on conditional cash transfers for education and conditional health benefits in Turkey.

Conditional cash transfer programs were first launched in 1995 in Brazil on the regional basis and then were broadly implemented in 1997 in Mexico (Silva 2017, p. 3; Uchiyama 2019, p. 1), and since then it has been practiced mainly in many low- and middle-income countries (Bastagli et al. 2016, p. 5). Today, more than 80 countries have now implemented such programs as part of their social protection policies (Parker and Tom Vogl 2018, p. 1).

Conditional cash transfers (CCT thereinafter) are, however, different from conventional poverty reduction and social protection programs in two main respects

T. Akdemir (✉)
Ankara Yıldırım Beyazıt University, Ankara, Turkey
e-mail: takdemir@ybu.edu.tr

B. Alpaslan · H. Kıral
Social Sciences University of Ankara, Ankara, Turkey

H. Kıral and T. Akdemir (eds.), *Public Financial Management Reforms in Turkey: Progress and Challenges, Volume 1*, Accounting, Finance, Sustainability, Governance & Fraud: Theory and Application, https://doi.org/10.1007/978-981-15-1914-7_7

(Lettenhove 2012, p. 6): Firstly, CCT are in general given as cash transfers rather than in-kind aid with the exception of some countries where they are provided in the form of in-kind transfers, such as food and nutritional supplements. Secondly, poor families are targeted, yet transfers are provided on the basis that the beneficiary families meet the requirements set out. CCT are also believed to facilitate social integration of people who feel that they are socially excluded, especially following an economic downturn because having no access to basic services in health and education can lead people at risk of poverty to have a feeling of social exclusion. Lastly, CCT serve as an external financial source for beneficiary families in easing pressure on the household budget at bad times.

In essence, CCT have two fundamental objectives: they are first used as a tool to generate additional income for households who live in extreme poverty in an attempt to reduce poverty and inequality. In fact, contrary to conventional social protection programs which are concerned about poverty reduction only in the short term, CCT are basically involved in reducing long-term poverty (Rawlings and Rubio 2005, p. 33). In addition, CCT are aimed at improving the human capital formation of the future generation through its potential benefits on education and health outcomes as it is envisaged that it will break the poverty cycle (Silva 2017, p. 3). In other words, beneficiary families who receive cash transfers can send their children to school and take them to hospital for health and nutrition checkups on a regular basis through these transfers (Pantelic 2011, p. 797). In addition to its main objectives, CCT could also be a contributing factor to the empowerment of women (Yildirim et al. 2014, p. 63). More precisely, these transfers could put women in a position where they can have a more say on the allocation of family resources towards children because mothers are the main recipient of these transfers, as discussed further later. Indeed, this is especially the case in countries, such as Turkey where gender-based social protection programs are implemented.

Given that CCT are increasingly recognized as a worldwide social protection program and budget appropriations allocated to these transfers have, in recent years, increased, the effective management of these transfers is subject to considerable debate. Indeed, the question of whether countries have successfully implemented conditional cash transfer programs is closely related to how effectively these programs are managed. As a result, the design and implementation aspects of CCT appear to be of vital importance and need to be discussed. In particular, the following issues will be addressed in this paper: amount of cash benefits, conditionality, target beneficiaries, frequency of payments, and monitoring.

The amount of cash benefits can vary from country to country depending on the household size as well as age and gender composition of beneficiaries. For instance, the amount of transfer payments made would be different based on the number of children in the family.

Transfer payments are only made to the beneficiaries provided they meet certain requirements. In other words, these payments are generally conditional on education indicators, such as school attendance or enrolment rate or other indicators like grade averages or exam scores (Medgyesi and Temesváry 2013, p. 5) or on regular clinic visits or attending nutrition and health seminars (Fiszbein et al. 2009, p. 45).

Cash transfers are usually targeted at families in need or those living in extreme poverty. However, there are some exceptional cases where target beneficiaries are elderly or disabled people (Cecchini and Madariaga 2011, p. 14). In relation to families, these transfers are commonly made available to mothers who are believed to use them for the benefit of their family members (Handa and Davis 2006, p. 513). They can also be given to its direct users, family representatives or family members responsible for making decisions or earning money (Cecchini and Madariaga 2011, p. 15).

In general, cash transfers are paid on a monthly basis. This is evident in the case of Turkey. There are, however, countries like Colombia (Familias en Acción), Mexico (Prospera), and Philippines (4Ps) where transfer payments are made every two months whereas in countries, for example, the Republic of El Salvador (Comunidades Solidarias) and the Republic of Honduras (Bono Vida Mejor) they are provided three times a year or at less frequent intervals (Catubig et al. 2015, p. 243; Medellín and Tejerina 2017, p. 57).

The final element concerning the implementation of conditional cash transfer programs is the monitoring process which ensures that beneficiaries meet the specified criteria and therefore the programs are successfully implemented (Pacassi and Maurer 2015, p. 10). The overall evaluation of these programs is undertaken by a unit responsible for operational monitoring or by an external agency (Parodi and Vásquez 2017, p. 85).

The above section has provided a brief overview of conditional cash transfer programs. Since the purpose of this study is to review in detail the available information on conditional cash transfers for education and conditional health benefits in Turkey, we will, therefore, move on to discuss how this program is in particular implemented in Turkey.

7.2 Conditional Cash Transfer Program in Turkey

Conditional cash transfer program was part of the Social Risk Mitigation Project funded by the World Bank and was put into practice on November 28, 2001 (Dama and Sundaram 2018, p. 47). The program was initially implemented in 6 pilot provinces in 2003 and has been gradually expanded across the country since 2004. However, after the Social Risk Mitigation Project came to an end in 2007, the program then continued to be supported by the Social Assistance and Solidarity Fund (Aile ve Sosyal Politikalar Bakanligi[1] and UNICEF 2014, p. 13).

The program was primarily initiated to alleviate the effects of the Turkish 2000–2001 banking crisis on the poor. In addition, it was aimed at increasing the enrolment rate and duration of schooling for children living in a low-income family as well as ensuring that women during and after pregnancy, and children after birth benefit from basic healthcare and nutrition services.

[1]The Ministry of Family and Social Policies in English.

The discussion is now divided into two parts in the following sections: conditional cash transfers for education and conditional health benefits, respectively.

7.2.1 Conditional Cash Transfers for Education

Conditional cash transfers for education (CCTE thereinafter) have been designed for families at risk of poverty to send their children to school. The stringent criteria for accessing CCTE is that school-aged children are registered at school, that primary and secondary education aged children (from 6-year-old to age 18) meet attendance of a minimum 80% of the classes during each month of the school period, and that they do not repeat the same class more than once, these transfers are given to the poorest 6% of the population who are not covered by any social security and cannot send their children to school due to financial difficulties (Uzun 2012, p. 44). Transfer payments are, on the other hand, stopped temporarily or permanently if the expected requirements that have been mentioned previously are not met. In order to determine continued eligibility, school attendance records are therefore held by the Ministry of National Education for children who receive cash transfers.

In this regard, Social Assistance and Solidarity Foundations serve as the representative body of the Ministry of Family, Labor and Social Services (formerly named as the Ministry of Family and Social Policies) to help families in need have access to cash transfers. The main principle is that the application for cash transfers is made by the mother but in her absence for any reason it can also be made by the father or by any family member aged over 18, and each applicant is required to provide information in the application form about their socioeconomic status, such as the income, expense, property, housing and employment status, etc. (Esenyel 2009, p. 55). However, the most important eligibility criteria for CCTE is that families have no social security (Dama and Sundaram 2018, p. 51).

Transfer payments are made primarily to mothers through a post office and their amount is determined according to gender and school levels. Girls are paid more than boys in order to ensure that girls stay at school for a longer period and that gender equality in education is achieved in the long run. According to the most recent data by the Ministry of Family, Labor, and Social Services, at the time of writing this paper, 35 Turkish Lira and 40 Turkish Lira are monthly paid for boys and girls, respectively who continue their primary education, whereas they are 50 Turkish Lira and 60 Turkish Lira for boys and girls at the secondary education, respectively.[2]

The amount of money allocated to CCTE and the number of beneficiaries between the years 2003–2018 are shown in Table 7.1, whereas the number of beneficiaries by gender and school levels is reported in Table 7.2.

As can be seen from Table 7.1, CCTE have become a social assistance program by which more students have benefited over the years. What is important for us to

[2]2018 Annual report (in Turkish). See page on 143: http://www.sp.gov.tr/upload/xSPRapor/files/RqI2i+ACSHB_2018_FAALIYET_RAPORU.pdf (Accessed on June 26, 2019).

Table 7.1 The amount of money allocated to CCTE and the number of beneficiaries by years

Years	The amount of money allocated to CCTE (Million Turkish Lira)	The number of beneficiaries
2003	1.59	59,206
2004	66.76	697,307
2005	180.13	1,266,331
2006	240.27	1,563,253
2007	224.45	1,757,187
2008	290.64	1,951,420
2009	345.05	2,066,869
2010	267.11	2,172,750
2011	397.49	1,863,099
2012	488.37	1,916,276
2013	486.09	2,018,879
2014	570.75	2,068,869
2015	670.06	2,449,392
2016	605.77	2,132,741
2017	761.46	2,340,374
2018	643.10	2,517,680

Source Data were gathered from multiple sources
Saglam (2016, p. 114, Table 3.7), the Ministry of Family and Social Policies (2016, p. 54, Tables 21 and 22) (2016 Annual report (in Turkish): https://www.ailevecalisma.gov.tr/Uploads/sgb/uploads/pages/arge-raporlar/2016-yili-faaliyet-raporu.pdf (Accessed on June 26, 2019)), and the Ministry of Family, Labor, and Social Services (2018, p. 144, Table 63) (2018 Annual report (in Turkish): http://www.sp.gov.tr/upload/xSPRapor/files/RqI2i+ACSHB_2018_FAALIYET_RAPORU.pdf (Accessed on June 26, 2019))

recognize here, however, is that the increase in the total amount of money allocated to CCTE is mainly due to the increase in the number of beneficiaries. To put it another way, although from 2003 to 2018 the number of beneficiaries has significantly increased, the increase in the amount of money allocated to CCTE has generally remained limited during the same period.

It can be seen from the data in Table 7.2 that there is no particular trend in the number of beneficiaries at all education levels over the period 2013–2018. In fact, the number of girls who benefit from CCTE is lower than that of boys at both primary and secondary school levels, but quite the opposite is the case at the high school level. On the other hand, according to the latest national education statistics published by the Ministry of National Education (p. 1, Table 1.1.a), in the 2017–2018 school year, schooling rate at the primary school for girls was 91.68% as opposed to 91.42% for boys. Similarly, it was 94.69% for girls and 94.26% for boys at the secondary school, while these rates were relatively lower at the high school: 83.39% for girls and

Table 7.2 The number of beneficiaries by gender and school level between 2013 and 2018

Years	Primary school		Secondary school		High school	
	Girls	Boys	Girls	Boys	Girls	Boys
2013	489,114	504,983	502,111	520,964	185,505	197,805
2014	454,088	469,634	479,466	496,841	221,282	228,570
2015	450,358	465,210	489,260	504,546	253,065	255,950
2016	453,310	469,547	449,982	463,340	246,407	244,783
2017	472,967	489,647	570,683	584,086	267,685	266,774
2018	535,879	556,440	544,035	553,035	266,460	260,362

Source Data were obtained using multiple annual reports published by the Ministry of Family and Social Policies (now named as the Ministry of Family, Labor and Social Services) for 2013 (p. 119, Table 34) (2013 Annual report (in Turkish): https://www.ailevecalisma.gov.tr/Uploads/sgb/uploads/pages/arge-raporlar/2013-yili-faaliyet-raporu.pdf (Accessed on June 26, 2019)), 2014 (p. 84, Table 18) (2014 Annual report (in Turkish): https://www.ailevecalisma.gov.tr/Uploads/sgb/uploads/pages/arge-raporlar/2014-yili-faaliyet-raporu.pdf (Accessed on June 26, 2019)), 2015 (pp. 125–126) (2015 Annual report (in Turkish): https://www.ailevecalisma.gov.tr/Uploads/sgb/uploads/pages/arge-raporlar/2015-yili-idare-faaliyet-raporu.pdf (Accessed on June 26, 2019)), 2016 (p. 54, Table 21) (2016 Annual report (in Turkish): https://www.ailevecalisma.gov.tr/Uploads/sgb/uploads/pages/arge-raporlar/2016-yili-faaliyet-raporu.pdf (Accessed on June 26, 2019)), and 2018 (p. 144, Table 62) (2018 Annual report (in Turkish): http://www.sp.gov.tr/upload/xSPRapor/files/RqI2i+ACSHB_2018_FAALIYET_RAPORU.pdf (Accessed on June 26, 2019)). There is no annual report for 2017 published by the Ministry so we rely on the study of Dama and Sundaram (2018, pp. 52–53, Graph 4 and Table 3) for the figures in 2017
Note that data for pre-2013 years are not available

83.77% for boys, respectively.[3] According to the same statistics, in the 2003–2004 school year when CCTE were initiated, schooling rates at primary and secondary education were a lot lower than what they were in the 2017–2018 school year. These data suggest that Turkey has made significant progress in access to education at all levels, and this observed improvement in education could be attributed to the implementation of CCTE.

7.2.2 *Conditional Health Benefits*

Conditional health benefits are also given to the poorest 6% of the population as in the case for CCTE but it is conditional in the sense that beneficiary families are expected to take their children aged 0–6 years to hospitals or health clinics for regular checkups and receiving immunizations. Since 2005, these benefits have been, however, extended to include expectant mothers (Yildirim et al. 2014, p. 66). In summary, conditional health benefits consist of the following components: child

[3]2017–2018 National Education Statistics https://sgb.meb.gov.tr/meb_iys_dosyalar/2018_09/06123056_meb_istatistikleri_orgun_egitim_2017_2018.pdf (Accessed on June 26, 2019).

health benefits, and maternity benefits during pregnancy, childbirth, and post-delivery period.

As long as there is no individual with social security in the household and children are regularly taken to health centers for checkups, regardless of their gender for children aged 0–6 years (unlike CCTE which cover children aged 6–18 years), a health benefit of 35 Turkish Lira per child is monthly given primarily to the child's mother through a post office but under very specific circumstances, such as maternal death, health benefit can also be paid to the father or the majors, who live in the same household with the child and bear the childcare. The application is also subject to the approval of Social Assistance and Solidarity Foundation's Board of Trustees in the sense that members of the Board of Trustees need to be convinced that the household applying for the child health benefit is really in need.[4]

There are, however, a number of reasons why child health benefits are stopped temporarily or permanently. Examples are, if the child is not taken to hospitals for checkups on the specified dates by the Ministry of Health or if the child is older than 72 months or 6-year-old. This is also the case when the residence address of the child is subject to change without giving notice to the Social Assistance and Solidarity Foundation. There are also other reasons for such a situation, such as if the Board of Trustees believes that the family is no longer in need or if the child or beneficiary parent dies.[5]

Conditional maternity benefits are given to pregnant women during their pregnancy, childbirth, and post-delivery (postpartum) period as long as they visit health clinics for regular checkups and follow-up care after delivery. At the time of writing this paper, according to official figures published by the Ministry of Family, Labor, and Social Services, 35 Turkish Lira is paid during pregnancy conditional on regular visits to health clinics for checkups but it is limited to a maximum period of 9 months. In the same vein, a one-time payment of 75 Turkish Lira is made as long as the birth is given in hospital, and 35 Turkish Lira is paid two times during the postpartum period.[6]

In order for expectant mothers to receive benefits on a regular basis, they are expected to submit medical reports to the Social Assistance and Solidarity Foundation during the first three months of their pregnancy. They should also give birth in hospital and visit health clinics for regular checkups during pregnancy and a two-month postpartum period (Esenyel 2009, p. 63). Overall, process monitoring is therefore operated by the Ministry of Health through the family medicine information system in order to ensure that beneficiaries meet the expected requirements.

The total amount of money allocated to conditional health benefits (child health benefits and maternity benefits during pregnancy, childbirth, and post-delivery

[4]Further information (in Turkish) is available on its website https://ailevecalisma.gov.tr/sss/sosyal-yardimlar-genel-mudurlugu/sartli-egitim-saglik-yardimi/ (Accessed on June 26, 2019).

[5]Further information (in Turkish) is available on its website https://ailevecalisma.gov.tr/sss/sosyal-yardimlar-genel-mudurlugu/sartli-egitim-saglik-yardimi/ (Accessed on June 26, 2019).

[6]Further information (in Turkish) is available on its website https://ailevecalisma.gov.tr/sss/sosyal-yardimlar-genel-mudurlugu/sartli-egitim-saglik-yardimi/ (Accessed on June 26, 2019).

Table 7.3 The total amount of money allocated to conditional health benefits and the number of beneficiaries by years

Years	The total amount of money allocated to conditional health benefits (Million Turkish Lira)	The number of beneficiaries
2003	0.8	24,644
2004	16.67	329,833
2005	62.08	731,784
2006	104.31	899,454
2007	96.61	1,029,703
2008	118.85	1,033,840
2009	138.78	836,506
2010	73.73	829,464
2011	143.30	757,757
2012	202	787,987
2013	236.23	968,360
2014	287.43	1,159,824
2015	363.08	1,262,564
2016	422	1,418,486
2017	395.25	1,348,240
2018	398.46	1,325,972

Source Data were obtained using 2016 (p. 56, Tables 27 and 28) (2016 Annual report (in Turkish): https://www.ailevecalisma.gov.tr/Uploads/sgb/uploads/pages/arge-raporlar/2016-yili-faaliyet-raporu.pdf (Accessed on June 27, 2019)) and 2018 (p. 146, Tables 68 and 69) (2018 Annual report (in Turkish): http://www.sp.gov.tr/upload/xSPRapor/files/RqI2i+ACSHB_2018_FAALIYET_RAPORU.pdf (Accessed on June 27, 2019)) annual reports published by the Ministry of Family and Social Policies (now named as the Ministry of Family, Labor, and Social Services, as noted earlier) as well as the figures compiled by Saglam (2016, p. 114) in her dissertation

period) and the number of beneficiaries between the years 2003–2018 are shown in Table 7.3.

Turkey has made considerable progress in health outcomes and reduced its maternal mortality over the last decade. Indeed, from 2005 to 2015, maternal mortality rates per 100,000 live births declined by nearly one-third (from 57 deaths to 16 deaths).[7] Likewise, according to the 2017 health statistics report by the Ministry of Health (p. 80, Table 5.2), hospital delivery rates were 75% in 2002 as compared to 98% in 2017.[8] The latest health data from UNICEF also suggest that while antenatal care coverage (at least one visit during pregnancy) was 80.9% in 2003 when conditional

[7]UNICEF data: https://data.unicef.org/topic/maternal-health/maternal-mortality/ (Accessed on June 30, 2019).

[8]T.C. Saglik Bakanligi, Saglik İstatistikleri Yilligi 2017 (in Turkish).

health benefit scheme was initiated, it was observed to be 97% in 2013.[9] In conclusion, considering the improvement in both the total amount of money allocated to conditional health benefits and its beneficiary numbers over the period 2003–2018, it could be argued that these results may partly be explained by the positive effects of conditional health benefits.

7.3 Concluding Remarks

In this paper, we have provided a brief review of conditional cash transfer programs in general and of its implementation in Turkey. In particular, as stated earlier, the purpose of this study was to review in detail the available information on conditional cash transfers for education and conditional health benefits in Turkey. CCT are generally considered to be an additional income source for beneficiary families and therefore allow their children to have access to education and health services, thereby breaking the intergenerational transmission of poverty. Despite its exploratory nature, we, however, believe that this study raises intriguing issues regarding the nature and extent of CCT in Turkey in a number of important ways.

Firstly, even though CCTE were aimed at increasing the enrolment rate and duration of schooling for children at risk of poverty, children's school attendance is not closely monitored so we believe that this may well affect the overall success of the program in the long term. Secondly, although the descriptive statistics suggest that there has been a gradual increase in the number of beneficiaries for both conditional cash transfers for education and conditional health benefits over serves (2003–2018), the total amount of resources allocated to conditional cash transfers in other social protection programs is still limited.

Last but not least, further investigation into the impact analysis on conditional cash transfers is required to evaluate whether or not the conditional cash transfer program is generally implemented in an efficient manner.

References

Aile ve Sosyal Politikalar Bakanligi & UNICEF. (2014). *Turkiye'de Sartli Nakit Transferi Programinin Iyilestirilmesine Yonelik Politika Belgesi.* Ankara (in Turkish).

Bastagli, F., Hagen-Zanker, J., Harman, L., Barca, V., Sturge, G., Schmidt, T., & Pellerano, L. (2016). *Cash Transfers: What Does the Evidence Say? A Rigorous Review of Programme Impact and of the Role of Design and Implementation Features.* London: Overseas Development Institute.

Catubig, M. C., Villano, R., & Dollery, B. (2015). Payment Schemes in Conditional Cash Transfer Programs: The Case of 4Ps in the Davao Region, Philippines. *Administrative Sciences, 5(4),* 240–259.

[9]UNICEF data: https://data.unicef.org/topic/maternal-health/antenatal-care/ (Accessed on June 30, 2019).

Cecchini, S., & Madariaga, A. (2011). *Conditional Cash Transfer Programmes: The Recent Experience in Latin America and the Caribbean.* Santiago, Chile: United Nations.

Dama, N., & Sundaram, D. T. (2018). *Yoksulluk Dongusunden Cikis: Sartli Egitim Yardimi.* Istanbul: SETA (in Turkish).

Esenyel, C. (2009, Haziran). *Turkiye'de ve Dunya'da Sartli Nakit Transferi Uygulamalari.* Ankara: T.C Basbakanlik Sosyal Yardimlasma ve Dayanisma Genel Mudurlugu (in Turkish).

Fiszbein, A., Schady, N., Ferreira, F. H., Grosh, M., Keleher, N., Olinto, P., & Skoufias, E. (2009). *Conditional Cash Transfers: Reducing Present and Future Poverty.* Washington DC: World Bank.

Handa, S., & Davis, B. (2006). The Experience of Conditional Cash Transfers in Latin America and the Caribbean. *Development Policy Review, 24(5)*, 513–536.

Lettenhove, M. K. (2012). Conditional Cash Transfers in Latin America. *Reflets et perspectives de la vie économique, 51(2)*, 5–18.

Medellín, N., & Tejerina, L. (2017). Benefit Structure, the Payment Process, and Financial Inclusion. In P. Ibarrarán, N. Medellín, F. Regalia, & M. Stampini, *How Conditional Cash Transfers Work: Good Practices after 20 Years of Implementation* (pp. 52–74). Inter-American Development Bank.

Medgyesi, M., & Temesváry, Z. (2013, August). *Conditional Cash Transfers in High-Income OECD Countries and Their Effects on Human Capital Accumulation.* AIAS GINI Discussion Paper No.84.

Pacassi, S. E., & Maurer, S. (2015, May 14). Practical Project in Development Cooperation. *Conditional Cash Transfers (CCT): Potential for Development Cooperation? The Case of Bolivia.* University of St. Gallen.

Pantelić, A. (2011). A Comparative Analysis of Microfinance and Conditional Cash Transfers in Latin America. *Development in Practice, 21(6)*, 790–805.

Parker, S. W., & Tom Vogl. (2018, February). *Do Conditional Cash Transfers Improve Economic Outcomes in the Next Generation? Evidence from Mexico.* Cambridge, MA: NBER Working Paper No.24303.

Parodi, S., & Vásquez, M. (2017). Foundations of the Operational Cycle. In P. Ibarrarán, N. Medellín, F. Regalia, & M. Stampini, *How Conditional Cash Transfers Work: Good Practices after 20 Years of Implementation* (pp. 77–97). Inter-American Development Bank.

Rawlings, L. B., & Rubio, G. M. (2005). Evaluating the Impact of Conditional Cash Transfer Programs. *The World Bank Research Observer, 20(1)*, 29–55.

Saglam, A. (2016, Temmuz). *Yoksullukla Mucadelede Sosyal Politika Araci Olarak Sartli Nakit Transferi (SNT) ve Brezilya Ornegi.* Ankara: T.C. Maliye Bakanligi Butce ve Mali Kontrol Genel Mudurlugu (in Turkish).

Silva, M. M. (2017). *Poverty Reduction, Education, and the Global Diffusion of Conditional Cash Transfers.* Switzerland: Palgrave Macmillan.

Uchiyama, N. (2019). Do Conditional Cash Transfers Reduce Household Vulnerability? Evidence from PROGRESA-Oportunidades in the 2000s. *Economia*, 1–19 (in press).

Uzun, C. B. (2012). Turkiye'deki Sartli Nakit Transferi Yardimlarinin Bolgesel Dagilimi. *Sosyal Politika Calismalari, 7(28)*, 37–59.

Yildirim, J., Ozdemir, S., & Sezgin, F. (2014). A Qualitative Evaluation of a Conditional Cash Transfer Program in Turkey: The Beneficiaries' and Key Informants' Perspectives. *Journal of Social Service Research, 40(1)*, 62–79.

Tekin Akdemir is Professor of Public Finance at the Ankara Yıldırım Beyazıt University, Faculty of Political Science. Before this post he was an Associate Professor at the Erciyes University. Professor Akdemir is also a member of the Turkish Tax Council. He received his Ph.D. in Public Finance Department at the Institute of Social Sciences, Dokuz Eylul University in 2006. His research focuses on budgeting and financial management, Government cash and debt management, and local government finance. Professor Akdemir has authored and contributed to numerous books, book chapters, articles, and reports on intergovernmental finance, public financial management, and public debt and cash management. In addition to his academic research and expertise in the management and provision of technical assistance, Prof. Akdemir has considerable experience in the development and delivery of academic courses and professional training programs in the areas of public sector finance, (fiscal) decentralization and government budgeting and financial management issues.

Barış Alpaslan is an Associate Professor of Economics in Social Sciences University of Ankara Department of Economics. Dr. Alpaslan has also been serving as an Associate Dean at the Faculty of Political Science. Prior to this post, Dr. Alpaslan was a faculty member at Ankara Yildirim Beyazit University Department of Public Finance. Dr. Alpaslan completed his M.Sc. (Econ) on which he received an award of distinction at the University of Manchester, and holds a Ph.D. (Econ) from the same university. Dr. Alpaslan is also a research associate at the Global Development Institute (GDI), University of Manchester, Centre for Applied Macroeconomic Analysis (CAMA), Australian National University, and the Sheffield Institute for International Development (SIID), University of Sheffield, as well as Economic Research Forum (ERF) in Cairo, Egypt. In addition, Dr. Alpaslan is serving on an expert committee for the 2030 agenda for Sustainable Development Goals at the Turkish National Commission for UNESCO and undertakes consultancy work at the World Bank. His research interests focus broadly on the macroeconomics of growth, inequality and development.

Halis Kıral is an Assistant Professor at the Social Sciences University of Ankara in Turkey. He is also Head of Audit and Risk Management Department and Director of Center for Audit and Risk Management (ASBÜDRM) at the ASBU. He was a visiting scholar at the Duke Center for International Development (DCID) for the 2017–2018 academic year. He has also worked in the Ministry of Finance of Turkey as a state budget expert, public finance expert, head of the department of Central Harmonization for Internal Audit, and head of the Budget Policy Department. As the Head of Central Harmonization Unit for Internal Audit, he led several projects including developing Public Internal Audit Software (İçDen©) for public internal auditors and publishing Public Internal Audit Manual, Information Technology Audit Manual, Quality Assurance and Improvement Manual and Performance Audit Manual for Public Internal Auditors. He wrote a number of articles, books and book chapters on topics such as public finance, public financial management and control, specifically internal audit and risk management, and applied economics.

Part III
Budget

Chapter 8
Program Budgeting in Turkey

Ebru Yenice

8.1 Introduction

Program budgeting delivers information to decision-makers to aid in the identification of spending priorities among a diverse range of programs. Program budgeting comprises three main phases: program classification, program performance identification, and program evaluation. Program classification refers to the modification of the budget coding system so as to include a program budget classification. Program classification reforms should not only involve changes in the budget classification system, but should also serve as the basis for such budget decision-making processes as the creation of a medium-term expenditure framework, the determination of the spending authority in budget management, and the implementation of such budgetary procedures as appropriation transfers. The cornerstones of the program budget classification reforms in Turkey are discussed and evaluated, and a comparison is made with international practices.

Secondly, program aims, objectives, and indicators should be established in line with government-wide policy priorities. Public institutions in Turkey have accumulated experience in the implementation of performance-based budgeting since 2003, which in Turkey includes the preparation of strategic plans, performance plans, and annual accountability reports. Accordingly, the present study determines the problems encountered in performance management in Turkey, and discusses the issues to be taken into account when determining performance information in a program budget system.

Finally, the third component of program budgeting involves the evaluation of programs. While program monitoring refers to the regular and systematic collection and recording of performance data, program evaluation involves the analysis of programs in terms of their impact on society by comparing the situations before and

E. Yenice (✉)
Ministry of Treasury and Finance, Ankara, Turkey
e-mail: ebruyenice@hotmail.com

H. Kıral and T. Akdemir (eds.), *Public Financial Management Reforms in Turkey: Progress and Challenges, Volume 1*, Accounting, Finance, Sustainability, Governance & Fraud: Theory and Application, https://doi.org/10.1007/978-981-15-1914-7_8

after implementation. With this in mind, this article reports on an examination of program monitoring and evaluation processes, along with spending review issues.

The Presidency of Strategy and Budget (PSB) and line ministries prepare proposals for program classifications, and program aims, targets and performance indicators based on legislation related to organizational structures, as well as the national development plan, strategic plan and performance plan. A proposal is to be prepared for the Central Government Budget Law 2021 that takes into account the principles of program budgeting in Turkey. Performance plans of public institutions in year 2020 will be prepared in accordance with the principles in the program budget guide prepared by PSB (PSB 2019, 2020).

8.2 History of the Budgeting and Public Financial Management System in Turkey

The Turkish public financial management system was built mainly around General Accounting Law No. 1050, which was enacted in 1927 (Law No. 1050, 1927), and maintained its influence over budget and accounting management up until 2003. Although amendments were made, Law No. 1050 maintained its overall integrity and continued to play a key role in the management of public finances. Over time, however, the number, scope, and organizational structures of public administration institutions changed. As was the case in the widespread extrabudgetary fund implementations, many expenditures were taken out of the scope of the law, leading to deviations from the general budget principles and disciplines.

Law No. 1050 focused on the control and inspection of the expenditures of public institutions, and limited the initiatives and responsibilities of public institutions in budget expenditure decisions. In other words, all expenditures and procurement processes above a certain limit were subject to pre-expenditure control by the Ministry of Finance and the Court of Accounts. Most financial transactions were carried out by branches of the Ministry of Finance that, despite being located within the line ministries, were manned by personnel of the Ministry of Finance.

One of the most groundbreaking budget reforms in Turkish budgeting history took place in 1971 during the efforts to adopt the Program Budgeting approach. After the introduction of program budgeting that year, the approach developed in a very comprehensive manner in line with international practices. The transition to program budgeting was planned in three stages: the first stage involved the determination of the programs of each organization or administrative unit; the second stage involved the creation of a costing, accounting, and administrative structure that was appropriate to the program classification structure; and the final stage involved a program evaluation of each individual program. Although first stage of the reform was completed, the other reform stages could not be applied, and no program evaluations were made in the years following the adoption of the program budget classification. Since no regular review was made of whether or not the programs were being carried out effectively, the program budging system could not be improved. Accordingly, budget resources were allocated to the same programs repetitiously, and this has led in time to distortions in applications, with programs becoming less based on results, and in time equivalent almost to intuitional units in their classification (Yenice 2006, p. 126).

An examination of international practices in this regard reveals that the rationale behind public financial management has changed in many countries, and that public institutions are now able to manage their own spending initiatives, but with increased accountability. Budgets have in time become a management tool, and a budgeting concept that associates institutional outputs and results with budgets has gained prominence. In recognition of this, Law No. 5018 was entered into force with the aim of introducing a new public financial management approach to Turkey and strengthening the principles of budget discipline.

The public financial management reforms started in 2003 with the enactment of Law No. 5018—the Public Financial Management and Control (PFMC) Law—in Turkey, which dramatically altered the basic understanding of public administration in Turkey in line with the principles of the "New Public Financial Management Reforms". Accordingly, a strategic planning and performance budgeting approach was introduced in which, it is stated, strategic and performance plans should be taken as the basis in the preparation of budgets within the public sector.

The Ministry Finance carried out ex-ante control of all budget expenditures above certain limits made by the line ministries prior to 2003. With the enactment of the PFMC Law, Strategy Development Units (SDUs) were established within the line ministries to replace the dismantled budgeting units, and were made responsible for overseeing the preparation of strategic plans, performance plans, budget and accountability reports, and for the provision of internal control services (Regulation on Working Principles of Strategy Development Units 2006). As a result of these reforms, very important steps have been taken toward the decentralization of budget services and the delegation of budgeting authority to line ministries. Concurrently, the central budget authorities have organized regular training programs and conferences to empower the budgeting management and reform capacity of the SDUs within the line ministries. The basic intention behind these reforms was to transfer management responsibility to the line ministries by making them accountable for their actions. Furthermore, the financial management, performance-based budgeting, internal control, and internal auditing systems in the line ministries have been strengthened by the Central Harmonization Units of the Ministry of Finance.

At the beginning of the 2000s, international organizations were having trouble obtaining data for statistical purposes from the budgeting and accounting system, since the classification system was incompatible with the international classification system. In 2004, the Analytical Budget Classification (ABC) system was adopted in place of the then-current program budget classification approach, which had degenerated over time.

The ABC system makes government statistics more reliable and consistent, and incorporates institutional, functional, financial and economic classifications. The

Institutional	Functional	Financial Type	Economic
Administrative Hierarchy	Governmental Functions	Source of Expenditure	Types of Goods and Services used by the Government
Source: Budget Call and Budget Preparation Guide for 2019-2021 Period (MoTF, 2018b)			

Fig. 8.1 Budget preparation and implementation level

institutional classification is based on Turkey's administrative structure; the functional and economic classifications are based on Government Financial Standards (IMF 2001); and the financial classification is developed based on Turkey's financial legislation. The budget preparation and implementation level of the ABC is reflected in Fig. 8.1. With the transition to the ABC, some specific problems related to budget applications were resolved, and the budget automation system (e-budget) was improved substantially during the associated reforms.

As can be seen from Fig. 8.1, there is no program classification within the current ABC. Although in the design stage of the ABC, the last digit of the functional classification was assigned for program classification, it is not used for this purpose. When the functional classification, which has been designed for statistical purposes, is used instead of the program classification in budget classification, budgeting loses its strength as a management tool. The need for program classification became apparent when public institutions in Turkey started to apply performance-based budgeting in 2003.

At the time the performance-based budgeting implementation was being designed, there was no program classification on which the performance system could be built. For this reason, the strategic planning and performance-based budgeting systems were built around institutional and economic classifications. In the performance-based budgeting system, performance plans, which include objectives, targets, and performance indicators and activities, are separate documents with no links to the traditional budget structure. This situation has led the budget and performance systems to progress along completely different trajectories. Since there is no link between the budgeting and performance systems, performance-based budgeting has lost its purpose as a budget accountability tool. While the strategic plans and performance plans were established based on a result-based management and costing system, the budget documents—based on an Analytical Budget Classification approach—have followed a detailed line-item budget structure with strict input controls.

Within the budgeting process, the determination of appropriations in budget law, budget approval, the transfer of appropriations and budget accountability are all carried out based on an Analytic Budget Classification. That said, the performance-based budgeting system operates only for presentation purposes, with no link to the budgeting system. The strategic plans and performance plans function as detailed intuitional managerial documents, but are not directly utilized as decision-making tools at a governmental level.

With the increasing need to strengthen the link between the budgeting and performance systems, program budgeting studies were initiated in 2012 with the founding of a program budget working group within the Ministry of Treasury and Finance (MoTF). After an intensive review of international practices, a program budgeting model for Turkey was proposed entitled the "Program Structure and Justification Guide (draft version)", published in 2017 by the MoTF and submitted to all public institutions for their opinions and contributions. In addition "The Program Budgeting Guide" was published by PSB to lead public institutions in the transition process to program budgeting (PSB 2020).

The two most important components contributing to the success of budget reforms are the solution to organizational fragmentation problem, and the structure of standard budget procedures in Turkey. The *organizationally fragmented* state of the authority leads to problems in coordination, which is necessary for the successful implementation of complex government policy (Grizzle and Pettijohn 2002, p. 58). In practice, there has been an ongoing problem of fragmentation in the central budgeting authorities in Turkey. While the general management of budget expenditures, including recurrent expenditures, were directed by the General Directorate of Budget and Fiscal Control under the Ministry of Finance, the management and monitoring of capital expenditures was carried out by the Ministry of Development, and all duties related to government cash and debt management were carried out by the Undersecretariat of the Treasury.

In the implementation of program budgeting, it is necessary to consider the coordination of activities and projects that serve the same program. Furthermore, expenditures should be evaluated based on their goals and objectives rather than on the expenditure type, such as recurrent or capital expenditures. Program budgeting and the performance-based budgeting reforms ran into problems of implementation in practice as a result of inconsistencies in the reform implementation approaches of the separate budgeting authorities. This fragmented organizational budget structure in Turkey and the associated coordination problems brought about a need for organizational structure reforms.

After the launch of the Presidential System in Turkey, the Ministry of the Treasury and Finance (MoTF) was established through a merger of the units of the Undersecretariat of the Treasury and the Ministry of Finance (Presidential Decree on the Organization of the Presidency No. 1 2018). The PSB was established under the Presidency, and was given the responsibility for the preparation and management of budgeting, including both recurrent and capital expenditures (Presidential Decree on the Organization of the Presidency of Strategy and Budget No. 13). As a result, one of the most important obstacles in the way of the implementation of the program budget—organizational fragmentation—was reduced in Turkey. These organizational structure reforms sought to resolve the problems of coordination arising out of the fragmented landscape in budget and economy management.

8.3 The Potential Benefits of Program Budgeting Reforms for Turkey's Budgeting System

The program budgeting reforms cleared the way for evidence-based budgeting, and served as a basis for other budget reforms. The advantages of the launch of program budgeting and how program budgeting can resolve budget application problems in Turkey will be set out below:

- *Determining expenditure priorities*: Program budgeting forms a solid basis for discussions geared toward evidence-based decision-making and the prioritization of expenditures at a government level. For example, instead of engaging in input-based discussions of such subjects as the necessary expenditures for cleaning services, equipment or security, budget discussions may involve policy debates; for example, whether or not to spend more on the area of curative or preventative health in the Ministry of Health, or whether regular high schools or vocational schools should be given more support.
- *Government-level performance management tool*: Strategic plans and performance plans are highly detailed institutional documents, although there is a need for macro-level performance monitoring instruments in Turkey. In practice, too much micro-scale performance information can prevent the use of performance indicators as decision-making tools. Programs are government-level decision-making tools and reflect government priorities, and so include key macro-level performance information.
- *The budget as an expenditure-analysis tool*: The absence of activities and programs in budget classification means that the budget is completely input-oriented, and that the cost of government programs is not seen in budget documents. Accordingly, the costs of activities and projects that serve specific purposes cannot be analyzed through the budget system and cannot be monitored throughout the year. The necessary tools in evidence-based budgeting, such as performance monitoring, and evaluation and spending reviews, are built on a program budgeting structure. It is thus possible to carry out program evaluations and other budget analyses through the use of program intervention logic, based on program goals, objectives and indicators.
- *Parliament's budgetary authority*: One of the most appropriate means of increasing Parliament's budgetary authority would be to engage in budgetary debates related to government policies involving an inspection of program expenditures. The current input-oriented budgets, which are highly detailed and technical, far from creating the necessary basis for parliamentary discussion.
- *Strengthening the Medium-Term Expenditure Framework*: The medium-term expenditure system works best when budgets are based on programs. In such cases it is possible to remain in line with long-term government policies through a program budgeting approach. In contrast, in input-oriented systems, budgets will only be increased incrementally in subsequent years in the medium term, and medium-term forecasts that fail to take into account future output levels will be

unreliable, as they take into account only increases in input costs (Kraan 2008, p. 4).

- *The main service units of an organization come to the forefront*: In ABC (institutional classification), the main and supporting service units are reflected at the same level of importance. The main services, being those that directly serve the stakeholders, should be emphasized more in the budget structure. In the current budget classification and performance budgeting system in Turkey, all units are afforded equal status. For example, in application, human resources units have their own performance targets, such as in-service training times, while in-service training serves to improve the quality of the main services provided to the stakeholders, and should not be targeted by itself (Robinson 2013a).
- *Increasing the effectiveness of the central budgeting authorities*: When program budgeting comes into effect, budget discussions and budget controls should focus on public policies rather than being input-based. Such a change in the budgeting approach would increase the role and effectiveness of the central budget authorities in policy-making.
- *Providing transparency and accountability*: With the transition to program budgeting, the budget becomes more understandable by the public. With an output and result-oriented budget structure, the public is able to scrutinize how their taxes are being spent. Also, while determining the programs and the program objectives, targets and indicators, public institutions consider the target groups of their services and their specific expectations.

8.4 Program Budgeting Design

In the Program Structure and Justification Guide, "program" is defined as "a group of activities, products and services that are coherently/appropriately combined and allocated to contribute to a specific policy objective" (MoTF 2017, p. 14). Programs are determined based on public service outcomes. If the main service units of the institutions follow a result-oriented approach, meaning that the organizational units are determined based on the services provided to the stakeholders, the institutional and program structures will coincide. However, if the organization units are not result-oriented, the program structure will need to be defined separately from the organizational structure. In the long term, it is generally expected that the organizational structure will change in accordance with the program structure (Robinson 2013a, p. 35). The most significant exception to the result-oriented program structure is "the management and support services program," which includes the expenditures of organizational units that do not directly serve the stakeholders, but rather contribute to the provision of the institution's result-based services.

The program hierarchy is formed by the program, subprogram and activities. The determination of activities is largely in line with the principles set out in the performance plans, but since the programs and activities will be coded in the budgeting system and monitored regularly throughout the year, the role of the central budget authorities will be of considerable importance. The central budget authorities play a key role in determining the program hierarchy of public institutions. Program implementation structure created by PSB in Turkey in cooperation with the public administration and approved by the President (Presidential authority approval No. 67 dated 07/08/2019 and No. 2 dated 16/01/2020).

Finally, how the program classification will be included within the existing coding structure, which is illustrated in Fig. 8.1, can be discussed. If the program classification code is located at the beginning of the classification structure, resources can be allocated to programs directly, and can be followed at the highest priority level. However, this structure is only practically applicable if the programs are defined at a macro-level, and when the program includes the participation of many organizations. If programs are defined only generally under ministries, it is more convenient to define the program classification after the institutional classification.

8.5 What Should Be the Level of Budget Flexibility in Program Budgeting Reform?

The traditional budget, which is referred to as a line-item budget, is very detailed, containing appropriation items based on various government expenditures. A traditional budget is input-based and enables tight budget controls in expenditure management. In a traditional budget, ex-ante controls are made, budget allocations are determined in detail and appropriation transfers are made in accordance with strict rules. With program budgets, since transition to an output- and result-oriented budget management is targeted, budget elasticity should be increased, and over time, budget control should be shifted from input to output and outcome (Kraan 2008, pp. 4–5). Budget flexibility is increased by reducing the number of line-items that are prepared and approved within the budget. The degree of budget elasticity depends on the country's budgeting traditions and the applied management structure.

There are both negative and positive consequences for increasing budget elasticity. Increasing budget flexibility generally leads to a growth in public spending, weakens spending controls and increases the risk of corruption (Dorotinsky 2004). On the other hand, the main advantages of budget flexibility are its focus on issues that need to be decided upon through the reduction of excessive detail, while a boost to efficiency is provided by increasing the authority of line ministries over their expenditures. For this reason, it is necessary to increase budget flexibility in the implementation of the program budget reforms. Full budget flexibility is provided through the application of a "block budget" approach that does not even include programs in budget law, and this has seen practical use in some developed countries. The implementation of "block budgets" threatens budget discipline. Since budget programs are a means of implementing public policies, the legislative body should be included in the program-level allocation process.

In the transition to a program budgeting process, how budget flexibility can be increased in Turkey has long been discussed. With the institutional classification in Turkey, budget appropriations are allocated to public institutions and their subordinate units at a very detailed level. For example, in each line ministry, the appropriations of each general directorate, provincial unit and foreign branch (such as foreign representative offices of the organizations) are indicated in the budget document. With Law No. 5018, the highest administrator of each expenditure unit to which the appropriation is allocated within the budget is defined as the spending authority. In the above example, each director general within the line ministry has their own budget and the authority to spend, and likewise, each spending authority is held accountable for their expenses through the annual accountability reports of the organization.

Budget accountability is provided at the highest level through the existing institutional budget coding system in Turkey, since it specifies the budget of each subunit separately. However, this system limits the authority of the topmost manager in public institutions. As the budget preparation and implementation process in this system is very detailed, the focus of the budget is on detailed line items rather than policy development and expenditure prioritization. The central budgeting authority and Parliament could focus more the possible impacts of public policies on the future of the country, rather than how much a subunit of an institution has spent on, for example, electricity or cleaning supplies. Another disadvantage of this spending system is that each spending unit has its own expenditure and procurement procedure, leading to higher prices and inefficiencies in the public procurement mechanism.

For these reasons, whether or not the institutional classification will be simplified with the transition to a program budget is an important field of discussion. In other words, if the budget appropriations of subunits is not covered by the budget law, the highest level manager of the organization will decide upon the budget appropriations of the subunits of the organization. Following the transition to the program budget, it will be important to link spending responsibility to the program manager if the program budgeting approach is to function well in practice. Thus, when designing program budgeting, all elements of the system, including the budgeting, spending, accounting, monitoring, and evaluation processes, should comply with the program structure.

Another issue under discussion is whether the functional classification will be included in the budget coding or not after the program classification has been added to the coding system. The functional classification approach serves as a budget accounting and reporting tool rather than as a budget management tool. The Classification of the Functions of the Government (COFOG) system, which permits international comparisons, is used in many countries, but is not required to be included in the budget classification. As stated by Robinson (2013a, p. 46), "COFOG is not a budget classification of expenditure, but purely a statistical classification for ex post reporting". Accordingly, it is possible to report functional classification results via links to be formed; however, the program budget expenditures should be included in the coding system for day-to-day budget administration and accounting (Dorotinsky 2004).

Keeping all existing classification sections in the budget preparation and implementation process in the program budgeting reforms has the advantage of allowing the continued production of statistical data, allowing comparisons with the historical statistical values. However, simplifying the existing coding system after the transition to the program budget is generally preferred by countries, since statistical information can be produced through ex-post links.

8.6 Cross-Organizational Programs

Programs are generally determined in line with the organizational structure, as public institutions are usually organized on the basis of their services to stakeholders. For this reason, programs are defined under an organizational structure, although "cross-organizational programs" require the cooperation of various institutions. Such programs are defined as a group of products and services of similar nature that are produced by different administrations and submitted to the same target group (MoTF 2017, p. 25).

Program budgeting is based mainly on the classification of appropriations in terms of what the expenditures are trying to achieve, rather than how administrations use resources. For this reason, all activities that contribute to the same target should be included in the same program, regardless of which institution is carrying out the activities. For example, a program entitled "fighting against crime" would include such organizational units as the police department, courts and prisons, all of which are under the responsibility of different public institutions. A program determined in this way allows for the analysis of the various aspects of the targeted service. For example, increasing the appropriations provided to the police force could lead to a reduction in the crime rate, and thus a reduction in the budget allocations to prisons (Schick 2007, p. 115).

One example of a cross-organizational program could be a "coping with climate change program". Climate change is a multidimensional concept that necessitates the collaboration of different parties in both the public and private sectors. Studies into coping with climate change in Turkey are conducted under the leadership of the Ministry of Environment and Urban Planning, but with the cooperation of the Ministry of Energy and Natural Resources, the Ministry of Agriculture and Forestry and the Ministry of Transport and Infrastructure, along with many other public and non-governmental organizations. All of these intuitions are engaged in activities serving the common goal of coping with climate change within the scope of their assigned duties, and so there is a need for a cross-organizational program for the management of climate change issues.

One of the struggles related to the cross-organizational program is to take an organizational unit responsible for reporting upon the success or failure of the program. Since cross-organizational programs fall under the area of responsibility of many institutions, institutional program accountability may be defined at a subprogram level. Each ministry determines the activities that serve the cross-organizational program under an institutionally defined subprogram.

Turkey has adopted a similar approach to the cross-organizational programs applied in Korea, although program classification in Korea is linked with functional classification, different from Turkey's current program classification approach. Discussions in the literature on cross-organizational programs and details of the implementation of cross-organizational programs in Korea are presented in Box I.

Box I: Cross-organizational Programs in Korea

Public financial management reforms, involving medium-term spending frameworks, top-down budgeting, enhanced performance management systems and the establishment of a digital budget information system that includes a transition to a program budget, have been implemented in Korea. While the medium-term spending plan in Korea imposes tight spending limits on the spending ministries, it leaves lower-level budget spending decisions to the line ministries up to a specified spending ceiling. Thus, while more authority is given to public institutions through increased budget flexibility, accountability is provided through the developed performance management system. The performance management system was developed after analyzing the performance of expenditure programs and increasing the connections between budget and performance information. The new budget and accounting reform, including a transition to a program budget, was developed in 2005 and entered into full effect in 2007 (Kim and Park 2007).

In the Korean program budgeting case, as a general rule, programs remain within organizational boundaries and cross-organizational programs are avoided. However, in some exceptional cases, when more than one institution can serve the same goal, large cross-organizational programs are created. In cross-organizational programs, problems can arise in the generation of performance targets and indicators and in providing accountability.

It is therefore recommended that each organization's responsibility be specified with subprograms in larger programs in Korea (Korea Institute of Public Finance [Korea IPF] and The World Bank 2007). In this way, organizational accountability is reflected within the sub-programs, with program responsibility shared among the different institutions through subprograms. However, in some exceptional cases, sub-programs may be used by different organizations at the same time. For example, the sub-program including activities related to medical education under the higher education program will appear in the budgets of many universities in the same way, but in this case, administrative codes will define an institution's appropriation separately, and each university will be responsible for its own sub-program (Korea IPF and The World Bank 2007).

8.7 Program Performance Information

The second component of program budgeting relates to performance information. The implementation of performance-based budgeting reforms often fails in both developed and developing countries, with one of the main reasons for this being that performance-based budgeting assumes the rationality of the budgeting process. Budget decisions are made based on optimization behaviors, and on information gathered through scientific and rational methods, although performance-based budgeting ignores the fact that budgetary decisions are inherently political, and are made as a result of compromise rather than optimization (Hijal-Moghrabi 2018).

Furthermore, the implementation of performance budgeting requires not only technical information but also a cultural change. Political and bureaucratic authorities are generally reluctant to carry out such reforms since they limit their level of budget control. Line-item budgeting allows authorities to directly control the allocation of resources.

Performance results must systematically affect budget funding in performance-based budgeting, and a presentational approach that does not aim to influence budget funding cannot be classified in this way (Robinson 2013b, p. 238). The performance-based budgeting structure that was introduced in Turkey was applied mostly with a presentational goal, and has a highly complex and hierarchical structure that consists of strategic goals, strategic objectives, performance targets, and performance indicators and activities.

Studies of performance-based budgeting reforms first appeared in Turkey in 2003. While public intuitions now have experience in determining their organizational aims, objectives, and performance indicators, there is still a need for intensive efforts to link performance information and budgeting. The performance-based budgeting system entered into practice in Turkey with the preparation of strategic plans, performance plans, and annual accountability reports.

With the adoption of Law No. 5018, all public institutions are now obliged to prepare strategic plans, gradually, and with a predetermined agenda. Public institutions have determined their missions, visions, strategic goals and strategic targets through a strategic planning process and involving participatory methods, and strategic plans are expected to be compatible with such high-level policy documents as national plans and strategy papers. Strategic plans are drawn up for five years with the aim of deciding upon the main goals to be reached by the organization.

Performance Plans[1] are prepared on an annual basis, and in accordance with the strategic plans, and include strategic goals and objectives. Performance plans include annual performance targets, performance indicators, the activities to be achieved in order to fulfill these performance targets, and the costs of these activities. Furthermore, in order to ensure fiscal transparency and accountability, public administrations are mandated to prepare accountability reports that explain the levels of attainment of

[1]The annual application period of strategic plans is referred to as the performance program in Law No 5018. In parallel with general international usage, the term "performance plan" is adopted in this article.

the performance targets, the resources used, the budget targets and realizations, and the reasons for any deviations from the performance targets. Accountability reports are shared publicly in order to inform the public of the kind of services provided by public administrations.

In Turkey, after a sound program structure has been created, selective performance information related to the programs should be determined, and a system should be designed that allows for the simple and effective setting of program targets for the budget. Performance indicators should be determined that include the most important issues related to the program, and the performance targets should be monitored and evaluated regularly. Information on the performance of the program should be formulated in such a way that the identified indicators can be used as a tool for prioritizing expenditures.

Information on the performance of the program is to be included in the program justification document in Turkey, detailing the progress, importance, performance and cost information of the program. The aim in program justification is to systematically produce, use and report performance information related to the program in order to support budget decisions. The performance information of the program details the goals, objectives, performance indicators, and costing information about the activities and programs.

The performance information contained within the program justification differs in scope and content from the strategic and performance plans. As strategic and performance plans are currently used as an organizational governance tools, they are prepared in a substantially detailed manner and include many performance indicators at different levels of the target hierarchy, such as strategic goals or yearly performance targets. The performance information contained within the program budget should be limited in number, making it easier for the government to determine the key spending priorities. Cooperation between the central budgeting authorities and line ministries when determining performance indicators is a key factor in the success of the implementation of performance-based budgeting.

8.8 Activity-Based Costing Approach in Turkey

To summarize the basic principles of the costing approach in Turkey and their reflection on the performance plans (MoTF 2009), first of all, the concept of the activity is defined in a broad sense as an umbrella term that includes similar sub-activities, different from activity-based costing literature. Furthermore, the concept of the activity includes both recurrent and capital expenditures that serve the same purpose.

Activity costs cover both operational and administrative activities, and so the total cost of activities is the entire budget of the institution. Where applicable, output-based costing is applied based on unit cost, but when this is not possible, the institutional and economic budget classifications are used to allocate costs directly to the related activities.

Indirect costs are not allocated, but are included as general administrative expenses. Management expenditures that serve the needs of the internal units are classified as support activities. In application, the expenses of support activities that are not directly related to performance goals and targets in Turkey account for some 70–80% of the total budget in some organizations. For example, in 2018, the general administrative expenses of the Ministry of National Education (MoNE) amounted to 79.36% of the total budget appropriations (MoNE 2018), while general administrative expenses accounted for only 16.25% of the total expenditures of the Ministry of Environment and Urbanization (MoEU) (MoEU 2018) compared to 1.11% for the Ministry of Transport and Infrastructure (MoTI) (MoTI 2018).

The difference in these ratios stems from the cost allocation methods used in the individual ministries. While some ministries determine performance targets and activities for internal services and allocate costs to these activities, others set these costs apart as administrative expenses. Factors such as in which field the ministry operates, the size of the provincial organizations of the institution, and the scale of the economic and social transfers made from their budgets to other organizations and stakeholders all affect the ratio of administrative expenses within the budget. The support programs of the core ministries are more stable, being generally less than 10% of the overall budget in countries applying program budgets (Kraan 2008, p. 9). These facts reveal the lack of standardization in the application of costing of activities related to performance plans in Turkey.

The most significant problem in activity costing is the manual calculation of activity costs by the institution, since it is not included in ABC as a budget figure. The absence of programs and activities in the budget codes prevents the use of activities as a management tool, and make it impossible to monitor and evaluate activity costs within the year. Furthermore, since activities are not coded, it is not possible to make transfers between the line items of the budget when based on programs and activities.

8.9 Evaluation of Programs

The final component of program budgeting is the evaluation of programs. Programs are determined taking into account the expectations of the target recipients of the public services. As social expectations change, the continuity of program in subsequent years and the resources allocated to the program should be assessed regularly. In countries that have been implementing a program budget for many decades, systems for the monitoring and evaluation of programs have been established.

The number of countries carrying out spending reviews increased after the global financial crisis. Spending reviews focus mainly on budget savings in times of crisis, and have turned progressively into a tool for the creation of fiscal space in public finance through the termination of ineffective and inefficient expenditure programs. The results of program evaluations and spending reviews provide information to decision-makers, allowing them to prioritize government spending based on the analytical methods used for expenditure analyses. The program monitoring, evaluation and spending review approach is summarized below, including international experiences and the implementation in Turkey.

8.10 Program Monitoring and Evaluation

Program monitoring refers to the systematic collection and following of performance information related to ongoing programs. Programs are monitored regularly through the information management systems created by the spending units through a program evaluation, which is a systematic study of the effects of programs, activities, and projects on society and an analysis of the level of achievement of the program aims and objectives.

Program monitoring and evaluations are conducted primarily by line ministries, given their knowledge of the programs they apply. The central budget authority also evaluates public programs to determine spending priorities at a government level, and the programs are evaluated further by the Court of Accounts in order to inform Parliament and the public. Since program monitoring and evaluations are based on an intervention logic, it is important to create programs that are in line with the theoretical rules of program intervention logic, and to identify realistic and achievable goals and targets and to set key performance indicators beforehand to aid in the program evaluation.

A program evaluation, which is an evidence-based expenditure analysis tool, cannot be expected to directly determine the budget and the resource allocation, but does provide inputs for decision-making since government decisions are affected by various information sources (Lahey 2010). The results of the program evaluation also contribute to the accomplishment of the spending review process. Only limited time and resources can be allotted to a spending review of a specific program, in that a large number of programs are reviewed within a government-wide analysis. Program evaluations increase the success of spending reviews, since they provide the necessary detailed background information.

In Turkey, in the creation of a performance information and evaluation system, an online platform was established within budgeting system. The "Performance Budget Module" was developed within the e-budget system for the monitoring of the information in the performance plans, to aid in the creation of cost tables, to strengthen the connection between the budget and the performance plans, and to facilitate the collection of performance information on public institutions. In order to monitor, evaluate and report the performance plans of the Ministries and other public administrations, a "Performance Monitoring and Evaluation" module section was added in 2012.

The performance plans submitted by the public administrations to the Ministry of Finance were evaluated in 2012 and in subsequent years, and the results of the evaluations were shared with the public administrations. The evaluation results, however, did not include remarks related to specific program expenditures, but made rather only general remarks regarding the overall performance of the budgeting system. Additional performance audits were carried out by both internal auditors and the Turkish Court of Accounts. In designing the program evaluation approach in Turkey, the lessons learned from international experience have been vital. The program evaluation approach applied in Canada, and the changes applied to the structure of the Canadian program in recent years, are discussed in Box II.

Program budgeting, costing, monitoring, and evaluation are the main instruments in ensuring the effective, economic, and efficient utilization of public resources, as defined in PFMC Law No: 5018. Accordingly, the MoTF launched a project[2] in which international practices were analyzed with a view to preparing a model for estimating and assessing program costs, and to establish program monitoring and evaluation systems in line with international practices. These studies have made important contributions to increasing the existing knowledge on public financial management reforms in Turkey.

Box II: Program Evaluation in Canada

In Canada, the monitoring and evaluation system has a long-established history that dates back to 1969 when the first formulated and centrally-led evaluation was introduced. In 1977, the government-wide implementation of the Evaluation Policy was initiated, and served as the basis for the current evaluation practices in Canada (Lahey 2010).

In Canada, the main responsibilities in the evaluation process are borne by Departments, the Treasury Board of Canada Secretariat (TBS) and the Auditor General of Canada (AGC). Departments prepare five-year rolling evaluation plans that are approved and released annually and submitted also to the TBS, and carry out program evaluations of their own organizations. Within its oversight function, the TBS leads the departments in the scope of performance management and evaluation and, when needed, conducts centrally-led evaluations of departmental expenditures. The AGC carries out annual systematic performance audits and provides information to Parliament related to the functioning of government programs (TBS 2016).

In Canada, the Strategic Outcomes and the Program Alignment Architecture (PAA) is a multi-layered and hierarchical program structure consisting of Strategic Results, Programs and Sub-programs. The programs, which comprise activities and input sources, form the basis of a budget unit. The "Policy on Result" approach launched by the TBS in 2016 changed the budgetary

[2]The Grant Agreement (Project No: TF019355) titled "Public Finance Management Reform Implementation Support Project" entered into force with its publication in the Official Gazette dated December 22, 2015 and numbered 29570. In line with the agreement, the Ministry of Finance received a grant from the International Bank for Reconstruction and Development (IBRD) with the purpose of enhancing transparency and accountability in the Turkish public sector through the provision of support to its administrations in addressing the challenges faced in the implementation of public financial management reforms.

framework from a PAA to a Departmental Result Framework (DRF) structure. A DRF structure, which focuses on the responsibilities of Departments, was adopted rather than a PAA structure which is hierarchical in nature and is hampered by vague responsibility allocation.

The DRF structure is simpler and more flexible, and provides a clearer picture of the differences made by Departments in society, as well as how they accomplish these core responsibilities through their applied programs. With the "Policy on Result" approach, the dispersed and unclear responsibilities related to performance management in the various Departments are clearly defined (Pagan 2016). The DRF structure identifies the core responsibilities of Departments and defines Program Inventories (PI) that describe how the departments' core responsibilities are to be fulfilled. The "Policy on Results" also requires the development of the Performance Information Profiles (PIP) which identifies the performance information of the program.

8.11 Spending Review

Systematic spending reviews were made in only a limited number of countries prior to the global financial crisis, but were applied in many countries in which the balance of public finances deteriorated after the crisis. Spending reviews are defined as "the process of developing and adopting savings measures, based on the systematic scrutiny of baseline expenditures" (OECD 2013, p. 38), and permit the determination of savings options in budget expenditures. Budget appropriation cuts in traditional budget applications are made by reducing the allowances of certain expenditure items at a certain ratio, without taking into account the aims and objectives of the specific expenditures. Spending reviews examine government programs and activities to identify potential saving areas that do not serve the government's priorities.

A spending review focuses mainly on baseline expenditures, as in most countries the budget preparation process takes into consideration almost exclusively new expenditure proposals, and fails to consider the rationale behind any ongoing financing of baseline expenditures. While the budget process traditionally focuses only on new budget offers, ongoing spending is preserved, and continues to be financed, even when unproductive. Maintaining current expenditures without analyzing or adding new programs and activities in line with the needs of the society each year will lead inevitably to a tendency for budget increases (Robinson 2018, p. 306).

Spending reviews can be applied either comprehensively or selectively. In a comprehensive review, all government programs and activities are reviewed within a certain period of time, while in a selective review, reviews are made only of predetermined policy areas. Comprehensive and selective reviews differ in terms of whether or not the review topics are determined before the review process. If spending review areas are identified in the design stage of the assessment, then a selective review is applied, while in a comprehensive review, the review is not limited to ex-ante issues (Kennedy and Howlin 2017). These two assessments are applied simultaneously in some countries, which make it possible to conduct a comprehensive review while also determining policy areas at each review cycle. The implementation approach in Ireland can be put forward as an example in which both evaluations are carried at the same time. Box III provides a summary of the expenditure review process in Ireland.

In expenditure reviews, the analytical analysis techniques adopted in the evaluation include effectiveness, allocative efficiency, technical efficiency, and functional coherence analyses. An effectiveness analysis examines whether the program or activity is achieving the desired results; a technical efficiency analysis focuses on the costs of existing goods and services; an allocative efficiency analysis examines the level of compliance of programs or activities with government strategies and policies; and a functional coherence analysis scrutinizes whether duplications have occurred in the execution of programs, and identifies any inefficiencies in the sharing of duties and responsibilities among public organizations (Fallov et al. 2018).

The MoTF in Turkey has carried out studies into the establishment of a spending review system in Turkey in which countries with spending review experience have been examined and infrastructure works have been carried out with a view to creating a spending review model for Turkey. Subsequently, further spending review studies have been initiated in Turkey in line with the New Economic Program (2019–2021). The Public Finance Transformation Office has been established within the MoTF to ensure the efficient use of public resources, to reduce costs and expenditures, and to improve the quality of revenues. The Savings and Revenue Transformation Program, which will be prepared and followed by this office, aims to bring permanent improvements to public finance, targeting savings of approximately 76 billion TL for 2019 by means of increases in income and reductions in expenditures (MoTF 2018a).

Box III: Spending Review Practice: Ireland Case

Ireland's public finance balance deteriorated significantly in the aftermath of the global financial crisis, which led to a general government deficit that reached 13.8% of GDP in 2009 (OECD 2015). Spending reviews in Ireland aim to identify inefficiencies in the public sector and to improve the management of scarce public resources as part of the comprehensive reforms being implemented within the restructuring of the budgeting system.

At the beginning of the 2009 financial crisis, a Special Group on Public Service Numbers and Expenditure Programs (Special Group) was launched, and published an expenditure review report that contained an analysis of government expenditures. The subsequent Comprehensive Review of Expenditures (CRE11) and Comprehensive Review of Expenditures (CRE14) were conducted, and from 2017 onwards a yearly spending review has been made covering a rolling three-year period, with selective spending reviews published covering government expenditures up to 2019.

The spending reviews were carried out by the staff of the Irish Government Economic and Evaluation Service (IGEES), and spending review studies of line ministries are also supported by IGEES. Almost all of the ministries have had IGEES units working to increase capacity in policy development and evaluation. The IGEES network that has been established in all line ministries aims to increase the evaluation capacity of these ministries (OECD 2015). In the review process, each ministry has reviewed its current programs and activities based on a predetermined principle, and has submitted its spending review results to the Ministry of Public Expenditure and Reform (PER) to provide input for the determination of expenditure ceilings.

Spending reviews are a relatively new process in the Irish budgeting system, with those carried out prior to 2008 being limited in number with a specific purpose, including policy reviews of such specific areas as industrial programs, and performance reviews and audits conducted for internal use in spending ministries (Kennedy and Howlin 2016). Ireland's spending review practices reveal that although the spending review working groups lacked adequate analytical support in the earliest years in which comprehensive reviews were made, in time they have gained experience in the development and analysis of public policy.

In the Ireland system, comprehensive and selective spending reviews were applied together. All programs and activities were fully evaluated, with thematic in depth evaluations made of selected ministries and programs. Thus, beside the comprehensive review, in-depth thematic evaluations covering multiple ministries and programs identified were conducted. Lastly, in Ireland, expenditure reviews were initially intended to lead to budget cuts under the fiscal discipline applied during the financial crisis, but have now become a tool for increasing the efficiency and effectiveness of public spending. The increased capacity for analysis and the improved fiscal conditions have allowed Irish administration to focus on efficiency and effectiveness through more complex analytical expenditure analysis tools.

8.12 Conclusion

Turkey has spent more than 15 years engaged in intensive efforts aimed at establishing a new approach to the management of public finance. In order to achieve this reform, the organizational structure of financial management has been changed, such that the branches of the Ministry of Finance in the line ministries have been closed and fiscal units specific to the individual line ministries have been created. The budget coding system has been reclassified to be included in the detailed institutional classification, meaning that spending authority has been delegated to each subunit. Budget management has been automated, and budget preparation and implementation operations are now fulfilled through electronic budgeting systems.

Within this process, studies to change the budgeting system from being input-based to performance-based have been carried out. For more than 10 years, strategic plans and performance plans have been prepared by all public institutions and local administrations, leading public institutions to gain considerable experience in performance management. As a consequence, their strategic plans and annual performance plans have become important tools in their organizational governance approach. However, the failure to link performance budgeting with either planning or resource allocation in Turkey has led to a situation in which performance information is not the focus of the budgeting negotiations with the central budget authority, neither is it at the center of budget discussions in Parliament, being used mostly for presentational purposes at a governmental level in the country.

Program budget studies have sought to make active use of the garnered performance information to strengthen the link between planning and budgeting and to reflect the policy priorities of resources in budget documents. To this end, international practices have been examined, and the lessons learned in terms of best practices are being reflected in Turkey's program budgeting transition process. It is important to simplify the budgeting and performance information system while designing program budgeting so as to reflect the government priorities in the budget documents.

The program budget is not limited by a coding system, and so is not just a budgeting concept consisting of budget appropriations. The program budgeting reforms should include other accompanying reforms, along with a modification to budget classifications. During the design phase of the program budget, the link between planning and budgeting should be strengthened and the program objectives should be determined based on key performance indicators. The efficiency of the Medium-Term Expenditure Framework should be increased and a program costing framework should be developed that considers the diversified needs of public institutions. Moreover, the simultaneous implementation of the program budget with the spending review and program evaluation reforms will increase the chances of success of the new management reforms. In the design and implementation of the program monitoring approach, and the evaluation and spending review systems in Turkey, it is important to make use of the lessons learned in the countries that have been using these tools for decades.

References

A. Grizzle, Gloria & D. Pettijohn, Carole (2002). Implementing Performance-Based Program Budgeting: A System-Dynamics Perspective. *Public Administration Review*, 62. 51–62. https://doi.org/10.1111/1540-62https://doi.org/10.00154.

Dorotinsky, Bill (2004). Public Expenditure and Financial Management: An Integrated Perspective: Chapter 3: Budget Systems and Expenditure Classification. *Public Expenditure Analysis and Management Course (Fall 2004)*, World Bank. Retrieved from http://www1.worldbank.org/publicsector/LearningProgram/PEAM/DorotinskyBackCh3.pdf

Fallov, Jonas Ar, Georgieva-Andonovska, Elena Georgieva (2018). Bulgaria - Spending review manual (English). Washington, D.C.: World Bank Group. Retrieved from http://documents.worldbank.org/curated/en/940921532366222268/Bulgaria-spending-review-manual

Hijal-Moghrabi, Imane (2018). Why Is it So Hard to Rationalize the Budgetary Process? A Behavioral Analysis of Performance-Based Budgeting. *Public Organization Review*, 1–20. https://doi.org/10.1007/s11115-018-0410-1.

IMF (2001). Statistics Department's Government Finance Statistics Manual 2001 (GFSM 2001). Retrieved from https://www.imf.org/external/pubs/ft/gfs/manual/

Kennedy, F. & J. Howlin (2016). Spending Reviews in Ireland: Lessons for the future. *Department of Public Expenditure and Reform*, Staff Papers 2016. http://www.budget.gov.ie/Budgets/2017/Documents/6.%20Spending%20Reviews%20in%20Ireland-%20Lessons%20for%20the%20Future.pdf

Kennedy, F. & J. Howlin (2017). Spending reviews in Ireland – Learning from experience, *OECD Journal on Budgeting*, vol. 16/2. https://doi.org/10.1787/budget-16-5jg30cchf0g0.

Korea IPF & The World Bank (2007). John M. Kim (edd.), *From Line- item to Program Budgeting: Global Lessons and the Korean Case*. Korea IPF & The World Bank. http://www1.worldbank.org/publicsector/pe/bookprogrambudget.pdf

Kraan, Dirk-Jan, (2008). Programme Budgeting in OECD countries. *OECD Journal on Budgeting*, 7, issue 4, p. 1–41. https://EconPapers.repec.org/RePEc:oec:govkaa:5kznbht3nc7b

Lahey, Robert (2010). The Canadian monitoring and evaluation (M&E) system: lessons learned from 30 years of development (English). *Evaluation Capacity Development working paper series*; no. ECD 23. Washington, DC: World Bank. http://documents.worldbank.org/curated/en/865531468226748462/The-Canadian-monitoring-and-evaluation-M-E-system-lessons-learned-from-30-years-of-development

Law No. 1050 (1927). Law No. 1050 on Accounting General. Official Gazette dated 9/6/1927 and numbered 606. http://www.mevzuat.gov.tr/Metin.Aspx?MevzuatKod=1.5.3483&MevzuatIliski=0&sourceXmlSearch=

Law No. 5018 (2013). Law No. 5018 on Public Financial Management and Control. Official Gazette dated 24/12/2003 and numbered 25326. http://www.mevzuat.gov.tr/MevzuatMetin/1.5.5018.pdf

M. Kim, John & Park, Nowook (2007). Performance Budgeting in Korea. OECD Journal on Budgeting. 7. 21–21. https://doi.org/10.1787/budget-v7-art21-en.

MoEU (2018). 2018 Performance Plan. Retrieved from http://www.sp.gov.tr/upload/xSPRapor/files/dA1Ds+2018-yili-performans-programi-20180131101510.pdf

MoNE (2018). 2018 Performance Program. Retrieved from https://sgb.meb.gov.tr/meb_iys_dosyalar/2018_03/19144448_2018_PP_-_13.02.2017_2.pdf

MoTI (2018). 2018 Performance Plan. Retrieved from http://www.uab.gov.tr/images/duyurular/2045ed1f6ed6a78.pdf

MoTF (2009). Performance Program Preparation Guide. Retrieved from https://ms.hmb.gov.tr/uploads/2019/01/Performans-Programı-Hazırlama-Rehberi.pdf

MoTF (2017). Program Structure and Program Justification Guide. Retrieved from https://ms.hmb.gov.tr/uploads/2019/07/10763programyapisiveprogramgerekcesirehberitaslagisurumii.pdf

MoTF (2018a). New Economy Program, Balance-Discipline- Transformation 2019–2021 (Medium Term Program). Ministry of Treasury and Finance. https://ms.hmb.gov.tr/uploads/2019/04/Yeni-Ekonomi-Programı-2019-v5.pdf

MoTF (2018b). Budget Call and Budget Preparation Guide for 2019–2021 Period. https://ms.hmb.gov.tr/uploads/2019/04/1126501-2018-10-8taslak-rehber-aciklamalar2019 2021pdf.pdf

OECD (2013). 3rd Annual Meeting of OECD Senior Budget Officials Spending Reviews. *Working Party of Senior Budget Officials*. OECD Conference Centre, Paris, 3–4 June 2013, GOV/PGC/SBO(2013)6.

OECD (2015). Performance Budgeting Practices and Procedures: Case Studies. *Working Party of Senior Budget Officials*. OECD Conference Centre, Paris, 26–27 November 2015, GOV/PGC/SBO (2015) 12.
Pagan, Brian (2016). Treasury Board Policy on Results: A Results and Delivery Culture in the Government of Canada. *Financial Management Institute* – PD Week November 24, 2016.
PSB (2019). 2020 Year Presidential Program http://www.sbb.gov.tr/wp-content/uploads/2019/11/2020_Yili_Cumhurbaskanligi_Yillik_Programi.pdf
PSB (2020). Program Budget Guide (Program Classification and Performance Information). January 2020 http://www.sbb.gov.tr/wp-content/uploads/2020/01/programrchber_ocak2020.pdf
Presidential Decree on the Organization of Presidency No. 1 (2018). Official Gazette dated 10/7/2018 and numbered 30474. http://www.mevzuat.gov.tr/MevzuatMetin/19.5.1.pdf
Presidential Decree on the Organization of the Presidency of Strategy and Budget No. 13 (2018). Official Gazette dated 24/7/2018 and numbered 30488. http://www.mevzuat.gov.tr/MevzuatMetin/19.5.13.pdf
Presidential authority approval No. 67 dated 07/08/2019
Presidential authority approval No. 2 dated 16/01/2020
Regulation on Working Principles of Strategy Development Units (2006). Number of Decisions: 2006/9972. http://www.resmigazete.gov.tr/eskiler/2006/02/20060218-2.htm
Robinson, Marc (2013a). Program classification for performance-based budgeting: how to structure budgets to enable the use of evidence (English), Washington, DC: World Bank Group. http://documents.worldbank.org/curated/en/627581468322141749/Program-classification-for-performance-based-budgeting-how-to-structure-budgets-to-enable-the-use-of-evidence
Robinson M. (2013b). Performance Budgeting. In: Allen R., Hemming R., Potter B.H. (eds) *The International Handbook of Public Financial Management*. Palgrave Macmillan, London. https://doi.org/10.1057/9781137315304_12
Robinson, Marc (2018). The Role of Evaluation in Spending Review. *Canadian Journal of Program Evaluation*, 32. https://doi.org/10.3138/cjpe.43177
Schick, Allen, (2007). Performance Budgeting and Accrual Budgeting: Decision rules or Analytic Tools? *OECD Journal on Budgeting*, 7, issue 2, p. 109–138. https://EconPapers.repec.org/RePEc:oec:govkaa:5l4fghkq206d
TBS (2016). Policy on Result. ISBN: 978-0-660-09947-7. https://www.tbs-sct.gc.ca/pol/doc-eng.aspx?id=31300
Yenice, Ebru (2006). Kamu Kesiminde Performans Değerlendirmesi. *Maliye Dergisi*, Sayı 150, Ocak – Haziran 2006. https://dergiler.sgb.gov.tr/calismalar/maliye_dergisi/yayinlar/md/150/e_yenice.pdf

Ebru Yenice is a Treasury and Finance Expert in the General Directorate of Public Financial Management and Transformation of the Ministry of Treasury and Finance. She completed her master degree at Carnegie Mellon University, H. John Heinz III College with highest distinction award in public management. She is currently Ph.D. candidate at Hacettepe University, Department of Economics. Her research interests include financial economics, public financial management and budgeting. She has published many articles and book chapters on the determination of performance indicators, performance measurement, program budgeting, monitoring and evaluation and performance auditing in the public sector. She worked at the manual preparing studies and projects on the program budgeting, activity based costing and program evaluation. She also participated as a trainer to many training programs for public officials on the subjects of Turkish budgetary system, performance measurement and program evaluation.

Chapter 9
Judicial Review of Budget in Turkish Law

Nahit Yüksel

9.1 Introduction

The Republic of Turkey was founded in 1923 and the first constitution of the Republic entered into force the following year. The Constitution of 1924 brought together the legislative and executive powers under the Grand National Assembly of Turkey (GNAT), the only representative of the nation. The legislative power was to be exercised directly by the GNAT. It was adopted as a principle that the laws could not be in conflict with the Constitution, yet no mechanism responsible for inspecting existence of any violation or no sanction against any violation was included in the Constitution. The executive power was to come out from inside the legislature and be responsible vis-a-vis the legislative power. The system established by the Constitution of 1924 also had the characteristics of parliamentary system, as it stipulated that the executive power could be exercised by a separate body headed by the President and the Prime Minister to be determined by him. During this constitutional period, which would remain in force until 1960, multi-party democratic political life was adopted in 1946.

The 1961 Constitution defined the Republic of Turkey as a democratic, secular, social state of law based on the human rights and the fundamental principles set forth in the Preamble of the Constitution. Again, sovereignty belonged to the nation. The nation was to exercise its sovereignty through the bodies in line with the principles laid down by the Constitution. The Constitution of 1961, which included the constitutional judgment (judicial review of the laws, rules of procedures of GNAT and decree-laws after 1971 in terms of their compliance with the Constitution) as a requirement of the rule of law, stipulated the establishment of a Constitutional Court for this purpose (Kaboğlu 1994; Öden 1999) and the rights and freedoms were regulated comprehensively.

N. Yüksel (✉)
Ministry of Treasury and Finance, Ankara, Turkey
e-mail: nyuksel08@gmail.com

H. Kıral and T. Akdemir (eds.), *Public Financial Management Reforms in Turkey: Progress and Challenges, Volume 1*, Accounting, Finance, Sustainability, Governance & Fraud: Theory and Application, https://doi.org/10.1007/978-981-15-1914-7_9

The Constitution of 1982, just like the Constitution of 1961, defined the Republic of Turkey, as a democratic, secular, social state of law based on the human rights and the fundamental principles set forth in the Preamble of the Constitution. As was the case in the previous two Constitutions, sovereignty, according to this Constitution, unconditionally belongs to the nation. The nation shall exercise its sovereignty by means of the authorized organs in accordance with the principles laid down by the Constitution. This Constitution further strengthened the executive body against the legislature in terms of exercise of sovereignty, and adopted the principle of protecting the "indivisible integrity of the state with its country and its nation" rather than the individual in terms of fundamental rights and freedoms, and showed a pro-authority understanding. In the catalogue of fundamental rights and freedoms, firstly the principle of homework is highlighted, which is followed by right. With regard to the constitutional jurisdiction, the Constitution of 1982 maintained, until June 24, 2018, the stance of 1961 Constitution adopted following the 1971 amendment (judicial review of the laws, rules of procedures of GNAT and decree-laws in terms of their compliance with the Constitution). Following a constitutional amendment to be effective from this date, the constitutional jurisdictions are texts, laws, the Rules of Procedure of the Turkish Grand National Assembly and Presidential Decree. To take effect as of the mentioned date following the Constitutional amendment, the texts which are subject to constitutional jurisdiction are the laws, rules of procedures of GNAT, and the Presidential decrees. A minor amendment (amendment in the characterization of parties) was also made in the list of those authorized to file an annulment action.

According to the constitutional jurisdiction adopted by the 1982 Constitution, the decisions of the Constitutional Court are final; decisions cannot be disclosed without providing rationale in writing. The court, when annulling the provision of law or Decree, cannot establish a provision in a way that will lead to a new application, acting as a legislator. Court decisions are not backward. The court decisions are not retrospective. The decisions of the Supreme Court bind the legislative, executive and judicial bodies, administrative authorities, and real and legal persons.

The State of Law, with the shortest expression, refers to ensuring the rule of law. The rule of law is not enough, it is also necessary to improve the rights and ensure that the legal system is fair. In its many decisions in the 1961 and 1982 Constitutional periods, which adopted the principle of the rule of law and the constitutional jurisdiction, the Turkish Constitutional Court defined the rule of law in its Decision Docket No. 1963/124, D. 1963/243 (D.R.: 11.10.1963) as follows: a state which respects human rights and establishes a fair legal order protecting these rights and considers it necessary to maintain this, and which acts in compliance with the law and constitution in all its activities. One of the prerequisites for being a state of law is to adopt the principle of separation of powers, and another one is that the state equips its legal system with constitutional jurisdiction. The constitutions of 1961 and 1982 adopted the principle of separation of powers and carefully drawn the duties and jurisdictions of the legislative, executive, and judicial powers. The constitutional jurisdiction established by the 1961 Constitution was also regulated by the 1982 Constitution. For more than half a century, the Constitutional Court has fulfilled its function as a constitutional jurisdiction and supervises the legislature's compliance with the law.

Power of the purse was introduced into the Turkish legal system by the Constitution of 1876 in the period of the Ottoman Empire, much earlier than the principle of rule of law. Some of the budget provisions of this Constitution were amended in 1908, and thus, power of the purse was rendered more functional.

These three powers, whose powers and responsibilities are regulated, in detail, based on the principle of separation of powers in the current Constitution, play an important role in the audit of the budget.

As required by "power of the purse", an audit is conducted on the budget by the legislative power at various stages, namely, submission to the legislative body by the executive body of the draft budget (after 24 June 2018 budget "proposal"), debate on the proposal, the implementation of the adopted budget, and debate on finalization of draft final act (after June 24, 2018, "proposal") which indicates the results of the implementation. Direct audit on the executive within the scope of the budget process is mainly carried out through questions, motions of censure, general interview, parliamentary research, parliamentary inquiry and vote of confidence (after June 24, 2018, question, general interview, parliamentary research), and other audit methods such as making legal arrangements on public expenditure, revenues, and assets are also applied. The indirect audit of the legislature on the executive within the scope of the budget process is carried out by having all public accounts and assets examined by the Court of Accounts. The Constitution regulates how the legislature will audit the results of the budget implementation. The Law No. 5018 also states that the audits carried out by the legislative body after the implementation of the budget are conducted over the accountability reports, final account draft laws and statements of general conformity ("direct audit" and "external audit").

The audit of the budget by the executive power is carried out by the competent authorities of the administration during the implementation of the budget. Such audit can be conducted either during the undertaking and realization stages of the expenditures or over the spending documents, other documents and accounts after the expenditure is made.

The audit of the budget by the judiciary power is the examination and inspection by the Court of Accounts, which is an independent judicial organ, after the powers delegated to the executive by the legislative power through executive budget law have been exercised, over their reflections in the account records. In other words, the judicial review of the budget (budget implementation) is mainly carried out by the Court of Accounts. Such audit is performed on the accounts and transactions of the responsible persons after the implementation of the budget.

After evaluating the arrangements on the power of the purse in Turkey from a historical perspective, this study will discuss judicial review of the budget in the following two axes: judicial review (the Court of Accounts) of the budget (budget implementation) and judicial review (Constitutional Court) of the constitutionality of the budget laws. In the "Conclusion" section, a situation analysis will be carried out on the audits conducted by the Court of Accounts and the Constitutional Court, and an evaluation will be made in this regard.

9.2 An Evaluation from Historical Perspective: Regulations Regarding the Power of the Purse in Turkey

Most of today's constitutional institutions (by the way, budget) are based on the Magna Carta Libertatum (the Great Charter of the Liberties) proclaimed by King Homeless John in England in 1215. This is considered to be the first document regarding "power of the purse."

> ...In the UK, the king was frequently demanding tax to cover the costs of the ongoing battles in the 12th and 13th centuries. The British people and the barons began to complain about the heavy taxes that the king demanded and feel uneasy. On the request and insistence of the Barons, King John had to sign the Great Charter, called Magna Carta Libertatum, on 15 June 1215 near London. This charter became a constitutional rule in the following years not only in the country where it was born, but also in many countries of the world. (Mutluer et al. 2011, p. 44)

As a political institution evolving, in eight-hundred years, from the proclamation of Magna Carta to the present, the parliaments have been the places where the power of the purse is represented the most (Canbay and Gerger 2012). The power of the purse held by the parliaments still maintains its dignity and is mostly regulated in constitutions.

The power of the purse is, in its simplest definition, the right to determine and approve the type and amount of public revenues and public expenditures.

One of the issues widely discussed in our public finance literature is "state budget." The state budget refers to a document containing the revenue and expenditure estimates of the state for a certain period of time and the permission (authorization) given for this document or for the use of this document (Yüksel 2011, p. 1211).

Our country's public finance met the concept of power of the purse and budget organization, in modern sense, for the first time, in the middle of nineteenth century, that is, during the Ottoman Empire and 20 years before the first Constitution proclaimed in 1876. Inspired by the financial system of Western countries, it was aimed to modernize and improve Ottoman finance. However, the budget implementation in the Ottoman Empire from 1855 to 1876 was unsuccessful, despite all efforts, according to some financiers (Erçin 1938).

Divan-ı Muhasebat, which formed the core of the Court of Accounts, was founded in 1863 during the Ottoman Empire.

The constitution of 1876, which allowed the Ottoman Empire to shift to parliamentary monarchy, naturally regulated the "power of the purse". The constitution adopted the principle of the legality of taxes. It was highlighted that the budget was the law showing annual revenue and expenditure estimates, and that imposing, distribution and collection of taxes would be based on the budget law to be enacted every year. The method of discussing the budget in parliament was indicated and the content of the budget law (articles and annexed tables) was specified (Kili and Gözübüyük 1985, pp. 41–42).

Divan-ı Muhasebat has become a constitutional institution when its duties and authorities were regulated in Article 105 of the Constitution of 1876. According to this article, *Divan-ı Muhasebat* would be established to examine (audit) the accounts of the civil servants who are authorized to purchase and spend state assets and inspect the accounts prepared by the departments, and to present its final assessment in this regard to the *Heyeti Mebusan* (chamber of Deputies) each year by means of a special report. In 1878, a Decree was issued to regulate the formation and duties of *Divan-ı Muhasebat.*

Since the Ottoman Parliament was abolished within two years of its inauguration, in 1878, they had to wait until 1908, (Second Constitutional Period) when the Constitution was put into force, to fulfill the requirement of the power of the purse. After that date, efforts were made to modernize Ottoman finance. In 1910, a provisional law (General Accounting Provisional Law) was enacted, which envisaged equipping of public finances and budget with modern principles. The modernization efforts in this area were hampered by the eruption of World War II (Ministry of Finance 2000; Öner 2007)

The 1921 Constitution, composed of very few articles, issued by the Turkish Grand National Assembly under the conditions of the War of Independence, contained no provision related to the power of the purse or other financial issues. In the years of the War of Independence, the yearly budget laws issued by the Grand National Assembly of Turkey took Ottoman budget law as basis and the budgets were carefully discussed in the Turkish Grand National Assembly (Ministry of Finance 1994; Yüksel 2010).

Following the proclamation of the Republic, *Divan-ı Muhasebat* (Court of Accounts) was re-established with the "Law on the Election Procedures of *Divan-ı Muhasebat*" of November 24, 1923 and no. 374. In Article 1 of this Law, which totally consists of 6 articles, it was stated that *Divan-ı Muhasebat* was affiliated to the Grand National Assembly and was obliged to inspect the government revenues and expenditures on its behalf. Apart from the election and dismissal procedures of the president and members, the law did not make any other arrangements.

The provisions of the 1924 Constitution on the power of the purse were largely a repetition of the provisions of 1876 Constitution. The most important difference was that the Constitution of 1924 gave the sovereignty to the nation. According to Article 100 of the 1924 Constitution, *Divan-ı Muhasebat* was established, as affiliated to the Grand National Assembly, which was responsible for auditing the government revenues and expenditures according to a special law.

In 1927, the General Accounting Law, which regulates the management and accounting of all state properties and which will remain in force for approximately 80 years (until the end of 2005), was enacted. According to that Law, which is also referred to as "Constitution of finance," the state property consisted of all kinds of taxes and duties imposed and collected by the State and all cashes, bills and all kinds of movable and immovable properties and their proceedings and yields and sales prices. The budget was defined as "the law that indicates the annual revenue and expenditure estimates of government institutions and organisations and authorises their implementation." The Law, which includes budgetary principles, determines in detail the principles that revenues and expenditures will be subject to, and lists the actors (**authorizing officer**, **assessment officer** and **accountant**) in the financial affairs and transactions together with their duties, powers and responsibilities, and stipulates that the taxes to be collected and the expenditures to be made each fiscal year will be determined by the budget law. The General Accounting Law stipulated that the state budget (budget law) would consist of a text and 7 tables annexed to it.

The General Accounting Law included two other types of budgets, other than the "**general budget**" law: budgets whose expenditures are covered by their own revenues and those managed outside the general budget ("**annexed budget**") and budgets including local expenditures and revenues ("**special budget**"). Draft annexed budget (for example, General Directorate of Post, Telegraph and Telephone) would be submitted to the Parliament by the Ministry of Finance, along with the general budget draft law. The accounts and transactions of annexed and special budgets were subject to the provisions of the General Accounting Law, without prejudice to the written statements in their special laws (Ministry of Finance and Customs 1992). A separate budget law was enacted for each of the annexed budgets of more than 30.

According to Article 1 of the General Accounting Law No. 1050 enacted in 1927, the administration and accounting of all State properties would be subject to this Law. In articles 8, 9, and 10 of the Law, **three important actors of the financial system (assessment officer, bookkeeper/accountant, and authorizing officer)** are defined and in Article 11 the duties of the actors are listed. Accordingly, revenue assessment officers were responsible for assessing and accrual of revenues and proceedings and enabling their collection; expenditure assessment officers were responsible for accrual of expenditures; authorizing officers were responsible for having the accrued expenditures paid; and the accountants (treasurer) were responsible for executing collection and payments. This article and other provisions of the Law on the duties of these actors were of great importance for judicial review of the accounts by *Divan-ı Muhasebat*.

"Law on Court of Accounts" No. 2514, which was enacted in 1934, rearranged the establishment and functioning of the Court of Accounts and abolished the scattered legislation applied until that date. As stipulated in Article 1 of the Law, *Divan-ı Muhasebat* was responsible for inspecting all revenues, expenditures, properties, and accounts of the State on behalf of the Parliament in accordance with the provisions of this law and reviewing and judging the accounts of those who buy and spend State property. Article 11 of the Law lists the duties of *Divan-ı Muhasebat*. The article also provides for the judicial task against the three important actors of the financial system (authorizing officer, assessment officer and accountant), other than auditing duty: the prosecution of the accountants (treasurers) and, where appropriate, the second degree authorizing officers and the accrual officers.

The Constitution of 1961, which adopted a two-assembly parliament, included among the duties and powers of GNAT under Article 64 the following duty and power: "debate and adopt the bills on the State budget and final accounts" in addition to "enacting, amending and abolishing laws." This Constitution regulated the procedure of debate on and adoption of the laws in Article 92, and regulated the procedure of debate on and adoption of the budget laws in Article 94. Another important regulation governing the power of the purse was Article 126. Expenditures of the State and of public corporate bodies other than public economic enterprises would be effected in accordance with the annual budgets. The manner in which the general and annexed budgets are to be drawn up and applied would be defined by law (General Accounting Law). The following sentence of the article was very important in terms of constitutional jurisdiction: "No provisions other than those pertaining to the budget shall be incorporated in the budget law."

Divan-ı Muhasebat was re-established and its functions were redefined under its new name, Turkish Court of Accounts (TCA), by the Constitution of the 1961 in Article 127. Mentioned article assigned the TCA the duties of "auditing all revenues, expenditures and properties of general and annexed budget administrations on behalf of the Grand National Assembly of Turkey, reaching final decision concerning the accounts and transactions of those responsible, and examining, auditing and deciding matters stipulated by laws".

In order to comply with the provisions of the 1961 Constitution, the Turkish Court of Accounts Law No. 832 was enacted in 1967. According to Article 1 of Law No. 832, the TCA The Court of Accounts shall be charged with auditing, on behalf of the Turkish Grand National Assembly, the revenues, expenditures, and property of the government offices financed by the general and annexed budgets; taking final decision by trying the accounts and acts of the responsible officials; and performing other tasks conferred on it by various laws in matters related to examining, auditing, and passing judgement. Article 28 states its judicial duty as, "TCA takes final decision by trying the accounts and acts of the responsible officials."

During the 1961 Constitutional period, the main principles of budget law were set out in the relevant articles of the Constitution, in the General Accounting Law and in the budget laws enacted each year. Yearly draft budgets of annexed budgets of more than 30 were enacted separately. In the 1950s, the number of articles in the "general budget" law, which is between 20 and 25, increased rapidly in the period of 1961 Constitution, reached 105 in 1975, followed by 89-93 articles in the subsequent years. The number of articles in the budget law was 75 in 1981 and 77 in 1982, just before the enforcement of 1982 Constitution.

The Constitution of 1982 also gave the GNAT the duty and power of "discussing and adopting the state's budget and final account laws, other than the duty and authority to "discuss, adopt and repeal laws." Article 161 and the following articles were related to the budget law: The expenditures of the government and public legal entities other than the public economic enterprises, shall be made in accordance with the annual budgets, the beginning of the fiscal year and how the general and annexed budgets will be prepared and implemented will be determined by law. No provisions other than those pertaining to the budget shall be incorporated in the budget law. The manner in which the Budget Commission was established and the way in which the budget would be discussed in the GNAT committees and in the General Assembly were also elaborated.

In the 1982 Constitutional period, the implementation of a separate budget law for each of the annexed budget administrations was quitted and a single annexed budget law was enacted to cover all of the annexed budget administrations: "1985 Fiscal Year Budget Law" and "1985 Fiscal Year Budget Law for Annexed Budget Administrations." This practice continued until 2005 (including 2005).

Public Financial Management and Control Law No. 5018, which abolished the General Accounting Law, abrogated funds and all government revenues and expenditures and the debts were completely covered by the budget and it was ensured that they were subject to legislative review. This way, an important step was taken in order for the Court of Accounts to pass to an audit concept that focuses on the whole financial structure of the institution rather than addressing the transactions individually and to turn it into a more comprehensive report-generating structure. (https://www.sayistay.gov.tr/tr/?p=2&CategoryId=120, Date of access/28.12.2018).

In 2006 and the following years, only one budget law (Central Government Budget Law) started to be enacted for "general budget," "special budget" and "regulatory and supervisory agencies" all of which together constitute "central government" within the framework of the definitions in Law No. 5018. Law No. 5018 has adopted the procedure of Law No. 1050 on the content of budgets: a text and tables annexed to it.

With the TCA Law No. 6085, all activities using public resources were included in the audit scope of the Court of Accounts and the Prime Ministry Supreme Auditing Board, which audits state-owned enterprises, was incorporated into the Court of Auditors, and thus, the dual structure in external audit was terminated. With this Law, the TCA has been repositioned in line with today's conditions, international standards and contemporary developments in management and auditing.

Considering the number of articles in the budgets (general budget) enacted during the 1982 Constitutional period, it is obvious that in the period of 1984–1995 the number of articles was between 60-70. In the period of 1984–2001, the number of articles was 70 and over and in 2002–2005 such number constantly fell down from 63 to 39. During 1984–2005 the number of articles in the annexed budget law was in the range of 10–20. In 2006 and the following years, when the central government budget law was enacted, the number of articles in the budget law fell steadily: 34 in 2006 and 15 in 2018.

Power of the purse which was introduced to Turkish legal system by the Constitution of 1876, has been rendered even more functional by the constitutional and legal regulations and through implementations within 143 years, and it became a constitutional principle of the legal system. The Court of Accounts, which is authorized and charged with the judicial review of budget implementations, has an important function in the establishment of the power of the purse. With the introduction of the rule of law to the Turkish legal system under the 1961 Constitution, the Constitutional Court started to conduct the constitutional review of the budget law. Constitutional review of the budget law in Turkey has a history and experience of over half a century.

9.3 Judicial Review of Budget (Budget Implementations) in Turkey

The duty and power of determining whether public expenditures are duly made in the Turkish legal system and whether they are made in a way intended for performance or not (Mutluer et al. 2011) is assigned to the TCA. Today, TCA is one of the most fundamental and respected institutions of the Constitutional system, with the auditing and judicial function it assumes on behalf of the GNAT.

The auditing duty and the judicial function of the TCA are regulated in Article 160 of the Constitution. Accordingly, the Court of Auditors is in charge with auditing all revenues, expenditures, and properties of the public administrations included in the central government budget and those of social security institutions and taking final decision about the accounts and transactions of those responsible to check on behalf of the Grand National Assembly of Turkey, reaching final decision concerning the accounts and transactions of those responsible, and examining, auditing, and taking final decision concerning the matters stipulated by laws. The TCA shall also audit and finalise the accounts and transactions of local administrations.

During the Ottoman Empire, the duties and powers of the responsible in the Turkish public financial management established in 1910 were strictly regulated and subject to the judicial review of *Divan-ı Muhasebat*.

In the General Accounting Law No. 1050, which was enacted in 1927, **assessment officer, bookkeeper/accountant, and authorizing officer** were considered three important actors of the financial system. Revenue assessment officers were responsible for assessing and accrual of revenues and proceedings and enabling their collection; expenditure assessment officers were responsible for accrual of expenditures; authorizing officers were responsible for having the accrued expenditures paid; and the accountants (treasurer) were responsible for executing collection and payments. This article and other provisions of the Law on the duties of these actors were of great importance for the judicial review of the accounts by *Divan-ı Muhasebat*.

Article 2 of the TCA Law No. 6085, which was enacted in 2010, defines regularity audit as a type of regularity audit, defines **compliance audit** as, "audit pertaining to the examination of the compliance of accounts and transactions related to the revenues, expenditures and assets of public administrations with laws and other legal arrangements" and defines **trial of account** as, "taking final decision by judicial procedure on whether the accounts and transactions of those responsible specified in laws are in compliance with the legislation, and the legal remedies related to this." According to the TCA Law, the public loss refers to the "public loss specified in the Public Financial Management and Control Law".

Article 71 of Law No. 5018 defines the public loss as "bringing an obstacle to the increase or causing a decrease in the public resource as a result of a decision, transaction or action that violates the legislation and that stems from intention, flaw or negligence of public officers" and regulates in detail the issues to be considered when determining the public loss.

According to article 5 of TCA Law no. 6085 the duties of TCA are as follows:

(a) to audit the financial activities, decisions and transactions of public administrations within the framework of accountability and submit accurate, sufficient, timely information and reports to the Turkish Grand National Assembly on the results of these audits;
(b) to audit whether or not accounts and transactions of public administrations within the scope of the general government with respect to their revenues, expenditures, and assets are in compliance with laws and other legal arrangements, and **take final decision on matters related to public loss arising from the accounts and transactions of those responsible;**
(c) to submit the Statement of General Conformity to the Grand National Assembly of Turkey;
(d) to perform the duties of examining, auditing, and taking final decision prescribed by laws.

The TCA fulfills its duties in accordance with the mentioned provision of the Constitution and the TCA Law No. 6085. In the event of any conflict during the audit, which is its main function, the matter is transferred to the TCA judiciary.

Articles 48–53 of the TCA Law regulates the "Trial of Account." "Where a matter resulting in public loss is detected by auditors in the course of audits of the accounts and transactions of public administrations within the scope of the general government, defence statements of those responsible shall be taken, and judicial reports shall be prepared as of the end of the fiscal year (Article 48). The procedure for the execution of TCA writs is provided in Article 53. Accordingly, the writs of TCA shall be executed within 90 days after they become final. Heads of public administrations to whom writs are sent shall be responsible for the implementation of the writ. The amount of indemnification stated in the writ shall be subject to interest, as defined in laws, as of the date of decision, and shall be collected in accordance with the provisions of Law on the Execution and Bankruptcy.

The judicial activity of the TCA begins with the results of compliance audits. In its Decision Docket No. 2011/21, D.: 2013/3 taken upon a request for annulment concerning TCA Law, the Constitutional Court stated, "… TCA carries out a judicial activity in terms of its duty of taking final decision about the accounts and transactions of the responsible persons and in this framework, its decisions are deemed rulings as which are final, and no application to or appeal in any authority or institution including the judicial bodies is allowed against such rulings, and it is concluded that TCA is a court of account which takes decisions with judicial results." According to the Constitutional Court, the TCA carries out a judicial activity with respect to the duty of finalising the accounts and transactions of those responsible. TCA is a court of account that makes decisions with judicial results.

In terms of trial of account, the Law no. 1050, which remained in force until 2006, did not consider whether there had been any intent, flaw or negligence of the officer performing the transaction, except for some special cases; i.e., perfect responsibility was taken as basis. Law No. 5018, which has been in force since 2006, is completely different from the Law no. 1050 on this matter and has made the responsibility a defective responsibility (Mutluer et al. 2011, p. 482).

The actors in the public financial management introduced by the Law No. 5018 are the **head of public administration, authorizing officers, realization officer and accounting officer**.

According to Article 11 of Law No. 5018, the head of public administration is the highest administrator in the ministries and other public administrations, whereas it is the governor in special provincial administrations and the mayor in municipalities (Until June 24, 2018, head of public administration was the undersecretary in the ministries). The President determines the highest administrator in the ministries.

The heads of public administrations are accountable to the Minister for fulfilling the duties and responsibilities set out in the second paragraph of Article 11, and to their local councils in local administrations. The heads of public administrations fulfills the requirements of this responsibility through authorizing officers, the financial services unit and internal auditors.

In accordance with Article 31 of the Law, Head of each spending unit to which appropriation is allocated with the budget is the **authorizing officer**. The article indicates how to determine the authorize spending and the authorizing officers in different situations. Authorizing officers may effect expenditures up to the amount of the appropriation foreseen in the budget and authorizing officers who are supplied with the appropriations via appropriation dispatch document may effect expenditures up to the amount of appropriation allocated

According to Article 33 of the Law, The realization of the expenditures shall be completed when the payment order, which is prepared by the person determined by the authorizing officers, is signed by the authorizing officer and upon the payment of the due amount to the rightful person. Upon the spending instruction, **realization officers** shall perform the duties of having the work to be done, receiving goods or services, completing the receiving formalities, documenting and issuing the documents required for payment. Realization officers shall be responsible for the duties and transactions they should perform in the framework of this Law.

According to the Article 61 of the Law, accounting services include; collecting revenues and receivables; making payments to the payees; receiving, keeping, and sending to the concerned authorities the deposits and the values that can be expressed as money; and keeping records of all other financial transactions as well as issuing reports thereon. Persons performing these transactions shall be **accounting officers**. The civil service positions and titles shall have no effect on being qualified as the accounting officer. The accounting officer is responsible for performing these services and duly keeping accounting records transparent and accessible.

Accounting officers are responsible for the provisions regarding payment included under second paragraph of article 34 and for controlling of payments stated in the third paragraph of this article. The duty of the authorizing officer and accounting officer cannot be combined on one person. Those performing ex-ante control duty in the financial services unit cannot be on duty in the financial transaction process.

According to Law No. 5018, the main responsibility rests with the authorizing officer. However, the accounting officer and the realization officer assume some responsibilities within the framework of the duties stipulated in the Law No. 5018. In accordance with Law No. 5018, ministers are accountable to the President of the

Republic for effective, economic, and efficient use of public resources (from 2006, when the Law no. 5018 entered into force, to June 24, 2018, they were accountable to the Prime Minister and the Parliament).

The heads of public administrations are accountable to the Minister for fulfilling the responsibilities set out in Article 11 of the Law no 5018, and to their local councils in local administrations.

Law No. 5018 enacted in 2003 reorganised the Turkish public financial management and control system with a different approach, which directly affected the TCA's judicial review of budget implementations. Arrangements have been made in line with international norms with regard to auditing and the responsible who are subject to audit as well as their responsibilities, and the principle of conducting financial management and control under the management responsibility of public administrations has been adopted. It is envisaged that public administrations be subject to regularity and performance audits, and public officials be accountable for both in terms of compliance and performance due to their financial transactions. The balance of authority and responsibility was tried to be established during the public spending process, and the audit was conducted before, during, and after the implementation phase; and it was intended to create an efficient internal control, internal audit, and ex-ante financial control system. The scope of the external audit was extended in a way to be left to TCA. Law No. 5018 stipulated reporting activities to ensure the transparency of public activities, introduced the accountability rule, advised the budget to be formulated in a certain scope, avoiding going beyond that scope and tried to ensure fiscal discipline this way, foresaw performance indicators and made accounting systems accrual based. The new TCA No. 6085 was enacted in 2010 in accordance with the approach adopted by Law No. 5018. The Law No. 6085 both modernized the audit procedure of the TCA and expanded its audit area.

Law No. 5018 tried to establish the balance of authority and responsibility during the public spending process and accountability was highlighted. However, it drew up a responsibility area which was too wide and the responsibilities have not been clearly defined. The law mostly refers to fiscal responsibility under the name of accountability. With the entry into force of the Law No. 5018, "internal control" gained importance, and importance was also attached to making the financial decisions and transactions be subject to performance audits in order to determine whether public resources are managed within the framework of the principles of economy, effectiveness, and efficiency, apart from being subject to audit in terms of their compliance with the legislation. However, the fact that the institutions do not have an adequate infrastructure and adequate knowledge and experience limit the feasibility of performance audits.

Risk analysis should be conducted in order to establish, implement, monitor, and develop internal control systems in public administrations. In line with the organizational structure, authorities, duties, and responsibilities of the institutions defined in the legislation, a large number of business processes and a large number of control products are available, yet the infrastructure for ensuring the existing structures to meet the criteria set has not been completed. Therefore, internal control systems in public institutions cannot be adequately audited and generating data or making evaluations related to internal control systems in public administrations are not sufficiently possible.

As internal control standards have not been established yet, internal audit units of institutions have not yet been able to adequately assess their internal control systems. The current audits are performed by internal audit units within the framework of relevant legislation and activities carried out. Furthermore, the existence of an independent internal audit system will ensure the establishment of an efficient and transparent financial management and control system. However, internal audit units do not yet have an independence at international standards. There are also deficiencies in the perception of internal audit. What the internal auditing focuses on is to ensure that the system operates at a desired level in a way to obtain and use the institutional resources effectively, economically, and efficiently, not to find the shortcomings, defects or errors of the employees. Failure to clarify the organizational structure of the internal audit units and how they will be managed cause the internal audit units to remain weak.

9.4 Judicial Review of the Constitutionality of Budget Law (Constitutional Court)

9.4.1 1961 Constitutional Period

Upon the first application made in 1965, the Constitutional Court first looked for answers to the following questions on the nature, scope, and situation of the budget laws: Can the "budget laws" be considered as "laws" before the Constitution and the legal system? Can the tables contained in the budget laws be considered as a whole together with the text of the law? Are the budget laws subject to constitutional jurisdiction?

According to the Constitutional Court's statement in its Decision Docket No.1965/19, D. 1965/42, although there are debates in the doctrine over the definition of formal and material law, the provisions of the Constitution and the General Accounting Law clearly and unquestionably show that the budget is a law. The articles of budget law and the tables annexed to these articles together form the "budget law." Like other laws, budget laws may be subject of annulment cases.

The Court, having examined the request for annulment on the merits (on the basis of the spending formulas included in R-signed tables annexed to Article 16 of the Budget Law), rules that the spending formulas were in violation of Article 82 of the Constitution and annulled the spending formulas.

The second lawsuit in constitutional jurisdiction was filed in 1968 for the 1968 Fiscal Year Budget Law with the claim that the provisions of budget law were in conflict with the Constitution. The subject of the case was the request for annulment of relevant provision of the Budget Law with the claim that the Budget Law provision which stipulated that the Civil Servants Law would not be applied in the fiscal year of 1968 and until entry into force of General Cadre Law was in conflict with the last paragraph of Article 126 of the Constitution (No provisions other than those pertaining to the budget shall be incorporated in the budget law).

As stated by the Court in its Decision Docket No. 1968/24, D. 1969/4, the provision of the Budget Law, which is requested to be annulled, postpones the enforcement of some provisions of the Civil Servants Law to an indefinite date in the fiscal year of 1968. The regulation subject to annulment request includes a provision which has been duly discussed and approved and which amends an "ordinary" clause of the law declared in accordance with the Constitution.

According to the Court, the statements "enacting, amending and repealing laws" and "debating and adopting the "draft budget laws" included in Article 64 of the Constitution are two separate power groups. In other words, enacting laws, making amendments to a law that enacted before or repealing a law is the savings of the GNAT with the same nature. Budgets are a kind of "special nature" power of the GNAT. As a natural result of the powers stated separately for "budget laws" and "ordinary laws" under Article 64 of the Constitution, the draft budget laws or draft amendments to the budget laws are debated and adopted in accordance with the procedures the budgets are subject to, whereas other draft laws and draft amendments to such laws are debated and adopted in accordance with the procedures they are subject to. The provision of Article 64 of the Constitution considers budget laws as a kind of law different from ordinary laws. One of the rules of the law is that to amend or abolish a document created in accordance with certain procedures is only possible by going through the same procedures. If it is necessary to change the enforcement dates of the law by postponing entry into force of some articles of the Civil Servants Law, a draft law to be prepared in this way shall be submitted to the GNAT, be subject to the procedures on draft laws and enacted in accordance with the principles under Articles 91–93 of the Constitution. The fact that the regulation to be made by the ordinary law is made by the budget law is in conflict with the intent of Article 64. The Budget Law arrangement which is the subject of the request must be annulled.

The Court draws attention to the enactment processes during 1924 and 1961 Constitutional periods.

> "… The Constitution of 1924 contained exactly the same and a single procedure for debating and adopting budget laws and other laws in the Grand National Assembly of Turkey. (…)
>
> Therefore, in the former practice, it was possible and common to place, in any law, an appropriation item related to budget, and to place, in budget laws, a provision related to other laws.
>
> However, as per the provisions of the 1961 Constitution, it was not possible to place, in the draft laws, an appropriation clause related to budget. Because, as explained above, the debate and adoption procedures of the articles of a draft law which are not related to budget are different from the articles related to budget. In this case, it is not possible to combine the provisions of a separate nature in a draft arrangement…"

The Court examined the request within the framework of the statement "No provisions other than those pertaining to the budget shall be incorporated in the budget law" included under article 126 of the Constitution.

> "...The statement of the last sentence of Article 126 of the Constitution (the provision related to budget) must be considered as explanatory provisions with regard to the budget implementations, facilitating or completing the practice, not in the sense of the provision of a financial nature, provided that it is not a new provision which may be a subject of law.
>
> Accordingly, the fact that a provision of law requires spending from the budget cannot be a reason for it to be considered a provision related to budgetary provision provided for in Article 126. Because almost every law can have one or more provisions that require spending from the budget..."

The Court ruled that the provision of the Budget Law which was subject of annulment request was in conflict with the provisions of Articles 64, 92, and 126 of the Constitution. This assessment based on the distinction of "ordinary law-budget law" and the criteria of "being relate to budget" stated in the relevant provision was transformed into case-law for the 1961 and 1982 constitutions (Yüksel 1993).

"Provisional" budget law no. 1789, which was enacted for 1974, was argued to be contrary to various articles of the Constitution and these articles were requested to be annulled.

The Court firstly examined the constitutionality of the provisional budget organization which was not regulated in the Constitution and the Law No. 1050. According to the Court, Law No. 1789 was a real "budget law" in the sense of both a provisional law and in terms of its main issues, and it was enacted in accordance with the methods laid down by the Constitution for the debate on budgets. The fact that the provisional budget law is not, as envisaged in Article 126 of the Constitution, annual and covers a maximum period of three months cannot change its nature. In exceptional cases entailed by the requirements and necessities of state life, although the main rule is annual budget, the work may be carried out with provisional budgets, and under the condition that ordinary budgets are made on annual basis, a mandatory and provisional measure such as "provisional budget" is not in violation with the Constitution.

The Court found that the provisional budget law was amending a provision of an ordinary law and annulled the articles which are subject of annulment request, on the basis of its justifications in its Decision Docket No. 1974/9, D. 1974/22 on the 1968 Budget Act. The provisional budget organization was included in the Public Financial Management and Control Law, entered into force in 2006, and also in the Constitution, through 2017 amendment.

9.4.2 *1982 Constitutional Period*

During 1982 Constitutional period, the first of the Constitutional Court decisions on the budget laws was given on the annulment request for a total of 5 articles of the 1990 Fiscal Year Budget Law. The importance of the mentioned first Decision Merit 1990/6, D. 1990/17 of the 1982 Constitutional period was to show the stance of the Court regarding the annulment requests for budget laws in the new constitutional period. The decision commented on the constitutional jurisdiction as follows:

> ...As stated in the rationale of Article 161 of the Constitution, budget laws are separate from other laws. If, as a requirement of this constitutional principle, a rule of law can be amended by a rule of law of the same nature, then the budget laws can also be made in the same manner with a budget law amended drafted and adopted in the same way, as a natural result of that, a rule of law cannot be amended and abolished with a budget law nor a budget law can be amended and abolished with a rule of law in general sense. The term 'provisions related to budget', which must be understood as explanatory provisions, also points at an obligation provided that the budget does not cover a rule which is related to the implementation of the budget, which facilitates implementation and which may be the subject of a law. ...

The Court did not consider as facilitating the implementation of the budget or explanatory the provision of the 1990 Fiscal Year Budget Law which was subject of request for annulment, and it annulled that provision which was not related to the budget and in conflict with the constitutional principle, especially Article 161 of the Constitution. Considering the Decisions Docket No. 1991/16, D. 1991/19 and Docket No.1991/37, D. 1991/44, the interpretation made by the Court in 1961 Constitutional period on "Provision related to budget" was stuck to in 1982 constitutional period.

According to the 1982 Constitution, the annulment decisions of the Constitutional Court could not be explained without justification. However, the writing of decisions involving long justifications lasted a month, sometimes a few months. An article which had been annulled by the Court could not be enforced because of the delay in writing the justification of annulment.

With the application made to the Constitutional Court in 1993 with the request of the annulment of certain provisions of a decree, it was also requested to cease the execution of the provisions of which are subject of the request for annulment.

Upon that request, the Court stayed the execution of the provision of Decree which it had annulled with its Decision Docket No. 1993/33, D. 1993/40-1, in order to prevent any situation which could be difficult and impossible to remedy which might stem from application, until the annulment decision took effect. The inclusion of the institution "stay of execution" in the constitutional jurisdiction somehow was important not only for other laws and decrees but also for the budget laws; maybe even more important. Because, the rationale of the decisions that ruled the requests for the annulment of the budget law provisions was explained mostly after the end of the fiscal year and the annulment decisions were not functional since the fiscal year ended. In the new case, when the annulment of the provision of the budget law was decided in March, the Court could stay the enforcement of the provision on the same day in a short decision, to prevent any situation which could be difficult and impossible to remedy which might stem from application, until the annulment decision took effect. As a matter of fact, shortly afterward, on the same day with the annulment decision of June 1995 with regard to 1995 budget, the execution of 13 clauses of the budget law was stayed with Decision Docket No. 1995/2, D. Stay of Execution 1995/1. Upon stay of execution of many articles of the 1996 budget in the middle of the fiscal year, a draft law was rapidly enacted by Law No. 4160 to ensure that some provisions included in the budget laws are regulated in the relevant laws. Stay of execution is a meaningful and effective institution for disciplining budget law.

In its Decision Docket No. 2015/7, D. 2016/47 as a result of request for the annulment of some provisions of 2015 Central Government Budget Law, the Constitutional Court added a new criterion, "**power of the purse**," to its other two criteria which it had been using for a long time.

According to the court, power of the purse means that the legislature vests the authority, with set limits, to the executive to collect and to spend government revenues on behalf of the public and audits the results. "Power of the purse" refers to the power to determine and approve the type and amount of taxes, similar revenues, and public expenditures. Such power belongs to the legislative body composed of representatives elected by the public. The budget is the basic responsibility mechanism of the government against the Parliament. The Parliament authorizes the government, through budget, to collect revenues and spend, and audits the proper use of this power through final account law, which is part of the budget process.

According to the Court, considering the structure of the budget, it is possible for the budget to function well as long as the basic budgetary principles are respected. Budgetary principles mean the rules to be considered in relation to preparation, debate on, approval and auditing of the budget. These principles are nationally and internationally recognized principles that are essential for the realization of the basic characteristics and objectives of government budgets.

The Court, explaining power of the purse approach this way with reference to the budgetary principles, decided that the power vested to the legislature to collect and spend government revenues on behalf of the public, had partly been given to the ministers or institutions concerned with the rules which are subject of the case, and thus vested broad powers without being subject to any limitations in an unspecified area. In addition to the principle "No provisions other than those pertaining to the budget shall be incorporated in the budget law," the Court stated that **it also violates power of the purse of the Parliament**. Even though the power of the purse criterion has been used alongside the other two criteria, an innovation has emerged in the case-law of the Constitutional Court regarding this issue. The court can now use the power of the purse criterion more frequently in terms of budgetary laws.

Until recently, the provisions contained in the tables annexed to the budget laws were not much of a subject for annulment requests. Especially after 2010, it is observed that the annulment requests for the provisions of table (E) have increased and some of these requests have resulted in annulment.

At least one annulment and/or stay of execution decision was taken regarding almost every year's budget law between 1990–2018. Number of the articles annulled, either wholly or partly, was 11 in 1996, 18 in 1991, and 19 in 1995 (Yüksel 2007, p. 135).

It is understood that 4 articles were annulled in 1990, 1 article was annulled in 1993'te, 3 articles were annulled in 1994, 1 article was annulled in 1997, 5 articles were annulled in 1998, 1 article was annulled in 1999, 6 articles were annulled in 2001, 4 articles were annulled in 2002, 11 articles were annulled in 2003, 8 articles were annulled in 2004, 2005, and 2006 per each, 2 articles were annulled in 2007, 1 article was annulled in 2009, 3 articles were annulled in 2015, 2 articles were annulled in 2016, and 1 article was annulled in 2017.

Budget laws consist of a text and annexed tables. From 1962 to 1984 when the constitutional jurisdiction began functioning, a budget law (general budget) and more than 30 annexed budget laws were enacted in each fiscal year, each of which was amended at least once during the fiscal year. As of 1984, as a requirement of the approach of the 1982 Constitution, a budget law (general budget) and only one "annexed budget administrations budget law" were started to be enacted in every fiscal year. In 2006 and the following years, in accordance with the provisions of the Law No. 5018, only one budget law (Central Government Budget Law) was started to be enacted for the administrations within the scope of general budget and the annexed budget administrations.

In 2005 and previous years, the total number of articles of the "general budget" and "annexed budget" laws enacted in accordance with the General Accounting Law was around 80–90. In 2006 and the following years, several laws have been enacted in order to eliminate budgetary provisions that are not related to the budget. As a result of this elimination and the fact that the Public Financial Management and Control Law stipulated that only one budget law shall be issued under the name of "Central Government Budget Law" for each fiscal year, number of articles in budget laws began to fell firstly to 30s and then 15, as was the case in 2018. "Considering the ideal number of articles in the budget laws, current constitutional provisions and interpretation style in constitutional jurisdiction, it should not exceed 15" (Yüksel 2007, p. 153). When "maximum 15 articles" was foreseen, it was assumed that the subjects which are obliged to be governed in budget laws, as a minimum requirement, (expenditure, revenue, balance, table notes, explanations of budgetary transactions and Treasury transactions and some other issues provided that the Constitutional limits are respected) would be subject of separate articles. This reduction in the number of articles was similarly reflected in the decrease in the number of pages and words (Yüksel 1999, 2000, 2012).

9.5 Conclusion and Evaluation

This chapter addresses judicial review of budget implementations (accounts and transactions of the responsible) by TCA and the audit by the Constitutional Court on compliance of budget laws with the constitution.

From the founding of the Republic until 2003, in nearly 80 years, the TCA has carried out a judicial review of the budget implementations within the framework of the relevant constitutional arrangements, the TCA Law and the provisions of the Law no. 1050 and the approach adopted by them. In 2003, Law No. 5018 with a different approach was enacted. The prerequisite for the success of judicial review of the Court of Accounts is the good construction and good functioning of the new public financial management and control system stipulated by Law No. 5018.

It is difficult to say that the new approach introduced by Law No. 5018 is sufficiently internalized in public financial management and an efficient internal control system has been created. As mentioned in the relevant section, many problems are encountered. The internalization of the approach will obviously take some more time. While the fact that the audit procedure of the TCA is amended and modernized and the judicial review area of TCA on budget is expanded through new TCA Law in 2010 is a positive development, some problems are encountered regarding the mentioned audit. With its increased duties regarding audit and reporting, the TCA should increase its administrative capacity and make its audit approach compatible with the new approach envisaged by the Law No. 5018 shortly. More importantly, the success of the external audit of a public administration (TCA audit) is related to the success of internal control and internal audit. The success of the TCA reporting and the level of importance attributed to these reports by the legislative body have a direct impact on the success of external audit.

The number of decisions on which the Constitutional Court concluded requests for the annulment of certain provisions of the budget laws upon the requests submitted to itself in the period of 1962–2018 has already exceeded 100. Except for the inclusion of the stay of execution in constitutional jurisdiction in 1993, no material amendment was made to the Constitutional provisions governing the constitutional jurisdiction, and the arrangements of 1961 and 1982 Constitutions on constitutional jurisdiction were, in a way, maintained. In 2006, the law regulating the financial system (General Accounting Law) was replaced by another law with a different content and philosophy (Public Financial Management and Control Law). The criteria developed by the Court in assessing the constitutionality of the provisions of the budget law remained the same in both constitutional periods, despite the minor changes in the constitutional arrangements and the replacement of the Law 1050 by the Law No. 5018. It can easily be said that the case-law has stabilized.

In its numerous decisions in which it finalized the requests for the annulment/stay of execution of the provisions of the Budget Law, the Constitutional Court used two criteria referred to below in the period of 1962–2018 and based its decisions on its case-law based on these criteria ("violation of power of purse" was used as the third criterion in 2016 and 2017).

- Budget law is a type of law different from other laws, as can be understood from the provisions of the 1961 and 1982 Constitutions that regulate the duties of the GNAT. The Constitution maker regulates the procedures for the enactment and amendment of these two types of laws in different ways. The procedure set for a type of law should not be applied to another type of law (**separation of ordinary law—budget law**).
- No provisions other than "those pertaining to the budget" shall be incorporated in the budget law as clearly laid down in 1961 and 1982 Constitutions. Provided that it does not cover a rule that may be the subject of a law, the words "those pertaining to the budget" are the regulations that explain the budget and facilitate its implementation **("relevancy" of provision to the budget)**.

The articles included in the budget laws in the period of 1962–2018 can be gathered under three groups in terms of the possibility of being subject to annulment/stay of execution.

The first group of provisions are the provisions that are explicitly stated in "ordinary" laws or in the laws regulating the financial system (General Accounting Law/Public Financial Management and Control Law) to be included in budget laws. To the extent that they comply with the reference in "ordinary" laws or in the laws regulating the financial system and do not exceed the limits specified therein, it is almost impossible for the provisions of this group to be subject to annulment/stay of execution.

"Provisions not applicable" as referred to in the 1990s, "Provisions not applicable either wholly or partly" as referred to in the following years or "other provisions related to revenues or expenditures" as referred to in the last few years constitute the **second group provisions**. These are the articles that are subject to claims of unconstitutionality the most, since they are the provisions of "ordinary laws" which are stated to be not applicable, not applicable either wholly or partly, or applicable in different manner. Provisions included in this group are those with the highest probability of annulment.

The articles which are not included in the two groups above and which regulate different subjects constitute **third group of provisions** (other articles). In court decisions, dissenting vote letters are written the most when finalizing the requests for annulment of such kind of articles. This proves the fact that the members of the Court often hesitate about the constitutionality of the provision subject of the annulment request and that they cannot reach a decision easily (Yüksel 2007, p. 139).

Why the unconstitutional provisions are still inserted in the budget laws, despite the case-law of the Constitutional Court and even its stabilized case-law (Soysal 1986)?

- As the unconstitutionality of the provisions concerned cannot be understood, some provisions that are in violation of the constitution may have been inserted in the budget draft law/budget proposal text. Even members of the Court cannot agree on certain provisions.
- Due to blockages in ordinary law-making processes, the provisions which will probably be subject of an annulment request are included in the budget laws. Because, this way relevant provision is guaranteed to be enacted without causing any dispute between the articles of budget law (through concealing to some extent) and before the fiscal year begins. In the 1990s, when the coalition governments were in the scene, it was sometimes so difficult to enact ordinary law that the governments preferred to put into the budget laws the issues which included any measure that they intended to put into practice together with the fiscal year and that they attached importance. Without prejudice to the legislative process, it is necessary to review the Rules of Procedure of the GNAT and to ensure the efficient functioning of the GNAT in order to eliminate the blockages in the ordinary law-making process.
- The fact that the provisions annulled in previous years are inserted into the budget laws in the following year or years, despite clear and explicit stance of the Supreme Court on that matter is an evidence of the low degree of diligence shown in taking

into account the decisions of constitutional jurisdiction or stubborn approach taken from time to time.

As is known, the budget laws only apply to the fiscal year which they relate to. After the end of the fiscal year, the annulments and/or annulment decisions made regarding the budget laws will not function. For this reason, and in order to make the constitutionality audit of budget laws more efficient, the Constitutional Court should promptly finalise the requests related to the budget law and efficiently make use of stay of execution.

References

Canbay, T., Gerger, G. Ç. (2012), Batı'da Bütçe Hakkının Gelişiminin Toplumsal Yapının Değişimi Üzerindeki Etkileri, In K. Gerger (Eds.), *Mali Sosyoloji Üzerine Denemeler* (pp. 159–194). Ankara, Turkey: Maliye Bakanlığı Strateji Geliştirme Başkanlığı.

Erçin, C. (1938). *Bütçe Nazariyat ve Tatbikatı*. İstanbul, Turkey: Devlet Basımevi.

https://www.sayistay.gov.tr/tr/?p=2&CategoryId=120 Erişim/28.12.2018.

Kaboğlu, İ. Ö. (1994), *Anayasa Yargısı*, Ankara, Turkey, İmge Kitabevi.

Kili, S., Gözübüyük, A. Ş. (1985). *Türk Anayasa Metinleri 'Senedi İttifaktan Günümüze'*. İstanbul, Turkey: Türkiye İş Bankası Kültür Yayınları.

Maliye Bakanlığı (1994). *Milli Mücadele Dönemi Bütçeleri ve Mali Mevzuatı (1920–1923)*. Ankara, Turkey: Maliye Bakanlığı Bütçe ve Mali Kontrol Genel Müdürlüğü.

Maliye Bakanlığı, (2000). *Osmanlı Bütçeleri: 1909–1918*. Ankara, Turkey: Maliye Bakanlığı Araştırma Planlama ve Koordinasyon Kurulu Başkanlığı.

Maliye ve Gümrük Bakanlığı (1992). *Genel Bütçe Kanunları: Kanun Maddeleri, A (Ödenek) Cetvelleri, B (Gelir) Cetvelleri, H (Harcırah) Cetvelleri, Cilt I (1924–1970), Cilt II (1971–1991)*. Ankara, Turkey: Maliye ve Gümrük Bakanlığı Bütçe ve Mali Kontrol Genel Müdürlüğü.

Mutluer, M. K., Öner, E., Kesik, A. (2011). *Bütçe Hukuku*, İstanbul, Turkey, Bilgi Üniversitesi.

Öden, M. (1999). Cumhuriyetin 75. Yıldönümünde Anayasa Yargısı, *A.Ü.H.F. Dergisi*, 49(1), 23–37. (DERGİ j.)

Öner, E. (2007). *Osmanlı Bütçeleri Osmanlı Muvazene Defterleri (1864, 1868, 1877, 1880, 1897)*. Ankara, Turkey: Maliye Bakanlığı Strateji Geliştirme Başkanlığı.

Soysal, M. (1986). *100 Soruda Anayasanın Anlamı*. İstanbul, Turkey, Gerçek Yayınevi.

Yüksel, N. (1993). *Bütçe Kanunlarının Anayasaya Uygunluğunun Yargısal Denetimi ve Anayasa Mahkemesi Kararları (1961–1992)*. Ankara, Turkey: Maliye ve Gümrük Bakanlığı Bütçe ve Mali Kontrol Genel Müdürlüğü.

Yüksel, N. (1999). *Anayasa Yargısında Bütçe Yasaları (1993–1998)*. Ankara, Turkey: Maliye Bakanlığı Bütçe ve Mali Kontrol Genel Müdürlüğü.

Yüksel, N. (2000). 1990'lı Yıllarda Bütçe Yasaları. *Mülkiye*, 225, 162–168. (j.1305-9971.x)

Yüksel, N. (2007). Türk Anayasa Yargısında Arındırma(ma) Sorunu: Bütçe Yasası ve Anayasa Yargısı. *Yasama Dergisi*, 6, 113–155. j.1306-6250.x.

Yüksel, N. (2010). Cumhuriyetin İlk Bütçesi: Coşku, Gurur ve Kaygı. *Maliye Dergisi*, 159, 299–322. (j.1300.1323.x)

Yüksel, N. (2011). Bütçe Üzerinden Dört Tarz-ı Siyaset, In Serdar Şahinkaya & İ. Ertuğrul (Eds.) *Bilsay Kuruç'a Armağan* (1211– 1240). Ankara, Turkey: Mülkiyeliler Birliği.

Yüksel, N. (2012). Anayasa Yargısında 'Olağan'lık ve 'İlgili'lik: Bütçe Yasaları, In Alparslan Altan & Engin Yıldırım & Erdal Tercan & Hikmet Tülen & Ali Rıza Çoban (Eds.) *Anayasa Mahkemesinin 50. Yılına Armağan*. (599–640). Ankara, Turkey: Anayasa Mahkemesi.

Nahit Yüksel Ph.D. is a Treasury and Finance Specialist at General Directorate of Public Financial Management and Transformation, Ministry of Treasury and Finance, Republic of Turkey. He has a Ph.D. degree in political science. He is a published professional with four books and various chapters of books as well on political financing, provisional budget and public housing in Turkey and other countries, and constitutional jurisdiction. He has been a Certified Public Internal Auditor since 2011. His proceeding on the "pursuits of democracy in 1930s Turkey" was submitted to the VI. International Congress on Ataturk and published in the Proceeding Book of the Congress. Besides, he has published many articles on various themes including public administration, budget law, regulatory impact analysis, Turkish law of parliament, history of Budget Committee of Grand National Assembly of Turkey, constitutional jurisdiction, political financing, law of parliament, rule of law and ideological orientations in Turkish media, and all these were published in journals. His article on legislative performances of Turkey and Eurpean countries has already been at publishing stage.

Chapter 10
The Role of Parliament in Budget Process

Hilal Tezcan

10.1 Introduction

As is known, parliaments or congresses are one of the three main powers in a democracy and the checks and balances in a government are crucial to control the governmental branches. Developments in public finance history since the Magna Carta brought the notion power of the purse in the limelight and made the budgets one of the most important mediums for the legislation to control the execution branch of the governments. The budget process consists of various stages such as social demands, determination of the major policy priorities, legislation, execution, auditing, and control. Participation of the parliament in the budget process is normally concentrated on two of these stages which are the examination and approval of budget bill and the auditing of the public accounts (Yılmaz and Biçer 2010). Within this context, legislation reflects the whole society's preferences and makes governments more accountable via power of the purse.

Since budgets are technical documents as well as being political, parliaments should be eligible to scrutinize those documents and should play an active role in budget process. Otherwise, budgets reflect the preferences of the execution branch of the government and more particularly the preferences of bureaucrats rather than people's (Lienert 2013). For this reason, the legislature's active engagement in the budget process is of utmost importance for good governance and fiscal transparency. If budgets are debated and approved by legislation, they are more likely to be owned by the most (Lienert 2010).

In practice, however, there are two main problems related to legislation's involvement in the budget process. One of these problems is the budget illiteracy of the deputies to scrutinize budgets since the budgeting systems are getting more complicated in modern governmental systems (Posner and Park 2007). The other one is that

H. Tezcan (✉)
Head of Department, Presidency of Strategy and Budget, Ankara, Turkey
e-mail: hilaltezcan@gmail.com

H. Kıral and T. Akdemir (eds.), *Public Financial Management Reforms in Turkey: Progress and Challenges, Volume 1*, Accounting, Finance, Sustainability, Governance & Fraud: Theory and Application, https://doi.org/10.1007/978-981-15-1914-7_10

deputies represent their own electorates and they may try to increase funds for their constituencies rather than ensuring fiscal discipline and seeking for the whole society's well-being (Lienert 2013). Therefore, the legislation may favor ensuring fiscal discipline or neglects discipline at the expense of increased budget deficit (Schick 2002).

Yet, OECD asserts that even if the general view is that the strong parliaments undermine fiscal discipline, the experiences of OECD member countries show that legislative supervision through committee reviews, plenary debates, parliamentary questions, and interpellations in budget process is essential for establishing and maintaining fiscal discipline (OECD 2014). Even if legislative activity in budget process creates some risks for fiscal discipline, those risks cannot be considered as a reason to inactivate legislatures. Furthermore, there are various ways—such as limiting the legislative amendments, setting process rules, providing qualified information, and establishing nonpartisan budget offices—to reduce the risks arising from legislative engagement in budget process. Overall, enhancing the activeness of legislatures and setting institutional rules that optimize its role can help to create better budgetary outcomes (Fölscher 2006).

In Turkey, the Grand National Assembly of Turkey (GNAT) uses the legislative power on behalf of Turkish Nation[1] and the role of the GNAT in budget process is mainly defined both in the Constitution of 1982 and Law no. 5018.[2] Constitution of the Republic of Turkey was ratified through referendum of the Turkish People on November 7th in 1982 and was amended several times since then. The last amendment was made through the referendum of April 16, 2017.

The major change made through the 2017 referendum was transition of the governmental system from parliamentary to the presidential which was put into effect after the elections of June 24, 2018. Another significant amendment made through the referendum—that affects the role of the parliament in budget process—was the amendment to the articles 161, 162, 163, and 164 which used to regulate the budget preparation and implementation, debate on the budget, principles governing budgetary amendments and final accounts. Those four articles were consolidated in article 161. According to the amended article 161 the Plan and Budget Committee (PBC) is still the only parliamentary committee identified in the Constitution but the provision on the structure of the Committee has been repealed.

The details related to public financial management system including budget process had been regulated by Law no. 1050[3] which was enacted in 1927. On the other hand, Law no. 1050 was repealed by Law no. 5018 that was enacted in 2003 and fully put into effect in 2006. The medium-term expenditure framework, multiyear budgeting, strategic planning, performance-based budgeting, accountability, and transparency were all introduced through Law no. 5018. It has been amended several times since then, and the last amendment was made in 2018 in accordance with the Constitutional amendment.

[1] Constitution of the Republic of Turkey, Article 7.

[2] Public Financial Management and Control Law.

[3] General Accounting Law.

This study aims to examine the role of the GNAT in budget process including budget calendar, budgetary documents submitted to the Parliament by the President of the Republic and the tools of legislative oversight within the context of transition of the governmental system.

10.2 Legislative Oversight in Different Governmental Systems

One of the main functions of legislatures is overseeing the executive branch through monitoring and scrutinizing its policy implementations to ensure transparency and hold the governments accountable. On the other hand, legislative oversight differs from country to country in line with the constitutional and institutional structure as well as the legitimacy of the legislature (The World Bank 2002). Therefore, it can be said that the oversight function of a legislature mainly depends on the governmental system of a country which determines the relationship between executive and legislative branches. However, there is no one type of parliamentary or presidential system. In general, parliamentary systems are mainly grouped into as Westminster-style parliaments and others while the presidential systems are grouped as presidential and semi-presidential systems.

Presidential and parliamentary systems both aim at efficient management of government even if the philosophy behind them and the structure of the organization they have adopted differ from each other. The main difference of these two systems is the formation of government. In parliamentary systems the government is formed from among the members of the parliament, while president and legislature are elected separately in presidential systems. Therefore, contrary to the parliamentary systems, the head of executive is independent from legislature in presidential systems. Additionally, the structure of the government is fragmented in parliamentary systems since the governments consist of head of government, cabinet, and the head of state (a monarch or a parliamentary elected president in republics). However, in presidential systems, there is only one president who is the head of both government and state (Puig 2002). On the other hand, the semi-presidential systems differ from these two governmental systems since it is a mix of them that includes a directly elected fix term president and a prime minister and cabinet. In the countries with semi-presidential systems; president, prime minister, and cabinet are all subject to legislative oversight (Elgie 2011).

Another characteristic difference between parliamentary and presidential systems is the relationship between the executive and legislative branches. In parliamentary systems, the executive branch needs legislative confidence to stay in office. On the other hand, "the terms of the chief executive and of the assembly are fixed, and not subject to mutual confidence" in presidential systems (Carey 2008). But this separation is also ambiguous since parliamentary systems also differ from each other.

For instance, executive power is concentrated in one party and cabinet in Westminster-style parliaments. Even if it is expected that the parliament can remove the cabinet, in practice, it is not the case. Since the leaders of the majority party are generally the members of cabinet, it is commonly supported by the majority and stays in office (Lijphart 2012).

Generally in presidential systems, legislatures are more influential when compared to parliamentary systems in determination of taxes and expenditures because of the strong separation of powers. However, political context is an important determinant on the activeness of legislatures in both systems depending on the distribution of members among political parties (Fölscher 2006). There are several factors that influence the role of legislature in the budget process, such as political and electoral system, legislature's formal power, political environment, and the budget literacy of the parliament (Johnson and Stapenhurst 2008). For example, strong separation of power between the executive and legislature in presidential systems may create conflict or improve the quality of oversight through decreasing the collusion experienced in parliamentary systems (Desposato 2008).

As is mentioned above Turkey has transformed its governmental system from parliamentary to presidential. Since the differences between governmental systems affect the legislative oversight function of parliaments, it is important to examine the constitutional amendments made through the latest referendum. For this reason, legislative oversight in Turkey will be examined in consideration of those amendments.

10.3 Legislative Oversight in Turkey

As is mentioned above parliaments are one of the three main powers of a democracy. They consist of equal members representing the electorate and their major function is controlling the executive branch of the governments. To perform this oversight function, parliaments use several tools such as ombudsmen, committees of inquiry, auditing institutions, specialized parliamentary committees, public hearings, interpellations, and procedures for questioning ministers in many ways (Damgaard 2000).

In Turkey, the tools of legislative oversight are defined and regulated in both Constitution and some other laws. While the Constitution regulates the establishment of the Institution of the Ombudsperson, ways of obtaining information and supervision by the GNAT, the Turkish Court of Accounts (TCA), PBC and legislative budget process; the organization of the Ombudsperson Institution, the organization, authorization and duties of the TCA and the details of the budget process are regulated in other special laws.

As is regulated in the Constitution and other various laws, Turkey has various legislative oversight tools such as ombudsperson, parliamentary inquiry, general debate, parliamentary investigation, and written question. In addition to those, Turkey has a budget committee to carry out both ex-ante and ex-post oversight that is supported by the TCA. Therefore, in this section, the tools used by the GNAT to perform its oversight function will be examined.

Ombudsperson

As is known, "an ombudsperson is a person who heads a constitutional or statutory public institution that handles complaints from the public regarding the decisions, actions or omissions of the public administration" and in the countries that adopt the parliamentary model, ombudspersons are appointed by legislature (Yamamoto 2007). According to the International Ombudsman Institute (IOI), the best practices have several features:

- An independent ombudsman institution should be introduced that has a legal basis,
- The ombudsman should be appointed by the parliament, preferably through the election that require a qualified majority,
- The ombudsman should not be removed before the end of the term appointed for, except in the case of incapacity, misconduct, or other good cause,
- Ombudsman positions should have fixed mandates that is not shorter than five years,
- The ombudsman should have the power to cooperate with any individual and institution to receive support in his or her investigations and the institutions should be able to access to all service users and should be available for all,
- The ombudsman should examine the legality and compliance, promote human rights and good administration and should be able to make recommendations as well as having the power to enforce those recommendations,
- The ombudsman should submit annual reports to the parliament that should be discussed at Plenary or at a Committee,
- The Ombudsman may be appointed on a renewable, fixed-term basis but "the IOI has adopted a formal policy encouraging a public, staged approach to the management of the renewal of mandate" (IOI 2017).

In Turkey, the Institution of the Ombudsperson is introduced through the constitutional amendment made in 2010. According to the article 74 of the Constitution, the Institution is established under the organization of GNAT and the duty of the Institution is to consider the complaints about the public administrations. The Chief Ombudsperson is elected by the GNAT for a term of four years by secret ballot. Three ballots can be held for the election of the Chief Ombudsperson and in the first two ballots qualified majority (two–thirds) of the total members is required. If the qualified majority cannot be constituted in first two ballots, the majority of the total members are required in the third ballot (GNAT 1982).

Also, the code 6328[4] was enacted in 2012 to establish the Institution of Ombudsperson that indicates any authority or person cannot issue orders, instructions, or give advice to Chief Ombudsperson or ombudspersons related to their duties. The ombudsperson can request any information related to the issue under examination or investigation and the institutions have to submit that information within 30 days following the date of request. On the other hand, the Chief Ombudsperson can be

[4]Law On the Ombudsperson Institution.

removed from the office if he or she no longer holds the qualifications that required to be elected. Also the Chief Ombudsperson can be removed from the office in the case of a sentence or restriction which would damage the eligibility to be elected. According to the code 6328, the Institution prepares a report about its activities and recommendations at the end of every calendar year and submits it to a joint commission which is comprised of the members of the Petition Committee and the Human Rights Inquiry Committee of the GNAT. The commission discusses this report and prepares another report—which includes a summary of the previous report and the commission's own views and convictions—to be submitted to the Plenary (GNAT 2012).

Therefore, the model adopted by Turkey is the parliamentary ombudsperson model in which the chief ombudsperson is appointed by the parliament. Additionally, the system adopted by the code 6328 is in line with the IOI best practices, except for the term of office which is four years.

General Legislative Oversight Tools

Generally, the other tools of legislative oversight are regulated in the article 98 of the Constitution. According to the article, the GNAT performs its oversight function by means of parliamentary inquiry, general debate, parliamentary investigation, and written question. In this regard, the GNAT may carry out an examination to obtain information on a particular subject which is called parliamentary inquiry. General debate is defined as the consideration of a particular subject related to the community and the State activities at the Plenary. In addition, absolute majority of the GNAT may table a motion requesting the investigation of Vice Presidents of the Republic and ministers on allegations of perpetration of a crime regarding their duties which is called parliamentary investigation.[5] And finally, members of the GNAT can ask questions in written form to the Vice Presidents of the Republic and ministers which have to be answered no later than 15 days (GNAT 1982).

In the article 98, the Constitution also indicates that the form of presentation, content, and scope of parliamentary inquiry, general debate and written question, and the procedures for answering, debating and inquiring them are regulated by the Rules of Procedure of the GNAT. Besides, relating to the supervision of President of the Republic, the article 105 regulates that absolute majority of the GNAT may table a motion requesting the investigation of President of the Republic on allegations of a crime (GNAT 1982). On the other hand, the article 99 was repealed through the amendment in 2017 which used to regulate the censure[6] as a tool of legislative oversight.

Budget Committee and Plenary Sessions

Role of the GNAT in the budget process is particularly determined in the article 161. In accordance with the Constitution, the expenditures of the State and of public

[5] Article 106.

[6] The question used to be asked by the members of the GNAT to the prime minister or one of the ministers on a specific issue that had to be negotiated in the Plenary and at the end of negotiations members of the parliament could request an investigation or vote of confidence.

corporations (except for the state-owned enterprises) are determined by annual budgets. And the fiscal year,[7] processes related to the preparation, implementation, and control of the central government budgets and procedures for investments, works and services which take more than one year are regulated in the law. Also, provisions which are not related to budget cannot be included in budget laws. The main regulations in the constitution related to ex-ante legislative oversight in the budget process are listed in the table below including previous situation (Table 10.1).

However, there is an important restriction on the budgetary amendments made by the legislation that the members of the parliament may express their opinions in the

Table 10.1 Legislative Budget Process

Before constitutional amendment	After constitutional amendment
The budget bills are submitted to the GNAT by the Council of Ministers at least 75 days before the beginning of the fiscal year	The budget bills are submitted to the GNAT by the President of the Republic at least 75 days before the beginning of the fiscal year
The budget bills are debated and approved at the PBC within 55 days. According to the Constitution the PBC used to consist of 40 deputies, 25 of them were from the ruling party and the remaining 15 deputies were from the opponent parties	The budget bills are debated and approved at the PBC within 55 days. Since the article relating to structure of the PBC is repealed from the Constitution, the number of the members of the Committee is determined in line with the Rules of Procedure of the GNAT. Therefore, the number of the members of the parliamentary committees is determined in the Plenary and the distribution of the seats between the ruling and opponent parties in the Committee is determined according to percentage of their seats in the Plenary. For now, the PBC has 30, 15 of them are from the ruling party and the other 15 are from the opponent parties
The budget bills approved by the PBC are submitted to the Plenary for further debate and adopted by the Plenary before the beginning of the fiscal year. Therefore, the Plenary has 20 days to debate and adopt the budget bills. Budget bills used to be voted by functions of each institution	The budget bills approved by the PBC are submitted to the Plenary for further debate and adopted by the Plenary before the beginning of the fiscal year. Therefore, the Plenary has 20 days to debate and adopt the budget bills. Budget bills are voted on institutional bases in current situation
If budget laws cannot be put into force on the 1st of January,[a] provisional budget laws used to be enacted which did not used to long more than six months	If budget laws cannot be put into force on the 1st of January, provisional budget laws are enacted. If the provisional budget law cannot be enacted either, previous year's budget will be implemented with an increase depending on the revaluation rate until the budget law is adopted

Source: Derived from the Constitution of 1982 (GNAT 1982)
[a]The beginning of the fiscal year according to the code 5018

[7]The calender year is considered as the fiscal year in the Law no. 5018.

Plenary on budgets of public administrations but they cannot propose amendments that increase expenditures or reduce revenues (GNAT 1982). Therefore, even if the PBC has the legal power to amend the budgets without any restrictions, in terms of the Plenary it can be said that there is an institutional arrangement made through the Constitution to reduce the risks arising from legislative activity in the budget process.

Wehner conducted a study to calculate an index to assess the power of the purse that is the sum of powers, reversion, flexibility, time, committees, and research. Those variables can be explained as formal amendment power of legislatures, occurrence of legislative amendments, reversionary budgets, executive flexibility in the budget implementation process, budget and audit committees, a dedicated legislative budget unit and the time allocated to budget negotiations. According to the study, even if there is a high recognition of the importance of the power of the purse constitutionally, the financial scrutiny level of the legislative bodies differs widely from country to country. For example, USA has the highest score (88.9) and the legislative bodies of Hungary (66.7), Sweden (65.3), Norway (61.1), and Switzerland (61.1) follow US Congress. On the other hand, Ireland (16.7), France (18.1), Greece (19.4), United Kingdom (20.8), and Australia (20.8) have the lowest scores. Turkey's score (36.1) is at the middle such as Poland (37.5), Iceland (38.9), Finland (38.9) Portugal (38.9), and Spain (38.9). According to Wehner's study, the main problems related to Turkey's score are the high level of executive flexibility during budget execution and lack of capacity of the legislature (Wehner 2010).

The process for the ex-post legislative oversight of the GNAT through the final accounts bill is also determined in the article 161 of the Constitution. In that vein, the central government final accounts bill is submitted to the GNAT by the President of the Republic within six months of the end of fiscal year. Additionally, the TCA has to submit its statement of general conformity to the GNAT within 75 days of the submission of the final accounts bill. The final accounts bill is debated and adopted in the same procedure as the budget bill in both the PBC and Plenary (GNAT 1982). As is seen, there is not a separate committee which is responsible for the final account bills. Thereby, the GNAT can evaluate the budget bill, the previous year's realizations, and the statement of general conformity of the TCA at the same time that may affect the quality of debates negatively because of the time limit.

On the other hand, even if there is a dedicated parliamentary budget committee to scrutiny the budget and final account bills, the GNAT does not have an independent analytic budget unit such as a parliamentary budget office that provides information to the parliament to eliminate the domination of the budget information by the executive branch. Those parliamentary offices can perform independent economic forecasts, prepare expenditure and revenue projections, analyze the executive's budget proposals in medium term. Budget offices can also analyze policy proposals, prepare options for spending cuts based on program effectiveness and efficiency, and make long-term analyses. Indeed, there are several benefits in establishing this kind of units such as simplification of the complexity, promoting transparency and accountability, enhancing credibility, improving budget process, providing information to both majority and minority groups in the parliament, and providing rapid responses to budget inquiries from the legislature (Anderson 2008). For instance, in the US, the

Congressional Budget Office (CBO) assists to Congress in budget process through preparation of analysis and estimations related to economy and budget. The CBO also presents options and alternatives to the Congress to consider in decision-making process (Shaw 2016). Considering the strong role of US Congress in budget process, it can be said that the CBO is an important unit that facilitates the Congress's work in this process.

The Court of Accounts

The TCA is responsible for auditing revenues, expenditures, and the assets of the public administrations financed by the central government budget and social security institutions as well as taking final decisions on the accounts and acts of the responsible officials on behalf of the GNAT. Auditing and taking final decision on the accounts and activities of local administrations are also under the responsibility of the TCA (GNAT 1982). The purposes of the ex-post external audit carried out by the TCA are stated as auditing of the financial activities, decisions and transactions of public administrations in terms of their compliance with the laws, institutional goals, objectives and plans, and reporting the audit results to the GNAT (GNAT 2003).

The Law no. 6085[8]—enacted in 2010—regulates establishment of the TCA and repealed the previous law on the organization of TCA which was enacted in 1967. According to the Law no. 6085[9]; public administrations within the scope of general government,[10] companies that use public sources, off-budget funds, special accounts, accounts and transactions of international institutions and organizations,[11] borrowing, lending, repayments, grants, treasury guarantees, treasury receivables, cash management, domestic and foreign resources and funds (including European Union funds) are subject to TCA audit. The TCA also carries out performance audit which is described as "measurement of results of activities with respect to objectives and indicators determined by public administrations within the framework of accountability" (GNAT 2010). On the other hand, International Organization of Supreme Audit Institutions (INTOSAI)—the TCA is a member of it—describes performance auditing as "an independent, objective and reliable examination of whether government undertakings, systems, operations, programs, activities or organizations are operating in accordance with the principles of economy, efficiency and effectiveness and whether there is room for improvement" (INTOSAI 2013). Therefore, the definition made in the Law no. 6085 is narrower than the definition made by INTOSAI.

Performance audits carried out by national audit offices produce performance information that can lead a political consideration through the procedural obligations that makes ministers or committees of legislature to respond those reports. However, it is not guaranteed that those obligations create a substantive impact but at least they can lead a kind of formal consideration and reply (Pollitt 2006). Since the

[8]Law on the Court of Accounts.

[9]Article 4.

[10]Includes public administrations within the scope of central government, social security institutions and local governments.

[11]Within the framework of the principles set out in the relevant treaty or agreement.

performance auditing carried out by supreme audit institutions such as the TCA serves the legislature rather than executive, it can facilitate the role of parliaments in budget process and increase accountability (Robinson 2011). Therefore, considering the performance audits in a broader scope and increasing the capacity of TCA in this area are important to enhance the quality of legislative oversight.

10.4 Budgetary Actors and Budget Preparation Process

Budget preparation and implementation process in Turkey is determined both in the Constitution and the Law no. 5018. On the other hand, the budgetary actors within the government and their roles have changed because of the transition of the governmental system. Therefore, it is important to apprehend the budgetary actors for a good understanding of the budget cycle.

Before the constitutional amendment, Ministry of Finance used to be responsible for the current budget and overall preparation and implementation process while the Ministry of Development used to prepare investment budget and annual public investment programs. Also, there was a division in the preparation process of the medium-term expenditure framework in which the Ministry of Development used to be responsible for the preparation of medium-term programs (MTP), while the Ministry of Finance used to be responsible for the preparation of medium-term fiscal plans (MTFP). Additionally, the Undersecretariat of Treasury used to be responsible for the debt and cash management. Therefore, there was a fragmented structure within the executive budgeting process in which current budget, investment budget and debt-cash management used to be carried out separately by three main governmental bodies.

After the constitutional amendment, the Ministry of Development is abolished and the Presidency of Strategy and Budget (PSB) is established under the Presidency of the Republic. According to the Presidential Decree on Organization of the Presidency of Strategy and Budget, this newly established body is jointly responsible for the preparation and implementation of both mid-term expenditure framework and budget with the Ministry of Treasury and Finance[12] (Presidential Decree 2018a, b). As a result, the number of the budgetary actors in the budget preparation process is reduced to two bodies instead of three. One is the PSB and the other is the Ministry of Treasury and Finance.

As is mentioned above, the budget preparation and implementation process in Turkey is defined both in the Constitution and the Law no. 5018. According to the Law, the President of the Republic[13] is responsible for the preparation of the budget bill and the coordination among the governmental bodies. As it is clear in

[12]The Undersecretariat of Treasury and Ministry of Finance are united under the Ministry of Treasury and Finance through the Presidential Decree after the constitutional amendment.

[13]The PSB is the responsible institution to coordinate the budget process on behalf of the Presidency of the Republic.

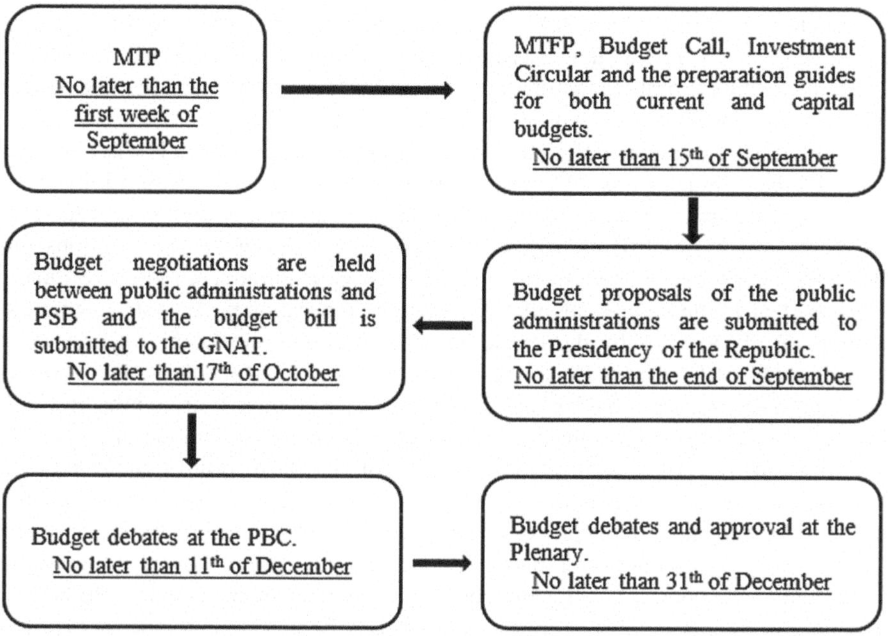

Fig. 10.1 Budget Calendar Source: Derived from the Constitution of 1982 and the Law No. 5018, (GNAT 1982; GNAT 2003)

the Fig. 10.1, budget preparation process starts with the approval and publication of the MTP by the Presidency of the Republic at the end of first week of September at the latest. The MTP is the main document in the multiyear budgeting process that is important to establish a linkage between the policies adopted in the development plans and budgets. Therefore, the MTP includes macroeconomic policies, principles, and basic macroeconomic figures as targets and indicators in accordance with the five-year development plans, institutional strategic plans and the requirements of general economic conditions of the Country (Fig. 10.1).

After the publication of the MTP, MTFP is prepared and published by the President of the Republic no later than 15th of September which has to be consistent with the MTP and includes budget deficit and targeted borrowing, total revenue, and expenditure estimations for the budget year and the following two years, as well as the institutional ceilings within the scope of central government budget. In addition to this, the budget call and the budget preparation guide, the investment circular and the investment program preparation guide are prepared and published by the Presidency of the Republic at the same time with the MTFP.

The PBC has 55 days to debate the budget and final account bills. The budget deliberation agenda is declared by the Presidency of the Committee and debates are held with the participation of the Committee members from the ruling and opposition parties and the representatives of the TCA, GNAT, PSB, and line ministries. The representatives of the TCA, GNAT, PSB, and line ministries attend to the Committee meetings to explain technical issues related to budget and final account bills if requested by the Committee members. At the end of the Committee meetings, budget and final account bills are voted on institutional bases.

Following the approval of the PBC, the budget and final account bills are submitted to the Plenary. Plenary has 20 days to debate budget and final account bills since they have to be approved and published before the beginning of the fiscal year. As is noted above, while the PBC has a right to amend budget bills without restrictions, the Plenary cannot propose amendments that increase expenditures or reduce revenues.

As is clear in the budget calendar, the budget preparation process starts with the publication of the MTP by the President of the Republic no later than first week of September and ends by December 31 at the latest. The whole budget process including both executive and legislative branches takes almost four months in which legislature has only 75 days that is quite short in comparison with the other OECD countries and does not allow the legislature to scrutinize the medium-term framework and budget in detail. For example, in Canada, even if there is no legal basis for the budget calendar, the budget process starts with the submission of forecasts to the Cabinet by the Department of Finance about 12 months before the beginning of the fiscal year.[14] The parliamentary budget process is held in two stages: pre-budget consultation and approval. The consultation process begins in September or October and ends in early December. Even if there is not a legal deadline to submit the budget to the parliament, in practice it is submitted about one month before the beginning of the fiscal year and traditionally it is approved in late June—after the beginning of fiscal year—as is inherited from United Kingdom (Lienert and Jung 2004). Therefore, the whole budget process in Canada takes more than one year which is quite longer than the Turkish budget preparation process.

10.5 Budgetary Documents Submitted to the Parliament

According to the Law no. 5018, budgets are prepared and implemented in line with the classification system adopted by the Presidency of the Republic that is also in accordance with the international standards and shows the institutional, functional, and economic results. Therefore, the Analytical Budget Classification (ABC) is introduced in 2004 that includes institutional, functional, source of financing and economic classifications of expenditures, and the economic classification of revenues. The estimations for expenditures are demonstrated in Appropriation Schedule (Schedule A) and the estimations for revenues are demonstrated in the Revenue Schedule (Schedule B) in line with the ABC. Also, there are other schedules which are submitted to the GNAT as a part of budget bill and show the details, procedures, and principles related to the budget such as Schedule C that includes the list of laws on public revenues and ensures pre-authorization to the executive to collect revenues.

[14] Fiscal year starts on the 1th of April.

In addition to this, government administrations have to prepare performance programs in accordance with their five-year strategic plans and submit them to the GNAT as a requirement of the performance-based budgeting system described in the Law no. 5018. Institutional performance programs include performance targets and indicators as well as cost of activities and projects of the administrations. The institutions also have to submit their accountability reports to the GNAT that shows the results of their activities. Therefore, the information flow to the GNAT is ensured through the Schedules within the budget bills, final account bills, performance programs, accountability reports, and the other supplementary documents listed in the Law no. 5018.

The documents have to be submitted to the GNAT as supplements of the budget bills are listed below:

- Budget justification including MTFP,
- Annual economic report,
- List and estimations of tax expenditures (tax exemptions, exceptions, reductions, etc.),
- Public debt management report,
- Last two years' budget realizations and next two years' revenue and expenditure estimations of the institutions within the scope of general government,
- Budget estimations for the local governments and social security institutions,
- List of the institutions funded through the central management budget which are not within the scope of central government (GNAT 2003).

As is mentioned before, in Turkey, public administrations within the scope of central government prepare performance programs in line with their strategic plans and budgets and submit them to the GNAT. Performance programs and budgets are submitted to the GNAT separately and the budget classification (ABC) does not include a program classification. Therefore, at the moment, incremental and line-item budgeting is applied in Turkey (Çatak and Çilingir 2010). Traditional line-item budgeting serves to the prioritization of expenditures only in a limited manner. On the contrary, program-based budgeting provides information on costs and benefits of different programs to meet public needs that facilitates decision-making processes (Robinson 2013).

As a result of lack of program structure and submission of the performance programs as a separate document from the budgets, performance information is rarely considered in the budget debates both at the PBC and Plenary which could increase the quality of the budget debates and assist the legislature in budget decision-making, if it was considered frequently. For this reason, Turkey has been working to adopt program-based performance budgeting system since 2012. A Draft Program Structure and Justification Guide was prepared first in 2014, revised in 2017 and shared with the government administrations and public. Also, one of the "policies and measures" expressed in the MTP (2019–2021) is the introduction of program-based performance budgeting that enhances the effectiveness in the use of public resources and increases transparency and accountability (Presidential Decree 2018a, b). In addition to this, in the Annual Program of Presidency of Republic, it is stated that program-based classification studies will be completed at the end of December in 2019 and the budget for the fiscal year 2020 will be prepared in line with program-based classification (PSB 2018). Therefore, it can be said that establishment of the program structure is adopted at the highest level of the government and a significant step is taken in 2020 to increase the use of performance information in budget decision-making processes. As a result, in 2020 budget, program structures—including programs-subprograms and activities—for the administrations in the scope of central government budget are prepared in cooperation with budgetary authorities and line ministries; approved by the President of Republic and included in performance programs. And the program classification will be fully adopted in budget law as of 2021.

10.6 Conclusion

As is known Turkey has transmitted its governmental system from parliamentary to presidential through the referendum in 2017. This transition affected the legislative oversight function of the GNAT as well as government's administrative structure. Even if the budget calendar did not change, the structure of the budgetary actors and the PBC has changed dramatically. Budget bills are submitted to the GNAT by the President of the Republic instead of Council of Ministers, and the number of administrative actors within the budget process is decreased from three to two. Additionally, since the article related to constitutional structure of PBC was repealed, the number of members and the distribution of the seats among the ruling and opponent parties have changed in accordance with the constitutional amendments. The main purpose of the constitutional amendments is to empower the GNAT in the budget process through the governmental system transition, since according to literature legislatures are seen more powerful in presidential systems.

Furthermore, in Turkey, program structure is approved by the President of Republic and included in performance programs in 2020 and it will be fully adopted in budget laws as of 2021. It is expected to simplify the budget bills to increase the understanding of the budgets by both public and the GNAT and enhance the use of performance information in both executive and legislative budget processes through the adoption of the program classification.

On the other hand, the budget calendar is still quite short in both executive and legislative phases, and it does not allow for detailed examinations of the institutional budget proposals by the budgetary actors and the scrutiny of the budget bills by the GNAT. Also, the lack of an independent budget office within the GNAT that can support legislative oversight process through detailed examination of the executive's budget is an important drawback in terms of the role of the GNAT in budget process. In addition to this, there is not a separate committee in the GNAT that is responsible for the final account bill and the final account bills are debated in the same process with the budget bills. Therefore, in general, final account bills are shadowed by the budget bills because of the time limit.

In conclusion, Turkey has transmitted its executive and legislative structures tremendously through the constitutional amendment, and it is expected that this transition is going to enhance the power of the GNAT in terms of legislative oversight and contribute the checks and balances which is sine qua non in a democracy. However, there are some steps that should be taken to enhance the legislative activity in budget process. At first, the budget calendar should be longer to provide enough time to the GNAT to scrutinize the budget bills. Secondly, an independent budget office within the GNAT should be established which can increase the budget literacy of the parliament and support the PBC in budget process.

References

Anderson, B. (2008). The Value of a Nonpartisan, Independent, Objective Analytic Unit to the Legislative Role in Budget Preparation. In R. Stapenhurst, R. Pelizzo, D. M. Olson, & L. von Trapp (Eds.), *Legislative Oversight and Budgeting: A World Perpective* (pp. 131–139). Washington DC: The World Bank.

Carey, J. M. (2008). Presidential versus Parliamentary Government. In C. Ménard, & M. M. Shirley (Eds.), *Handbook of New Institutional Economics* (pp. 91–122). Berlin, Germany: Springer.

Çatak, S., & Çilingir, C. (2010). Performance Budgeting in Turkey. *OECD Journal on Budgeting, 2010*(3), 7–45.

Damgaard, E. (2000, April 14–19). Representation, Delegation and Parliamentary Control. *Paper prepared for the workshop on "Parliamentary control of the executive", ECPR Joint Sessions.* Copenhagen.

Desposato, S. W. (2008). Explaining Patterns of Oversight in Brazilian Subnational Governments. In R. Stapenhurst, R. Pelizzo, D. M. Olson, & L. von Trapp (Eds.), *Legislative Oversight and Budgeting: A World Perpective* (pp. 193–200). Washington DC: The World Bank.

Elgie, R. (2011). Semi- Presidentialism: An Increasingly Common Constitutional Choice. In R. Elgie, S. Moestrup, & Y.-S. Wu (Eds.), *Semi-Presidentialism and Democracy* (pp. 1–20). New York: Palgrave Macmillan.

Fölscher, A. (2006). A Balancing Act: Fiscal Responsibility, Accountability and the Power of the Purse. *OECD Journal on Budgeting, 6*(2), 1–20.

GNAT. (1982). *Constitution of the Republic of Turkey.* Retrieved 12 15, 2018, from https://global.tbmm.gov.tr/docs/constitution_en.pdf.

GNAT. (2003, 12 10). *Public Financial Management and Control Law.* Retrieved 11 25, 2018, from Legislation Information System: http://www.mevzuat.gov.tr/MevzuatMetin/1.5.5018.pdf.

GNAT. (2010, 12 3). *Law on the Court of Accounts.* Retrieved 11 27, 2018, from Legislation Information System: http://www.mevzuat.gov.tr/MevzuatMetin/1.5.6085.pdf.

GNAT. (2012, 06 14). *Law On the Ombudsman Institution.* Retrieved 12 20, 2018, from Legislation Information System: http://www.mevzuat.gov.tr/MevzuatMetin/1.5.6328.pdf.

INTOSAI. (2013). *Fundamental Auditing Principles—ISSAI 300.* Retrieved 12 16, 2018, from International Standarts of Supreme Audit Institutions: http://www.issai.org/en_us/site-issai/issai-framework/3-fundamental-auditing-priciples.htm.

IOI. (2017, June 24). *Developing and Reforming Ombudsman Institutions—An IOI Guide for Those Undertaking These Tasks.* Retrieved 12 23, 2018, from International Ombudsman Institute: http://www.theioi.org/publications/best-practice-papers.

Johnson, J. K., & Stapenhurst, R. (2008). Legislative Budget Offices: International Experiences. In R. Stapenhurst, R. Pelizzo, D. M. Olson, & L. von Trapp (Eds.), *Legislative Oversight and Budgeting: A World Perspective* (pp. 141–158). Washington DC: The World Bank.

Lienert, I. (2010, April). *Role of the Legislature in Budget Processes*. Retrieved 11 11, 2018, from https://www.imf.org/en/Publications/TNM/Issues/2016/12/31/Role-of-the-Legislature-in-Budget-Processes-23722.
Lienert, I. (2013). Role of the Legislature in Budget Process. In R. Allen, R. Hemming, & B. H. Potter (Eds.), *The International Hand Book of Public Financial Management* (pp. 116–136). New York: Palgrave Macmillan.
Lienert, I., & Jung, M.-K. (2004). *OECD Journal on Budgeting Special Issue: The Legal Framework for Budget Systems* (Vol. 4). Paris: OECD Publishing.
Lijphart, A. (2012). *Patterns of Democracy: Government Forms and Performance in Thirty-Six Countries* (Second edition ed.). New Haven, USA: Yale University Press.
OECD. (2014, May 12). *Budgeting Practices and Procedures in OECD Countries*. Retrieved 12 15, 2018, from http://dx.doi.org/10.1787/9789264059696-en.
Pollitt, C. (2006). Performance Information for Democracy The Missing Link? *Evaluation, 12*(1), 38–55.
Posner, P., & Park, C.-K. (2007). Role of the Legislature in the Budget Process: Recent Trends and Innovations. *OECD Journal on Budgeting, 7*(3), 1–26.
Presidential Decree. (2018a, 9 20). *Medium Term Program*. Retrieved 12 25, 2018, from Official Gazette: https://www.resmigazete.gov.tr/eskiler/2018/09/20180920M2-1.pdf.
Presidential Decree. (2018b, 7 24). *Presidential Decree on Organization of the Presidency of Strategy and Budget*. Retrieved 12 9, 2018, from Legislation Information System: http://www.mevzuat.gov.tr/MevzuatMetin/19.5.13.pdf.
PSB. (2018). *2019 Annual Program of Presidency of Republic*. Retrieved 01 29, 2019, from Presidency of Strategy and Budget: http://www.sbb.gov.tr/wp-content/uploads/2018/11/2019_Yili_Cumhurbaskanligi_Yillik_Programi.pdf.
Puig, G. V. (2002, Sep.–Oct.). Parliamentary versus Presidential Government. *Australian Quarterly, 74*(5), 9–11.
Robinson, M. (2011). *Performance-Based Budgeting*. Retrieved from Public Expenditure Management Peer Assisted Learning: https://www.pempal.org/sites/pempal/files/event/attachments/pb-budgeting-manual_eng.pdf.
Robinson, M. (2013). *Program Classification For Performance-Based Budgeting: How to Structure Budgets to Enable the Use of Evidence*. Retrieved 12 25, 2018, from Independent Evaluation Group—World Bank Group: https://ieg.worldbankgroup.org/sites/default/files/Data/reports/performance_based_budgeting_bb.pdf.
Schick, A. (2002). Can National Legislatures Regain an Effective Voice in Budget Policy? *OECD Journal on Budgeting, 1*(3), 15–42.
Shaw, T. (2016). Performance Budgeting Practices and Procedures. *OECD Journal on Budgeting, 15*(3), 65–136.
The World Bank. (2002, October). *Strengthening oversight by legislatures*. Retrieved 02 04, 2019, from The World Bank: http://documents.worldbank.org/curated/en/790611468136805203/pdf/267480premnote74.pdf.
Wehner, J. (2010). *Legislatures and The Budget Process The Myth of Fiscal Control*. New York: Palgrave Macmillan.
Yamamoto, H. (2007). *Tools for Parliamentary Oversight A Comparative Study of 88 National Parliaments*. Geneva: Inter-Parliamentary Union.
Yılmaz, H. H., & Biçer, M. (2010, Ocak-Haziran). Parlamentonun Bütçe Hakkını Etkin Kullanımının Yeni Bütçe Sistemi Çerçevesinde Değerlendirilmesi. *Maliye Dergisi*(158), 201–225.

Hilal Tezcan is a Ph.D. candidate of Public Finance at Ankara University, Faculty of Political Science. She holds a master's degree in international development policy (MIDP-specialization on public financial management) from Duke University, Sanford School of Public Policy. She also has more than twelve years experience in public budgeting at the Turkish Ministry of Finance as a public finance expert responsible for different ministries' budgets in various sectors such as transportation, health and education. As of December 2018, she has been working for the Presidency of Strategy and Budget. She is especially interested in public budgeting systems, project appraisal and risk management, fiscal transparency and public financial management systems.

Chapter 11
Fiscal Transparency in Turkey: Lessons Learned from International Evaluations

Ali Yıldırım Eker

11.1 Introduction

Fiscal transparency ensures the availability, comprehensiveness, timeliness, and clarity of the data produced by public financial management and the comparability of state activities in the international arena, and thus plays an important role in the proper evaluation of the state's financial status by the electorate and financial markets. The globalized world economy and the financial crisis that broke out in Southeast Asia in 1997 caused some serious consequences in the economic, social, and political areas and led to questioning the structures of international financial institutions and fiscal policies of the countries.

The financial crisis also brought to light the need for fiscal transparency in the international platform and took the concept to the top of the agenda of international organizations. For this purpose, the standards established by international organizations such as International Monetary Fund (IMF), Organization for Economic Cooperation Development (OECD), World Bank and International Budget Partnership (IBP) have enabled the evaluation of the transparency of the countries and comparison among countries.

In the aftermath of the 2008 global crisis, countries had the opportunity to evaluate their own public financial management systems and institutions have learned some lessons from the crisis. In this context, many international institutions, particularly the IMF, made amendments to the standards they had adopted to measure the countries' fiscal transparency levels. For example, in 2014 the IMF revised its Fiscal Transparency Code, which was first issued in 2007. Again, International Budget Partnership (IBP) made some changes to the open budget survey.

In Turkey, the concept of fiscal transparency was brought to the agenda as a result of the standby agreements concluded with IMF and restructuring of the public

A. Y. Eker (✉)
Ministry of Treasury and Finance, Ankara, Turkey
e-mail: ekeraly@yahoo.com

H. Kıral and T. Akdemir (eds.), *Public Financial Management Reforms in Turkey: Progress and Challenges, Volume 1*, Accounting, Finance, Sustainability, Governance & Fraud: Theory and Application, https://doi.org/10.1007/978-981-15-1914-7_11

financial management system was jointly executed with the European Union. With these restructuring efforts, many legal arrangements were made and Public Financial Management and Control Law No. 5018, accepted as the constitution of public financial management, entered into force.

The study will discuss the steps taken by Turkey toward fiscal transparency and the status of the international organizations within the framework of fiscal transparency, and it will also seek the answer to the question, "What should Turkey do in order to meet the fiscal transparency standards of international organizations and to be ranked higher in fiscal transparency indexes?".

The study consists of three main parts: The first part examines why fiscal transparency is important by taking into account the definitions in the international literature. The second part discusses the steps taken in Turkey toward ensuring fiscal transparency. The third part examines the international standards for fiscal transparency and the status of Turkey in the international fiscal transparency indexes.

11.2 Why Fiscal Transparency Matters

Fiscal transparency is commonly defined as the government's structure and functions, its intentions regarding the fiscal policy to be implemented, public sector accounts and fiscal objectives are open to the public (Kopits and Craig 1998, p. 1). In Emil and Yılmaz's (2004, p. 15) studies, fiscal transparency is defined as "*the government does not hide the facts about fiscal transactions it performs.*"

According to the IMF (2018, p. 1), "*Fiscal transparency refers to the information available to the public about the government's fiscal policy making process. It refers to the clarity, reliability, frequency, timeliness, and relevance of public fiscal reporting and the openness of such information.*" OECD (2002, p. 7), "*Budget transparency is defined as the full disclosure of all relevant fiscal information in a timely and systematic manner.*"

The importance of fiscal transparency for governments stems from the fact that it provides comprehensive and understandable information for the past, present, and future activities of governments and it enhances the success of the fiscal policies to be implemented. Thanks to fiscal transparency, accountability of all actors using public resources has increased. It is observed that in nontransparent areas where there is no accountability, unethical activities come to the forefront and corruption increases. Fiscal transparency is one of the key factors for governments to ensure fiscal discipline, and a transparent public financial management system and timely publication of budgetary information facilitate the evaluation of the government's objectives by the markets.

There is mounting empirical evidence showing the proposition that fiscal transparency allows the government to improve its credibility in terms of management of public finances and gain market confidence. Dabla-Norris and others (2010) and Hameed (2005) have investigated that more transparent developing countries have better credit ratings and better fiscal discipline. Similar finding is also showed by Alt and Lassen (2006). They find the relationship between fiscal transparency and lower public debt and deficit in 19 advanced economies. Arbatli and Escolano (2012) are looking at the relationship between transparency and credit ratings in developing and advanced countries. According to the findings of the study, the abovementioned relationship has a direct impact via reducing current uncertainty over fiscal position in developing countries and has an indirect impact to improving primary balance in advanced countries. In terms of causality between transparency and outcomes, Glennerster and Shin (2008) found a significant causal relationship between publication and quality assurance of fiscal information (IMF's fiscal data and reports) and lower government bond yields. In terms of the political determinants of transparency, Wehner and de Renzio (2011) found the role of free and fair elections.

In countries where fiscal transparency is ensured, the trust on the governments and the public's support for the policies to be implemented is increasing. With fiscal transparency, governments are becoming more responsible and accountable to society. On the other hand, fiscal transparency strengthens the audit system and increases the efficiency in management and adherence to the law. With the development of international standards for fiscal transparency, government activities become internationally comparable and countries can evaluate their economic and financial situation in a transparent manner. Fiscal transparency is one of the most important elements of the structural reforms that countries are applying to eliminate the instability experienced after each financial crisis. The recent global crisis once again demonstrated the importance of the concept for national economies. Fiscal transparency makes it possible that the state is more responsible and accountable against the society.

In the next section, the steps taken within the scope of the structural reforms carried out in Turkey will be evaluated in order to make use of the abovementioned benefits of the fiscal transparency.

11.3 Implementation of Fiscal Transparency in Turkey

As in many structural reform efforts, requirement of legal arrangements related to "fiscal transparency" has not automatically emerged in Turkey, it was rather formed under the influence of external factors. The concept of fiscal transparency was taken into the national agenda following the Southeast Asian crisis after it was frequently emphasized by international organizations which is followed by the country's commitments regarding structural reforms within the scope of the Standby agreement between the IMF and Turkey.

On the other hand, at EU Heads of State or Government Meeting held in Helsinki in 1999, Turkey was unanimously accepted as a candidate for EU full membership and accelerated the process of establishing fiscal transparency in public financial management system, as it has accelerated its efforts in various areas toward the target of full membership. In particular, the EU's emphasis on increasing "transparency" and "accountability" for the use of funds has pushed all countries in the process of

EU accession into making arrangements in these matters according to international standards (Emil and Yılmaz 2004, p. 18).

With the impact of these external factors, the concept of fiscal transparency was taken into the Turkey's structural reform agenda and it has now been accepted by all circles that the transparency should be ensured with satisfactory measures. With regard to fiscal transparency, the most important work done in Turkey is the report issued by Restructuring the Public Financial Management and Fiscal Transparency Specialization Commission established within the frame work of "Seventh Five-Year Development Plan". In this report, the important deficiencies identified in terms of fiscal transparency for Turkey are summarized as follows (SPO 2000, pp. 84–85):

- Due to the very limited scope of the budget, a small portion of public resources are used with the approval of the parliament within the framework of power of the purse and then audited on behalf of the parliament.
- The budgetary text presented to the Parliament includes non-budgetary public sector activities. The contingent liabilities, tax expenditures, and semi-financial activities of the central government are not published together with the budget text.
- The financial risks that may arise due to the deviations in the assumptions and estimates related to the macroeconomic framework and budget, and the contingent liabilities, etc., are not reported.
- The classification of transactions does not allow the evaluation of managerial responsibilities in the collection and use of public funds.
- There are no documents showing accounting standards. The fact that the accounting system is cash-based creates problems in the evaluation of the economy.

In addition, it is stated in the abovementioned report that fiscal transparency is an important tool in ensuring budgetary results such as ensuring fiscal discipline, allocating resources according to strategic priorities, and using them efficiently. On the other hand, it has been stated that the Turkish Public Financial Management System does not function efficiently and responsibly due to the fact that budget covers only a part of the public expenditure area, accounting, reporting and coding structure is insufficient and standards are not developed.

11.4 Legal Arrangements Contributing to Fiscal Transparency in Turkey

Many legislative arrangements have been made regarding fiscal transparency since the 2000s in parallel with: the letter of intent within the scope of the standby arrangements concluded with the IMF in Turkey, external factors intensified as a result of candidacy negotiations with the EU and "Fiscal Transparency Specialization Commission" report emerged within the scope of Eighth Five-Year Development Plan as well as the internal factors revealed by the political will.

11.4.1 Public Financial Management and Control Law no. 5018

In Turkey, the most important legal regulation regarding fiscal transparency that took effect is Public Financial Management and Control Law No. 5018. The law sets out the framework of the public financial management system and highlights many concepts such as strategic planning, performance-based budgeting, medium-term expenditure framework, fiscal transparency, and accountability.

Main purpose of this Law is to regulate structure and functioning of the public financial management, preparation and implementation of the public budgets, accounting and reporting of all financial transactions, and financial control in line with the politics and objectives covered in the development plans and programs, in order to ensure accountability, transparency and the effective, economic, and efficient collection and utilization of public resources. According to the Law No. 5018; in order to ensure supervision in the acquisition and utilization of all types of public resources, the public shall be informed timely. Accordingly, the following are compulsory:

- To clearly define the duties, authorities, and responsibilities;
- To prepare government policies, development plans, annual programs, strategic plans and budgets; to negotiate them with the authorized bodies; to implement them and to make the implementation results and the relevant reports available and accessible to the public;
- To publicize the incentives and subsidies provided by the public administrations within the scope of general government, in periods not exceeding one year,
- To establish public accounts in line with a standard accounting system and an accounting in order in accordance with generally accepted accounting principles.

With the Law No. 5018, the following principles of modern public finance were included in the Turkish Public Financial Management System, and thus creating a more transparent, accountable and strong economic and managerial structure in line with international standards.

- The Scope of Financial Management and the budget are broadened.
- The principles of accountability and fiscal transparency are strengthened.
- Transition to strategic planning and performance-based budgeting are foreseen.
- Multi-Year budgetary framework is put into implementation within the framework of medium-term expenditure framework.
- Principles and procedures for the preparation of accountability reports have been determined.
- The principles of final account law are defined.
- Public accounts are ensured to be generated in accordance with a standard accounting system.
- Financial statistics started to be published in accordance with international standards.
- Internal control and internal audit systems are set up.

- The audit scope of Turkish Court of Account is broadened.
- The principles of the effective, economic, and efficient utilization of the resources are introduced.

There are many reports shared with the public under the law and contributed to the fiscal transparency. Medium Term Program, Medium Term Fiscal Plan, General Accountability Report, Expectations Report and Monthly Budget Realizations are important documents shared with the public. Medium Term Program covers basic macro policies, principles, and economic figures and indicators. Medium Term Fiscal Plan covers targeted deficit and borrowing positions, total revenue of appropriation proposals of public administrations. General accountability report covers results of the activities of public administrations within the scope of central government and social security institutions in one fiscal year. Report has also included general evaluations regarding the financial structures of the local government. Through the Expectations Report, the financial situation covering the first six months of implementation of the central government budget law, financing condition, expectations for the second six months and targets are disclosed to the public as a requirement of transparency.

All in all, Law No. 5018 brought a new breath to Turkish public financial management system in parallel with the developments in the international arena and accelerated the adoption of modern practices in this field in the country. The Law establishes mechanisms to ensure the efficient, economic, and effective use of public resources, and internal control, internal audit, and external audit are reconstructed and thus, the financial control process is developed. Thus, it is aimed to create a more transparent and powerful economic and managerial structure. On the other hand, it is important in terms of fiscal transparency to determine and eliminate the deficiencies of the Law that are not in line with the spirit of the Law at the point of implementation of a law which steers the public financial management system and which has been tried to be applied since 2006 and can be called as the financial constitution.

11.4.2 Public Procurement Law

Public Procurement Law No. 4734 which has been put into force in order to align public procurement arrangements with EU and international practices and to minimize the problems encountered in practice and Public Procurement Contracts Law No. 4735, which constitutes the legal basis of the contracts to be made in accordance with Law No. 4734 are significant legal arrangements. New arrangements introduced by the Law No. 4734 for ensuring transparency are mainly listed below:

- Arranging adequateness criteria for entering the tenders in detail.
- Introducing the obligation of announcing the tenders in Official Gazette.
- Announcing the tenders on Internet.
- Introducing the obligation of announcing the tender results above a certain amount in Official Gazette.

- Introducing the obligation of informing all bidders of the tenders about the tender result.
- Introducing the obligation of answering the questions posed by relevant bidders to the administration about any phase of the tender in a way to encompass all the participants.
- Introducing the obligation of providing the reasons by the administrations to the bidders whose bids were not evaluated or not deemed appropriate provided that they make a written request.
- Setting up a complaint mechanism and publishing the Board Decisions on the complaints in the Official Gazette.

Even though the Law No. 4734 broadens the scope, applies competition conditions more efficiently, highlights transparency and accountability when compared to the previous law and most importantly ensures unity in implementation, it has still some deficiencies. Some exceptional arrangements brought to some purchases due to the fact that some of the public administrations tend to go out of the system following the entry into force of the law damages the system, the integrity of the Law must be maintained to resolve the mentioned problem. The State, which plays a regulatory role in the economy due to public procurement, which has an important place in public expenditures, needs to eliminate the shortcomings in this area by making the public procurement transparent and ensuring economic and efficient utilization of the resources.

11.4.3 Public Financing and Debt Management Law

With the adoption of Law No. 4749 on Regulating of Public Finance and Debt Management, public debt management system, which has a fragmented structure for many years and carried out under various laws, has been gathered under a single roof and fiscal discipline has been introduced for borrowing, and new financial instruments and techniques have been started to be used. Law No. 4749 also introduces some arrangements to ensure fiscal discipline and transparency within the scope of public financial management, in general, except for debt management. Erdoğan (2005, pp. 177–189) explains these arrangements as follows:

- Fragmented legislation on debt management was consolidated.
- Statutory restrictions were introduced for the limits of borrowing and providing guarantee.
- A "Risk Account" has been established at the Central Bank of Turkey to mitigate the risks that may arise as a result of the failure of the repayment of Treasury guaranteed liabilities by the related institutions.
- In accordance with the Law, Public Debt Management Reports began to be issued and submitted to the Parliament on a quarterly basis to ensure a transparent and accountable debt policy from 2003 onward.

Within the framework of the fiscal transparency, the reports prepared under the law to be informed about the public can be summarized as "Monthly Public Debt Management Report," "Annual Public Debt Management Report," "Annual Treasury Financing Program," and "Domestic Borrowing Strategy and Auction Calendar". Monthly public debt management report includes basic information, indicators, and statistics. In the annual public debt management report, information is provided within the scope of debt management activities and various analyses are made. At the end of each year, the annual treasury financing program for the next year is published. With this program, the financing activities carried out within the scope of the previous year's financing program, along with the Medium Term Program and Central Government Budget projections, the debt service, financing activity information and the borrowing strategy are planned to be carried out the following year. At the end of each month, the domestic borrowing strategy and auction calendar for the next three months are shared with the public.

With the Law No. 4749, an important gap in the area of debt management was eliminated and an area that financial management could not control was taken under control and an important step was taken to ensure fiscal discipline.

11.4.4 Right to Information Law

The right of citizens to obtain information is important and necessary in terms of fiscal transparency and the necessity to determine the limits of the right to information and the protection of this right in a legal framework is a prerequisite for fiscal transparency in contemporary public financial management systems. Putting the recognition of this right and putting it in a legal framework in Turkey has been ensured with the Right to Information Act Law. 4982.

With the law, the principle of "everyone has the right to information" is accepted and it is stated that the foreigners also hold this right in the framework of the principle of reciprocity. The law stipulates that all institutions and organizations are obliged to provide information, except for the exceptions. Some information within the scope of exception is: transactions falling outside the scope of judicial control, information or documents relating to the state secret, information or documents related to the country's economic interests, information or documents related to intelligence, information or documents related to administrative investigation, information or documents related to judicial investigation and prosecution, privacy of private life, confidentiality of communication, and trade secrets.

The Right to Information Law is one of the most important steps taken by Turkey in terms of transparency, and openness and transparency are only possible by citizens' ability to access the information and documents. Citizens, nongovernmental organizations and the media, briefly all public opinion, will have more power to call to account for when they are more informed about public administration. Therefore, providing the requestors with the information will contribute to the formation of some new dynamics in the society. The most important of these dynamics is ensuring participation together with the concepts of transparency and accountability.

11.4.5 Council of Ethics for Public Service

In Turkey, the administration can function effectively and efficiently when the principles of openness, transparency, accountability, impartiality, honesty, and objectivity are ensured and operate in favor of public interest during the execution of public services. Honest, reliable, and fair public services increase the confidence in public sector and create a favorable environment within the business world. Therefore, ethics in public administration is recognized as the key to good governance.

Law No. 5176 on the Establishment of a Council of Ethics for Public Service filled an important gap in the field of transparency in Turkey. To ensure transparency in the establishment of the ethical principles which the public officials will be subject to is a requirement sought. Yüksel (2005, p. 181) states, "*No step has contributed to increasing the ethics level in public sector as much as ensuring transparency in the administration, including the adoption of codes of conduct in public administration.*" The fact that the ethical principles are set by their legal dimension is a positive step for fiscal transparency, although not enough efficiency has been achieved in practice.

Considering the best practices in the developed countries, there are many methods for the establishment of ethical values in the public sector. All these practices, in essence, emphasize the importance of a good educational infrastructure for internalizing ethical values by public officials. The best practices include attaching importance to ethical values in recruitments for public service, giving trainings on ethical issues in the institutional sense, making use of technology for adoption of the said, introducing penal sanctions in the event of noncompliance with ethical principles or rewarding other situations. At this point, it is important to implement the best practices of the developed countries in Turkey, apart from legal regulations. Ethical concepts should not remain in the form of abstract concepts, but should be associated with indicators to materialize them.

11.4.6 Turkish Court of Accounts Law No. 6085

The desire of citizens to be provided, effectively and efficiently, with the services they expect from the government in return for the taxes they have paid comes with a different understanding of the parliaments' auditing and supervision obligation on public resources. For this reason, the Courts of Auditors, which fulfill the obligation of auditing and supervision on behalf of the parliaments, need to keep up with the change. In parallel with the changes in the organizational structure and the functions of the constitutional supreme audit institutions, the changing public financial management approach has revealed the necessity of introducing some changes in the

Turkish Court of Accounts (TCA) on a legal basis. With a view to supporting the innovations introduced within the scope of reform efforts in Turkey in the field of public financial management, former Turkish Court of Accounts Law No. 832 was repealed, and the TCA Law No. 6085 which is in compliance with the Law No. 5018 took effect in 2010.

With the TCA Law No. 6085, the TCA started to implement the techniques of performance audit as well as regularity audit techniques and had legal authority to audit all public funds, resources, and activities. With the performance audit, activity results are measured in relation to the targets and indicators determined by the administrations within the framework of the accountability responsibility, and as a result of the audits, other issues that are related to the audit or arising from the audit and which are deemed necessary to be disclosed are reported. With the law, the TCA had the opportunity to perform audits in accordance with internationally accepted auditing standards. On the other hand, the TCA contributes to the development of transparency and accountability in public sector by presenting the reports they prepare to the parliament in a timely manner and under certain procedures. In addition, within the scope of the new duties of the TCA, the organizational structure has been improved by the Law as inspired by the TCAs in developed countries.

In Turkey, ensuring effective, efficient, and economic use of public resources through ensuring accountability and transparency is one of the fundamental tasks of the TCA which perform audits on behalf of the parliament. The public is able to learn to what priorities the institutions allocate their resources and how they use it from the reports generated as result of the audits performed by the Court of Accounts, which is an independent external audit body. Therefore, the importance of TCA in the new public financial management system is increasing day by day, in terms of ensuring fiscal transparency and accountability.

11.5 Important Infrastructure Work on Fiscal Transparency

In order to analyze the journey of fiscal transparency in Turkey, it is necessary to evaluate the studies on the development of the fiscal transparency infrastructure as well as the legal arrangements for the embracement of fiscal transparency. At this point, Web Base Accounting Automation System (Say2000i) and Analytical Budget Classification System (ABC) are among the important infrastructure work carried out in order to ensure fiscal transparency in Turkey.

11.5.1 Web Base Accounting Automation System (Say2000i)

With the development of information technologies since 2000s, many practices have been in place in the private and public sectors in order to ensure transparency. Many activities in the public sector have been made available to the public via the Internet, and the information has contributed to public awareness and to the citizen's demand for more information. Citizens' access to information on various issues has always increased in line with the development of information technologies. In parallel with the developments in information technologies, the Ministry of Finance has also implemented the Web Base Accounting Automation System (Say2000i) to ensure transparency and to provide timely and reliable information to everyone who wants to learn about the state's financial structure.

With Say2000i;

- All of the accounting units throughout the country spending and collecting the revenues have shifted to automation.
- Accounting information is monitored daily.
- Financial statements are generated in line with international standards.
- Efficiency is ensured with regard to implementing the budget policies decided.
- Economy management and decision-makers make use of efficient decision support mechanisms.
- Health spending is monitored on central database.

The need for comprehensive and comparable information was not so much due to the relatively low impact of the state on the national economy in the past and for the fact that the international markets were not in as many interactions with each other as today. In Turkey, with the introduction of say2000i, growing need for regular information regarding public finance has been met and one of the most important criticisms made, in the past, by the international organizations in the field of fiscal transparency has been met.

11.5.2 Analytical Budget Classification System

One of the important steps taken in order to ensure the fiscal transparency infrastructure in Turkey is switching to Analytical Budget Classification which enables preparation of budget prepared by the government as based on institutional, functional, financing, and economic classification in compliance with international standards. In the past, a functional classification did not exist and program-based classification which was initiated in the 1970s was not efficient in Turkey. The reason why the budget classification was a significant problem in the past is that the Turkish budget system did not have a classification which enables to generate data at international standards, which weakens the expected function of the budget, eliminates the opportunity of cost-benefit analysis of the activities, limits the strategic decision-making skills of decision-makers, and hinders making connection between the policies and budgets.

Analytical Budget Classification (ABC) was introduced as of 2004 in Turkey with the aim of eliminating mentioned problems and having a contemporary budget code system. ABC is composed of four levels: Institutional, Functional, Financing, and Economical. With the introduction of ABC, a remarkable progress has been made in terms of Turkish budget system and our budget system has been made compliant with European Union acquis (ESA 95 and GFS). The benefits of ABC can be seen as follows:

- to define the program responsible,
- to provide a functional classification which is not covered by current classification system,
- to provide a detailed instructional classification,
- to do international comparisons,
- to create appropriate environment for analyzing,
- to implement modern budgeting systems,
- to increase the elasticity of budget policies,
- to monitor some kind of issues which are undertaken by government, such as costs, financial sources, and services.

One of the most important objectives of the reform efforts undertaken in the budget sector in Turkey is to ensure the fiscal transparency. As for ensuring financial transparency ABC enables increasing flexibility of budget policy, detailed and systematic planning, monitoring and evaluation of the budget implementation results and monitoring of the state-run services, financial resources, and costs.

11.6 Fiscal Transparency Measurement in Turkey

In terms of international comparisons, it became a necessity to put forward the fiscal transparency levels of countries and therefore common criteria or standards were determined by various international organizations and nongovernmental organizations such as IMF, OECD, World Bank, and IBP, and it became possible to compare the countries' levels of fiscal transparency by using different methodologies. Figure 11.1 shows the basic international norms and standards published by the mentioned institutions in terms of budget and fiscal transparency.

In this study, IMF and IBP's standards have been preferred due to the fact that they carry out country-specific fiscal transparency assessments and their reports are up-to-date and open to the public.

Official standards/legal instruments	
IMF Code	IMF (2014) Fiscal Transparency Code
OECD Budget Principles	OECD (2015) Recommendation of the Council on Budgetary Governance
Other core reference materials	
GIFT High Level Principles	GIFT (2012), High Level Principles on Fiscal Transparency, Participation, and Accountability
IBP Open Budget Survey	IBP (2017), Guide to the Open Budget Questionnaire
OECD Best Practices	OECD (2002), Best Practices for Budget Transparency
PEFA	PEFA (2016), Framework for Assessing Public Financial Management
Other key international guidance	
CPA Benchmarks	Commonwealth Parliamentary Association (2015), Recommended Benchmarks for Democratic Legislatures
EITI	EITI (2016), The EITTI Standard 2016
GIFT Public Participation	GIFT (2015), Principles of Public Participation in Fiscal Policy
G20 Open Data	G20 (2015), G20 anti-corruption Open Data Principles
IMF GFSM	IMF (2014), Government Finance Statistics Manual
IPSAS	IPSASB (2016), International Public Sector Accounting Standards

Fig. 11.1 Basic international standards on fiscal transparency. *Source* OECD (2017, p. 41)

11.6.1 IMF Fiscal Transparency Code

After the last global crisis, the countries have had the opportunity to assess their public fiscal management systems and institutions have learned from the crisis. In this framework, in the post-crisis period, in 2014, the IMF revised the Fiscal Transparency Code which was issued in 2007. The main reasons behind this change can be summarized as follows (IMF 2014):

- To focus on outputs rather than the processes,
- To assess the capacities of member states at different levels,
- To give more room to fiscal risks in the IMF's evaluation,
- To include recent developments on fiscal management and international standards.

According to the new Code (2014), the IMF carries out its Fiscal Transparency Assessment for the member countries through four main sections. These sections are; "Fiscal Reporting," "Fiscal Forecasting and Budgeting," "Fiscal Risk Analysis and Management," and "Resource and Revenue Management." The fourth section of the report, "Resource (Revenue) Management" is not yet taken into account by the IMF in country assessments. After the evaluation made according to the new code by the IMF, an assessment is made according to the criteria under three importance levels, "High," "Medium," and "Low," stated before an evaluation map is generated at the end of the report. Red colors on the map mean that the criteria are not met, yellow colors mean that the criteria are met at basic level, light green means that the criteria are well met and dark green means that advanced criteria are met. Considering this map placed at the end of the report, as for showing the level of fiscal transparency, the red-colored areas are desired to be narrow while dark green areas are desired to be large.

LEVEL OF IMPORTANCE	LEVEL OF PRACTICE		
	1. FISCAL REPORTING	2. FISCAL FORECASTING AND BUDGETING	3. FISCAL RISK ANALYSIS AND MANAGEMENT
HIGH IMPORTANCE	1.1. Coverage of Institutions	2.1. Fiscal Legislation	1.1. Macroeconomic Risk
	1.2. Coverage of Stocks	2.1. Timeliness of Budget Documentation	1.2. Specific Fiscal Risks
	1.3 Coverage of Flows	3.2 Performance Information	1.3. Long-term Fiscal Sustainability
	4.3. Comparability of Fiscal Data	4.2. Supplementary Budget	3.4. Public-Private Partnerships
MEDIUM IMPORTANCE	2.2. Timeliness of Annual Financial Stat	1.1 Budget Unity	2.1. Budgetary Contingencies
	3.2. Internal Consistency	3.3 Public Participation	2.5. Financial Sector Exposure
	3.3. Historical Revisions	4.1. Independent Evaluation	3.1. Subnational Governments
	4.2. External Audit	4.3. Forecast Reconciliation	3.2. Public Corporations
LOW IMPORTANCE	1.4. Coverage of Tax Expenditures	1.2. Macroeconomic Forecasts	2.2. Asset and Liability Management
	2.1. Frequency of In-Year Reporting	1.3. Medium-term Budget Frameworks	2.3. Guarantees
	3.1. Classification	1.4. Investment Projects	2.6. Natural Resources
	4.1. Statistical Integrity	3.1. Fiscal Policy Objectives	2.7. Environmental Risks

LEVEL OF PRACTICE	RATING			
	NOT MET	BASIC	GOOD	ADVANCED

Fig. 11.2 Turkey's map in terms of fiscal transparency measurement level. *Source* IMF (2017, p. 12)

Turkey has been subject to the IMF's evaluation in 2000, 2008, and 2015 in terms of fiscal transparency. After the amendment to the Regulation made in 2014, new fiscal transparency evaluation was requested by Turkey, and the IMF mission in 2015 made a new fiscal transparency evaluation according to the new Regulation and the evaluation report was published in July 2017. Since the first IMF's evaluation in 2000, Turkey has improved the quality of fiscal information in terms of comprehensiveness, timeliness, and reliability. Figure 11.2 shows a map showing the fiscal transparency measurement level published after the fiscal transparency evaluation.

At the published measurement level, in the field of "**Fiscal Reporting**," "**Historical Revisions**" could not be met and remained as red area. Again, in the field of "**Fiscal Forecasting and Budgeting**," "**Supplementary Budget**," "**Public Participation**," and "**Independent Evaluation**" were not met and remained as red area, as well. "**Specific Fiscal Risks**," "**Long-Term Fiscal Sustainability**," and "**Natural Resources**" were not met in the field of "**Fiscal Risk Analysis and Management**" and remained as red area. Within the scope of IMF's transparency evaluation report in 2017, seven red areas that were not met can be explained as follows:

- **Historical Revisions**: Major revisions to historical fiscal statistics are not reported in Turkey.
- **Supplementary Budget**: According to Law, in the event that appropriations in the budgets of public administrations included in the central government turns to be insufficient, or in order to carry out unforeseen services, a supplementary budget can be prepared in a way to capture revenues to meet expenditures. In terms of material changes regarding approved budget are not generally authorized by the parliament in Turkey.
- **Public Participation**: In Turkey, government provides a summary of the implications of budget figures via citizen budget. On the other hand, to participate in budget deliberations are not possible for citizens in line with IMF's criteria.

- **Independent Evaluation**: There is no independent entity evaluating the credibility of fiscal forecast in Turkey.
- **Specific Fiscal Risks**: The government does not publish a regular report regarding specific fiscal risks to its fiscal forecasts in Turkey.
- **Long-term Fiscal Sustainability**: The government does not publish projections of the sustainability of main public finance in the long term.
- **Natural Resources**: The volume and value of major natural resource assets are not valued, managed, and disclosed.

11.7 International Budget Partnership Open Budget Survey

The International Budget Partnership (IBP), a nonprofit NGO founded in 1997, measures the country's budget transparency via Open Budget Index. By means of its survey, IBP measures whether the countries' central governments share their budget information with the public, the timing and content of the basic budget documents to be prepared in the budget process, their scope, whether they are up-to-date and useful, etc., and reveals the results by indexing the countries in terms of fiscal transparency. The Open Budget Survey (IBP) has been organized every two years since 2006.

There are eight basic budget documents that must be generated by the countries according to open budget index:

(1) Pre-Budget Statement
(2) Executive's Budget Proposal
(3) Enacted Budget
(4) Citizen Budget
(5) In-Year Reports
(6) Mid-Year Review
(7) Year-End Report
(8) Audit Report.

Turkey has participated in open budget surveys since 2006, and the latest survey results were published in 2017. According to the results of the last index, with 58 points Turkey has ranked 32nd among 115 countries. In 2015, Turkey ranked 58th with 44 points among 102 countries. Therefore, 2017 index results indicated an improvement in fiscal transparency in Turkey. Figure 11.3 shows Turkey's Open Budget Index scores for each year.

Figure 11.4 shows the knowledge of whether the eight basic documents produced by Turkey (within the framework of the methodology adopted by the Open Budget Index) are made available to the public.

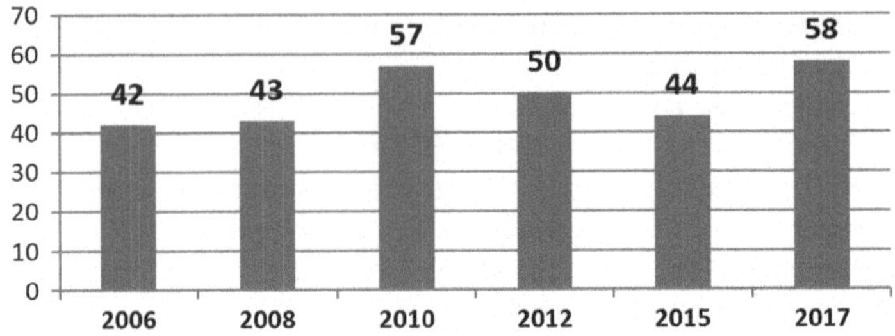

Fig. 11.3 Open Budget Index scores for Turkey (2006–2017). *Source* Turkey Open Budget Survey Country Summary (2017). Retrieved from https://www.internationalbudget.org/wp-content/uploads/turkey-open-budget-survey-2017-summary.pdf

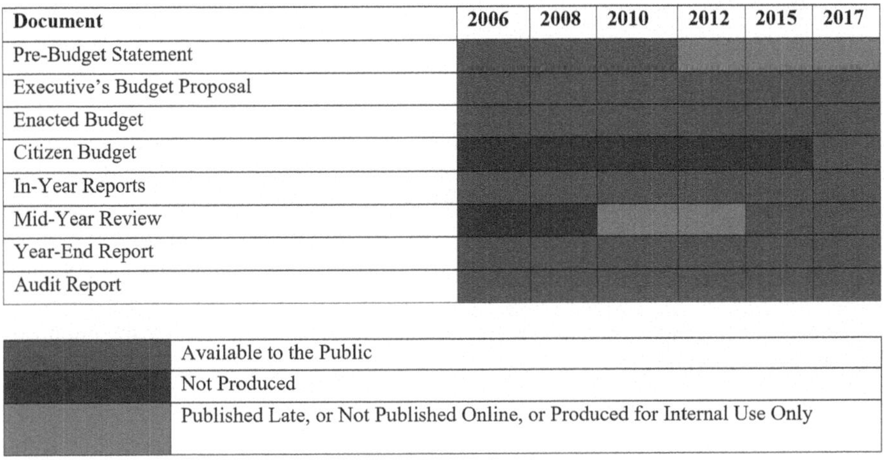

Fig. 11.4 Public availability of budget documents (2006–2017). *Source* Turkey Open Budget Survey Country Summary (2017). Retrieved from https://www.internationalbudget.org/wp-content/uploads/turkey-open-budget-survey-2017-summary.pdf

As it is clear in Fig. 11.4, Turkey received lower scores in relevant questions of the survey conducted in 2012, 2015, and 2017 due to the late publication of Pre-Budget statements. Again, since it did not have Citizen Budget in 2006, 2008, 2010, 2012, and 2015, it received a lower score from the relevant question, yet it received a full score since it published Citizen Budget in 2017. Another development with respect to the Mid-Year Review is that, in 2010 and 2012, Turkey improved its poor performance of 2006 and 2008, and received full scores in the surveys during the last two years.

11.8 Conclusion

With the global crisis of 2008, public financial management reforms were once again on the agenda of the countries, and the rush for eliminating "public policy failures" that undermines fiscal discipline started on financial policy side. The recent crisis has shown that the deficiencies in the field of fiscal transparency have again been one of the major causes. Therefore, it is important to determine the countries' fiscal transparency level within the framework of the evaluations made by their own and international organizations, and to eliminate the shortcomings in terms of fight against future crises and maintaining fiscal discipline.

At this point, as is the case for other developing countries, Turkey should resolve the shortcomings in the area of fiscal transparency in a manner consistent with international standards draw lessons from fiscal transparency evaluations and do its homework on time. The abovementioned shortcomings can be summarized as the supplementary budget, credibility of fiscal forecast, fiscal risk assessment, budget calendar, institutional scope of fiscal reports, program classification, and quality of citizen's budget.

The first homework to be done within this scope is to broaden the institutional scope of the fiscal reports in such a way to include all public institutions and to make an overall evaluation on the fiscal performance of the public sector. Then, major changes to the budget appropriations are made through a "supplementary budget" to be approved by the parliament within the year, and thus, a tighter budget discipline should be ensured.

In order to increase the reliability of the economic and fiscal estimates, macroeconomic estimates of the government should be compared with the figures estimated by the independent organizations. The Ministry of Treasury and Finance should enhance the quality of citizen's budget which has been published since 2017 in order to encourage policy-based and result-oriented debates on budget priorities. Turkey should publish an annual statement including annual macro-fiscal scenarios and certain fiscal risks, along with a medium-term fiscal risk statement. Turkey should take necessary steps to publish Medium Term Program and Medium Term Financial Plan in a timely manner.

Turkey should change budget calendar in a way to ensure that the Medium Term Program and Medium Term Fiscal Plan are submitted in spring, final accounts are submitted in summer and annual budget is submitted in early autumn, with the aim of providing the Parliament with sufficient time to conduct audit on each document. On the other hand, it is considered that it would be appropriate to classify the expenditures under the programs and the general level of economic classification and allocate appropriation on this basis, in order to encourage the policy-based and result-oriented discussions on budget priorities. Finally, Turkey should increase the quality of information provided in audit reports.

References

Alt J.E., & D.D. Lassen. (2006). Fiscal Transparency, Political Parties, and Debt in OECD Countries. European Economic Review, 50 (6), 1403–39.

Arbatli, E., & Escolano, J. (2012). Fiscal Transparency, Fiscal Performance and Credit Ratings. IMF Working Paper No. 12/156. Washington DC, Usa.

Dabla-Norris, E., and others. (2010). Budget Institutions and Fiscal Performance in Low-Income Countries. IMF Working Paper No. 10/80. Washington DC, USA.

Emil, F. & Yılmaz, H. (2004). Mali Saydamlık İzleme Raporu. Tesev Yayınları. İstanbul, Türkiye.

Erdoğan, İtibar. (2005). Kamu Mali Yönetiminde Mali Saydamlık ve Türkiye Açısından Değerlendirilmesi. Devlet Bütçe Uzmanlığı Raporu. Ankara, Turkiye.

Glennerster, R., & Y. Shin. (2008). Does Transparency Pay? Staff Papers, IMF, 55(1), 183–209.

Hameed, F. (2005). Fiscal Transparency and Economic Outcomes. IMF Working Paper No. 05/225. Washington DC, USA.

IMF. (2014). Policy Paper Update On The Fiscal Transparency Initiative New Fiscal Transparency Code, Fiscal Affairs Department, policy paper. Washington DC, USA.

IMF. (2017). Turkey Fiscal Transparency Evaluation Report, Country Report No. 17/208. Washington DC, USA.

IMF. (2018). Fiscal Transparency Handbook. Fiscal Affairs Department staff. Washington DC, USA.

Kopits, G. & Craig J. (1998). Transparency in Government Operations, Occasional Paper 158. Washington DC, USA.

OECD. (2002). OECD Best Practices in Budget Transparency. OECD Journal of Budgeting, 1(3):7–14.

OECD. (2017). Budget Transparency Toolkit: Practical Steps for Supporting Openness, Integrity and Accountability in Public Financial Management. Paris, France.

SPO. (2000). Specialisation Committee Report: Re-structure of Public Financial Management and Fiscal Transparency. State Planning Office. Ankara, Turkey.

Wehner, J., & P. de Renzio. (2011). Citizens, Legislators, and Executive Disclosure: The Political Determinants of Fiscal Transparency. IBF Working Papers 3. Washington DC, USA.

Yüksel, Cüneyt. (2005). Devlette Etikten Etik Devlete: Kamu Yönetiminde Etik. Tüsiad, Devlette Etik Altyapı Dizisi No:2. İstanbul, Turkiye.

Ali Yıldırım Eker is an Internal Auditor at Ministry of Treasury and Finance. Prior to this post, he was a budget expert at Ministry of Finance for 15 years. Ali completed his BA at Ankara University, School of Political Sciences with major in public finance and holds a master degree from Duke University (Master of International Development Policy/Public Finance Management). Ali is a Ph.D. (Public Finance) candidate at Ankara University, School of Political Sciences. Being a budget expert allowed him to gain huge experience in preparing important policy documents such as medium-term fiscal plan, budget, and to lead budget preparation and implementation process. He participated in technical discussions on macroeconomic and fiscal issues with the officials from EU, IMF and other international organizations. His former position in the Ministry of Finance gave him a chance to execute and participate in EU projects. In this regard, he executed "Effective Budget Analysis Project", funded by EU/National Agency, in 2007–2008 as the project coordinator. Ali's professional experiences regarding central government budget, medium-term fiscal framework, fiscal transparency, internal audit, internal control and public financial management issues enabled him to produce articles, reports and book chapters. His ongoing Ph.D. dissertation research broadly focuses on fiscal openness and open budget index issues.

Part IV
Government Financial Management Information Systems

Chapter 12
Integrated Public Financial Management Information Systems in Turkey

Habip Demirhan

12.1 Introduction

The rapid change in technology gives governments an opportunity to develop their financial systems. Governments in developing countries are increasingly exploring methods and systems to modernize and improve their financial systems. Over the years, the governments have aimed at producing an effective, efficient, accountable, transparent, secure, and comprehensive financial reporting and management system. Financial management information systems—the oldest record-keeping methods, dating back hundreds of years—include the recording of financial information based on accounting practices. In other words, it is not a new concept either in the literature or for implementation. However, with the rapid development of information technologies, developed countries have shown an increased tendency to digitize and transfer activities related to public financial management onto the electronic environments. One of the most important activities is the Integrated Financial Management Information System (IFMIS), which allows public institutions to digitize key aspects of budget implementations and accounting procedures. IFMIS is a budgeting and accounting system that manages spending, processing, payment, reporting and budgeting for governments and other entities, based on information technologies. An IFMIS bundles significant financial management functions into one software suite of applications (Chado 2015). The governments implement IFMIS to increase the efficiency and the effectiveness of their financial management. The system helps the governments to facilitate adoption of modern public expenditure's best practices for keeping with international standards and benchmarks (Chado 2015; International Consortium on Governmental Financial Management 2008).

H. Demirhan (✉)
Hakkari University, Hakkari, Turkey
e-mail: habipdemirhan@hakkari.edu.tr

H. Kıral and T. Akdemir (eds.), *Public Financial Management Reforms in Turkey: Progress and Challenges, Volume 1*, Accounting, Finance, Sustainability, Governance & Fraud: Theory and Application, https://doi.org/10.1007/978-981-15-1914-7_12

The IFMIS has become one of the most important financial management reform practices. The aim of this reform is to promote efficiency, effectiveness, accountability, transparency, comprehensive financial reporting, and security of data management. The IFMIS represents an enormous, complex strategic reform process. Therefore, the scope and functionality of the system varies across countries (Chado 2015). Developing countries face major challenges of institutional, political, technical, and operational nature. As a result, the IFMIS has been promoted as a core component of public financial reforms in developing countries. Successful case studies are available for countries such as Kosovo, The Slovak Republic, Tanzania, and Ethiopia. These studies indicate that supporting successful implementation of an IFMIS should include a clear commitment from the relevant authorities to the objectives of the financial reform (Chêne and Hodess 2009).

This chapter examines the reform process of IFMIS in Turkey. The chapter aims to explain the current situation and challenges of the applications of IFMIS in Turkey. Our methodology used literature studies to investigate and solve the research problem. The results indicate that there are numerous challenges concerning the implementation of IFMIS in Turkey.

12.2 Integrated Financial Management Information System

Financial Management System (FMIS) is an information system that tracks the financial events and summarizes information. FMIS generally refers to automating financial operations and it supports policy decisions, adequate management reporting, and preparation of auditable financial statements. An effective FMIS needs to be designed with good relationships between software, hardware, personnel, controls, procedures, and data. The FMIS may include cost management, fund management, and financial reporting. Public financial management system is designed to support all financial operations, collect accurate timely, complete, reliable and consistent information on all public financial events, provide adequate management reporting, support government-wide and agency policy decisions, and produce auditable financial statements.

An Integrated Financial Management Information System (IFMIS) is an automated system that is used for public financial management. Generally, IFMIS applies high technology to enhance financial management and reduce mismanagement of corruption. IFMIS is defined as a system that can provide a rapid and an effective access to reliable financial data and enhance the financial control of the state/public authorities, improve the effectiveness and efficiency of public activities, move the budget process to a higher level of transparency and accountability, and accelerate public activities (Diamond and Khemani 2006). In another definition, IFMIS is defined as a set of automation solutions that enable governments to plan, execute, and monitor the budget (Dener and Min 2013). The first generation of public financial management reforms concentrated on establishing well-functioning Treasury and Treasury Single Account to solve operational issues.

In order to implement IFMIS, international organizations such as International Monetary Fund and World Bank support the projects that provide a combination of technical assistance, training, financial resources, and procurement supports. Thus, they play an important role in supporting and shaping the financial management systems of the member countries through international incentives (Uysal and Aldemir 2018). There are four characteristics of IFMIS (US Government Accountability Office 2001):

- Classification of standard data for recording events.
- Common processes for similar transactions.
- Internal control over the data entry, reporting, and transaction processing applied consistently.
- A design to avoid unnecessary duplication of transaction entry.

The system should have an ability to collect timely, accurate, complete, reliable, consistent information and provide adequate management reporting. Additionally, the system should support preparation and execution of budget and government-wide and agency policy decisions. It should facilitate the preparation of financial statements and provide complete audit trail to facilitate audits. As a result, in a digitalized world, the implementation of IFMIS has proved a real challenge. The Information and Communication Technologies (ITCs) have a significant role in fighting corruption for the states by promoting transparency of information and greater comprehensiveness across public institutions (Chêne and Hodess 2009). IFMIS is a core component of financial reforms to promote security of data management, efficiency, and comprehensive financial reporting.

IFMIS refers to the system formed by the software programs supporting functional processes related to public financial management, working interactively with each other and sharing information while it needs. As a result, a fully functioning IFMIS contributes to improved governance by providing real-time financial information that financial and other managers can utilize to effectively administer programs, develop budgets, and manage resources. The IFMIS has increased public sector legitimacy, produced timely and efficient accounting of public resources, increased government accountability and transparency and made it possible to audit public accounts and strengthen internal control in government units.

12.3 Benefits and Challenges of IFMIS

IFMIS processes financial management transactions on a single software platform and a single database, facilitates sharing of common data and flow of information among different functions and processes of an enterprise, allows users to track and analyze trends in a wide range of events in an integrated fashion to plan for future performance improvements across enterprises (International Consortium of Governmental Financial Management 2009). Besides a number of ways that IFMIS can improve public finance management, the most important role of IFMIS is to enhance credibility and confidence of budget through greater comprehensiveness and transparency of information (Chêne and Hodess 2009). The governments need timely and accurate data for budget management and decision-making process to improve the planning and execution of their budget. Numerous benefits of IFMIS were cited by the researchers. The most important goals for an IFMIS acquisition are effectiveness and improved outcomes. According to Parry (2005), IFMIS improves management of resources, reduces fraud and corruption, improves transparency and accountability, provides optimal resource allocation opportunity, lowers transaction costs, and finally provides a better fiscal management. Some researchers claim that there are no systematic assessments of the impact of IFMIS on corruption. However, IFMIS can have a deterrent function on corruption by increasing the risks of detection. A well-designed IFMIS can provide a number of features that may help detect excessive payments, fraud, and theft (Chêne and Hodess 2009). On one hand IFMIS implies efficiency reforms and on the other hand implies reforms that change existing procedures. For a successful IFMIS implementation, IT reforms are crucial. Mostly, IT reforms are perceived as complex, resource intensive, risky, and require major procedural changes, often involving high-level officials, and lacking incentives for reform. Decision-makers should be convinced that benefits exceed risks. The agencies should recognize the need for a new system. Therefore, the IFMIS must be carefully designed to meet agency's needs and functional requirements, including the accounting and financial managements the system should perform (Chêne and Hodess 2009).

Fiscal transparency, fiscal discipline and accountability are the most important elements for financial management. The achievements of these elements depends on open data accession. IFMIS can improve fiscal transparency through disclosure of public finance information to citizens. Therefore, the data of published budget should be accurate, timely, easily accessible, and meaningful to ordinary citizens (Dener and Min 2013). The accession of data also improves the accountability and fiscal discipline while fiscal transparency can improve trust in government. Consequently, the benefits of IFMIS implementation can be summarized as below (ICPAK 2017; Hendriks 2013):

- Enables efficient resource allocation mechanisms;
- Improves management information for decision-making;
- Establishes effective links between key players in accounting and financial management;
- Improves financial controls by availing reliable and timely financial information;
- Improves accounting, recording, and reporting through timely, accurate financial data provision;
- Accelerates the pace/scope of economic growth;
- Enhances development of partners' confidence.

In addition to the benefits mentioned above, IFMIS also enables government reforms; improves efficiency and controls, budget planning and decision-making, and confidence through transparency; increases government revenue; and reduces costs.

12.4 The IFMIS Experiences in Turkey

In Turkey, the public financial management reforms started in the early 1990s. In 1995, an agreement was signed between Turkey and the World Bank to restructure public financial management. In 2000, the government of Turkey requested the support of the World Bank for Public Expenditure and Institutional Structure Review (PEIR). PEIR is intended to take place in two stages. In the first phase, the government planned to focus on public expenditure reforms. In the second phase, they concentrated on institutional issues related to the development of public sector management. Since then, various regulations have been made to emphasize the necessity of the system. Finally, with the leading decision Number 2002/3, the Ad Hoc Committee on Restructuring of Public Finance Management and Fiscal Transparency prepared a report and explained the requirement of a new system.

In 2003, the Public Financial Management and Control Law No: 5018 was adopted. This law has been one of the most important reforms of the administrative transformation of the public sector. In 2010, The Court of Accounts Law No: 6085 was adopted. Both of these laws mention accounting, reporting, and budgeting as the core concepts of new integrated system. In order to meet the basic requirements of the new system, public administrations try to make use of information and communication technologies as much as possible and to develop and operate information systems related to their respective fields. However, the system remained at the institutional level rather than covering the whole of public financial management, which led to creation of redundant jobs and expenditures in some areas, and the inefficient use of public resources (Uysal and Aldemir 2018). For this reason, the 10th Development Plan (2014–2018) determined the prior transformation programs. In 2015, the core concept of Prior Transformation Programs has been issued. The 10th Development Plan also included the Rationalization of Public Expenditure Program which was coordinated by former Ministry of Development and Ministry of Finance.

The Ministry of Finance is responsible for "Keeping the Current Expenditures Under Control" and "Strengthening Program-based Budget Link." Strengthening the Program-based Budget Link was the fifth component of the Rationalization of Public Expenditure Program. The "Integrating Management Information System" was mentioned as the first policy and the establishment of Integrated Public Management Information System as the first action under the fifth component of the Program. Then, it was mentioned both in Medium term program (2016–2018) and Medium-term Fiscal Plan (2016–2018). In National e-Government Strategy and Action Plan, the responsible and related institutions for integration of information systems for public financial management have been determined. The main aim of these plans and programs is to develop an integrated public financial information system. On May 16, 2017 Prime Minister's Circular was published in Official Gazette No. 20068 in order to increase the efficiency of public expenditures and integrate information systems infrastructures in public financial management to achieve this aim. The basic principles of the IFMIS project can be summarized as below (Prime Minister's Circular 2017):

- An innovative and process-oriented approach will be adopted in order to restructure the system.
- All financial management processes will be established together with the stakeholders that have the authority and responsibility.
- The Ministry of Finance will deliver services related to expenditure processes within the framework of a process-oriented approach.
- The administrations having the necessary technical infrastructure and performing the pre-financial process transactions through their own information systems will develop integration solutions that will enable them to perform their financial process through their own information systems.
- The integrated system design will be built on electronic document–electronic signature structure on the purpose of all of works, and transactions within the scope of Law No. 5018 could be carried out in electronic environment.
- The integrated financial management information system will be designed to include modern practices and methods such as e-Procurement, e-Invoice, e-Collection, e-Audit, financial statement analysis, risk analysis, decision support system, and early warning system.

The main objective of the project is to provide a technological integration of automation systems, electronic documents, electronic signatures, automated accounting, and the process-oriented integrated IT system infrastructure for financial management system from the beginning of budget preparation to the Turkish Grand National Assembly's legislative process. Also, the project determined the observed problems with the existing automation systems developed by different institutions as below:

- Limited integration between information systems,
- There are redundant work processes and different implementation can be observed for the same process,
- Inadequacy of the expected level of benefit from information technologies,
- Labor-intensive processes and productivity loss,
- There is no common data dictionary for information systems,
- Difficulty in target-budget-performance and accountability through plan-program-budget linkage,
- failure to create the data set needed in decision-making processes,
- Facing with difficulties in allocation of resources according to priorities and with tracing these transactions,
- Using new technologies and adaptation problem due to existing structures of systems,

- Limitation of accessing financial information produced by central systems.
- The responsibilities, obligations, and standards have not been clearly defined,
- Inadequate utilization of information technologies in audit processes,

Expected Outcomes are (IFMIS Policy Paper and Action Plan 2017; Yıldırım 2017)

- To obtain and use public resources effectively, economically, and efficiently;
- Increased level of control in expenditure processes;
- Development of financial reporting opportunities in the public sector;
- Effective and widespread use of statistical analysis methods in decision-making processes;
- Faster and more accurate processing of works and transactions in financial processes;
- Minimizing paper use and eliminating problems due to paper-based processes with the widespread use of electronic document;
- Evaluation of human resources in productive areas due to increase in automation level;
- Increasing the use of computer-based techniques in internal and external audit activities;
- Accelerating the e-Transformation process of our country.

The integrated Public Financial Management Information System consists of integrated systems composed of softwares that interact with each other with regard to some functional processes. These systems are: Macroeconomic forecasting and planning, Budget management, Financial planning, Cash management, Debt management, Revenue management, Public staff management, Asset management, Expenditure management, Accounting and financial reporting, Monitoring and Evaluation, and Audit (IFMIS Policy Paper and Action Plan 2017). In our study, the structure of some of these important systems will be explained and examined.

12.5 The IFMIS Policy Paper and Action Plan

Public Financial Management and Control Law No. 5018 constitutes the basic legal framework for public financial management and aims to ensure accountability and fiscal transparency as well as effective, economic, and efficient use of public resources. For this purpose, the law regulates the structure and operation of public financial management, preparation and implementation of public budgets, accounting, reporting, and financial control of all financial transactions. Law No. 5018 -prepared with the aim of creating a public financial management and control system in compliance with international standards and European Union norms- aims to increase efficiency in the process of budget preparation and implementation, ensure accountability and transparency in financial management, establish an effective internal control system. The new financial structure established by Law No. 5018 brings a new approach of which financial management and control will be carried out under the management and responsibility of the institutions, and increases the functions and responsibilities of public institutions. In this context, political responsibility and administrative responsibility are separated from each other and the political responsible (Minister or Mayor) and the administrative officer (undersecretary, mayor, other top managers) of each public institution budget are determined separately.

The rapid transformation of information and communication technologies brings new opportunities for the public institutions to develop their automation systems. In Turkey, each institution has developed its automation system independently and this situation brings out various problems. Some of these problems can be listed as below (IFMIS Policy Paper and Action Plan 2017):

- The development and management of related automation system independently lead to a limited level of integration between the public financial management information systems. Therefore, it becomes difficult to provide the required information timely, completely, and accuratcly. In addition, it also causes the creation of redundant job processes and different implementations for the same process.
- The process of basic financial transactions cannot be executed completely in electronic environment despite the developed automation systems, and some stages of the processes are still paper-based. Paper-based processing steps affecting the organizational structure of public financial management eliminate the expected level of benefit from information technologies significantly.
- Most of the routine procedures carried out based on paper are labor-intensive and this causes the productivity loses in terms of human resources utilization.
- There is no common data glossary for public financial management information systems.

In order to solve the problems mentioned above and solve the problems related to the automation systems developed and operated by different institutions, development of an integrated public financial management information system in line with the principles stipulated in Law No. 5018 is required. For this reason, IFMIS Policy Paper and Action Plan was released in 2017 within the context of Prime Minister Circular No:2017/7. The Policy Paper and Action Plan covers the 2017–2020 period and determines all actions and policies clearly.

The Regulation on Implementation Procedures and Principles of the Integrated Public Financial Management Information System published in Official Gazette on June 26, 2018 within the context of the Prime Minister Circular No:2017/7. The IFMIS project is coordinated by the Ministry of Finance. The purpose of this regulation is to create, record, deliver, save, and submit; and keeping accounts, records, and similar contents on electronic environment; and to determine the interoperability standards and security policies between the information systems related to the processes covered by the Law in order to ensure that the transactions mentioned in the Public Financial Management and Control Law No: 5018 are carried out electronically and in an integrated manner.

12.6 New Accounting Information System

The integrated Public Financial Management Information System (BKMYS) projects bring with it a comprehensive renewal and transformation process that directly concerns institutions within the scope of general administration institutions. The division of a project of this scale into certain stages is essential for obtaining successful results. For this purpose, at first stage, a new accounting system that is compatible with the principles of interoperability and e-document is being designed. For this reason, the Ministry of Finance has already renewed the public accounting information system called "Say2000i." The basic principle of the new accounting system is to register the administrative ledgers with a rowed per diem number. In this manner, the system provides flexibility to do changes on the existing job processes and organizational structure. The New Public Accounting Information System was developed in order to make automatic registration of jobs and transactions of public administrations' accounting units with a process-oriented approach (Table 12.1 and Fig. 12.1).

The new accounting system is administration based. It is appropriate to use Financial Management Approach and it also supports institutional transformation. The new system is accountable, open to integration, and uses smart accounting processes. In other words, the new system is interoperability based and it removes the paper-based processes. It offers the opportunity to reorganize the accounting units. The payment information and accounting information are separated. The processes are proper to the staff's expertise.

Table 12.1 A brief comparison of old and new accounting system

Say2000i	New accounting system
Accounting of accounting unit	Institutional Accounting, Multiple Account Plan Management
Accounting record form	Process-based Accounting
Process steps based on paper	Electronic document (preparation for applications such as e-procurement, e-invoice, e-collection, etc.)
Traditional data exchange methods	Improved integration possibilities
Desktop/Thinclient	PC + Mobile

Source IFMIS Policy Paper and Action Plan 2017

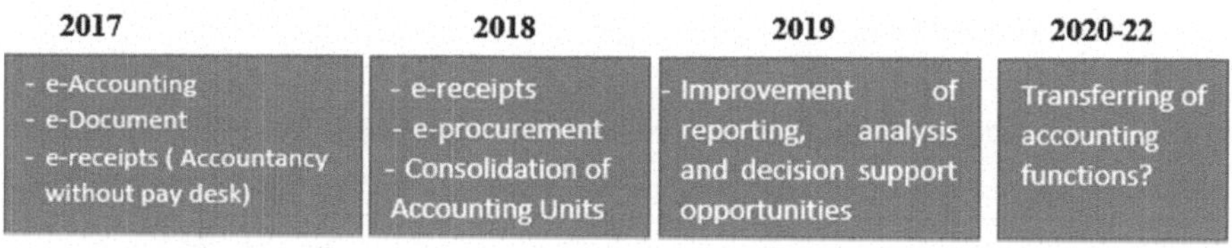

Fig. 12.1 The Transformation of Accounting Process. *Source* Gathered from IFMIS Policy Paper and Action Plan 2017; Uysal and Aldemir 2018; Polat 2007

12.7 New Expenditure Management System

The New Expenditure Management System is an information system that allows public administration to prepare “Spending Instruction Approval Document 1” and “Payment Order Document” electronically in accordance with e-document standards. The spending instruction, approval certificate, and tender approval certificate that are used in the old system are redesigned as a single electronic document format named spending instruction approval document based on the Universal Business Language. This definition is also a preparation for the e-procurement infrastructure which is planned to be formed in the later stages of the project.

The Expenditure Management System consists of the following modules:

1. **Expenditure Management Module**
   - *Expenditures*: Expenditures and Payment Orders;
     Definitions: Subscriptions, e invoice;
   - *Travel Allowance Transactions:* List of audit task, List of Audit Advance, Entrance of travel allowance information;
   - *References:* query of expenditure unit, query of payment code.
2. **Movable Management Module**
   - Movable transactions.
3. **Assistance Module**

Ongoing Studies: e-procurement processes, Asset management, Reporting module.

The main purpose of the New Expenditure Management System is to fulfill the expenditure processes, which are carried out on the basis of the wet signed documents in accordance with its legislation, with the e-document prepared according to the determined standards. It is aimed that transactions in financial processes can be carried out in an integrated manner with the New State Accounting Information System, thanks to the Spending Instruction Approval Certificate and the Payment Order Document, which is designed to provide a structured file format (Table 12.2).

12.8 E-Document Standards & Standard Documents and Reporting

The standard document and reporting refer to the framework for e-document standards defined in the New Accounting Information System. The old documentary process was paper-based and the documents were transferred physically. The e-document definition is based on functional differentiation. The functional differentiation allows to define e-document definitions for other regulatory institutions. Standard Document and Reporting process is defined as a result of the development

Table 12.2 The differences between old expenditure system and new expenditure management system

Old expenditure system	New expenditure management system
There are accounting records in the payment order document issued by the spending unit	There are no accounting records in the payment order document. Reference values containing verbal expressions that can be easily understood by the personnel of the spending unit are used
There is no process logic of expenditure	The system starts with the expenditure order and ends with the payment order certificate and the payment order certificate attachments can be kept on the system
The system does not support e-document	The system design is based on e-document.
The users that make transactions in the system are the authorizing officers and realization officers	The system users that make transactions are data entry officers, realization officer, strategy officer, and authorizing officer. The documents prepared by the data entry officer shall be approved electronically by the realization Officer and the authorizing Officer. Besides, Ex ante financial that did not exist in old system is added to the system as a new function. The edited documents can be sent to the Strategy User optionally. These documents can be viewed and examined by the strategy user on the system

Source IFMIS Policy paper and action plan 2017; http://bkmybs.maliye.gov.tr/ (accessed date, 04.01.2018)

of electronic document standards within the scope of "Integrated Public Financial Management System Project was carried out under the coordination of Ministry of Finance General Directorate of Accounting. Standard Document and Reporting is the technical and administrative process for determination and publication of standards related to electronic document circulation and other relevant standards among IT systems as a part of IFMIS project. The e-document formats are determined by the Ministry of Finance based on the studies of Public Financial Management Information System Steering Committee. Process and organizational responsibilities are taken into consideration during the development of the relevant e-document formats. The e-document standards are determined in accordance with the core component technical specification of The United Nations Centre for Trade Facilitation and Electronic Business. Also, the e-documents to be used in public e-procurement applications are determined within the scope of the Universal Business Language (UBL) and the formats for documents used in financial transactions such as Payment Order Document and Accrual Document are developed within the framework of XBRL—The Business Reporting Standards.

As a result, the main objectives of e-document can be listed as below:

- To remove paper-based processes
- To ensure institutional transformation
- To submit required data set
- To create end to end integrated business process
- To provide an interoperability environment.

12.9 Conclusion

We witnessed the rapid development in ICTs recently. This development process forces government to regulate their service delivery methods. Financial management is a core concept for the governments. In early 1990s, Turkey started to transform its financial management system with various reforms. One of these reforms—Public Financial Management and Control Law No. 5018—was accepted in 2003. The main objective of the reform was to strengthen financial discipline and provide transparency and accountability in financial processes. In 2017, Prime Minister's Circular was released in order to ensure that the transactions in Public Management and Control Law No. 5018 are carried out electronically in an integrated manner. The implementation of Integrated Public Financial Management Information System will create an institutional perspective, provide sufficient data sets, eliminate the lack of a common language with a common data glossary, eliminate the creation of redundant job processes, and eliminate paper-based and labor-based processes. There are various benefits of IFMIS project. Some of these benefits are

- It combines different sources of information in a single environment.
- It allows an analytical evaluation.
- It shortens and accelerates decision-making process.
- It develops the financial reporting opportunities in public sector.
- It reduces paper use due to increased use of electronic documents and reduces costs due to paper-based processes.
- It increases transparency and accountability due to accessible information data sets.

We can conclude that the international best practices and regulations are taken into consideration during the project. For example, e-document standards are determined in accordance with the core component technical specification of The United Nations Centre for Trade Facilitation and Electronic Business. Also, public e-documents for public e-procurement applications are determined within the scope of the Universal Business Language (UBL) and the formats for documents used in financial transactions such as Payment Order Document and Accrual Document are developed within the framework of XBRL—The Business Reporting Standards. These regulations are the strengths for the IFMIS project. However, many public institutions still don't have enough information about the whole processes. For this reason, a series of trainings should be planned for the institutions to raise awareness of the project. There are three core components of information management systems. These are: job processes, personnel, and technology. For this reason, the achievement of IFMIS not only depends on technological development but also depends on qualified personnel and clearly defined job processes.

The IFMIS project is a core component for the financial management. It is a fact that all public services will be electronically soon. Therefore, the development of IT database is important. For the achievement of all project objectives, information and communication technologies database should be adequate institutionally. As a result, public resources will be used and obtained effectively, economically, and efficiently while the IFMIS, which will contribute to the more effective transactions of the internal control system in public sector, is fully implemented.

References

Chado, H. M. (2015). The effect of integrated financial management information system on the financial management of public sector in Kenya. *Unpublished MSC Project, University of Nairobi.*

Chêne, M., & Hodess, R. (2009). The Implementation of Integrated Financial Information Management Systems (IFMIS). https://www.u4.no/publications/the-implementation-of-integrated-financial-manage. ment-systems-ifmis.pdf (Accessed date: 02.01.2019).

Dener, C. & Min, S.Y. (2013). *Financial Management Information Systems and Open Budget Data: Do The Governments Report on Where the Money Goes?* Washington DC: The World Bank.

Diamond, J. & Khemani, P. (2006). Introducing financial management information systems in developing countries, *OECD Journal on Budgeting*. 5(3). 97–132.

Hendriks, C. J. (2013). Integrated Financial Management Information Systems: Guidelines for effective implementation by the public sector of South Africa. *South African Journal of Information Management*, *15*(1), 1–9.

Integrated Public Financial Management Information System Policy Paper and Action Plan (2018).

International Consortium of Governmental Financial Management (2009). Use of Financial Management Information Systems (FMIS) to improve financial management and accountability in the public sector. *Conference Proceedings*. December 2007. Washington DC. https://tr.scribd.com/document/10269078/Use-of-Financial-Management-Information-Systems-to-Improve-Financial-Management-and-Accountability-in-the-Public-Sector (Accessed date: 02.01.2019).

ICPAK (2017). The Benefits, Challenges and way forward of IFMIS in Kenya. *IPSAS Workshop*.18th-19th July. Kakamega. https://www.icpak.com/wp-content/uploads/2017/07./IFMIS-CPA-Andrew-Rori.pdf (Accessed 04.01.2019).

Parry, M. (2005). Why government IFMS procurements so often get it wrong. *ACCA International Public Sector Bulletin*, *4*, 4–7.

Polat, N. (2007). Management Information System and Implementations of the Court of Account (Yönetim Bilgi Sistemi ve Sayıştay'da Yürütülen Çalışmalar). *Sayıştay Dergisi*, 18(65). 187–198.

US Government Accountability Office (2001). *Federal Financial Management System Requirements*. The Joint Financial Management Improvement Program. November. No: A02576.

The Prime Ministry Circular No. 2017/7 on the Integrated Public Financial Management Information System Policy Paper and Action Plan.

Uysal, T. U. & Aldemir, C. (2018). Digital Public Financial Management System and Blockchain Technology (Dijital Kamu Mali Yönetim Sistemi ve Blok Zinciri Teknolojisi). *Muhasebe ve Vergi Uygulamaları Dergisi*. 11(3). 505–522.

Yıldırım, A (2017). *Integrated Public Financial Management Information System Project: General Description, Policy Paper and Action Plan* (Bütünleşik Kamu Mali Yönetim Bilişim Sistemi Projesi Genel Açıklamalar, Politika Belgesi ve Eylem Planı) https://www.bumko.gov.tr/Eklenti/10657,butunlesik-kamu-mali-yonetim-bilisim-sistemi-projesi-arif-yildirimpdf.pdf?0 (Accessed date: 07.01.2019).
The Courts of Account Law No:6085.
Medium-term program (2016–2018).
Medium-term Fiscal Plan (2016–2018).
National e-Government Strategy and Action Plan.
Public Financial Management and Control Law No. 5018.
10th Development Plan (2014–2018).

Habip Demirhan is Assistant Professor of Public Finance at Faculty of Economics and Administrative Science of Hakkari University. Dr. Demirhan has also been serving as Vice-Dean at Faculty of Economics and Administrative Science since January 2018. He graduated from Faculty of Political Sciences of Ankara University in 2005. During 2006–2011, he worked in local governments as project manager and foreign relation advisor. He wrote and coordinated many EU projects. Shortly after that he started his academic career at Hakkari University as a research assistant. Dr. Demirhan received his both MSc and PhD from Social Sciences Institute of Dokuz Eylul University. He has been working as an Assistant professor of public finance at Hakkari University since September 2017. Dr. Demirhan's research and teaching interests are primarily in the Budgeting and Fiscal Issues. He has various articles, book chapters in the field of public finance.

Part V
EU and Fiscal Compliance

Chapter 13
Alignment of Turkey with the European Union in Public Financial Management and Control

Nihal Samsun Karabacak

13.1 Introduction

Turkey was acknowledged as a candidate country of the European Union (EU) at the Helsinki Summit of December 10–11, 1999. Later in the European Council meeting of December 17, 2004, it was confirmed that Turkey fulfills the political criteria and on October 3, 2005, the accession negotiations officially started. There are 35 chapters for negotiations that aim at transposing the EU *Acquis* into national law. So far, 16 chapters were opened to accession negotiations, whereas only one chapter is temporarily closed (Current Situation in Accession Negotiations 2016).

The conditions for EU accession emphasize the requirement to establish a strong public administration in order to transpose and implement the EU *Acquis* effectively. In this regard, the European Commission outlined six key reform areas as the 'Principles of Public Administration'. The performance of the candidate and potential candidate countries in applying these principles is an indicator of their capacity for effectively implementing the EU *Acquis*. Public financial management (PFM) is one of the six areas mentioned above, for which the main requirements that should be followed during the European integration process are defined (SIGMA 2017a).

Public financial management is among the most important areas of reform achieved by Turkey in European Union accession process. While the progress in EU alignment on the general framework of PFM and the budget are assessed under the public administration reform, specific fields of public financial management are subject to different negotiation chapters.

The following sections will describe the general EU requirements and Turkey's level of alignment in the field of public financial management and its subsystems that are covered under different "chapters," namely, Taxation, Economic and Monetary Policy, and Financial Control, all of which have been opened to negotiations. Then,

N. Samsun Karabacak (✉)
Directorate for European Union Affairs, Ankara, Turkey
e-mail: nsamsun@gmail.com

H. Kıral and T. Akdemir (eds.), *Public Financial Management Reforms in Turkey: Progress and Challenges, Volume 1*, Accounting, Finance, Sustainability, Governance & Fraud: Theory and Application, https://doi.org/10.1007/978-981-15-1914-7_13

the projects that have been carried out in these fields under EU financial assistance will be briefly listed. In the end, there will be a section to discuss the progress achieved and further work to be done in these areas.

This study will not go into the details of the reforms carried out by Turkey in these areas, as they have already been discussed under various parts above. It will rather focus on Turkey's level of compliance in this area.

13.2 Alignment in the Main Pillars of Public Financial Management

The European Commission describes the three important pillars of EU enlargement process as public administration reform, rule of law, and economic governance. These pillars are interrelated and fundamental for the success of both political and economic reforms and implementation of EU legislation and standards. Public administration reform aims at increasing accountability, transparency, and effectiveness for better functioning of the state as well as implementing the reforms on the way to EU membership. Accordingly, public financial management (PFM) is an important element of public administration. In the enlargement process, PFM consists of a commitment to improving budget management through multi-year programs and also having a policy dialogue with the Commission (European Commission 2014c).

The public financial management system covers the whole cycle of budget from preparation to execution, accounting, reporting, external audit, and scrutiny. The system should be designed to achieve strategic allocation and efficient use of resources as well as fiscal discipline, and cover both revenue and expenditure management (European Commission 2018b).

SIGMA was asked by the European Commission to gather evidence and data to monitor the progress in the countries for the assessment of their public administration systems. In this context, SIGMA prepared, among others, key requirements and principles for a sound public financial management system as a guide for candidate countries. While preparing the key principles for its assessments on public financial management, SIGMA has also taken the Public Expenditure and Financial Accountability (PEFA) program as reference. PEFA identifies the key requirement for a good PFM system on budget management, internal control, internal audit, external audit, and public procurement (SIGMA 2017a).

Starting with early 2000s, significant reforms have been realized in Turkey in order to increase the quality of public services and the effectiveness of public financial management. The Law no. 5018 on Public Financial Management and Control (PFMC), which has been prepared in accordance with the EU *Acquis* and international standards, can be considered as the basis of these reforms. The reforms were strengthened by further legislation, such as the Law No. 4749 on Regulating Public Finance and Debt Management, Turkish Court of Accounts Law No. 6085 and Public Procurement Law No. 6518.

The main aim of Law No. 5018 is to ensure economic, effective and efficient acquisition, and utilization of public funds together with accountability and fiscal transparency. With the enactment of this Law, the scope of the budget has been broadened, multi-year budgeting, strategic planning as well as performance-based budgeting systems have been introduced, unification of public accounting has been ensured, effective internal control and internal audit systems have been established, and the scope of audit performed by the Court of Accounts has been extended. The Law No. 5018 regulates all phases of public financial management, from preparation to control and reporting.

In its latest assessment of public financial management in accordance with the above mentioned key requirements and principles, SIGMA stated that most of the key elements of a strong public finances are in place and broad public finances remain robust in Turkey. However, gaps have been found in terms of fiscal rules as well as establishment of an independent oversight institution to monitor these rules (SIGMA 2017b). The main findings of SIGMA (2017b) on public financial management are as follows[1]:

In relation to *budget management*, the medium-term budgetary process is criticized due to the lack of a single institution who owns the entire process, not including the IPA funded projects in projections and not publishing sensitivity analysis or fiscal risk assessment. The exclusion of the revolving funds from annual budget is also found risky, as it creates a weakness in relation to Turkish Grand National Assembly's (TGNA) role in approving the budget, and in successful implementation of fiscal policy.

The unity of treasury is also mentioned in SIGMA reports, saying that the Law No. 5018 provides for a single treasury account. While the report states that the system of cash management and flows are well organized, it is criticized that the cash flows are on a rolling three months basis rather than monthly.

As regards the *debt management*, while the establishment of a strategy and the downward path of debt-to-GDP ratio are mentioned, the coverage of controls around borrowing and the issuance of guarantees is identified as a point of concern. It is also stated that state enterprises and local authorities do not require prior approval for borrowing in the domestic market but does so for foreign borrowing. The increase of Treasury guarantees in recent years is also seen as a matter of concern.

On *budget transparency*, it is stated that the Ministry of Treasury and Finance publishes central government expenditure and revenue reports monthly and financial statistics of general government (central government, social security institutions, local authorities, and state-owned enterprises) quarterly and annually. The monitoring of revolving funds, however, is done by the Ministry of Treasury and Finance through Revolving Funds Financial Management System (SIGMA 2017b). Accordingly, the conditions are in place for budget transparency, and the TCA audits public

[1]This part covers the findings under PFM. The findings on internal control, internal and external audit will be discussed under Chapter 32-Financial Control section.

finances annually. Nevertheless, it is criticized that the monthly budget reports provide consolidated data only and variations from expectations are not explained in reports.

Furthermore, IMF's Country Report on Turkey also evaluates fiscal transparency in Turkey, mentioning that significant progress has been achieved in fiscal transparency practices over the past decade and a half and Turkey has substantially improved the comprehensiveness, timeliness, and reliability of fiscal information, which is publicly available. The report concludes that as a result of the reforms on fiscal transparency, Turkey has made significant progress against the principles of IMF's Fiscal Transparency Code (IMF 2017).

Regarding the *transparency of accounting and reporting practices,* SIGMA (2017b) emphasized that Turkey continued to improve and standardize accounting practices across the general government and further align with international standards and best practices.

Finally, in the area of *public procurement*, it is stated that the Public Procurement Law has been changed many times since its adoption and the main divergences from the EU *Acquis* include a number of exclusions from the Law and implementation of domestic preferences. The fragmented structure and non-alignment with the *Acquis* in public–private partnerships and concessions are also highlighted. It is also mentioned that a draft has been prepared for a new Public Procurement Law and a strategy is being prepared to harmonize public–private partnerships on concessions (SIGMA 2017b). These fields are worked on under Chapter 5: Public Procurement in accession negotiations. However, its details will not be discussed here as the chapter is not opened to accession negotiations yet.

Moreover, in the most recent Regular Report for Turkey, Turkey is criticized for not having an overarching public financial management reform program. Besides, budget transparency on especially public investment programs, civil society's participation in the budgetary process, and involvement of revolving funds into the budget process are stated as the areas to be improved (European Commission 2018a).

13.3 Alignment in Fiscal and Budgetary Surveillance

Sound public finances is one of the most important pillars in EU's economic governance system, which was broadly changed after the economic and financial crisis. As a result of the crisis, government deficits and debts in the member states increased, which revealed the weaknesses in surveillance of fiscal policies. As a response to these weaknesses, EU has taken a wide range of measures, the most important of which is the legislative packages known as the six-pack and two-pack. These two packages of measures aim at increasing economic policy coordination via strengthening budgetary surveillance under the Stability and Growth Pact with stronger sanction mechanisms as well as increased surveillance for Euro Area countries regarding national budgetary preparation under the European Semester process (European Commission 2014b).

European Semester, which was introduced in 2010, is a framework for coordination of economic policies in member states (Verdun and Zeitlin 2018). Through this process, the EU countries discuss their economic reforms and national budgetary plans and the progress is monitored by the European Commission at specific times during the year. The aim of European Semester is to ensure strong public finances; prevent and correct excessive macroeconomic imbalances; speed up structural reforms; and increase growth, jobs, and investment (Efstathiou and Wolff 2018).

The Stability and Growth Pact, which is considered as a supranational fiscal rule, is a part of the European Semester and can be regarded as the fiscal framework of the EU. It is built on a preventive and a corrective arm. The preventive arm aims to ensure that the member states' fiscal policies are consistent with principles of fiscal responsibility and prudence stated in Maastricht Treaty. The corrective arm describes the procedures to be followed when a country is already in the excessive deficit procedure after exceeding the budget deficit limit of 3% of GDP (Corbacho and Ter-Minassian 2013).

Another legislative measure included in the abovementioned packs is the Council Directive 2011/85/EU, which lays down detailed rules for national budgets of Euro Area countries. This Directive requires countries to make the fiscal data publicly available, ensure that their fiscal planning is based on realistic and up-to-date forecasts, operate specific fiscal rules to prevent excessive public deficit or debt, establish a credible and effective medium-term budgetary framework, operate comprehensive public accounting systems and ensure consistency of all accounting procedures in all areas of government activity (Council of the European Union 2011).

The EU strengthened its economic governance exercise also with the enlargement countries to prepare them for their participation in the European Semester after becoming an EU member. The European Commission's support to these countries includes improving economic governance and competitiveness. It is built on the experiences of European Semester process. The candidate countries are expected to improve economic governance systems (European Commission 2014c).

The level of alignment of the candidate countries to European Union's fiscal surveillance mechanisms is followed under Chapter 17, Economic and Monetary Policy. "The *Acquis* in this area covers the independence of central banks in Member States, prohibiting direct financing of the public sector by the central banks and prohibiting privileged access of the public sector to financial institutions. Moreover, Member States are expected to coordinate their economic policies and are subject to the Stability and Growth Pact on fiscal surveillance." (European Commission 2006a, p. 2).

Turkish legislation in the economic and monetary policy area is already significantly convergent with the relevant *Acquis*. Turkey implements a medium-term budgetary framework and the main documents that determine the general framework are National Development Plan, Medium-Term Program, Medium-Term Fiscal Plan, Annual Program, and Pre-accession Economic Program (called Economic Reform Program since 2015). Turkey participates in the pre-accession economic policy coordination and surveillance procedures since 2001, by submitting annual Pre-accession

Economic Programs and Fiscal Notifications to the EU. Accordingly, this Chapter was opened to accession negotiations on December 14, 2015, without any opening benchmarks.

Turkey has been successful in ensuring the sustainability of public finances in the last years. By the end of the year 2017, general government deficit/GDP was realized as 1.8% and the public debt/GDP ratio was 28.3%, which are below the reference values (3% and 60%, respectively) on public finances stated in the Treaty on the Functioning of the European Union. However, the economic and social incentives of the government as well as the high increase in exchange rates created some amount of cost on the fiscal balances. As a result, budget deficit and public debt/GDP ratios are expected to increase to 2.4% and 31.1%, respectively, by the end of 2018 (Hazine ve Maliye Bakanlığı 2018). According to the European Commission, although the public finances of Turkey had been improving until 2016, it has deteriorated in the last two years, due to temporary measures on both the expenditure and revenue side of the budget. However, government debt is considered to be sustainable (European Commission 2018d).

On the other hand, Turkish Statistical Institute has completed the work on transition to ESA-2010 system and revised national accounts were published on December 12, 2016 (TÜİK 2016). The revision of the GDP data to comply with the European System of National and Regional Accounts (ESA-2010) and improvement of the methods used to estimate the national accounts are mainly emphasized as progress in the most recent Regular Report for Turkey. The areas where further improvement is needed are stated as implementing ESA-2010 for also government accounts, introducing numerical fiscal rules or an independent fiscal council that monitors fiscal policy independently, increasing credibility of macroeconomic forecasts and publishing government finance statistics also on an accrual basis (European Commission 2018a).

13.4 Alignment in Public Financial Control

Starting with 2000s, public administration reform of many EU member states have been intensified in the area of public internal control. Internal control systems differ from country to country, as they need to adapt the country's own governance system (European Commission 2014a). Although some countries have a centralized system and some are more decentralized, the main principles for public financial management and control are implemented by all countries.

The EU encourages the candidate countries to reform their governance systems so as to bring managerial accountability and ensure sound financial management, including audit of public funds (European Commission 2018a). In this context, Chapter 32: Financial Control is one of the 35 negotiation chapters and "it covers four main policy areas, namely public internal financial control (PIFC), external audit, the protection of the EU's financial interests and the protection of the Euro against counterfeiting." In the first two areas, there is no specific EU legislation but candidate countries need to adapt their PIFC and external audit systems according to international standards (INTOSAI) and EU best practices (European Commission 2006b). Both systems are related to the entire public budget, especially central government revenue and expenditure as well as external funds. However, specific rules for the management and control of EU funds exist, which are subjects of other accession negotiation chapters (European Commission 2018c).

PIFC concept was developed by the European Commission with the aim of supporting candidate countries in reforming their public internal control systems (De Koning 2007). PIFC systems aim to give reasonable assurance that budgetary transactions in a country are implemented in accordance with the relevant legislation and the principles of sound financial management, transparency, efficiency, effectiveness, and economy (European Commission 2006b).

PIFC is founded on three pillars: managerial accountability through financial management and control systems, functionally independent internal audit and central harmonization unit(s) (CHU) for developing methodologies and standards relating to the first two pillars (European Commission 2006b).

Financial control can be regarded as one of the most important elements for effective implementation of the new public financial management system in Turkey as well. The adoption of the Law No. 5018 was the major step for founding a public internal control system in line with international standards. It provided a framework of responsibility and accountability for all relevant actors included in the management of public finances and established a decentralized system of financial management and control (European Commission 2004).

Turkey's level of alignment as regards the Financial Control Chapter is at a satisfactory level. The aim of the PIFC system and its three pillars are defined in Law No. 5018 in accordance with the EU requirement, which is to ensure effective, economic, and efficient utilization of public resources in conformity with policies and objectives of the Government, on the basis of accountability and fiscal transparency. In order to improve the implementation of the system, secondary and tertiary legislation have been put into effect and two central harmonization units, which are responsible for setting standards and methods in the fields of both financial management and control as well as internal audit were established. The Central Harmonization Unit (CHU) for Financial Management and Control, which is established under the Ministry of Treasury and Finance, prepares relevant legislation, ensures coordination, and provides guidance to public institutions in this field. The CHU for Internal Audit is the Internal Audit Co-ordination Board attached to the Ministry of Treasury and Finance and a department within the Ministry facilitates the activities of the Board and acts as its Secretariat. The duties of the Board are to coordinate and monitor the internal audit systems of public organizations, define and develop internal audit standards and procedures and provide guidance (SIGMA 2017b). In addition, internal auditors were appointed in public administrations.[2] In the field of financial management and

[2]As of 18 September 2018, 890 internal auditors are working in public administrations, however some of the administrations haven't appointed any internal auditors yet and 1188 of the internal auditor cadres are still empty (retrieved from the web page of Internal Audit Coordination Board).

control, strategy development units were established and financial services experts were recruited in public administrations.

Turkey's first PIFC Policy Paper was adopted in 2002 and needs to be updated. The updated Policy Paper should cover important issues such as the relationship between internal audit and inspection, link between internal audit of national budget and of EU funds, the precise definition of ex-ante financial control and the establishment of a permanent CHU for internal audit (European Commission 2018c).

Another area of Financial Control Chapter, which is relevant to the public financial management, is external audit. The external audit system in Turkey was reviewed with the Turkish Court of Accounts (TCA) Law No. 6085, which has been prepared in accordance with INTOSAI standards and principles and therefore complies EU requirements in this field.

The TCA's audit mandate is exhaustive and it is also authorized to audit EU and other international funds. According to the TCA Law, TCA is authorized, among other duties, for regularity audit (financial and compliance), performance audit, and also audit of performance indicators. TCA carries out its duties in accordance with generally accepted auditing standards (SIGMA 2017b).

After the screening meetings held in 2006, the level of compliance in Financial Control Chapter with regard to both legislation and institutional capacity has been considered adequate and the chapter was opened to accession negotiations on June 26, 2007 without any opening benchmarks.

In the most recent Regular Report for Turkey, the European Commission acknowledges that Turkey already has a good level of alignment in the area of financial control. On PIFC, it is stated that public administration of Turkey has a uniform management structure that combines managerial accountability and delegation of authority with results-oriented performance management system. Relevant legislation is mostly in line with the international standards and central harmonization units provide methodological guidance and supervise the implementation of the system. However, there is still work to be done, such as adopting the updated PIFC Policy Paper, establishing a formal monitoring and reporting framework on implementation, ensuring a systematic approach to risk management and quality assurance and improving the reporting on irregularities (European Commission 2018a). On external audit, it is indicated that the TCA Law is in line with international standards. The issues that need further improvement are stated as the need to increase the capacity of the TCA to audit local administrations, municipal companies, and associations, to develop an effective monitoring system to follow up implementation of audit recommendations, and also to increase the effectiveness of parliamentary follow-up mechanism for TCA's audit reports (European Commission 2018a).

13.5 Alignment in Taxation

The administration of revenues is another important area under public financial management. The European Commission published guidelines called 'Fiscal Blueprints' in 2007 to lay down criteria for tax administrations based on EU best practice. The blueprints were first published in 1999 with the aim of serving as an instrument for the candidate countries to develop their administrative capacity in adopting and implementing the Acquis for accession to the EU. They describe the main functions and systems of a tax administration and also provide a basis to design tax reforms (European Commission 2007b).

The European Union member states have the right to design their tax legislation according to their national priorities, while respecting the fundamental principles of nondiscrimination and respect for free movement in internal market. The European Union can propose an EU legislation on tax legislation where an EU-wide action is seen necessary for the proper functioning of the internal market (European Commission 2015).

The European Commission clearly stated in its Communication on Tax Policy of the EU that the member states do not need to fully harmonize their tax systems, but they should respect EU rules. As a result, member states may choose their tax systems according to their own preferences. Within this framework, the main priority for EU tax policy would be to address the concerns of individuals and businesses functioning in internal EU market by focusing on the removing tax obstacles to cross-border economic activities and in the meantime preventing harmful tax competition and endorsing cooperation between member states' tax administrations to fight fraud (European Commission 2001).

EU legislation in indirect taxes consist of harmonization of national laws in the fields of Value Added Tax (VAT) and excise duties, since different tax rules in goods and services can harm competition between businesses and make it hard to sell and buy products across borders (European Commission 2015). VAT legislation lays down the scope, key definitions, and principles. Tobacco products, alcoholic beverages, and energy products are subject to excise duties according to EU legislation, which establishes the structure of the tax and minimum rates (European Commission 2007a).

Legislation in direct taxation area, however, regulates approximation of legislation of the member states in order to improve the functioning of the internal market and prevent intra-Community tax evasion and tax avoidance (European Commission 2015). The *Acquis* on direct taxation focus on eliminating distortions for cross-border economic activities within the internal market and therefore covers effective taxation of income from savings and corporate taxes. Member States also need to complying with the principles set by the Code of Conduct for Business Taxation, with the aim of eliminating harmful tax practices. Administrative cooperation between Member States is also necessary. Member States are expected to increase their implementation capacities and connection to EU's computerized tax systems (European Commission 2007a).

The need for the approximation of Turkey's tax legislation and administrative procedures with the EU started even before the accession negotiations, with the Customs Union established between Turkey and EU by the Decision No. 1/95 of Turkey-EU Association Council. The Articles 49–51 of this Decision cover provisions on direct and indirect taxation, mainly aiming at preventing discriminatory taxation against each other (EC-Turkey Association Council 1995).

Chapter 16: Taxation was opened to negotiations on June 26, 2009, after meeting the opening benchmark. Turkey is gradually taking steps to harmonize with EU legislation and improving the institutional capacity of tax administration; including transition to electronic transactions. However, bearing in mind that taxation is an important tool in national policymaking, it is assumed that full alignment will only take place by the time of full membership.

Turkey's alignment is seen moderate in the field of taxation, as stated in the most recent Regular Report for Turkey. The areas of progress are stated as the elimination of discriminatory excise duties on alcoholic beverages and tobacco in accordance with the Action Plan, the ratification of the Convention on administrative assistance in tax matters and the plans for an integrated public finance management information system. The issues which were criticized by the European Commission (2018a) are the remaining differences on exemptions, structure, special schemes, and reduced rates in VAT legislation, the range of excisable energy products and the deficits in tax regimes that could be potentially harmful.

13.6 Support of EU Funds in Alignment Process

The European Union provides financial assistance to candidate and potential candidate countries in order to support them in adopting and implementing the reforms required for membership, using the Instrument for Pre-accession Assistance (IPA). One of the objectives of IPA is to strengthen the public administration and good governance at all levels. The reforms in public administration reform, including the improvement of economic governance and public financial management are supported under the 'democracy and governance' priority sector of IPA II (2014–2018) period (European Parliament and the Council 2014).

The projects funded by IPA that aim alignment in the field of public financial management as well as the Financial Control and Taxation Chapters support both legislative alignment and capacity building in Turkey's core administrations. These projects also help to raise awareness about EU accession process.

13.7 Conclusion

European Union accession process has been a driving force behind some of the fundamental reforms in Turkey. The reforms in the area of PFMC can be considered as one of the most important reforms in this regard, which affected the whole public administration. As a result of these reforms and commitment in maintaining fiscal discipline, sustainability of public finances was achieved to a great extent.

The public financial management and control reform, which was headed by the Law No. 5018, incorporated many new concepts to public administrations, together with a change in management culture dating back to 1920s. After the enactment of the Law, relevant implementing legislation have been published, new units were founded such as strategy development units, internal audit units, and central harmonization units, and appointments have been made for the new functions in these units. Moreover, several trainings were organized for relevant civil servants, some of which were funded under EU projects.

Considering the overall impact of this transformation and the size of Turkish public administration, it is reasonable to argue that might take time until the new system is fully adopted and implemented. In this regard, in order to improve the implementation of the new system, it is important to continue activities for the civil servants in both central government and local administrations such as organizing regular trainings, raising awareness of top managers, recruiting adequate number of staff in financial management and control units and finally establishing a robust monitoring and evaluation mechanism.

Although the foundations of this new system are based on the EU requirements under various areas, there are still some elements to be improved for full alignment with the EU. It could be observed from the assessment reports that the general legislative and institutional framework of Turkey's public financial management and control systems as well as its subfields which are studied under different negotiation chapters are aligned with the EU *Acquis* to a large extent. The only remaining factors are related to increasing the institutional capacity of relevant public administrations in order to improve the implementation and monitoring of the system. On the other hand, continuing to implement structural reforms while maintaining the fiscal discipline is of critical importance for both EU alignment and for maintaining the stability of Turkish economy.

Consequently, regardless of the current slowdown in accession negotiations, the efforts for full alignment should be continued in all areas where they would help rise the living standards of Turkish citizens, increase Turkey's credibility in international platforms and improve the business and investment environment.

References

Corbacho, A. and Ter-Minassian T. (2013). Public Financial Management Requirements for Effective Implementation of Fiscal Rules. In R. Allen, R. Hemming & B.H. Potter (Eds.), *International Handbook of Public Financial Management* (pp. 38–60). Hampshire, England: Palgrave McMillan.

Council of the European Union. (2011). *Directive 2011/85/EU of 8 November 2011 on requirements for budgetary frameworks of the Member States*, Official Journal of the European Union, L 306/41. Brussels.

Current Situation in Accession Negotiations (2016). Retrieved from https://www.ab.gov.tr/files/5%20Ekim/yatay_muzakere_tablosu_30_06_2016_tr.pdf.

De Koning, R. (2007). *Public Internal Financial Control*, Slovenia: Drs Robet P.J. de Koning.

EC-Turkey Association Council. (1995). *Decision No 1/95 of 22 December 1995 on implementing the final phase (96/142/EC)*. Retrieved from http://trade.ec.europa.eu/doclib/docs/2003/december/tradoc_115267.pdf.

Efstathiou, K & Wolff, G.B. (2018). Is the European Semester effective and useful? *Policy Contribution Issue*, 09, pp. 1–15.

European Commission. (2001). *EU Tax Policy Strategy, Communication of 23 May 2001 on "Tax policy in the European Union - Priorities for the years ahead*" (COM (2001) 260). Retrieved from https://ec.europa.eu/taxation_customs/general-information-taxation/eu-tax-policy-strategy_en.

European Commission. (2004). *2004 Regular Report on Turkey's progress towards accession,* Brussels, SEC(2004)1201. Retrieved from https://www.ab.gov.tr/files/AB_Iliskileri/Tur_En_Realitons/Progress/Turkey_Progress_Report_2004.pdf.

European Commission. (2006a). *Screening Report for Turkey on Chapter 17- Economic and Monetary Policy*, 9 October 2006. Retrieved from https://ec.europa.eu/neighbourhood-enlargement/sites/near/files/pdf/turkey/screening_reports/screening_report_17_tr_internet_en.pdf.

European Commission. (2006b). *Welcome to the World of PIFC*, European Communities.

European Commission. (2007a). *Screening Report for Turkey on Chapter 16-Taxation.* Retrieved from https://ec.europa.eu/neighbourhood-enlargement/sites/near/files/pdf/turkey/screening_reports/screening_report_16_tr_internet_en.pdf.

European Commission. (2007b). *Fiscal Blueprints, A path to a robust, modern and efficient tax administration*, Italy, Retrieved from https://ec.europa.eu/taxation_customs/sites/taxation/files/resources/documents/common/publications/info_docs/taxation/fiscal_blueprint_en.pdf.

European Commission. (2014a). *Compendium of PIFC Systems in EU Member States*, second edition, Luxembourg.

European Commission. (2014b). Communication From The Commission To The European Parliament, The Council, The European Central Bank, The European Economic And Social Committee And The Committee Of The Regions, *Economic governance review*, Brussels, COM(2014) 905 final.

European Commission. (2014c). *Enlargement Strategy and Main Challenges 2014–15*, Brussels, COM(2014) 700 final.

European Commission. (2015). *Taxation: Towards simple, fair and efficient taxation in the European Union*, Luxembourg.

European Commission. (2018a). *Turkey 2018 Report*. Strasbourg, 17.4.2018, SWD (2018) 153 final, Commission Staff Working Document. Retrieved from https://www.ab.gov.tr/siteimages/kapbtablolar/20180417-turkey-report.pdf.

European Commission. (2018b). *Budget Support Guidelines*. Luxembourg: Publications Office of the European Union.

European Commission. (2018c). Screening Report for Turkey on Chapter 32. Retrieved from https://ec.europa.eu/neighbourhood-enlargement/sites/near/files/pdf/turkey/screening_reports/screening_report_32_tr_internet_en.pdf.

European Commission. (2018d). *Commission Staff Working Document Economic Reform Programme of Turkey (2018–2020) Commission Assessment*, Brussels, 17.4.2018, SWD(2018) 130 final.

European Parliament and Council of the European Union. (2014). *Regulation (EU) No 231/2014 of 11 March 2014 establishing an Instrument for Pre-accession Assistance (IPA II)*, Official Journal of the European Union L 77/11.

Hazine ve Maliye Bakanlığı (2018). *Yıllık Ekonomik Rapor 2018*, Retrieved from http://api.maliye.gov.tr/wp-content/uploads/2018/10/YILLIK-EKONOMİK-RAPOR-2018-e.pdf.

IMF. (2017). Country Report No. 17/208, *Turkey Fiscal Transparency Evaluation*, July 2017, Washington, D.C. Retrieved from https://www.imf.org/~/media/Files/Publications/CR/2017/cr17208.ashx.

SIGMA. (2017a). *The Principles of Public Administration*, OECD, Retrieved from http://www.sigmaweb.org/publications/Principles-of-Public-Administration_Edition-2017_ENG.pdf.

SIGMA. (2017b). *Monitoring Report Turkey*, November, Retrieved from http://www.sigmaweb.org/publications/Monitoring-Report-2017-Turkey.pdf.

TÜİK. (2016). *Türkiye Ulusal Hesaplar Sistemi'nde SNA-2008 ve ESA-2010'un Uygulanması ve Ana Revizyon.*

Verdun, A. & Zeitlin, J. (2018). Introduction: the European Semester as a new architecture of EU socioeconomic governance in theory and practice. *Journal of European Public Policy*, 25:2, 137–148, https://doi.org/10.1080/13501763.2017.1363807.

Nihal Samsun Karabacak is working at the Directorate for European Union Affairs of the Ministry of Foreign Affairs as the Head of Economic, Financial and Social Policies Department. She graduated from the Economics Department of Middle East Technical University (ODTÜ). Later, she received her masters degree on European Union Economics and Finance in Ankara University. Previously, she worked at the EU and Foreign Affairs Department of the Ministry of Finance as a European Union Expert for ten years. She has experience on EU alignment in the fields of public financial management and control, economic and monetary policy, economic criteria, taxation and EU budget and takes active role in accession process.

Index

H. Kıral and T. Akdemir (eds.), *Public Financial Management Reforms in Turkey: Progress and Challenges, Volume 1*, Accounting, Finance, Sustainability, Governance & Fraud: Theory and Application, https://doi.org/10.1007/978-981-15-1914-7

The manufacturer's authorised representative in the EU is Springer Nature Customer Service Centre GmbH, Europaplatz 3, 69115 Heidelberg, Germany. If you have any concerns regarding our products, please contact ProductSafety@springernature.com

Printed and bound by CPI Group (UK) Ltd, Croydon, CR0 4YY
25/09/2026
02222903-0007